P. Hazell

D0849017

Success in Small
and Medium-Scale Enterprises

A World Bank Research Publication

Success in Small and Medium-Scale Enterprises

The Evidence from Colombia

Mariluz Cortes, Albert Berry, and Ashfaq Ishaq

Published for The World Bank
Oxford University Press

Oxford University Press

NEW YORK OXFORD LONDON GLASGOW
TORONTO MELBOURNE WELLINGTON HONG KONG
TOKYO KUALA LUMPUR SINGAPORE JAKARTA
DELHI BOMBAY CALCUTTA MADRAS KARACHI
NAIROBI DAR ES SALAAM CAPE TOWN

© 1987 The International Bank for
Reconstruction and Development / THE WORLD BANK
1818 H Street, N.W., Washington, D.C. 20433, U.S.A.

All rights reserved. No part of this publication
may be reproduced, stored in a retrieval system,
or transmitted in any form or by any means,
electronic, mechanical, photocopying, recording,
or otherwise, without the prior permission
of Oxford University Press.

Manufactured in the United States of America
First printing May 1987

The findings, interpretations, and conclusions expressed
in this study are the results of research supported
by the World Bank, but they are entirely those of the
authors and should not be attributed in any manner
to the World Bank, to its affiliated organizations, or to
members of its Board of Executive Directors
or the countries they represent.

Library of Congress Cataloging-in-Publication Data

Cortes, Mariluz.
  Success in small and medium-scale enterprises.

  Bibliography: p.
  Includes index.
  1. Small business—Colombia. 2. Colombia—Industries.
I. Berry, R. Albert. II. Ishaq, Ashfaq, 1953-
III. Title.
HD2346.C7C69 1987   338.6'42'09861   86-46296
ISBN 0-19-520593-6

Contents

Preface

Although the extent to which small-scale manufacturing generates employment has been increasingly recognized, most of the research on small enterprises has focused on the smallest units (those with less than 5 workers), which make up the informal sector. The next size larger (those with 5–99 workers), which we refer to as small and medium-size enterprises, has received far less attention. Yet both theoretical considerations and the little empirical evidence reported in the literature suggest that such enterprises are often economically efficient as well as labor-intensive, and that they have a significant role in achieving the rapid growth of both output and employment.

To understand that role better and examine the problems and prospects of small-scale enterprises in developing countries, the World Bank undertook a large research project in Colombia. This book is a product of that study. Colombia was chosen because the dynamism of its small and medium-scale manufacturing in the 1970s presents lessons for other developing countries in the 1980s and further into the future. Our objective in this book is to lay out the details of that experience and to probe beneath the figures by which the sector's success is judged. Specially designed surveys of small and medium-size firms in the metalworking and food processing industries were made in 1978 and 1979 to measure the levels of economic efficiency and to analyze the determinants of productivity and growth. Time series information on all small and medium-size manufacturing enterprises was also used. It throws some light on why this sector flourished so strikingly in the decade beginning in the late 1960s, in contrast to its more modest progress in earlier years.

The collaboration which produced this volume began with our recognition that much would be gained by integrating the sample survey evidence which Mariluz Cortes had collected and analyzed with Ashfaq Ishaq and the aggregate time series data on which Albert Berry had worked. Subsequently, all three authors participated in all components of the analysis and the writing.

Many people contributed to our effort at one stage or another. We are indebted, in particular, to Larry Westphal, chief of the Industry Division of the Development Economics Department during most of the work, for his guidance and unending support, and to I. M. D. Little for his incisive comments on earlier drafts. José Francisco Escandón was a valuable source of ideas and surveying expertise during the fieldwork in Colombia, as was Martha Bermúdez. The staff of the Corporación Financiera Popular helped with the surveys and the design of the questionnaire. Tom Bentley and James Tybout provided us with valuable information on the financial sector, and Sarah McPhee on the use of subcontracting arrangements in Colombia. Most helpful in the early stage were the comments of Dennis Anderson, and in the final stage the comments and suggestions of Howard Pack and two anonymous reviewers. Peter Bocock undertook the task of reorganizing and polishing the manuscript, and we owe him our special thanks. The manuscript has been through many drafts and the capable hands of many typists, particularly Maria Ameal, whom we also wish to thank.

Glossary

Firm or Plant Size

(Defined by the number of workers employed.)

CS Cottage-shop activities; manufacturing establishments with less than 5 workers.

F Factories; manufacturing establishments with 5 or more workers.

LI Large industry; manufacturing establishments with 100 or more workers.

MI Medium industry; manufacturing establishments with 50–99 workers.

SI Small industry; manufacturing establishments with 5–49 workers.

SMI Small and medium industry; manufacturing establishments with 5–99 workers.

Firm's Performance

(Assumed to be reflected by its benefit-cost ratio and its technical efficiency index; formal definitions are presented in the methodological appendix.)

BC Benefit-cost ratio. The ratio of the value of the firm's output to the cost of its inputs.

EBC Entrepreneurial BC. Measures the profitability of the entrepreneur's inputs (labor and capital). The precise definition is given in the text.

PBC Private BC. Measures the profitability of all inputs used by the firm (that is, those of the entrepreneur and those that are hired).

SBC Social BC. Measures the firm's BC when outputs and inputs are costed at social prices (or social opportunity cost).

STPBC Short-term PBC. Measures the ratio of value of output to variable costs. Differs from PBC in that fixed costs are not taken into account.

TEI Technical efficiency index. Measures the degree to which a firm maximizes output from a given set of inputs.

Efficiency frontier The locus of points characterized by the highest level of output per unit of input achieved within a sample of firms; different points on the frontier correspond to the use of inputs in different proportions.

Price (or allocative) inefficiency Measures the extent of the firm's failure to choose the input combination that would achieve a given level of output at minimum cost, given the firm's level of technical efficiency.

Production function The relation between inputs used and the resulting output of firms.

Productivity of labor (VA/L) Value added per equivalent unit of unskilled labor.

Technical inefficiency Measures the extent to which a firm fails to obtain the maximum output from its inputs, as judged by how far its output-input ratio falls short of the most efficient of the firms in the sample that use factors in the same proportions as it does.

Output, Input, and Noncategorical Variables

VA Value added.

K Total capital. Includes fixed capital plus working capital.

FK Fixed capital. Commercial or replacement value of the firm's machinery and equipment. (In the case of food processing firms, FK includes vehicles.)

WK Working capital. Includes working capital for inventories and working capital to finance sales credit.

Self-financed capital Capital financed by the entrepreneur's own resources, including reinvestments.

K/L Capital per unit of labor. Unless otherwise indicated, uses fixed capital (commercial value) per unskilled equivalent man-days of labor per year.

rK Capital services (or flows). Annual cost of capital including depreciation allowance. Capital services at private costs are calculated using real interest rates according to the firm's sources of funds and credit. Capital services at social costs are calculated on the basis of an assumed social opportunity cost of capital.

KWH Kilowatt-hour.

L Labor. Amount of labor used in a firm. Unless otherwise indicated, measured as unskilled equivalent man-days per year.

W   An index of the cost of labor in a firm relative to its cost in other firms. Defined as the weighted average of the level of wages paid by the firm (relative to the sector's average) in each skill category.

WL   Total cost of labor (wage bill). For employees, calculated using daily wages per skill category times total number of days in operation. Equivalent to the unskilled wage rate times the number of unskilled equivalent man-years. For entrepreneurs, estimated on the basis of level of education and labor market experience.

Fringe benefits   Social security and severance payments.

XP   Entrepreneur's experience. Number of years the entrepreneur has been in the labor force as employee or entrepreneur.

Proportion of secondhand equipment   Proportion of the firm's equipment, measured by value, which was bought secondhand from other producers or from dealers.

Main Categorical Variables

Entrepreneur's education   Indicates the level of formal education achieved by the entrepreneur. Categories are primary or less, secondary, university, and technical.

Entrepreneur's previous occupation   Indicates the entrepreneur's occupation before establishing or taking over his present firm. Categories are production worker (technician, skilled worker); owner of enterprise; manager, administrator, or salesman; independent professional; first job; and father's firm.

Entrepreneur's skills   Distinguishes among the activities performed by the entrepreneur in the firm: only production; only administration; administration and sales; and administration, production, and sales.

Food processing firms   Sample of firms including three product groups: guava paste; cheese, yogurt, and other milk by-products; and potato chips.

Labor mobility   Relative mobility of the firm's labor force according to whether most of the workers have been in the firm for less than one year (high), one to five years (medium), more than five years, or from the beginning (low).

Labor skills   Labor's level of proficiency as defined by the employer. In decreasing order the categories are foremen and technicians, skilled workers, semiskilled workers, and unskilled workers.

Metalworking firms   Sample of firms including three broad product groups: agricultural implements and sprayers; ovens, stoves, and integrated kitchens; and pumps and other agricultural capital goods.

Product quality   Compared with that of main competitors. Reflects the entrepreneur's judgment as to whether the quality of the firm's products is above that of its main competitors, about the same, or below.

Relative cost of materials   Compared with that paid by main competitors. Reflects the entrepreneur's judgment as to whether the prices the firm pays for its raw materials are above, about the same, or below those paid by its main competitors.

Relative price of products   Compared with that of main competitors. Reflects the entrepreneur's judgment as to whether the firm's prices are above those of its main competitors, about the same, or below.

Source of entrepreneur's skills   Indicates the source of the entrepreneur's knowledge. Categories are work in large firms, in small and medium firms, in training institutions, in universities, and self-taught.

Source of finance   Distinguishes between firms that are totally self-financed and firms that have access to external sources, such as public banks, private banks, moneylenders, and suppliers.

Type of technology   Indicates the level of sophistication of the equipment in the firm's main production stages. Categories are simple technology (most of the firm's equipment is manual); intermediate technology (the firm uses a combination of manual and simple powered equipment); and sophisticated technology (most of the equipment is powered and includes some special or more advanced machines). This last category is usually considered intermediate by international standards.

Institutions

ANDI   Asociación Nacional de Industriales. National manufacturers' association.

CFP   Corporación Financiera Popular. Parastatal development finance corporation, which supplies credit to small and medium enterprises.

DANE   Departamento Administrativo Nacional de Estadística. Central statistical office.

FICITEC   Fundación para el Fomento de la Investigación Científica y Tecnológica. Foundation for the support of scientific and technological research.

ICA   Instituto Colombiano Agropecuario. Colombian institute for crops and livestock.

ICSS   Instituto Colombiano de Seguros Sociales. Colombian social security institute.

IFI   Instituto de Fomento Industrial. Industrial development institute.

IIT   Instituto de Investigaciones Tecnológicas. Institute for technological research.

PROEXPO   Fondo de Promoción de Exportaciones. Export promotion fund.

SENA   Servicio Nacional de Aprendizaje. National training agency.

Note: Unless otherwise specified, the statistical material in the tables is drawn from the surveys of metalworking and food processing firms conducted by the authors in 1978 and 1979.

1
Issues and Perspectives

The manufacturing sectors of most developing countries are characterized by a wide range of technologies and of firm and plant sizes. It is important to distinguish between small and large firms, for although each group contributes significantly to employment and output, the two behave differently and have different factor proportions and productivities.

The Issues

Opinions on the merits and potential of the very small-scale or craft sector and of small and medium-size industry vary widely. Most decisionmakers and many economists consider the advantages of modern technology to be overwhelming.[1] In this view, since modern technology usually entails a larger scale of production and greater capital intensity, total factor productivity is presumed to be higher in large industry (LI). Among those who assume that modern technology could "have such great advantages in productivity and efficiency that the loss through stressing the use of scarce capital rather than abundant labor is more than offset,"[2] some believe that the continued existence of small enterprises is mainly the result of market imperfections and that the resources used by these enterprises are suboptimally allocated. The removal of imperfections such as inadequate information in labor or capital markets is expected to raise total output and reduce small-scale activity. But where imperfections cannot by affected by policy, the use of resources by small producers necessarily constitutes a second-best allocation of resources according to this view.

In the past decade or so, the above perception has been largely superseded among mainstream development economists by two alternative views. According to one view, although small producers may be efficient, their chief contribution lies in their use of resources not yet needed by the modern sector; their productivity is not likely to increase substantially over time, nor is it very sensitive to changes in public policy. Consequently, an appropriate attitude toward the sector would be one of benign neglect, though not active discouragement; in any event, this sector can be expected to decline in importance over time. The second view holds not only that the small-scale sector is or could be almost as efficient as LI is now, but also that it can remain competitive for a substantial period of time, if not permanently, and should therefore be encouraged and supported by public policy.[3]

Several factors have given impetus to the trend toward one or another of these relatively positive views. First, the pivotal role of up-to-date technology in the development process has been questioned as understanding has spread that new techniques can significantly increase output only with very much greater capital outlays than are at present available, especially in the poorer developing countries. This recognition has fueled the emphasis on the need for "intermediate" or "appropriate" technology.[4] Second, the growing concern of economists and decisionmakers with the problems of employment, unemployment, and income distribution has exposed a major shortcoming of LI—its inability to create significant amounts of productive employment in relation to the amount of capital it uses. The advantages of labor-intensive technology have been widely recognized for some time, as is reflected in the words of a 1951 United Nations report: "Labor saving technology is not of great value to an economy which is over-populated."[5] Indeed, undue emphasis on LI can lead to net job destruction, by replacing labor-intensive activities with capital-intensive ones. Some people doubt that LI is likely to be efficient at all under the conditions of labor surpluses and capital shortages that are typical of most developing countries, let alone be the panacea originally hoped for.[6]

In contrast, small enterprises are thought to be labor-intensive as well as more characteristic of and more likely to succeed in smaller urban centers and rural areas, where they can contribute to the more even distribution of economic activity in a region and can help to slow the flow of migration to large cities.[7] Because of their regional dispersion *and* their labor intensity, the argument goes, small-scale production units can promote a more equitable distribution of income than large firms can; the former are also likely to be complementary to and supportive of an equitable (unimodal) strategy of agricultural development.[8] Some authors have cautioned, however, that the working conditions in small enterprises are frequently bad and that such abuses as child labor are not uncommon.[9]

The recent surge of interest in small enterprise probably owes more to a heightened awareness among policymakers and international agencies of the problems of unemployment and poverty than to any change of heart among economists or specialists in industrial development. By the mid-1950s, the main qualitative arguments and debates were already on the table. Unfortunately, the issues involved have not been easy to resolve, because there is inadequate empirical evidence on the characteristics and economic value of small and medium enterprises and some of the issues are quite complex.

Some of the hopes raised in recent literature extolling the merits of small firms may turn out to be as unfounded as the claims made for large industry in earlier years. The extreme positions taken in the debate are perhaps not surprising in view of the lack of solid information.[10] Policy decisions affecting small and medium industry (SMI) in developing countries have from the start been plagued by this lack of information, which extends beyond the narrowly economic aspects of the issue to wider questions about the political economy of small enterprise. Writers of nearly every persuasion have expressed varying degrees of doubt as to whether the small-scale sector could provide significant benefits either to those directly involved in it or to the economy in general—for the very good reason that large enterprises or governments could be expected to move into any profitable niche identified by the politically weak small-scale sector and to extract the bulk of the available benefits. Thus, in the view of authors such as Gerry, so-called petty production is restricted to activities that are not attractive to the capitalist sector and inevitably operates under difficult conditions of inadequate access to inputs and markets; its relation to the capitalist sector is one of subordination.[11]

Other analysts have emphasized the exploitation suffered by the small sector and the way in which it subsidizes the costs of capitalist enterprises: by producing wage goods at very low returns to labor and hence at low prices, it enables the capitalist enterprises to pay lower wages than they otherwise might.[12] Schmitz notes, however, that this argument would seem to be much more plausible with respect to Africa than to South American countries; evidence from the latter suggests that the greater part of the worker's family budget there is spent on goods produced in the modern sector. In general, the more one believes that power is highly concentrated in a monopoly capital sector that is in coalition with or in control of the government, the less plausible it is to assume that public policy will do anything significant to further the interest of small producers. But, as Schmitz emphasizes in his valuable review of the constraints facing small-scale manufacturing, students of the political economy of that sector have been as prone to reach their conclusions (optimistic or pessimistic) without the aid of solid empirical evidence as have those who focus more narrowly on its economics.[13]

While we hope that our analysis of the Colombian experience provides some results of relevance to the broader debate centered on the political economy and the role and potential of small enterprise, the objective of this book is more narrowly economic. The principal issues discussed in the economic literature and on which our study touches can be grouped into five somewhat overlapping categories: the relation between size, capital intensity, and efficiency; the determinants of efficiency among small enterprises; the innovative capacity of small enterprises; the determinants of viability among small enterprises; and the contribution of small enterprises to the growth of modern manufacturing.

Relation between Size, Capital Intensity, and Efficiency

Economists have long recognized that the size of an enterprise is related to certain behavioral traits, and numerous interesting differences between firms of different sizes are mentioned in the literature. For example, it has generally been agreed that factor prices and therefore factor proportions (that is, the capital-labor ratio) vary with firm size. There is much dispute, however, as to how the level of economic efficiency varies with size, if indeed it does.

The most obvious stylized facts are that, for manufacturing as a whole, both labor productivity and the ratio of capital to labor are positively related to establishment size. These relations are less systematic at the two-digit level of industry; SMI is widely believed to be more labor-intensive than LI, but this notion has received too little testing with sound data and with appropriate distinctions between skill categories of workers to provide grounds for safe generalizations. Capital productivity is said to be higher in SMI than in LI, but here, too, the data are meager. Furthermore, little is known about the relationship between size and total factor productivity.

In part, the aggregate relations of labor productivity and capital intensity to size are due to differences in the industrial composition of LI and SMI, the latter tending to predominate in labor-intensive industries. The indivisibility of capital equipment, which is a cause of scale economies in some industries, suggests that the optimum ratio of capital to labor will change with the level of planned production, even when the relative prices of these inputs are unchanged.[14] Other factors could, of course, also contribute to a phenomenon of this kind. In such instances, factor intensities would be particularly likely to vary with size in the aggregate as a reflection of differences in industrial composition by size; where economies of scale are important, establishments would tend to be both large and capital-intensive.

There are several reasons why labor can be cheaper in small establishments. In family enterprises, income may be shared by family members, whether they work or not; this leaves the opportunity cost of their time at work quite low. Household or cottage-shop establishments are also better placed than larger production units to use cheap family or child labor.

Small units can often hire workers without being subject to labor legislation or union pressure and can thus keep wage costs down. At the same time, small establishments sometimes incur the cost of training workers and then lose them to larger firms.

By contrast, capital is commonly thought to be cheaper for larger establishments because they have better connections in organized financial markets. In reality the situation is more complex than this. The opportunity cost of an entrepreneur's own capital may be lower in a small firm than in a large one since the SMI entrepreneur's investment options outside his enterprise are likely to be more limited than those of his large counterpart. For most firms the supply price of capital presumably rises with the quantity of capital (there is thus no single "price of capital"); the supply price of small quantities may be lower for a small firm with some capital of its own than for a large firm, but will then probably rise more quickly for the former as it seeks funds from outside sources. Which firm has the lower marginal or average cost of capital thus depends on the amount used; if a small firm uses little enough capital, the average and marginal cost of that capital may be lower than for a large firm.

Imperfections in the product market have sometimes also been blamed for differences in factor intensity by size of firm. It has been argued that some businessmen prefer capital-intensive technology because, for example, they want to be modern or to avoid the problems associated with a large labor force. In the case of monopoly or oligopoly power in the relevant product market, abnormal profits create a situation in which such a preference can be satisfied; monopoly power is more likely to arise in large firms than in small ones. Products consumed by higher-income groups tend to be manufactured with more capital-intensive technologies, and in this market advertising and sales promotion costs tend to increase the minimum size of firms; again, a positive association between size and capital intensity may arise.

The relative role of these and other possible elements contributing to factor proportions that differ with firm size remains unclear; there has been too little research into the correlates of factor proportions to provide a solid understanding of the relation between size and capital intensity. Todd's finding that in Colombia juridical form (proprietorship, limited company, corporation, and so on) is strongly correlated with factor proportions, even when size is held constant,[15] does suggest that access to inputs, input prices, and perhaps technological knowledge may be more important than any underlying features of the production function. Studies focusing on factor substitutability give some feel for the variance of factor proportions,[16] but few go very far in tracking down the sources of that variance. A number of studies have reported quite capital-intensive small plants.[17] In their examination of the small-scale industrial sector in India, for example, Dhar and Lydall concluded that the most capital-intensive type of manufacturing establishments were small factories using modern machinery.[18] These and other findings have led some researchers to conclude that the most appropriate production unit for developing countries is the large labor-intensive plant, as exemplified, according to Sandesara, by the modern sector of the textile industry in India.[19] In most (perhaps all) of these discussions size is measured by the number of workers, although it has been noted that this can be misleading.[20]

In any case, it is clear that factor or product market imperfections can give rise to different factor intensities and different total factor productivity among firms. Some imperfections reflect real costs—for example, when product prices differ between markets because of transport costs or when wages differ because of moving costs. Others reflect government policies—such as minimum wage legislation or tariffs or subsidies applied to imports of machinery. Factor or product price differences can permit firms with low total factor productivity to exist. When the price differences reflect real costs, such as transport costs, it may be efficient for them to exist; when the price differences are induced by policy, the outcome is more likely to be inefficient.

Determinants of Efficiency among Small Enterprises

Low productivity of small enterprises—whether it be labor productivity (which is almost always relatively low) or capital or total factor productivity (the level of which, as noted above, has been a matter of debate)—has been linked with several possible causes: smallness per se, which precludes firms from reaping economies of scale;[21] weak management; and problems external to the firm, such as poor access to capital and inputs or market exploitation by monopsonistic buyers. These problems are also blamed for the frequency with which small enterprises go out of business.

Much debate has centered on the adequacy of entrepreneurship. Kilby, for example, argued that the basic obstacle to the development of modern, medium-scale manufacturing firms (which he said was a prerequisite for solid and enduring industrialization in Nigeria) was entrepreneurial deficiencies.[22] At the other extreme, Leff emphasized the elasticity of the supply response of entrepreneurship, which had permitted the high growth rates observed in many countries since World War II.[23] Many observers have also drawn attention to the enterprising nature of small businessmen in diverse parts of the developing world.[24] Anderson recently cautioned against either extreme view, citing evidence to show that there are indeed many potential entrepreneurs but that low levels of efficiency and endemic problems such as the lack of modern bookkeeping practices may prevent a good number of them from realizing their potential.[25] Although much evidence (including our own) suggests that the level of technical efficiency varies widely among small firms,[26] it is not easy to generalize about good management practice in the very small firm—for example, some small firms probably should have double-entry bookkeeping and others should not.[27] Clearly, the process of growing from a simple organization that forms part of the household economy into a larger and more hierarchical one is beset by many difficulties. Again the issue is not which type of organization is superior in a general sense, but rather which works better for a particular situation.[28] Perhaps the most time-honored observation about the small entrepreneur in manufacturing is that this pivotal figure is often very good at part of the job (the technological side is most frequently cited)[29] but deficient in some other area (such as marketing).

Rapidly rising levels of education in developing countries prompt another question—whether and how education contributes to entrepreneurial skills and performance. It is frequently argued, and there is at least scattered evidence to support the view, that education helps individuals assess and gain access to new technological developments.[30] It may also help entrepreneurs raise their marketing, personnel relations, and other relevant skills, although the causal linkage is not very clear. The skill composition of the work force also varies with size, certainly in the aggregate and probably within the typical industry, the larger firms having a higher share of professional and white-collar workers than small ones; thus some of the increase in average labor productivity and capital per worker with size is associated with higher-quality labor.[31]

The difficulty in obtaining raw materials is one of the most frequently cited "external" problems facing small business.[32] This problem may be the result of discrimination against small firms by the government, small businesses' lack of bargaining power against large companies, or a combination of the two (as in Senegal, for example, where a highly protected multinational was able to achieve a virtual monopsony in the purchase of fine leather and thereby force small producers to switch to synthetic materials).[33]

Innovative Capacity of Small Enterprises

Over the past century or more, technical progress has increasingly favored large-scale operations.[34] The ability to take advantage of efficient new technology is thus generally conceded to be highest among large capital-intensive firms, which can more easily engage in research and development. Moreover, since their technologies are relatively similar to those in use in industrialized countries, such firms can borrow a given technique more readily than can smaller firms. Discussion in the literature has therefore focused on the gap between large and small firms and on whether the small-enterprise sector with its typically labor-intensive technology has shown any significant technological advances at all. Some distant observers have described small-enterprise technology as stagnant or nearly so, whereas more knowledgeable students have emphasized the innovative character of many small entrepreneurs. King, in his study of machinemakers in Kenya's informal sector, compared their innovative capacity favorably with (larger-scale) foreign-controlled activities, noting that they had "the hallmark of improvisation that is so conspicuously absent from so much foreign production in Kenya."[35] For many small factories, the adoption of modern technology does involve a "discontinuous leap" from existing technologies and a quantum jump in total investment. The feasibility of this leap can depend on such factors as the availability of secondhand machinery, the ability to make repairs, and the availability of information (for example, from importers) about technological alternatives.[36] Although small industry clearly cannot be characterized as technologically stagnant, most students do believe that technological *change* is slower among small firms; some, however, argue that properly measured technological *improvement* may be as great or greater for them than for larger firms because the technology is more appropriate (that is, it has higher total factor productivity when factors are valued at their social opportunity costs). This is not to deny that some small firms move to expensive modern technologies when it is not efficient to do so, frequently because of a "more-modern-is-better" mentality.[37]

Both static and dynamic factors are relevant in assessing the relative merits of alternative technologies or firm sizes. The argument of Galenson and Leibenstein against labor-intensive technologies is essentially a dynamic one: they believe that capital-intensive technology is more likely to generate a high reinvestment ratio (that is, high savings) and to raise the quality of the labor force over time.[38] Gerschenkron has taken a similar view, which is based on his reading of the economic history of Europe in the nineteenth century.[39] Ranis's results from Pakistan have thrown doubt on Galenson and Leibenstein's argument for capital-intensive technologies with the finding that the reinvestment ratio was highest among medium-size firms rather than in the largest and most capital-intensive ones.[40]

Determinants of Viability among Small Enterprises

That small enterprises are more likely to be competitive with large firms in some industries than in others is not disputed. The question is, what determines whether the small enterprise will succeed? Staley and Morse have suggested that location, process, and the market strongly influence the success of small firms:

- Locational influences are predominant among factories that process a dispersed raw material (for example, dairy products, wines, grease and tallow, lumber, and stone); firms whose products have local markets and relatively high transfer costs (for example, bottled and canned soft drinks, carpentry such as door and window frames, concrete products, sheet metal items such as tanks, wood and paperboard boxes, bricks, and tiles); and service industries (small-scale printing, engraving and typesetting, electroplating, and shoe and watch repairs).
- Process influences are predominant among separable manufacturing operations (mostly specialized operations in machine metal working and repair, foundry products, and castings); firms that produce crafts or precision handiwork (jewelry, some textiles, and carpets); and simple assembly, mixing, or finishing operations (flavoring, disinfectants and polish, curtains and draperies, and miscellaneous wood products).
- Market influences are predominant among firms with differentiated products having low scale economies (women's and children's garments and some leather goods) and industries serving small total markets (certain woolen and canvas products, some food products such as fresh and frozen packaged fish, some pottery products, and many others, depending on the type of local market).[41]

An additional factor on the marketing side that may help identify the industries in which small enterprises can (and cannot) survive is the extent to which high-powered advertising is able to define the character of the market for a product or category of products. Advertising, especially by multinationals or by nationals trying to convert buyers to a modern, foreign, or otherwise higher-status set of preferences, often gives those firms a decided advantage. Langdon refers to the capacity of multinationals to "establish patterns of demand that are very hard for small-scale indigenous Kenyan industrialists to meet directly. In that sense, the . . . role [of multinational corporations] in Kenya seems responsible for blocking, in a general way, the development of decentralised local industry in a wide range of sectors."[42]

It is also generally assumed that small firms are more likely to be competitive in labor-intensive industries, either because they can tap lower-cost labor or because they can use labor more efficiently with less supervision. Furthermore, the small firm's greater flexibility may be an advantage in industries that face unstable conditions of demand, product specification, and the like.

The locational factor in small-enterprise development was recently discussed by Anderson and Leiserson.[43] Subcontracting has been studied in detail by Watanabe[44] and others; although it seems to be of lesser quantitative importance in most developing countries than in Japan, the true extent of subcontracting is not at all well know. Subcontracting warrants continued attention, especially given the point recently made by Mead that for "smaller, nascent 'parent firms,' particularly those based in Third World countries, the use of disintegrated production and distribution systems may be important in facilitating a movement to more complex products and more distant markets."[45] Ho has attempted, in the context of the Republic of Korea, to identify five-digit industries that seem to have one or more of the advantages for small industry identified by Staley and Morse and notes that the declining importance of small firms in several industries during the years of Korea's rapid economic growth could be attributed to the expansion of domestic markets and improvements in infrastructure, both of which reduced the previous locational advantages of small firms.[46]

No one would seriously argue that small firms can be efficient in all industries—or, at the other extreme, in none. The debate about their viability is a matter of degree, and the small-scale sector's potential for healthy participation in a national economy is defined primarily by the number of industries in which it can be competitive with imports or large firms. Another factor that helps to determine how well small producers will do in a given industry is the presence or absence of complementarity with large firms in other lines of production or in handling other stages of a production process. Such complementarity can lead to subcontracting or simply to a commonality of interest that means the political clout of large firms will probably be used to support objectives they share with their smaller colleagues.

Contribution of Small Enterprises to the Growth of Modern Manufacturing

Small enterprises represent the natural starting point for countries embarking on industrialization, a process more likely to succeed—and to remain under local control—if it is undertaken gradually and organically rather than with a sudden shift to modern technology and large-scale production. This view is, of course, opposed by those who see strong merits in large-scale capital-intensive production and by those who see a break with the past as the remedy for perceived inefficiencies in traditional technologies and styles of work.

It has often been argued that, whatever the merits of large-scale production, most large firms had their origins in small ones and that support for small firms today can therefore promote the evolution of productive large firms tomorrow. Hoselitz has noted that many small cottage and handicraft establishments in Europe and Japan "did develop into small and medium sized factories, and this process appears to be of special importance in under-developed countries. Though it is well-known that in the course of European industrial development the participation of craftsmen was significant, and in some countries, indeed, indispensable, we know little about the actual relative weight which may be assigned to the gradual evolution of small handicrafts shops into medium and ultimately into large plants."[47]

As Anderson notes, we now have widespread evidence from firm-level surveys that firms tend to begin "with low amounts of capital drawn from the savings of the owner or borrowings from friends and relatives; initial levels of employment are low, typically less than a dozen, though the figure varies with the nature of the business; the social and occupational backgrounds of the owners vary greatly; and the firms that expand into medium or large scale activities do so continually or in steps. Expansion can be very fast for some firms, though the growth rates appear as broadly distributed as their final sizes."[48]

The wide variation in the growth paths of small firms makes it difficult to generalize about their contribution as a group to the growth of total employment or output at a given point in time. And it is not clear how the importance of handicrafts and small factories as sources of modern medium and large firms varies with the level of development, the presence of foreign enterprise, and other contextual features of development.[49] Most indigenous large firms in developing countries originated in small factories, but to what extent the artisan or handicraft sector has contributed importantly to the growth of modern manufacturing capacity is not clear.[50] What does seem reasonable, however, is the suggestion that small enterprises often serve as training grounds for entrepreneurship, thereby creating a business-oriented middle class, spreading entrepreneurial attitudes throughout the population, and providing future managers for large firms and public sector entities. Of course, this phenomenon is not inconsistent with a reverse flow of entrepreneurial talent from large firms to smaller ones, a feature frequently discussed in the Japanese case. It would be interesting to see how far this latter process depends on whether large industry is domestically or externally owned and managed.

Drawing on the experience of industrialized countries, the theoretical and empirical literature on the growth of the firm provides a useful conceptual framework for analyzing the dynamics of small or medium factories and their potential contribution to employment and output growth. Penrose distinguishes between economies in operation and

economies in expansion.[51] Technological or managerial economies of
scale may permit larger firms to operate with lower production costs than
their smaller counterparts. But size may also give a firm advantage in its
expansion—into new products based on its research capacity, into new
processes requiring the ability to take substantial risks, or into new markets requiring a well-developed sales capability. Some of these factors
are ephemeral, in the sense that they are only needed for the expansion
process. Penrose also notes that the distinction between economies in operation and economies in expansion throws some light on the difficult
question of optimal firm size.[52] Although large firms are often able to
benefit from economies of expansion, small firms can sometimes show
greater flexibility; thus large firms may pave the way for a new product or
market but their scale advantages may then be reduced or disappear. We
shall discuss relevant examples from Colombia later.

The relatively simple conceptualization of the firm in traditional
microeconomics tends to overlook the complexities involved in a firm's
growth. On one hand, the problems and costs associated with moving to
a new level of operation—which would not arise were the firm's size to
be held constant—may be substantial. On the other hand, the benefits of
expansion may extend beyond the simple fact of reaching a higher level
of production; size can often provide a degree of security, especially
when combined with diversification.

The set of resources used in expansion is likely to be different in kind
from that used in operating at a given scale. In the managerial domain,
entrepreneurial skills—in the classical sense of the ability to see an opportunity, to innovate, and to assess and take risks—will be more
prominent than the comparatively routine skills needed for steady-state
operations. Moreover, the physical inputs needed for capital investment,
reorganization, and the like will also be different from those needed by a
stable firm. One implication of these differences is that the factor proportions of a firm may be expected to depend not only on its size but also on
its rate of expansion.

In the absence of any good reason to believe that the history of a firm
should essentially be the story of its growth to optimal size (except when
exogenous factors imply a change in that optimal size), it makes sense to
search for a theory that would attempt to specify the optimal size of a
firm at each point in time, that is, to specify an optimal rate of growth and
to predict the typical or average growth curves. After reviewing the relevant factors, Penrose suggested that "[w]e should expect the rate of
growth of medium-sized and moderately large firms to be higher than
that of the very new and very small firms and higher also than that of the
very large firms."[53]

The theory of the firm as presented in the economic literature has only
belatedly moved beyond the concept of a simple profit-maximizing static

entity toward a more realistic, comprehensive, and subtle conception of the firm as an organic unit, possibly with its own laws of growth. The concept of the satisficing firm, which is associated with the "behavioristic" approach to economic analysis pioneered by Simon and with organization theory, was a significant advance.[54] Marris has contributed to the refinement of an economic theory of firm growth.[55]

In addition to examining the nature and role of small-scale industry, economists have discussed ways to encourage this sector so as to maximize its contribution to welfare in general. At the economywide level, there has been a debate about the need for public intervention in support of small enterprise. The International Labour Organisation (ILO), notably in its Kenya report, has argued for a number of special measures to foster growth of the sector, as well as for the removal of public policies that seem to impede its growth.[56] India has gone as far as to reserve certain branches of industry for small producers.

Moreover, many economists now recognize that trade policy often discriminates against small firms in the choice of industries to protect, in the use of disequilibrium exchange rates or of licenses to allocate foreign exchange, and so on. Regulatory practices often have similarly harmful effects, although wage legislation—which is generally directed at relatively large production units—is an exception. Meanwhile, the organized financial system tends mainly to support relatively large and well-connected firms. Supporters of small enterprise have suggested various remedies, including better access to credit, greater availability of extension services designed to enhance managerial capacity and upgrade operational technology, and improvements in the working of input and output markets (so that small producers would less often be the victims of market distortions that typically favor larger firms).

Objective and Approach

This study attempts to shed some light on several of the issues just reviewed. The Colombian case is of particular interest, both because previous studies have suggested that small manufacturing plants there have had advantages over large ones with respect to total factor productivity and employment creation,[57] and because small-scale manufacturing experienced a boom during the 1970s, raising hopes for an active longer-run role in Colombia and structurally similar countries. Our objective is to examine the efficiency, contribution to employment, and other salient features of Colombian small and medium industry and to understand its dynamics, including its rapid growth during the 1970s.

The study of SMI tends to be comparative; assessments of its efficiency or ability to create employment, for example, are usually made in reference to large industry. SMI, as we define it, is the middle group of three broad size categories: households and very small firms—referred to here as cottage shops (CS)—SMI, and LI. SMI's defining characteristics are organizational simplicity and relatively small size. Neither the technical literature nor broader studies of the political economy of small enterprises provide clear and consistent definitions of the boundaries of the sector. The definitional issue is of some importance to this study, however, since our focus is on small and medium-size factories, not on household industry or the self-employed (though some of the firms we studied started out very small). Some students of the informal sector would say that the firms on which we focus share most of the relevant characteristics and problems of the smallest producers; others would not.

For practical reasons concerning the availability of data, our categories are based on the number of workers in establishments; thus cottage shop refers to establishments with fewer than 5 workers, SMI to those with 5–99 workers, and LI to those with 100 or more workers. These cutoff points are necessarily arbitrary but are adequate for our purposes.[58] In some contexts the level of output, of all inputs, or of capital inputs may be a more appropriate measure of size than employment. But the level of employment is the most easily and accurately measurable variable; moreover, its availability over time in Colombia and its frequent use in other countries permit a greater number of useful comparisons. We have tried to test the sensitivity of our results to the measures of size and have cautioned readers when our conclusions are sensitive to the measure used.

Having defined the size variable, one must also specify whether the analysis is to focus on the size of a plant, an establishment, or a firm. The "plant" or factory is usually defined as a single industrial unit, manufacturing one or more products as part of an integral operation. An "establishment" is a business or industrial entity at a single physical location; it can consist of several plants as long as these are located together under a single management. A "firm" may include more than one establishment in the same or separate physical locations, each having its own local management, although all establishments are coordinated by central management and subject to its decisions. It is especially important to make these distinctions when dealing with large-scale manufacturing, which includes many multiestablishment firms or enterprises. This question is less important for our purposes since the SMI sector in Colombia is essentially made up of single-plant firms, though a large proportion of entrepreneurs in small and medium industry have more than one business (see chapter 4). The aggregate statistics we use include some plants that are themselves relatively small but are part of larger firms, but this unavoidable complication is unlikely to affect our findings significantly.

Our detailed survey of the metal and food industries deals only with single-plant firms. For the purposes of this study, "plant" and "establishment" will be used interchangeably since neither our data nor our arguments involve a distinction between them. "Firm" will be distinguished from the other two concepts, however, and attention will be drawn to the distinction when it is important.

To study the evolution of SMI employment and output, together with its sectoral and regional distributions, factor proportions, and organization, we use relatively aggregated time-series data for all manufacturing industries. Statistics on such variables as output, wages, and investment are available by plant size over time and by branch of industry, but not normally by plant size within a given branch. Aggregate data of this kind can provide an overall picture of how SMI has evolved over time, but they do not permit a detailed examination of its structure and modes of operation or of the growth processes and life cycles of individual plants. We have therefore assembled more detailed evidence from samples of firms in the metalworking and food processing industries in order to study questions of efficiency, growth, innovative capacity, and the sources of entrepreneurship.

In studying SMI growth and the level and determinants of SMI efficiency, we have tried to take into account the economic relations between the existence, growth, and efficiency of SMI. For example, a finding based on input and output data that SMI in a given industry is very inefficient (that is, has low total factor productivity) would have to be viewed with caution if SMI accounts for a high share of employment and output in that industry. One might then hypothesize major market imperfections, or an error in the shadow prices assumed in the total factor productivity calculation, or both.

The next sections of this chapter examine evidence on the size structure of firms and possible explanations for changes over time in that structure along with criteria for evaluating a firm's contribution to the economy. The last section of chapter 1 presents a brief overview of the rest of the study and its principal conclusions.

Determinants of Size and Trends in the Factory Subsector

We are particularly interested in the generally negative relationship between the level of a country's development and the relative importance of smaller producers within manufacturing. The varying degrees of competitiveness of smaller establishments in different industries and at different stages of a country's development produce an evolutionary process in which, as Anderson puts it, the composition of manufacturing activities by size goes through three phases:[59]

(1) a phase in which household manufacturing is predominant, accounting for one-half to three-quarters or more of total manufacturing employment; (2) a phase in which small workshops and factories emerge at a comparatively rapid rate, and act to displace household manufacturing in several sectors; and (3) a phase in which large-scale production becomes predominant, displacing the remaining household manufacturing activities and a large share—though not the whole—of workshop and small factory production. This phase is partly a product of the second, since the recorded growth of output and employment in large-scale manufacturing can be divided into: (a) the growth of once small firms through the size structure, and (b) the expansion of already large domestic and foreign concerns.[60]

Anderson presents time-series data for four developing countries—Colombia, India, the Philippines, and Turkey—all of which he classifies in the second phase on the basis of the share of manufacturing employment in establishments of 5–49 or 5–99 workers. Only in Colombia was the level of employment in small factories not rising rapidly.[61] (Anderson's data on Colombia were for 1953–73; the present study focuses on the decade from the late 1960s to the late 1970s, when small factory employment *was* rising rapidly.) Hoselitz had earlier noted that, in contrast to Germany, Japan showed "the rather unusual feature of smaller plants growing faster than larger ones in a period of rising prosperity."[62] Staley and Morse also commented on the phase in which small factories grow rapidly.[63] It is evident that the share of CS in manufacturing output and employment falls with the level of development and eventually nearly disappears and that the share of LI rises from very low levels in the poorest countries to dominance in developed ones. The trends in the relative and absolute importance of SMI are less clear-cut, however, and experience seems to have varied considerably across countries.

In assessing the determinants of the size structure of factory establishments, the following stylized facts should be borne in mind:

- The ranking of industries by average size (number of workers per establishment) seems to be broadly similar across countries and appears to change little over time (see table 1-2); this is also true for other indicators of the relative importance of large establishments.
- The average size of establishments, both in the aggregate and for specific industries, tends to be larger in developed than in developing countries.
- In most industries, and especially in manufacturing as a whole, there is a very wide range of establishment sizes at any given time.

- Over time most manufacturing establishments tend to grow in terms of number of workers, but growth in capital and in output tends to be even more pronounced.
- In any given manufacturing sector, establishments are constantly being born and dying. Those arriving and departing tend to be small in relation to the average size of establishment in the sector concerned (see chapter 4).

Available historical evidence suggests that in many developing and developed countries, including Colombia today, SMI accounts for 20–40 percent of all manufacturing employment (see table 1-1). As noted earlier, its share of output and employment usually rises early in the process of development, at which point it often still exceeds that of large industry. This was the case in Colombia as late as the mid-1960s with respect to employment, although LI had probably already surpassed SMI in output by the 1940s. During this phase, SMI increases its role at the expense of CS. It is unclear whether, at this stage, the share of LI is likely to be increasing relative to that of SMI—in other words, whether within the factory subsector (SMI and LI together) SMI's share will already be falling.[64] Later, when CS has become relatively less important, SMI's gains at the expense of CS will become less than its losses to LI and its overall share will begin to decline. These trends over time contribute to an overall increase in the average size of establishments, a pattern that, on balance, gives SMI a larger role in the early stages of a country's development and a smaller role later. Thus, the first step in attempting to explain SMI's changing role is to determine why establishment size in general tends to rise; this in turn requires some understanding of what determines the distribution of establishment sizes.

A comprehensive effort to explain patterns and trends in firm-size distribution must take into account both static and dynamic factors; the wide range of firm sizes at any time and the general tendency of firms to grow suggest the importance of the latter factors.[65] A model used to explain size and its variance across establishments must, at a minimum, take into consideration the factors listed below and the ways in which they interact:

- Technological factors (each firm's production function). In the simplest microeconomics of pure competition, technology (as reflected in the shape of the average total-cost curve) is the sole determinant of firm size. But the incompleteness of a model based solely on the character of the production function is evident from the many different sizes of firms that coexist at any point in time. Nevertheless, the concavity of the average cost curve is a determinant of the vari-

Table 1-1. *Distribution of Manufacturing Employment among Cottage Shop, Small and Medium Industry, and Large Industry: Selected Economies and Years*
(percent)

Economy	Year	Cottage shop (1–4 workers)	Small and medium industry (5–99 workers)	Large industry (100+ workers)
United States[a]	1967	1.1	22.3	76.6
	1947	1.1	23.9	75.0
Canada[b]	1959	2.5	31.9	65.6
	1955	2.8	30.5	66.7
	1950	2.9	31.2	65.9
	1930	3.7	35.5	60.8
Japan[c]	1975	19.1[d]	36.6[e]	44.3
	1965	16.1[d]	37.1[e]	46.8
	1955	20.0[d]	40.2[e]	39.8
Taiwan[f]	1971	3.0[g]	33.0	64.0
	1966	4.0[g]	39.0	57.0
	1940	25.3	74.7	
	1920	60.6	39.4	
Korea[h]	1975	36	17	47
Colombia[i]	1978	42.5–47.5	28.7–29.9	24.0–27.6
	1970	53.7	21.7	24.6
	1964	51.4	25.9	23.7
Philippines[j]	1975	66.0[d]	8.0[e]	26.0
	1967	77.8[d]	7.2[e]	15.0
India[k]	1973	60[d]	18[e]	22
Indonesia[l]	1975	76	12	12
Nigeria[m]	1972	59[d]	15[n]	26[o]
Kenya[m]	1969	49	10[t]	41[o]
Ghana[m]	1970	78	7[n]	15[o]
Tanzania[m]	1967	55	8[p]	37[o]

a. Data refer only to paid employees and therefore underestimate the share of employment in CS and in the smaller size categories of SMI. U.S. Department of Commerce, Bureau of the Census, *1967 Census of Manufactures*, vol. 1, *Summary and Subject Statistics* (Washington, D.C.: U.S. Government Printing Office, 1971), p. 24.

b. Data are from M. C. Urquhart and K. A. H. Buckley, eds., *Historical Statistics of Canada* (Toronto: Cambridge University Press, 1965), p. 489. They appear to exclude unpaid workers.

c. Data are from Small and Medium Enterprise Agency, *White Paper on Small and Medium Enterprises,* various annual editions, as presented in Hiromitsu Kaneda, "Development of Small and Medium Enterprise and Policy Response in Japan: An Analytical Survey" (Davis: University of California, Department of Economics, 1980), p. 58.

d. Establishments with 1–9 workers.

e. Establishments with 10–99 workers.

ance of establishment size: where average costs are nearly independent of size, a wide range of sizes would be expected, whereas a strongly U-shaped curve should produce a narrower range. A monotonically and strongly decreasing curve should produce only large firms.

● Demand factors (the size of each firm's market). A national market fragmented by high transportation costs can limit growth opportunities and lead to the development of many small plants rather than a few large ones. Rapidly rising total demand for a product can encourage new small firms to enter and existing ones to grow. The relevance of demand factors implies the absence of perfect competition. We assume that the market structure in manufacturing involves elements of oligopoly and monopolistic competition. The size distribution of establishments at any given time will reflect past and expected demand for the output of each establishment as perceived by it.

● Input supply factors. Each firm's evolution is affected by the input supply curves it faces, including that of capital wherein part (or all)

Table 1-1 *(notes continued)*

f. Samuel P. S. Ho, *Small-Scale Enterprises in Korea and Taiwan,* World Bank Staff Working Paper 384 (Washington, D.C., 1980), pp. 5, 9. Original sources are cited there.

g. Includes establishments with 1–3 workers; for the earlier years this category included establishments with less than 5 workers, which did not use power and were not operated by the Monopoly Bureau.

h. Ho, *Small-Scale Enterprises,* p. 5. According to Ho, if all temporary or daily workers are excluded from manufacturing employment and it is assumed that all of these were in the household sector (it is not clear how exaggerated an assumption this is), the share in that sector would fall to 16 percent.

i. Figures are from table 2-2. For 1978, the lower of the total manufacturing employment figures of that table are used here. As discussed in chapter 2, there is considerable uncertainty about the comparability of figures for the various years, so the trends suggested here should not be taken as proven facts.

j. Figures from Dennis Anderson and Farida Khambata, *Small Enterprises and Development Policy in the Philippines: A Case Study,* World Bank Staff Working Paper 468 (Washington, D.C., July 1981), p. 9.

k. Dipak Mazumdar, "A Descriptive Analysis of the Role of Small-Scale Enterprises in the Indian Economy," World Bank, Development Research Department, 1980; processed, pp. 2, 54.

l. T. Otsuki, I. Ohara, H. Iwayama, T. Miki, M. Hondai, and A. Hasida, *Industrial Development in South East Asian Countries: Small and Medium Industries—Republic of Indonesia* (International Development Center of Japan, 1977–78), p. 3.

m. John M. Page, Jr., *Small Enterprises in African Development: A Survey,* World Bank Staff Working Paper 363 (Washington, D.C., 1979), p. 2.

n. Establishments with 19–49 workers.

o. Establishments with 50 workers or more.

p. Establishments with 5–49 workers (approximately).

of the supply may be self-generated; with perfect factor markets, firm growth would be unaffected by input constraints.
- Other constraints on the rate of change of output. Even if product demand and input supplies are consistent with one rate of growth, factors such as risk aversion or the need to reorganize management procedures may dictate a slower rate.

To the extent that the rate of output growth tends to be constrained within a certain range, the size distribution of establishments will reflect their relative age. Scenarios can be conceived in which current size distribution is much better understood as the outcome of a historical process, rather than as a reflection of technically optimal firm or plant sizes given the current capital-labor (K/L) ratio of the economy and other conditions. If the capital market is highly imperfect, for example, firms may tend to become large even though there are no technical advantages to being large. The growth process must thus be analyzed in detail. Further, if the market has monopolistic and oligopolistic features, the growth prospects of a given firm will normally be affected by the growth strategies and performance of its competitors. Any two firms in an industry will usually compete, in the sense that the expansion of one lowers the rate of growth of demand for the other; however, various types of complementarity may also exist.

The trend toward large establishments as development proceeds is fueled by a combination of technical economies of scale and increases in market size, the latter reflecting higher national income together with better transportation and communications networks. At very low levels of development, a country's population is mainly agricultural and likely to be widely dispersed, with the result that transportation is relatively costly. The demand for simple consumer goods (processed foods, clothing, furniture, and so on) is met mainly by small local producers. In industries where economies of scale exist, an establishment can be expected to grow when its market expands. One means by which markets expand is international trade. Historically, developed countries have had a comparative advantage in many manufactured products and many of them have been imperial powers; thus they have been best able to exploit international markets in manufactured items. This pattern is now changing as the higher-income developing countries succeed in moving into the manufactured export market.

Scale economies are much more important in some industries than in others, and it seems reasonable to suppose that they have something to do with the broadly similar ranking of industries by average plant size in different countries. Table 1-2 gives some illustrative figures. In 1967 average plant size (measured by number of workers) in tobacco products, for example, was 30 times as large as that in wood products (excluding furniture) in the United States, 19.4 times as large on the average for nine other high-income countries, and 11.5 times as large in thirteen middle- and low-income countries.

At the same time, the data in table 1-2 strongly suggest that technological factors are by no means the only or even the main determinant of average plant size. For any given two-digit industry, average size (measured by level of employment) is typically much smaller in developing countries than in high-income countries; for the sets of countries covered in the table, the differential is seldom less than 2:1 and often 2.5:1 or more.[66] The size of this ratio is partly due to spurious comparisons of heterogeneous items at the two-digit level of industry. For example, the transportation equipment industry in developing countries consists largely of firms producing bicycles and other small vehicles, whereas in developed countries it is dominated by automobile production. In most cases, however, other factors are also at work. Several possibilities come to mind. Optimal plant size may be larger in high-income countries as a consequence of a nonhomogeneous production function under which optimal size rises with capital intensity, and a higher ratio of wage costs to capital costs than in developing countries.[67] Plants may also be larger in developed countries simply because they have had more time to grow or because the larger markets in these countries permit them to take greater advantage of economies of scale.[68] Pryor suggests that smaller countries or ones that strongly encourage import substitution (often for balance of payments reasons) may have lower average plant sizes because they are likely to promote industries for which their domestic markets are too small.[69] Furthermore, high-income countries have more highly developed capital markets—including stock markets, large banks, and a range of financial intermediaries, all of which facilitate large-scale investment—which may also contribute to the relatively large scale of their plants.

Another factor contributing to the larger average size of manufacturing firms in the aggregate in developed countries may be that a number of industries producing modern consumer and intermediate goods originated in economies that were already developed. Thus large firms could have quick access to large markets and capital would have been relatively inexpensive compared with labor. Partly as a result, the technologies used might be expected to incorporate economies of scale and to be capital-intensive. Industries that had been important at earlier stages of a country's development might also become more capital-intensive and larger in scale during the process of development, but would be less likely to exhibit these tendencies than the newer industries. This consideration does not help to explain differences in firm size within spe-

Table 1-2. *Average Rank of Industries by Average Size of Plants and an Overview of Plant-Size Relationships* (average size of U.S. plants = 100)

	Average rank			High-income economies			Middle- and low-income economies			U.S. average plant size (number of workers)
Industry group	All economies in sample	High-income economies	Middle- and low-income economies	Mean of indices[a]	Sample size	Average size (number of workers)[b]	Mean of indices[a]	Sample size	Average size (number of workers)[b]	
All industries				40.8	9	51.8	10.0	14	12.7	127
Tobacco products	1	1	2	60.0	4	324.6	20.0	7	108.2	541
Basic metals	2	2	1	184.5	9	306.3	48.3	7	80.2	166
Chemicals	3	4	5	178.7	9	173.3	54.1	14	55.4	97
Paper and pulp products	4	6	4	90.1	9	139.9	22.4	13	34.7	155
Textiles	5	8	3	42.3	9	105.3	41.5	14	103.3	249
Petroleum	6	3	10	203.7	9	301.4	27.7	7	41.0	148
Electrical machinery	7	5	9	70.7	9	131.5	14.6	14	27.2	186
Rubber products	8	10	6	79.3	9	69.0	48.2	14	41.9	87
Nonelectrical machinery	9	9	8	120.5	9	61.5	51.2	14	26.6	51
Transport equipment	10	7	12	71.1	9	192.7	5.1	14	13.8	271
Nonmetallic mineral manufactures	11	12	7	76.8	9	42.2	40.0	14	22.0	55
Printing and publishing	12	18	7	31.4	9	28.3	19.8	14	17.8	90
Beverages	13	11	16	85.4	5	31.6	41.4	9	15.3	37

Leather products	14	13	24.2	9	44.0	9.0	14	16.4	182
Food processing	15	15	58.5	7	48.0	33.4	13	27.4	82
Fabricated metal	16	14	71.0	9	38.3	28.6	9	15.4	54
Diver industries	17	17	47.0	9	37.1	17.0	14	13.4	79
Apparel	18	18	89.6	9	43.0	28.0	14	13.4	48
Furniture	19	19	44.0	7	55.4	3.5	13	4.4	126
Wood	20	20	92.7	9	16.7	52.0	14	9.4	18
Food, beverages, and tobacco	—	—	84.8	9	55.1	20.7	13	13.5	65
Sample size (number of countries)	23	9	14	9			9		

— Not applicable.

Note: Plant size computed from the parameters of fitted lognormal distribution. The high-income economies sampled are Austria (1964), Australia (1968–69), Canada (1970), France (1966), Federal Republic of Germany (1970), Japan (1971), Norway (1963), the United Kingdom (1968), and United States (1967). The middle- and low-income economies are Brazil (1960, 1970), Cyprus (1967), Ghana (1962), Israel (1965–66), Republic of Korea (1967), W. Malaysia (1968), Mauritius (1967–68), Mexico (1965), Peru (1963), Puerto Rico (1963, 1967), Spain (1970), Taiwan (1960), Thailand (1963), and Turkey (1964).

a. That is, the mean of the indices for each of the economies in the sample, where the index base is given by U.S. = 100. The value of 40.8 for "all industries" thus means that the average of the average plant sizes of all economies was 40.8 percent as large as in the United States, that is, 0.408 times 127, or 52 workers.

b. Calculated on the basis of average U.S. plant sizes and the mean of indices.

Source: Adapted from Ranadev Banerji, "Average Size of Plants in Manufacturing and Capital Intensity: A Cross-Country Analysis by Industry," *Journal of Development Economics*, vol. 5, no. 2 (June 1978), p. 161. The figures were originally computed from industrial censuses.

cific industries; but it suggests that these modern industries, which are relatively more important in developed countries, will contribute to a greater manufacturing-wide average firm size there.

In any event, average plant size in an industry is clearly affected both by static factors (such as the character of the production function, relative factor prices, and market concentration) and by dynamic ones (such as the representative firm's age and the rate of growth of its market and of the economy as a whole). The relative importance of these and other factors and how they interact has not hitherto been satisfactorily explained, partly because of insufficient data. It is clear, however, that the interactions are likely to be close. For example, economies of scale are likely to promote market concentration, which in turn is likely to raise the average size of plants.

The average size differentials between plants in developed countries and in developing countries cannot be explained without some understanding of the process by which establishments grow. If firms have an inherent tendency to grow but are usually faced with constraints on the rate of growth—with the result that there exists a "normal" range of growth rates—this would help to explain the differential (because the average age of plants is greater in developed countries) and why plant sizes vary in any industry at any time (because some started earlier than others). Microeconomic data on the growth of firms or establishments are limited, however. Some clues to the nature of the growth process can be gleaned from data on the changes in average establishment size over time, but it should be kept in mind that such changes reflect the creation of new establishments and the disappearance of others, as well as the growth of existing ones. In most countries, births and deaths of plants tend to take place in the smaller size range, and the former tend to exceed the latter; consequently the net effect is usually a lower average plant size. Thus if average size increases over time, as appears to be the case in general, one can infer that the existing establishments have been growing.

Average establishment size has tended to grow over time in most developing countries and in developed economies already characterized by large establishments.[70] If diseconomies of scale do not constrain the growth of establishments in countries where the average industrial unit is already relatively large, it seems even less likely that these constraints will operate in developing countries; growth in the average size of establishments can therefore be expected to be the norm for both groups. In Colombia, the average size of factory establishments (those with five or more workers) rose from about 18 workers in 1953 to about 55 in 1975; without reliable data it is hard to give precise estimates for later years.

Most of the limited microeconomic research on the determinants of growth of individual manufacturing firms has referred to relatively large units in developed countries.[71] In a recent study of British joint stock companies in manufacturing, construction, distribution, and miscellaneous services between 1948 and 1960, Singh and Whittington found that the average growth rate of net assets was somewhat faster for larger than for smaller firms (8.4 percent a year for the largest category as opposed to 6.1 percent for the smallest).[72] These authors also reported that the standard deviation of growth rates declined with firm size. They found a definite though rather weak tendency for the rankings of firms' growth rates to be similar in the two subperiods 1948–54 and 1954–60. Most corporate births and deaths occurred in the smaller firms, while net losses were greatest in the smallest and largest classes.[73] Later chapters will show whether our Colombian data yield similar results.

Different explanations for the general tendency of firms to grow may have quite different implications. According to one hypothesis, the impetus for growth can be explained by the benefits to be reaped from economies of scale. These economies can exist in production, administration, marketing, or purchases of factors (for example, capital); they can provide a cost advantage over smaller competitors—and, on occasion, monopoly or oligopoly power within a given market (whether local or national).[74] This explanation implies that the eventual decline in the market share of SMI occurs because SMI is not competitive; firms must either expand or die. In another scenario, small firms may be efficient, but if capital markets are imperfect these firms may find it desirable to reinvest their profits internally and grow, even though this lessens the average profit rate. The fact that profit maximization is not the only objective of corporate policy also plays a part here. Size is frequently desirable for its own sake, in the minds of management if not in those of shareholders.

Since the tendency to growth does not by itself demonstrate the presence of scale economies, it is important to have other types of evidence on the advantages and disadvantages of size and on when they come into play. Apart from scale economies, possible advantages of size include the ability to exclude competitors by noneconomic means, such as legal advantages, bribery of government officials, threats to potential competitors, and the like; favorable factor market imperfections; and government regulatory systems that favor larger units. In a dynamic sense, the existence of LI at one point in time can increase its competitiveness in subsequent periods by promoting favorable market imperfections (for example, a capital market to which LI has better access than SMI does); technical economies of scale (perhaps realized as a result of research that improves LI's production processes); and government regulations or procedures beneficial to LI. As an industry's size structure shifts toward larger units, the political power of these units is likely to increase in relation to that of small firms; their pressure on the government for policies favoring them will, in turn, further increase their relative importance.

SMI owes its success relative to CS to the same kinds of factors as those outlined above, while any success SMI achieves relative to LI is likely to be a consequence of such factors as diseconomies of scale and product and factor market imperfections that are the opposite of those that favor it by comparison with CS. If most scale economies in a given industry are achieved when a plant has 50 workers, they may mainly encourage SMI against CS; if they are not achieved until the work force numbers 500, they will encourage LI.

The extent of economies of scale depends not only on technology, but also on the relative availability and prices of factors of production. If labor is cheap, labor-intensive technologies with limited scale economies are likely to be economically efficient in a number of industries. The availability of the entrepreneurial skills needed for smaller-scale operations may also affect optimal size if, as seems likely, the skills and preferences most relevant to the creation and management of small firms (such as the desire to run one's own business) are different from those needed in large firms. Attitudes to risk also have an effect on the availability of entrepreneurs, as do the institutions that help to determine the potential costs of risk taking.

There are many sources of entrepreneurial and managerial talents. In some household and small factory enterprises, these skills tend to be acquired and handed down on the job. In nontraditional small enterprises, entrepreneurs are more likely to be self-starters or former employees of other firms in LI or in SMI. Most managers in LI have had professional or technical education; higher executives have usually also had considerable work experience. At an early stage of a country's development, entrepreneurial skills are probably most frequently learned in the context of traditional SI. Later, increasing formal education and accumulated experience with LI will expand the pool of talent in that subsector. The talent available to manage modern SMI may expand in the wake of LI, as well as under formal and specialized educational programs. Although the pool of talent for LI normally rises fastest, this need not always be the case.

Market imperfections related to the spatial dispersion of economic activity will generally raise the share of manufacturing employment and output in small establishments. The advantages to LI of locating in a large urban center depend on such factors as transportation costs and the need for a wide range of inputs, as well as more general factors such as the locational preferences of entrepreneurs. Managers of large firms are usually high earners and their expectations are likely to include a relatively sophisticated living environment and good educational opportunities for their children. In most developing countries these preferences limit them to medium-size or large cities.

Since exporting normally requires an organization of some size with opportunities for the division of labor, international trade tends to be the preserve of large firms.[75] Some manufactured exports, especially those destined for developed countries, need to be similar to items normally consumed in the buying country; consequently they may require a relatively large-scale and capital-intensive production technology. This requirement is a barrier to participation by small producers. Thus SMI is unlikely to play a significant role in a developing country economy that is heavily engaged in the export of manufactured goods. In some countries, however, exports of products from small firms are facilitated by a strong intermediary system; Japan's trading houses have historically been a case in point. In other countries, when large producers move into world markets, their domestic markets may be partly taken over by smaller producers; those export activities may in turn be stimulated by the difficulty of competing in the domestic market. Despite such qualifications, heavy involvement in foreign trade in manufactured goods is likely to be associated with a size structure inclined toward LI.

Evaluating the Economic Effects of Firms

Several of a firm's effects merit separate consideration, including its effect on the total output of the economy (commonly referred to as the economic efficiency of the firm), on income distribution, and on other determinants of welfare, such as the stability of family income and employment. Some effects are taken into account and valued in the market, whereas others (externalities) are not. Both present and future contributions must be taken into account; firms may be ranked differently at different points in time or under different assumptions about their behavior.

Any assessment of the economic impact of a firm (or of a category of firms such as SMI) depends not only on the firm's own characteristics and those of the economy of which it is a part, but also on the policy questions prompting the assessment. Policymakers are likely to be interested in three questions about a particular firm or type of firm:

- Given a firm's present characteristics, should it continue to exist, and would it be desirable to have more firms like this one?

- Would it be desirable for the firm to expand or contract?
- Would it be desirable for the firm to change in a certain way—for example, to become more labor-intensive?

Many efficiency calculations (such as benefit-cost ratios) are directly relevant only to the first question, since they are estimates of the average efficiency of all factors used by a firm or group of firms, not of the efficiency of increases or decreases in factors used. The first question involves the "total conditions" responsible for a firm's efficiency, whereas the other two involve marginal conditions. The first question also has to do with the contributions this sort of firm now makes; the other two relate to how those contributions would change if the firm changed in size or structure. Some policies (credit policies, for example) are more concerned with the behavior and evolution of existing firms, others with the creation of firms.

Attempts to measure the economic worth of firms, industries, and public sector projects have tended to focus mainly or exclusively on questions of "efficiency"; some have also tried to assess the consequences for employment or income distribution.[76] Such measurements involve comparing total benefits to total costs, with the use of whatever formula is considered most appropriate to the structure of the economy and the particular questions being asked. Complexities arise when the social costs of a firm's activities differ from its private costs owing to market imperfections or externalities. When the economy suffers not only from imperfections that cause misallocation of resources among firms and industries but also from unemployment of resources, opportunity costs can fall to zero. In a Keynesian underemployment equilibrium with all the inputs in excess supply, the social cost of producing a unit of a product could be zero and the ratio of benefits to costs could be infinity. The estimation of social costs requires much information about the state of the economy in order to predict the decrease in output elsewhere that accompanies a given firm's increased use of inputs.

Further, the benefits and costs of the presence of a given type of manufacturing firm may depend not only on its own characteristics and on the overall state of the economy, but also on the characteristics of the firms with which it has direct or indirect linkages. The importance of linkages as a component of a firm's contribution to the economy depends on how the economy functions. Hirschman argues, for example, that when a firm's expansion raises demand for some of its inputs, the supply of savings and entrepreneurship is stimulated.[77] Under these circumstances, linkages can clearly be important. Unfortunately, there is little organized information on how linkages differ by firm size.[78] If small and large firms tended to have similar linkages to the rest of the economy, the difference in their total impact on the economy would be proportionately less than the difference in their direct effects. Differences in secondary effects via linkages might even tend to offset differences in direct effects. In Colombia, however, it appears that large manufacturing firms deal disproportionately with large financial, manufacturing, and commercial establishments; similarly, small firms tend to deal disproportionately with other small firms. If this general pattern holds, then any differences in the direct impact on the economy of small and large firms would be magnified if indirect effects were also to be taken into account. The existence of subcontracting suggests, however, that some links do exist between large and small producers.[79]

Large firms offer the economy one external benefit that may be of real value to countries in which too few resources are channeled through the public sector: such firms, especially incorporated ones, are relatively easy to tax. Consequently, they usually pay a much higher share of their value added in taxes than do small firms. Another possible externality associated with large firms is their contribution to savings. It has often been argued that large firms generate more savings per unit of value added because of their high ratio of profits to value added and the relatively high incomes of the capital earners and employees whom they support. Rates of savings derived from profits are generally held to exceed those derived from wages. It is also reasonable to expect that rates of savings are positively related to income levels for both capital earners and wage earners—and both groups tend to have higher incomes from larger firms than from smaller ones. There is little empirical evidence on these issues, however. Moreover, there is a good deal of employee mobility between larger and smaller firms—a phenomenon that we discuss further in chapter 4. This may produce important externalities in the form of experience gained in one firm that is subsequently used to benefit another. On one hand, labor tends to move from smaller to larger firms; in this case the externalities involved would flow from the former to the latter. On the other hand, small entrepreneurs often acquire skills as employees of large firms and then go into business on their own; here the externalities accrue to SMI. The existence of these two flows implies a degree of complementarity between large and small establishments.

Since its current contributions may not be typical of those in the longer run, allowance must be made for the firm's own evolution together with the expected changes in the structure of the economy and its functioning (for example, the level of utilization of resources). In some cases prediction may be so speculative as to be irrelevant. But in certain types of firms the stages of growth may be predicted with a reasonable degree of confidence. In that case it may be feasible to estimate a firm's long-run or life-cycle efficiency, which could differ considerably from its level of efficiency at a given point in time and would of course be a more meaningful measure.

The Present Study: Principal Findings and Structure

The main conclusions reached in this study are as follows:

• Colombia's SMI sector grew very rapidly in the 1970s, both absolutely and in relation to its own previous growth and that of large industry during the same period. Employment in plants with fewer than 100 workers appears to have expanded at around 8–9 percent a year between 1970 and 1978, and aggregate output grew at about the same rate; employment and output in large industry grew by about 6 percent annually during these years. The detailed data from our sample of metalworking firms are consistent with these aggregate figures.

• Our samples from the metalworking and food processing sectors together with aggregate data for 1976 suggest that the average return to investment in SMI was high in the late 1970s. These high returns help to explain the rapid expansion of SMI in the 1970s; they represented both an inducement to growth and a source of the investment funds needed for expansion. We do not know by how much the rate of profit has fallen in the subsequent recession, which began in 1980.

• The average return to investment in our sample of firms was quite high, but the variance around the mean was also very high; a significant minority of firms had negative private benefit-cost ratios. (For definitions of the terms used here and in later chapters, see the glossary.) A similar picture emerges from the growth of employment and sales in our subsample of metalworking firms in the 1970s (these data were not available for the food processing firms); while average growth was rapid, the variance was also high, with a significant minority showing declines in short periods of a few years. A large majority of firms registered net growth over the ten years preceding our survey, but many suffered temporary declines at one time or another during this period. In short, growth was not typically smooth.

• The private profitability of firms appears to have been more closely associated with their technical efficiency than with allocative or price efficiency or with absolute levels of input and output prices. (For definitions, see the glossary.) The wide variations in the profitability of firms thus reflect comparably wide variations in their technical efficiency.

• These observed interfirm variations in profitability and technical efficiency seem to have several causes. Some are associated with the dynamics of firm growth; where indivisibilities are important, for example, some small firms are likely to be inefficient because they are operating at levels well below the optimal scale of production. Levels of efficiency are also influenced by the differing expectations of entrepreneurs; those who were previously production workers, and whose alternative earnings were therefore relatively low, appear to have been satisfied with a lower income—and thus a lower level of technical efficiency—than those whose time had a high opportunity cost. Another source of inefficiency seems to be the fluctuation of sales over time. We found this to be especially true in the case of food processing, where sales formed the basis of our estimates of value added (see chapter 3). Purely seasonal fluctuations do not appear to affect the level of efficiency, however, to judge by their lack of explanatory power in our regressions.

• Personal characteristics of the entrepreneur—such as skills, education, and previous job—strongly influence both technical efficiency and profitability.

• In the metalworking and food processing sectors, SMI firms as a group tend to do better with intermediate technologies than with either the simplest or the most sophisticated techniques. In metalworking, the most profitable technology for MI is more sophisticated than that for SI. None of the technologies observed are sophisticated by the standards of developed countries, however.

• Technological improvements appear to be reasonably frequent and economically important in SMI. Our subsamples of both metalworking and food processing firms provided considerable evidence of design capability and capacity for innovation and adaptation. Aggregate data indicate a 45 percent increase in the labor productivity in small industry (plants with five to forty-nine workers) from the mid-1950s to the late 1970s; this increase implies either technological improvement or a rising ratio of capital to labor, or both.

• On the average, small plants operate at lower levels of economic and technical efficiency than medium-size ones. This finding, which emerges clearly from our firm-level data in metalworking and food processing, is also suggested by data from the manufacturing sector as a whole. This efficiency gap is probably related to static factors such as indivisibilities and the tendency for more efficient firms to grow more quickly than less efficient ones.

• During the 1970s, the employment elasticity of output growth in the manufacturing sector as a whole was above the level for the previous two decades. This increase, which represents a reversal of previous experience, is also apparent for SMI in general. The causal factors involved appear to include the constant or falling levels of real wages in the early 1970s, the increasing ability of Colombian entrepreneurs to develop or adapt labor-intensive technologies, and the high cost of capital for many of the firms that were expanding in the 1970s.

• Some government policies seem to have helped to promote the rapid growth of SMI, especially during the 1970s, even though this was by no means their main purpose, and their impact was less important than that of other causal factors. The satisfactory pace of overall economic growth beginning in the late 1960s helped SMI by expanding demand, by generating the savings needed to finance new firms, and by creating positive business expectations. Another helpful macroeconomic development was the increased supply of imports, which reflected the healthier state of the foreign trade sector—itself largely a result of the adoption in 1967 of a floating exchange rate and better exchange rate management.

• In addition to these contextual factors, several more specific developments favored SMI growth. Our survey showed the importance of the buildup of a nest egg in the form of the *cesantía* (severance pay) as a basis for starting up many small firms. The Corporación Financiera Popular (CFP) has performed relatively well and has assisted many firms. It is harder to assess the impact of the activities of the Servicio Nacional de Aprendizaje (SENA), the country's main vocational-technical training institution. Courses attended by employees of large firms appear to have helped some of them to start businesses of their own, and some SMI firms have benefited from SENA courses attended by their workers. Favorable attitudes toward SENA, although not universal, are widespread.

The chapters that follow discuss the nature and evolution of SMI in Colombia using historical data on the sector as a whole and detailed firm-level evidence drawn from surveys of the metalworking and food processing industries. Chapter 2 describes the SMI sector in broad economic terms and traces its evolution over the past half century. The reversal in the 1970s of SMI's former decline relative to large-scale industry is discussed in some detail. Chapters 3, 4, and 5 examine the microeconomics of SMI in Colombia, relying heavily on enterprise surveys taken in the metalworking and food processing industries in 1978 and 1979, respectively. Chapter 3 presents an evaluation of the static economic efficiency of SMI. Chapter 4 focuses on SMI entrepreneurs and on the patterns and determinants of SMI growth. Chapter 5 discusses the process of technological change in metalworking and food processing firms and suggests some elements of a theory of technological change for SMI. Chapter 6 reviews the main features of SMI detailed in earlier chapters, attempts to explain the special dynamism of SMI in the 1970s, and briefly examines some implications of the study's findings for policy toward the SMI sector.

Notes

1. The following remarks provide but one example of this view: "For almost any factor prices and in almost any industry, efficiently operated modern technology is more productive than craft production." R. R. Nelson, T. P. Schultz, and R. L. Slighton, *Structural Change in a Developing Economy: Colombia's Problems and Prospects* (Princeton, N.J.: Princeton University Press, 1971), p. 360.

2. Murray D. Bryce, *Industrial Development: A Guide for Accelerating Economic Growth* (New York: McGraw-Hill, 1960), p. 24.

3. An important expression of this view appears in International Labour Organisation (ILO), *Employment, Incomes and Equality: A Strategy for Increasing Productive Employment in Kenya* (Geneva, 1972).

4. This was one of the many issues considered by E. F. Schumacher in *Small is Beautiful* (London: Sphere Books, 1974).

5. United Nations, *Measures for the Economic Development of Underdeveloped Countries* (New York, 1951).

6. "It is worth noting in this connection that large scale modern industry is usually much less profitable than the small craft-type industries, in addition to being more costly in terms of capital and creating less employment." Ian Little, Tibor Scitovsky, and Maurice Scott, *Industry and Trade in Some Developing Countries* (London: Oxford University Press, 1970), p. 91.

7. This argument has had special appeal in India, where the economic considerations it embodies have been coupled with the Gandhian philosophical preference for rural and village life. See Indian Government, Ministry of Commerce and Industry, *Small Industry in a North Indian Town* (New Delhi, 1956); and Gunnar Myrdal, *Asian Drama: An Inquiry into the Poverty of Nations* (London: Allen Lane the Penguin Press, 1968), pp. 1217-20.

8. See Dennis Anderson and Farida Khambata, *Small Enterprises and Development Policy in the Philippines: A Case Study*, World Bank Staff Working Paper 468 (Washington, D.C., July 1981); J. W. Mellor, *The New Economics of Growth: A Strategy for India and the Developing World* (Ithaca, N.Y.: Cornell University Press, 1976); and F. C. Child and Hiromitsu Kaneda, "Links to the Green Revolution: A Study of Small-Scale, Agriculturally-Related Industry in the Pakistan Punjab," *Economic Development and Cultural Change*, vol. 23, no. 2 (January 1975), pp. 249-75.

9. For a description of the record in Japan, see W. W. Lockwood, *The Economic Development of Japan 1868-1938* (Princeton, N.J.: Princeton University Press, 1955), p. 212.

10. Useful reviews of what is known have recently been compiled by Anderson and Schmitz. See Dennis Anderson, "Small Industry in Developing Countries: A Discussion of Issues," *World Development*, vol. 10, no. 11 (November 1982); and Hubert Schmitz, "The Growth Constraints on Small Scale Manufacturing in Developing Countries: A Critical Review," *World Development*, vol. 10, no. 6 (June 1982), pp. 429-50.

11. Chris Gerry, "Petty Production and Capitalist Production in Dakar: The Crisis of the Self-Employed," *World Development*, vol. 6, no. 9-10 (1978), pp. 1147-60.

12. See, for example, Alejandro Portes, "The Informal Sector and the World Economy: Notes on the Structure of Subsidized Labour," *IDS Bulletin*, vol. 9, no. 4 (1978), pp. 35-40.

13. Schmitz, "Growth Constraints," p. 433.

14. In economic terms, this is known as a nonhomothetic production function, that is, a production function characterized by a changing marginal rate of substitution among factors of production for a given ratio of each factor to each other factor, as the level of output rises.

15. John Todd, "Plant Size, Factor Proportions, and Efficiency in Colombian Industry," in *Essays on Industrialization*, ed. Albert Berry (Tempe, Ariz.: Arizona State University Center for Latin American Studies, 1983).

16. Lawrence J. White, "The Evidence on Appropriate Factor Proportions for Manufacturing in Less Developed Countries: A Survey," *Economic Development and Cultural Change*, vol. 27, no. 1 (October 1978), pp. 27–60.

17. For example, A. S. Bhalla, "Galenson-Leibenstein Criterion of Growth Reconsidered: Some Implicit Assumptions," *Economia Internazionale*, vol. 17 (1964), p. 248.

18. P. N. Dhar and Harold Lydall, *The Role of Small Enterprises in Indian Development* (Bombay: Asia Publishing House, 1961), p. 19.

19. J. C. Sandesara, "Scale and Technology in Indian Industry," *Bulletin of the Oxford University Institute of Economics and Statistics*, vol. 28 (August 1966), pp. 194–95.

20. For a discussion of measurement problems, see R. B. Sutcliffe, *Industry and Underdevelopment* (Reading, Mass.: Addison-Wesley, 1971), chap. 5.

21. For a good discussion of economies of scale in manufacturing, see Sutcliffe, *Industry and Underdevelopment*, chap. 6.

22. Peter Kilby, *Industrialization in an Open Economy: Nigeria, 1945–1966* (London: Cambridge University Press, 1969).

23. N. H. Leff, "Entrepreneurship and Development: The Problem Revisited," *Journal of Economic Literature*, vol. 17, no. 1 (March 1979), pp. 46–64.

24. See, for example, Eugene Staley and Richard Morse, *Modern Small Industry for Developing Countries* (New York: McGraw-Hill, 1965), p. 233.

25. Anderson, "Small Industry," pp. 926–32.

26. For evidence from a sample of firms in Thailand, see D. J. LeCraw, "Choice of Technology in Low Wage Countries: A Non-neoclassical Approach," *Quarterly Journal of Economics*, vol. 373 (November 1979), pp. 631–54.

27. For insights on such matters, see Malcolm Harper, *Small Business in the Third World* (New York: Wiley, 1984). As Schmitz, "Growth Constraints," p. 432, notes, one must be aware of the possibility that the frequent reference to organizational deficiencies reflects more the background of the analyst than the true problem.

28. Michael Lipton, "Family, Fungibility, and Formality: Rural Advantages of Informal Non-farm Enterprises versus the Urban-Formal State," paper presented at the meeting of the International Economic Association, Mexico City, 1980.

29. See, for example, Schmitz, "Growth Constraints," p. 432.

30. Contributions to this discussion include Richard R. Nelson and Edmund S. Phelps, "Investment in Humans, Technological Diffusions and Economic Growth," *American Economic Review*, vol. 56 (May 1966), pp. 69–75; Finis Welch, "Education in Production," *Journal of Political Economy*, vol. 78, no. 1 (January-February 1970), pp. 35–59.

31. The different composition of the labor force may be due either to a nonhomothetic production function or to labor market imperfection.

32. In Ghana, it is reported to be the single most important constraint facing such firms. B. F. Steele, *Small-Scale Employment and Production in Developing Countries: Evidence from Ghana* (New York: Praeger, 1977).

33. For examples from India, see Dhar and Lydall, "The Role of Small Enterprises"; from Brazil, see Hubert Schmitz, *Manufacturing in the Backyard: Case Studies on Accumulation and Employment in Small Scale Brazilian Industry* (London: Frances Pinter, 1982); and from Senegal, see Gerry, "Petty Production and Capitalist Production in Dakar."

34. Sutcliffe, *Industry and Underdevelopment*, pp. 240–41; Kenneth King, "Kenya's Machine Makers: A Study of Small-Scale Industry in Kenya's Emergent Artisan Society," *World Development*, vol. 2, no. 4 (1974), p. 28.

35. King, "Kenya's Machine Makers," p. 28.

36. Schmitz, *Manufacturing in the Backyard*.

37. A. S. Bhalla, *Technology and Employment in Industry: A Case Study Approach* (Geneva: International Labour Office, 1975); and Frances Stewart, *Technology and Underdevelopment*, 2d. ed. (London: Macmillan, 1978).

38. Walter Galenson and Harvey Leibenstein, "Investment Criteria, Productivity, and Economic Development," *Quarterly Journal of Economics*, vol. 69, no. 3 (August 1955), pp. 343–70. Hirschman also commented on the higher productivity achievable through machine-paced technologies. See Albert O. Hirschman, *The Strategy of Economic Development* (New Haven, Conn.: Yale University Press, 1958).

39. Alexander Gerschenkron, "Economic Backwardness in Historical Perspective," in *The Progress of Underdeveloped Areas*, ed. Bert F. Hoselitz (Chicago: University of Chicago Press, 1952), p. 7.

40. Gustav Ranis, "Investment Criteria, Productivity and Economic Development: An Empirical Comment," *Quarterly Journal of Economics*, vol. 76 (May 1962), p. 302. In fact, Ranis's comparisons were limited to firm-size categories, not categories defined by degree of factor intensity.

41. Staley and Morse, *Modern Small Industry*, chap. 5.

42. Steven Langdon, "Multinational Corporations, Taste Transfers and Underdevelopment: A Case Study from Kenya," *Review of African Political Economy*, no. 2 (1975).

43. Dennis Anderson and Mark W. Leiserson, "Rural Non-farm Employment in Developing Countries," *Economic Development and Cultural Change*, vol. 28, no. 2 (January 1980).

44. Susumu Watanabe, "Reflections on Current Policies for Promoting Small Enterprises and Subcontracting," *International Labour Review*, vol. 110, no. 5 (November 1974); and Watanabe, ed., *Technology, Marketing and Industrialization: Linkages between Large and Small Enterprises* (New Delhi: Macmillan, 1983).

45. Donald C. Mead, "Of Contracts and Subcontracts: Small Firms in Vertically Disintegrated Production/Distribution Systems in LDCs," *World Development*, vol. 12, no. 11–12 (November-December 1984), p. 1101.

46. Samuel P. S. Ho, *Small-Scale Enterprises in Korea and Taiwan*, World Bank Staff Working Paper 384 (Washington, D.C., April 1980).

47. Bert F. Hoselitz, "Small Industry in Underdeveloped Countries," *Journal of Economic History*, vol. 19 (1959), p. 612.

48. Anderson, "Small Industry," p. 923. For surveys, see Peter Kilby, ed., *Entrepreneurship and Economic Development* (New York: Free Press, 1971); Enyinna Chuta and Carl Liedholm, "The Economics of Rural and Urban Small Scale Industries in Sierra Leone," African Rural Economy Paper 14 (East

Lansing, Mich.: Michigan State University Department of Agricultural Economics, 1976); and Child and Kaneda, "Links to the Green Revolution."

49. The recent literature on proto-industrialization is relevant in this context. See Franklin Mendels, "Proto-industrialization, the First Phase of the Industrialization Process," *Journal of Economic History*, vol. 32 (1972), pp. 241–61.

50. With respect to the Colombian case, see Albert Berry, "The Limited Role of Rural Small Scale Manufacturing for Late Comers: Some Hypotheses on the Colombian Experience," Working Paper B.4 (Toronto, Ont.: University of Toronto Development Studies Programme, 1984). See also Enyinna Chuta and Carl Liedholm, "Rural Non-Farm Employment: A Review of the State of the Art," Michigan State University Rural Development Paper 4 (East Lansing: Michigan State University, 1979).

51. Edith T. Penrose, *The Theory of the Growth of the Firm* (Oxford: Basil Blackwell, 1972), chap. 6.

52. Ibid., p. 98.

53. Ibid., pp. 212–13.

54. Among the contributions to the analysis of the implication of satisficing behavior was W. J. Baumol, *Business Behaviour, Value and Growth*, rev. ed. (New York: Harcourt, Brace and World, 1967). See also H. A. Simon, *Models of Man* (New York: Wiley, 1957); and Harvey Leibenstein, *Economic Theory and Organizational Analysis* (New York: Harper, 1960).

55. Robin Marris, *The Economic Theory of Managerial Capitalism* (Glencoe, Ill.: Free Press, 1964); and Richard Nelson and Sidney Winters, *An Evolution Theory of Economic Capabilities and Behaviour* (Cambridge, Mass.: Harvard University Press, 1982).

56. ILO, *Employment, Incomes and Equality.*

57. See especially Todd, "Plant Size, Factor Proportions, and Efficiency in Colombian Industry."

58. Depending on one's purpose, different ways of categorizing firms by size may be appropriate. One important distinction is that between family establishments and larger ones; within the latter group it may be useful also to distinguish between firms small enough to have a very simple managerial hierarchy and larger ones. For manufacturing as a whole, such distinctions do not coincide very closely with measures such as output levels, number of workers, or capital stock. They are more likely to do so at the level of specific industries. In any case, since many size-related characteristics change gradually rather than abruptly with size, it is often preferable to think of size as a continuous variable.

A limited number of categories do facilitate the discussion, however. In Colombia, both data availability and presumed structural differences suggest a distinction between small and medium factories on the one hand, and household or cottage-shop industries (with very small family-based units) on the other. Data on the latter are available only on a piecemeal and limited basis. For establishments of five or more workers (since about 1970, for establishments of ten or more workers), some useful information at an aggregate level can be found in the annual surveys of the Departamento Administrativo Nacional de Estadística (DANE, Central Statistical Office).

59. For discussions, see Hoselitz, "Small Industry in Underdeveloped Countries"; and W. N. Parker, "Industry," chap. 3 in *The New Cambridge Modern*

History, ed. Peter Burke, vol. 13 (Cambridge, England: Cambridge University Press, 1979).

60. Anderson, "Small Industry," p. 914.

61. Ibid., pp. 816–17.

62. Hoselitz, "Small Industry in Underdeveloped Countries," p. 205.

63. Staley and Morse, *Modern Small Industry,* pp. 137–40.

64. This is true in some of the countries for which Anderson ("Small Industry," p. 916) breaks down employment over time, but not in others.

65. The literature on the economics of the firm is relevant in this context; see, for example, Penrose, *The Theory of the Growth of the Firm;* and Marris, *Economic Theory of Managerial Capitalism.*

66. A comparison between Eastern European centrally planned economies and Western European market economies also reveals broadly similar industry rankings by average size of establishment, although average size tends to be much larger in the former than in the latter in relation to the size of their economies. See Frederick Pryor, "The Size of Production Establishments in Manufacturing," *Economic Journal,* vol. 28 (1972), p. 563.

67. Ranadev Banerji, "Average Size of Plants in Manufacturing and Capital Intensity: A Cross-Country Analysis by Industry," *Journal of Development Economics,* vol. 5, no. 2 (June 1978), pp. 155–66, shows that for a large number of two-digit industries, intercountry variations in average size of plant are positively correlated with nonwage value added per employee, used as a proxy for capital intensity.

68. In a cross-country analysis of high- and middle-income countries, Pryor ("The Size of Production Establishments," pp. 560–61) found that his indicators of establishment size (the mean size of establishment for those with 20 or more workers, the Niehans index, and the percentage of workers in establishments of 1,000 workers or more) were significantly related to the total size of the economy (GNP in U.S. dollars, using U.S. price weights) and also, in the case of the Niehans index, to a measure of openness, the ratio of nonagricultural merchandise exports to value added in manufacturing and mining. The Niehan index is defined as the sum of the sizes of the establishments with 20 or more workers, weighted by the fraction of the total labor force employed in all the units under consideration. Neither economic density variables (which measure the level of economic activity per unit of geographical area) nor per capita income appears to be of much importance. In short, the size of the market seems to have a crucial influence on average manufacturing establishment size, mainly by constraining establishment size in each industrial branch, but perhaps also to some extent by affecting industrial composition (countries with small domestic markets tend not to specialize in industries in which large establishments are the norm).

69. "The Size of Production Establishments in Manufacturing," p. 553.

70. Jewkes argued in 1952 that "there have in the past thirty or forty years been no very spectacular changes in size [of manufacturing establishments]." See John Jewkes, "The Size of the Factory," *Economic Journal* (June 1952), pp. 237–51. Pryor's more recent analysis ("The Size of Production Establishments in Manufacturing") demonstrates, however, that for a number of definitions (all involving employment) the average size of establishments of 20 or more workers rose in six market economies during the first five or six decades of this century.

The arithmetical average rate of growth for these six countries, with industrial composition held constant at its early-year level in each, was 16 percent; using late-year composition, it was 18 percent. For two of the three large countries included—the United States and France (the third was the Federal Republic of Germany)—the increase was very small or nonexistent (using early-year weights, the average for the United States fell). The share of workers in establishments of more than 1,000 workers rose sharply in both France and the United States, however. A relatively small proportion of the increases in average size was attributable to shifts in industrial composition toward industries typified by large establishments. Had output or total inputs been used to measure size, the increase would have been much greater than that observed. Inclusion of plants of less than 20 workers might also have led to higher estimates for the increases in average establishment size.

71. Much of the early discussion, including Gibrat's formulation of the law of proportionate effect—the proposition that the percentage change in the size of a firm is independent of its absolute size—was related to the fact that in practice size distributions tend to approximate closely the lognormal distribution, which is generated by the law. Robert Gibrat, *Les Inégalités Economiques* (Paris: Recueil Sirey, 1931).

72. Ajit Singh and Geoffrey Whittington, "The Size and Growth of Firms," *Review of Economic Studies*, vol. 42, no. 129 (January 1975), p. 18. Since some firms revalued assets for inflation and others did not, it is not clear whether these results more closely approximate the growth of assets in nominal or in real terms.

73. Ibid., pp. 19, 21, 23.

74. Since technical economies of scale are more relevant to plant size and other economies to firm size, some of this discussion may have more bearing on firm-size distribution than on plant-size distribution.

75. The concentration of Colombia's manufactured exports in the hands of large firms is documented, among other places, in Carlos Díaz-Alejandro, *Foreign Trade Regimes and Economic Development: Colombia* (New York: Columbia University Press, 1976). See also J. P. Wogart, *Industrialization in Colombia: Policies, Patterns, Perspectives* (Tubingen: J. C. B. Mohr, 1978), p. 121.

76. The concept of efficiency in western economics has traditionally been related to the very simple social welfare function in which the marginal utility of income is the same for everyone, and hence income distribution does not affect the level of social welfare. Some economists further assume that inefficient firms will be weeded out by the competitive process, in which case there would be little need, for policy purposes, to worry about measurement of efficiency at the firm level. In the real world, the existence of a given type of productive unit (for example, SMI) may signal some relatively acceptable level of efficiency or contribution to the economy, but the relationship may be weak. First, given product and factor market imperfections and externalities, social efficiency need not be closely related to private profitability, so efficient firms may be weeded out and inefficient ones may survive. Second, firms may have variable levels of efficiency over time.

77. Hirschman, *Strategy of Economic Development.*

78. Attempts have been made to differentiate levels of linkages by small and large producers, but these efforts generally assume that linkages per unit of output are the same for small and large firms in a given industry. They thus address only some of the sources of different linkages. See, for example, Patricio Meller and Manuel Marfán, "Small and Large Industry: Employment Generation, Linkages and Key Sectors," *Economic Development and Cultural Change,* vol. 29, no. 2 (January 1981), pp. 263–74.

79. The major work on this subject is Watanabe, *Technology, Marketing and Industrialization.*

2

The Role of Small and Medium Firms in Colombia's Industrial Development

Over the past half-century or so, Colombia's manufacturing sector has been radically transformed by rapid growth and major structural change. This chapter traces the evolution of small and medium industry in the context of that wider transformation and reviews some of the characteristics that distinguish SMI from cottage-shop industry and from large industry. The chapters that follow probe the SMI sector more deeply. To repeat the definitions set forth in chapter 1, CS is said to consist of establishments with fewer than 5 workers, SI consists of those with 5–49 workers, MI 50–99 workers, and LI 100 or more workers.

Taken individually, the various censuses and surveys that provide the data base for this chapter are of reasonable quality. Many types of information are available for only one or a few years, however, and the years in question vary with the type of information. Thus trends in two conceptually related variables often have to be analyzed with data from different years. The best aggregate information on the employment structure of manufacturing by sector and size of plant is for 1964; although it would obviously have been preferable to focus on a more recent year, 1964 is frequently used as a benchmark. More generally, when the data we use do not correspond to the years that would seem most appropriate to the task at hand, the reader is asked to accept that the appropriate figures are unavailable. Another point to mention again is that it matters in some contexts whether size is defined by level of employment, output, or capital. For most of the data arranged by size of plant, the employment measure is used; wherever other classifications are available and the relationship under discussion is affected by the measure used, we so indicate.

SMI in the Growth of the Manufacturing Sector

Modern economic growth in Colombia is rooted in the development of coffee production and exports in the late nineteenth century. More recently, however, it has come to rely more and more on the expansion of the manufacturing sector. Over the years, employment and output have risen in LI, SMI, and CS alike; in relative terms, however, large-scale industry has gained at the expense of the other two groups.

The interrelations among the three size categories differ from one industry to another. Some "modern" industries that use advanced technologies—for example, rubber, paper, and certain chemicals—have been dominated by large-scale producers from the outset, with their domestic output replacing imports over time. In some industries characterized by both small- and large-scale production systems, the latter have fairly quickly displaced the former once a certain combination of capital availability, entrepreneurship, and market size has been reached. Textiles are the outstanding example in this category. Other industries, such as wood furniture making and transport equipment repairing, have provided growth opportunities for very small operators.

Large- and small-scale units producing different versions of the same product often coexist over long periods of time. In many cases, small firms grow into large ones. Certain shifts in demand or in consumption patterns can create opportunities to which small firms, because of their greater operational flexibility, can respond more successfully than large ones. As background to our later discussion of the determinants of changing size structure and the interactions among size categories, we review below the growth patterns of manufacturing as a whole and of our three size categories.

Manufacturing Employment

The growth of modern factory manufacturing in Colombia is almost entirely a twentieth-century phenomenon. Attempts to operate factories in the nineteenth century were few and generally unsuccessful. Until the mid-nineteenth century, Colombia's international trade was small and the domestic supply of manufactured goods came mainly from household or artisan production rather than from imports. There was some internal trading of manufactured goods for agricultural goods, and pockets of artisan activity developed in Santander and some of the surrounding Andean departments (administrative regions). About the middle of the nineteenth century, exports began to rise, and policy was geared toward freer international trade and import liberalization. This trend reflected the belief that efforts to establish indigenous manufacturing plants had been mistaken, since the country could not compete with more efficient European industries.[1] The increasing availability of imported manufactures put considerable pressure on domestic artisan activity; in the second half of the nineteenth century there were job losses in some branches of artisanry,[2] although overall employment may not have fallen.[3] Later, domestic factories also began to displace artisan activity in some industries.

Since the turn of the century or perhaps a little earlier, manufacturing output has grown rapidly, averaging about 5.5–6.3 percent a year between 1900 and 1970.[4] Labor productivity rose by about 4.3–4.7 percent a year, and employment by perhaps 1.5 percent.[5] The growth of output during the 1970s was close to the long-run average—about 6 percent a year.

The proportion of the total labor force working in manufacturing appears to have fallen during the latter part of the nineteenth century and in the first years of the twentieth century, as factory manufacturing began to replace artisanry and cottage-shop production; during this period the share of manufacturing in total output probably rose little, if at all. The population census of 1870 suggests that at least 275,000–325,000 persons, perhaps 20 percent of the labor force, were engaged primarily in manufacturing. This share appears to have fallen to about 12 percent by 1950; it later rose to 16–18 percent in 1978.[6] Trends in the share of manufacturing output in GDP have been more consistently positive, since the sector's productivity has risen in relation to the rest of the economy over time—a trend that has been assisted by the shift away from small-scale artisanry and cottage-shop output toward modern factory production (table 2-1).

Factories (defined as plants of 5 workers or more) accounted for perhaps 5 percent of manufacturing employment in 1870, for 12–15 percent by the mid-1920s, and for 50 percent or so in 1978. Within the cottage-shop subsector, employment in rural areas has declined as a share of the total; in the first few decades of this century, it also fell in absolute terms. Urban cottage-shop employment appears to have risen by perhaps 3.5 percent a year between 1951 and 1978; during this period, urban factory employment rose at an annual average rate of 5.5 percent.

Within the factory subsector, the long-run growth of both employment and output has been greatest in LI; if one goes back far enough, very few plants were large. Since 1945, the first year for which a reasonably accurate estimate could be made, the variation in employment growth by firm-size category has been modest; between 1944–45 and 1978 LI employment grew at an estimated 5.1 percent a year (table 2-2) in comparison with 4.2–4.5 percent for SMI.[7] Small- and medium-scale factories clearly lost ground during the 1950s and 1960s, but this trend seems to have been reversed in the 1970s.[8] Although the events of this decade are hard to pin down owing to a variety of statistical problems, SMI seems to have been the more dynamic category.[9] In 1945 SMI plants generated about 59 percent of factory manufacturing employment,

Table 2-1. *Estimates of the Composition of Manufacturing Output, by Plant Size, 1939–41 to 1975*
(percent)

		Factory			
Years	Cottage shop	Total	LI^a	MI^b	SI^c
1939–41	34.7	65.3	n.a.	n.a.	n.a.
1953	25.6	74.4	40.2	12.7	21.5
			(54.0)	(17.1)	(28.9)
1956			[64.4]	[14.4]	[21.2]
1964	22.4	77.6	52.7	7.9	17.1
			(67.8)	(10.2)	(22.0)
1969–71	20	80	n.a.	n.a.	n.a.
1975	15.1	84.9	64.2	7.3	13.4
			(75.6)	(8.6)	(15.8)
			[81.7]	[8.9]	[9.2]

n.a. Not available.

Note: Figures in parentheses denote share of factory output; those in brackets denote share of factory output from unadjusted DANE statistics.

a. 100+ workers.
b. 50–99 workers.
c. 5–49 workers.

Sources: For 1953, 1964, and 1975 calculations, see appendix tables 5, 6, and 7, respectively. The figure for 1939–41 is from appendix table 1 and may not be quite comparable to those for subsequent years. The figure for 1969–71 is a guess based on the estimated CS employment share in 1970 reported in table 2-2.

about 20 percent of all manufacturing employment, and 2.5 percent of total employment in the economy; by 1970 these figures were 47 percent, 22 percent, and 3.3 percent, respectively. Tentative estimates for 1978 are 50–53 percent, 29–30 percent, and 4.5 percent, respectively.

Thus during much of the 1970s the growth rates of both SMI and total manufacturing employment appear to have been unusually rapid, with the fastest growth occurring in SI.[10] This constitutes a marked change in the growth pattern of Colombian manufacturing; whether it will continue for some time or turn out to be only a brief interruption of the long-run trend toward larger plants remains to be seen. In sum, the record for Colombia in the 1970s suggests that the evolutionary process outlined in chapter 1—consisting of a phase in which SMI is the main focus of dynamism in the manufacturing sector, followed by one in which that distinction passes to LI—is not immutable; SMI can be the most dynamic sector relatively late in the development process, provided that conditions are right (a point to which we shall return later).

Before we examine developments in the 1970s, longer-run patterns of growth merit a closer look. The secular trend toward large plants in the

Table 2-2. Estimates of Employment in the Manufacturing Sector, 1944-45 to 1978 (absolute figures in thousands)

Plant size	1944-45	1953	1956	1964	1970	1973	1975	1978	Annual growth rate (percent)				
									1953-78	1953-64	1964-73	1973-78	1944-45 to 1978
Factory	155.6	199.0	220.8	310.0	395.4	488.8	550.0	708.1-747.7	5.2-5.4	4.1	5.2	7.7-8.9	4.6-4.8
Small (5-49 workers)	74.5	92.9	95.7	125.7	139.2	148.8	188.1	288.1-322.1	4.6-5.1	2.8	2.2	14.1-16.7	4.1-4.5
Medium (50-99 workers)	17.6	23.6	25.8	33.1	46.7	57.0	60.3	80.0-85	5.0-5.3	3.1	6.2	7.0-8.3	4.6-4.8
Large (100+ workers)	63.4	82.6	99.3	151.2	210.5	279.0	301.6	340.0	5.8	5.7	7.0	4.0	5.1
Cottage shops	308.4	287.0	n.a.	327.5	457.6	496.2	n.a.	523.7-669.1	2.4-3.4	1.2	4.7	1.1-6.2	1.6-2.3
Very small enterprises (1-4 employees)	n.a.	n.a.	n.a.	n.a.	n.a.	176.2	n.a.	n.a.	n.a.	n.a.	n.a.	n.a.	n.a.
Household industries	n.a.	n.a.	n.a.	n.a.	n.a.	320	n.a.	n.a.	n.a.	n.a.	n.a.	n.a.	n.a.
Total	464	485.1	637.5	853	985			1,232-1,417	3.8-4.4	2.5	5.0	4.6-7.5	3.0-3.4

Percentage of total employment																
Cottage shop	66.5	59.2	n.a.	51.4	53.6	50.4	n.a.	42.5–47.2	—	—	—	—	—	—	—	—
Factory	33.5	40.8	n.a.	48.6	46.4	49.6	n.a.	50.0–52.8	—	—	—	—	—	—	—	—
LI	13.7	18.9	n.a.	23.7	24.7	28.3	n.a.	24.0–27.6	—	—	—	—	—	—	—	—
SMI	19.8	20.3	n.a.	24.9	21.7	21.5	n.a.	28.7–29.9	—	—	—	—	—	—	—	—

n.a. Not available.

— Not applicable.

Note: For all years, data for factories of 50 workers and more are from DANE, *Industria Manufacturera* or, before 1967, *Anuario General de Estadística*. Estimates of total factory employment (plants of five workers or more) are from Albert Berry, "A Descriptive History of Industrialization in Colombia," in *Essays on Industrialization in Colombia* (Tempe, Ariz.: Arizona State University, Center for Latin American Studies, 1983), table 2-5 (p. 25) and table A-130. That source estimates underreporting by a variety of cross-checks with other sources. Employment in plants of 5–49 workers is calculated as a residual.

Total manufacturing employment is based on the population censuses of 1938, 1951, 1964, and 1973 and various household surveys of the 1970s. The 1953 estimate used here is an interpolation between 1951 and 1964. The nonfactory sector is calculated as a residual. It is assumed here that no household industries are reported in DANE's manufacturing statistics. Some household operations have 5+ workers; in fact, the percentage of household employment accounted for by such cases in November 1973, according to the population census, was 35.4 (appendix table 2c). The number of unpaid family helpers reported in the censuses is very low relative to the number of workers in these household industries, after one excludes the household head (who is presumably defined as an independent worker or employer); the implication is that there are many paid employees (whether family members or not) in the household industries. In the 1964 population census, only 18,500 were listed as unpaid family helpers. (DANE, *III Censo Nacional de Población: Resumen General*, pp. 134–35.) The range estimated for most categories in 1978 results from the unexpectedly high figure for total manufacturing employment that emerged from DANE's June 1978 household survey of rural and urban areas. The upper limit estimates reflect the DANE data, while a 15 percent reduction seems reasonable for the lower limit estimates. The range widens for the smaller plant categories, for which DANE's annual surveys of manufacturers are less reliable.

factory subsector has had little to do with changes in the composition of factory manufacturing output. Major changes in composition have, of course, occurred—between 1956 and 1975, for example, food, beverages, tobacco, and nonmetallic minerals all lost ground markedly, whereas the metalworking industries gained strongly—but these shifts played little or no part in lowering SMI's share of factory employment.[11] Between these two years (chosen, incidentally, because they are the earliest and latest years for which reasonably comparable data are available), SMI lost ground to LI in nearly all industries; furniture and other wood products and leather goods were the main exceptions (table 2-3).[12]

There appears to be some correlation between the labor productivity disadvantage of SI within individual industries in 1956 and the rate at which its share of factory employment fell. The decline was atypically slow in wood, wood furniture, paper, printing, and transport equipment. In all of these but printing, the ratio of labor productivity in SI to that in MI or LI was above average. Meanwhile the share of SI fell atypically rapidly in food, tobacco, chemicals, and nonelectrical machinery; in tobacco, SI productivity was very low in 1956; and in the other three its relation to MI and LI productivity was more or less typical.[13]

As SMI has in the long run lost ground to LI in most industries, so CS has lost ground to the factory sector as a whole. Nevertheless, excluding the textiles, clothing, and footwear industries, our estimates imply long-term annual growth rates of about 3.2 percent for CS employment compared with 4.8 percent for factory employment between 1938 and 1964. CS employment fell sharply in textiles (from perhaps 90,000 in 1938 to 18,000 in 1964), and significantly in clothing and footwear (from about 150,000 in 1938 to 122,000 in 1964). At the other end of the spectrum, CS continued to dominate the wood and wood products industries (mainly furniture), in which employment actually grew at a faster rate in CS than in the factory subsector. The relative and absolute decline of CS employment in textiles, clothing, and footwear reflected competition from factory industry; the growth of wood and furniture employment occurred in spite of such competition. Some small-scale metalworking activities appear to be complementary to new consumption patterns (especially to those involving the automobile) and some to expanding factory manufacturing.

Labor Productivity

We noted above that labor productivity in manufacturing as a whole had risen rapidly during the twentieth century. Our rough output and labor force series suggest an increase of about 5 percent a year over the period

1900–50.[14] The rate of increase remained very high (over 4 percent a year) between 1951 and 1964, but has slowed markedly since that time and is probably under 2 percent a year now. This secular decline in labor productivity growth has been associated with changing relative rates of employment growth by firm size categories. The 1930s and 1940s witnessed wholesale replacement of traditional small-scale manufacturing by larger-scale units—especially in textiles—with significant positive effects on average labor productivity. The absolute level of CS employment leveled off in the 1950s, but then began to rise again; there appears to have been only a small subsequent decrease in the proportion of all workers in firms with fewer than five employees. In the 1970s the fall in LI's share of factory employment adversely affected the growth of labor productivity.

Labor productivity rises when the locus of manufacturing production shifts toward larger units because of the relatively high capital-labor ratio of these units—and sometimes their more efficient technology. Much of the increase in labor productivity in Colombian manufacturing seems to have been associated with advances in total factor productivity. One estimate allocated 15–22 percent of the labor productivity increase between 1944–45 and 1969 to increases in physical capital per worker, 11–19 percent to increases in labor skills (human capital), up to 10 percent to shifting composition of output among subsectors, and the residual (51–75 percent) to increases in total factor productivity within individual industries.[15] Some part of this residual can be accounted for by public sector investment and economies of scale, but the bulk of it is probably the result of improvements in technology per se. Total factor productivity rose by an average of perhaps 3 percent a year between 1925 and 1970, with output measured at Colombian prices. The increase seems to have been particularly rapid in the period before World War II; our figures suggest 4 percent a year or more, with a gradual decline to a little more than 2 percent a year during the 1960s.[16]

The role of establishment size in the growth of labor productivity in the manufacturing industry is shown by the fact that some size categories of establishments had productivity increases much smaller than the overall increase. Although annual movements of the labor productivity series are erratic, it is clear that between 1953–57 and 1977–79 labor productivity rose by about 65 percent in large plants, a much more rapid increase than that in medium and small ones, whose productivity growth seems to have been virtually nil and 45 percent, respectively (table 2-4).[17] For SMI as a whole, the increase was about 40 percent during this period.[18] About 70 percent of the increase in labor productivity for manufacturing as a whole was associated with the productivity gains within

Table 2-3. Composition of Factory Employment, by Size Category and by Industry, 1956 and 1975 (percent)

Industry	1956				1975			
	Share of total factory employment	Share of industry's employment[a]			Share of total factory employment	Share of industry's employment		
		SI (5–49)[a]	MI (50–99)	LI (100+)		SI (5–49)[b]	MI (50–99)	LI (100+)
Food	16.23	57.60	15.50	26.90	12.82	31.70	14.82	53.48
Beverages	5.64	18.06	15.91	66.03	3.89	4.65	5.03	90.32
Tobacco	2.57	51.01	13.67	35.32	0.86	5.97	6.44	87.59
Textiles	17.21	11.37	5.17	83.46	14.19	8.55	8.16	83.29
Footwear and clothing	13.74	60.48	16.31	23.21	12.28	41.46	13.37	45.17
Wood	2.77	50.51	10.02	39.47	1.61	57.21	4.81	37.98
Furniture and other wood products	2.29	70.08	16.12	13.80	2.87	64.49	15.08	20.43
Paper	1.40	28.93	16.47	54.60	2.08	21.01	18.13	60.86
Printing	4.11	51.28	8.74	39.98	4.06	41.12	7.07	51.81
Leather	2.03	43.35	15.95	40.70	2.00	32.40	15.37	52.23
Rubber	2.26	12.44	1.30	86.26	1.58	19.91	9.23	70.87
Chemicals	5.26	40.97	19.27	39.76	6.74	17.06	9.62	73.32
Oil and coal	0.96	10.61	0.00	89.39	0.84	8.97	2.72	88.31

Nonmetallic minerals	8.95	39.34	10.36	50.30	5.96	24.05	12.81	63.14
Base metals	2.31	13.63	3.14	83.23	3.11	8.05	6.07	85.88
Metal products	3.88	54.32	15.48	30.20	9.20	39.38	15.05	45.57
Nonelectrical machinery	1.04	68.26	11.58	20.16	2.74	31.02	22.23	46.75
Electrical machinery	1.44	57.64	14.53	27.82	4.29	42.54	14.94	42.52
Transport equipment	4.21	40.17	8.76	51.07	4.33	31.91	9.32	58.77
Other	1.72	54.29	21.84	23.87	4.55	37.71	15.60	46.69
Total	100.00	40.98	12.12	46.85	100.00	28.51	12.19	59.30
Total assuming 1956 share of employment in each industry		40.98	12.12	46.85		26.60	11.15	62.21

a. Data include 9,002 employees in plants of less than 5 workers. These have not been excluded as there was evidence of underreporting in the 1956 data and it would presumably fall in the same industries with some workers in the less-than-5 category.

b. Includes plants of less than 5 workers, for the reasons mentioned in note a. Usually the adjusted total employment figures of the Instituto Colombiano de Seguros Sociales (ICSS) were higher because of the more complete inclusion of small plants. Often the DANE figure for large plants is higher, however, and in such cases it seems desirable to accept it on the grounds of possibly more comparable treatment with the 1956 figures.

Source: Albert Berry and Armando Pinell-Siles, Small-Scale Enterprises in Colombia: A Case Study, Studies in Employment and Rural Development 56 (Washington, D.C.: World Bank, 1979), table A-17b (for 1956) and table A-18a (for 1975). The former contains unpublished DANE data from the Annual Survey of Manufacturers, 1956, and DANE, Anuario General de Estadística, 1957, p. 41. The latter contains adjusted and unpublished ICSS data.

Table 2-4. *Indices of Labor Productivity and of Remuneration
per Worker, by Size Category, Mid-1950s to Late 1970s*
(1956=100)

| Three-year period | Labor productivity | | | | Remuneration per person |
	SI	MI	LI	Total	(total)
1953 to 1956–57	0.95	0.92	0.96	0.94	0.95
1967 to 1968–69	1.41	1.13	1.58	1.55	1.65
1973 to 1975–76	1.17	0.90	1.41	1.51	1.75
1977 to 1978–79	1.38	0.94	1.59	1.70	1.88

Source: Labor productivity is based on annual output and employment data published in
DANE, *Industria Manufacturera.* Deflation of the output data is by the national accounts deflator for the manufacturing sector. The last column is from the same source, and deflation
is by the national cost-of-living indices.

SI and LI; the rest can be attributed to the increasing share of resources in
larger establishments.

Of course, the labor productivity figures cited above are calculated
on the basis of available aggregate data and do not necessarily reflect
changes over time in a representative plant within each category. The
percentages also include the effects of plants moving from one size category to another. For example, when MI loses plants to LI, this is likely to
lower average MI labor productivity; a similar effect will occur in the SI
category when MI gains plants from SI. This phenomenon of category
change probably produces figures that underestimate the true rate of
productivity growth for plants in each size category, but perhaps this is
least so for LI, since no plants leave this category for a larger one. There is
thus no reason to believe that labor productivity was not rising in the typical MI plant during the period under consideration.

In the early 1970s, labor productivity fell in all size categories and in
manufacturing as a whole, then rose again from 1975 to 1979; the 1977–
79 averages were not far from those of 1967–69, so this period can be
counted as one of little net change. The main cycles in labor productivity
correspond quite closely to movements in earnings per worker. Short-
term movements in the latter, especially the decline in the early 1970s,
have often been linked to changes in the rate of inflation.[19] Why labor
productivity should fluctuate in a parallel fashion is not clear; it seems
unlikely that this could be explained by firms raising employment and
pushing down the marginal product of labor when real wages fell and
vice versa, since the response of employment to wage movements would
have had to be implausibly quick. What other factors have been at work
is not clear.

The substantial increase in SI labor productivity may be part of a more
general pattern in which variations in productivity by establishment size

are tending to narrow, or at least are not widening. Average labor productivity in CS rose significantly between 1953 and 1975; a reasonable
estimate, if the relative prices of CS products did not change over this period, might be around 80 percent.[20] Part of the increase is associated with
changing output composition among these establishments (for example,
away from clothing, footwear, and textiles and toward food processing,
transportation repairs, and other industries); labor productivity increases
within specific industries have probably been substantial as well, and
some of the increase may be due to rising prices of CS output relative to
factory output.

Earnings

Earnings gaps appear to have followed a similar pattern to that of labor
productivity gaps. Once again, the gains have been largest in CS and in LI.
Earnings per paid worker in CS establishments are always substantially
lower than in the factory sector: the former were about 45 percent of the
latter in 1953, probably a little less in 1970, and back to or above the 1953
level in 1975 (table 2-5). The increase in average real earnings over the
period was probably above 100 percent (on the basis of wages in current
pesos deflated by the national blue-collar cost of living series), which was
roughly comparable to that for factory workers and for LI.[21]

   In any event, the 1970s seem to have been a time of markedly rising CS
earnings as well as of SI expansion. By 1975, after differences in workers'
personal characteristics are taken into account, the true wage differentials between establishments with more than five workers and those with
five or fewer were rather small for the urban economy as a whole (see the
discussion later in the chapter). Even if these true differentials are somewhat wider in manufacturing, the large gross earnings gap (that is, the
unadjusted differential when no account is taken of differences in labor
force characteristics between the two subsectors) would indicate a considerable difference in composition between the factory and CS labor
forces. The small size of the "true" wage gap in 1975 also suggests that
movements in the aggregate or gross earnings differential over time have
been mainly the result of changes in the relative composition of the two
labor forces. Within CS there has been a marked trend away from rural
production (often by women) of simple nondurable consumer goods to
urban production, often by better-educated, skilled workers who make
increasingly sophisticated products.

   Within the factory sector also, unadjusted DANE data show a gradual
widening of earnings differentials by plant size between 1956 and 1970
(see table 2-6) and a narrowing during the 1970s.[22] For the period 1953–
78 as a whole, earnings increases have not fully paralleled labor
productivity trends. There was an increase of 46 percent in real earnings

Table 2-5. *Average Annual Earnings of Workers, by Plant Size,*
Selected Years
(thousands of pesos)

			1975		1979	
Plant size	1953 *(with fringe benefits)*	1970 *(with fringe benefits)*	*Without fringe benefits*	*With fringe benefits*	*Without fringe benefits*	*With fringe benefits*
CS[a]	1.09	9.00–10.00[b]	26.00[c]	26.35[d]	n.a.	n.a.
SI	1.99	13.37	23.08	29.90	64.53	85.37
MI	2.30[e]	19.43	28.75	39.64	77.49	108.46
LI	2.82[e]	32.82	43.48	68.61	115.68	183.66
Factory	2.43	26.31	37.48	57.11	101.53	156.22

n.a. Not available.

Note: Employers, even if also workers, are excluded from the figures.

a. The figures for CS are artificially high relative to the factory sector in that they include capital income for independent workers. Were we to assume that two-thirds of independent workers' income was from labor and to exclude the other third, the average figure for cottage shop would typically fall by about one-quarter.

b. This range is a rough estimate. If the ratio of earnings in CS as a whole to those in the DANE survey of CS plants were the same in 1970 as the one we estimated for 1953 (1.12:1), the figure would be a little under 9,000. But the relative incomes of independent workers to paid workers in plants of 2–4 workers may have risen in the interim.

c. Assumes that a little more than half of income earners in CS are independent workers; employers are excluded from the calculation. Employers are assumed to constitute 5 percent of the total CS labor force. If unpaid helpers are included, the average falls by perhaps 7–9 percent, while that for the factory sector falls by perhaps 2 percent.

d. For the factory sector, data on fringe benefits come from DANE's annual statistics. For CS we assume 10 percent for paid workers and nothing for independent workers. In the 1970 DANE survey of very small establishments, fringe benefits were only 3.1 percent of base wages and salaries (appendix table 3). The DANE figure for the few plants of less than 5 workers was 25 percent of the base wage.

e. Estimates. The figure available was 2.70 for MI and LI together.

of SI employees, an improvement of 63 percent for those in MI, and a strong advance of 135 percent for those in LI. The apparently strong gain of CS relative to SI (as of 1975) is intriguing; the strikingly high incomes of independent workers in 1975 (see table 2-12) contributed strongly to this trend.[23] It is possible that the skill levels of independent workers have risen by comparison with those of paid workers in the smallest plants. The modest increase in earnings of the workers in SI suggests either little upgrading of skills in this category (perhaps because some of the better workers have been skimmed off by MI or LI) or slow growth in the wages of workers with a given skill.

Both dualistic models and radical interpretations of the evolution of manufacturing or of the urban economy as a whole in developing coun-

Table 2-6. *Index of Average Remuneration, by Plant Size,*
Selected Years
(category 100–199 workers = 100)

Plant size (number of workers)	1956	1962	1969–71	1975–76	1978
5–9	55.7	46.9	39.1	48.9	63.0
10–14	63.7	55.9	42.8	52.1	59.9
15–19	69.1	58.1	50.2	53.1	63.8
20–24	72.4	66.5	52.5	56.4	66.5
25–49	80.3	76.6	61.1	64.0	72.3
50–74	88.7	86.5	73.8	74.7	79.4
75–99	99.5	91.7	81.1	85.0	90.0
100–99	100.0	100.0	100.0	100.0	100.0
200+	121.6	118.8	132.1	144.8	154.3
Total	94.8	92.4	101.0	112.3	120.3

Note: Remuneration includes fringe benefits.
Source: Through 1967, DANE, *Anuario General de Estadística,* annual issues; for 1970, DANE, *III Censo Industrial 1970;* for other years, DANE, *Industria Manufacturera.*

tries often imply that employment growth in the smaller-scale sectors acts mainly as a safety valve—that it reflects poor employment prospects elsewhere and is consistent with stagnant or declining real earnings of the workers involved. The evidence presented above, especially for the 1970s, instead suggests that this phenomenon stems from increasing productivity and ability to compete on the part of CS and SI. To be sure, the situation has varied by period, by region, and by industry. For example, Urrutia and Villalba report decreases in CS workers' incomes between 1953 and 1964 in the departments of Caldas, Tolima, and Norte de Santander. But such cases appear to have been the exceptions.

Overall, developments during the 1970s appear to have included many elements of the "recipe" for terminating labor surpluses and for growth with distribution. Since manufacturing output grew rapidly but labor productivity did not, manufacturing employment also rose sharply. Developments in SMI were central to this overall result; their importance in the development of Japan and in its transition out of the labor surplus condition was emphasized by Fei and Ranis.[24] The fruits of growth during the 1970s seem to have been fairly widely shared among the population as a whole.[25] Meanwhile, wage trends and other labor market indicators suggested a tightening labor market and a drying up of labor surplus toward the end of the decade.[26]

What explains the competitive strength of smaller manufacturing establishments? In the rest of this chapter we use aggregate data to focus on their characteristics and to show how they differ from large firms.

Differences between SMI and Other Manufacturing

In addition to the characteristics of size and structure that we use to differentiate them, CS, SMI, and LI also differ in industrial composition, locational tendencies, factor proportions, and factor productivities. In some respects, SMI can be defined as a component of a size continuum that ranges from the independent worker to the giant corporation; in others, it is more a discrete grouping with features that clearly distinguish it from both CS and LI.

Location and Composition of Production

In the very early stages of economic development, manufacturing activity is undertaken largely in households and small shops.[27] These units are located mainly in rural areas or in small urban centers and serve basic consumer needs for clothing, food, furniture, and the like. As development and urbanization proceed, the location of CS activity gradually shifts to urban settings; its orientation also shifts somewhat to more modern products and to repair activities. In general, SMI seems to be urban from the start, as is LI; both tend to produce more modern and more complex goods than does CS. Shifts in the focus of manufacturing activity to larger establishments and more urban settings are associated with increases in average capital intensity and labor productivity over time.

A glance at Colombian manufacturing as of 1964 (the year for which the best data are available) shows that CS accounted for a little more than half of total employment, SMI a little more than one-quarter, and LI a little less than one-quarter (table 2-7). Because of the higher labor productivity of larger establishments, the corresponding shares of output were about 17 percent for CS, 27 percent for SMI, and 56 percent for LI. The composition of employment and output by industry group varied significantly across the three subsectors. Cottage-shop activity was and probably still is concentrated in four main subsectors—clothing and footwear, metal industries (especially nonelectric machinery and transport manufacturing and repair), wood and wood products (mainly furniture), and food—with repair work forming an important component of CS activities in general. In 1964, CS accounted for a majority of the total employment in these industry groupings, except for food; CS also dominated employment in the leather industry, although this industry was relatively small (table 2-8).[28]

The smallest factories (about 5–24 workers) tend to be important in the same industries as CS, though with some interesting differences. In 1964 the main employers in this firm-size range were food, clothing and footwear, nonmetallic minerals, and metal products excluding machinery.

Wood furniture and transport equipment (mainly repairs), in both of which CS predominates, accounted for relatively few small establishments in this size range. For these products, the growth process seems to have consisted of increases in the number of households or small shops, rather than the expansion of existing establishments into small factories; economies of scale are apparently unimportant. By contrast, the gradual decline of cottage-shop employment in textiles appears to have been associated with a shift toward larger plants rather than the growth of cottage-shop firms into small factories, to judge by the lack of small plants in the 1960s. If CS is important in an industry, however, SI or SMI employment tends to be large relative to LI employment, even if not as a share of the industry's total employment. SMI's share is highest in wood products (mainly furniture), footwear and clothing, food, nonmechanical products, nonelectrical machinery, and printing; of these, only printing is not also characterized by a high share of employment in CS (table 2-8).

The shares of CS, SMI, and LI in employment by industry group are reasonably closely reflected in their respective shares of output, despite the fact that the relative labor productivity of the three size categories differs somewhat by industry (table 2-11). Within the factory subsector (and especially between SI and MI) the labor productivity differential by firm size group tends to be below average in those industries in which the SI share of factory employment is very large, as with clothing and footwear and wood and wood furniture. This is also true for leather and, to some extent, for metal products, but not for electrical machinery or printing. In some cases (wood, leather, rubber, glass), labor productivity was actually higher in SI than in MI. As of 1975, LI's share of factory employment exceeded 75 percent only in the traditional consumer goods industries (beverages, tobacco, and textiles) and in two cases where economies of scale are very strong (base metals and petroleum and coal products).

To summarize, some two-digit industries are strongly and systematically oriented to small-scale production, as reflected by the fact that they have a lower share of total SMI employment or output than of CS employment or output and a still lower share of LI employment or output (table 2-9). On the basis of 1964 employment data (table 2-9) the clearest examples of this tendency were wood furniture and clothing and footwear, followed by nonelectrical machinery and transport equipment (mainly repairs). Several industries were strongly oriented to smaller plants, but less to CS; these included food (very notably), metal products, printing, wood products (excluding furniture), and leather. Tobacco and miscellaneous (of which plastics was an important component) were somewhat atypically represented in MI, as were chemicals in MI and LI. The other industries were oriented toward large-scale production; this orientation

Table 2-7. Selected Aspects of the Size Structure of Colombian Manufacturing, 1964

| | Plants of less than 5 workers | | | Plants of 5+ workers | | | | | | | | Total |
Item	Independent workers	2–4	Subtotal	5–9	10–25	25–49	50–74	75–99	100–99	200+	Subtotal	
Number of establishments	n.a.	n.a.	n.a.	6,100–7,635	2,961	869	315	167	261	223	10,806–12,431	n.a.
Number of workers (thousands)	169.3	153.2–163.2	322.5–332.5	40–50	40.7	29.6	18.9	14.2	36.0	115.2	294.6–304.6	627.1
Gross value added (millions of pesos)	1,073	1,036–1,100	2,109–2,173	580–725	749	764	637	452	1,841	5,407	10,451–10,576	12,540–12,749
Salaries (including fringe benefits) per paid worker (thousands of pesos)	n.a.	3.5–3.9	3.5–3.9	6.0	7.0	9.5	11.2	11.2	14.0	16.1	11.9–12.4	10.5–10.7

Gross value added per person (thousands of pesos)	8.0–9.0	7.4	7.7–8.2	14.5	18.4	25.8	33.7	31.8	51.2	46.9	34.2–35.9	20.0–20.3
Gross value added per horsepower (thousands of pesos)	n.a.	n.a.	n.a.	10.4	9.8	8.0	14.3	14.8	15.2	9.3	10.38–10.40	n.a.
Paid labor share of gross value added (percent)	n.a.	20.54–22.02	10.09–11.15	33.69	35.69	35.43	33.07	35.02	27.31	34.30	33.17–33.18	20.81–29.91

n.a. Not available.

Sources: For details see Albert Berry, "The Relevance and Prospects of Small-Scale Industry in Colombia," Yale Economic Growth Center Discussion Paper 142 (New Haven, Conn., 1972), table 1, p. 4. A few figures have been revised from that source. The basic source for all but the independent workers and the small plants (2–4 workers) not surveyed by DANE is DANE, Anuario General de Estadística, 1964. A number of adjustments were made to the DANE figures because of certain biases they are known to have. Data for the smaller plants and independent workers are based primarily on Miguel Urrutia and Clara Elsa Villalba, "El Sector Artesanal en el Desarrollo Colombiano," Revista de Planeación y Desarrollo, vol. 1, no. 3 (October 1969), pp. 43–78.

Table 2-8. *Distribution of Employment among Cottage Shop and Small, Medium, and Large Industry, by Branch of Industry, 1964*
(percent)

Industry	CS	SI	MI	LI	Employment (thousands)
Food	40.56	34.47	4.57	20.40	73.9
Beverages	10.01	10.42	7.09	72.48	19.2
Tobacco	52.38	17.41	7.43	22.79	8.6
Textiles	28.32	9.33	2.32	60.04	62.4
Clothing and footwear	78.35	12.58	2.61	6.46	153.3
Wood products (excluding furniture)	55.36	28.07	0.83	15.73	14.8
Wood furniture	91.35	6.98	0.18	1.49	63.4
Paper	7.23	20.94	12.90	58.93	5.6
Printing	24.44	38.49	3.82	32.63	16.9
Leather	52.63	22.07	2.63	22.66	9.5
Rubber	11.44	12.38	3.86	72.32	7.9
Chemicals	20.45	25.15	9.80	44.60	25.7
Petroleum and Coal	57.19	5.40	2.32	35.09	4.9
Nonmetallic minerals	27.29	31.33	4.85	36.54	36.9
Base metals	64.04	4.55	1.00	30.41	10.3
Metal products (excluding machinery)	29.42	33.95	9.74	26.89	28.7
Nonelectrical machinery	70.31	16.58	4.54	8.57	18.1
Electrical machinery	39.47	18.24	9.15	33.14	15.9
Transport equipment	75.14	10.61	2.51	11.75	64.0
Other	49.74	23.14	11.05	16.06	16.0
All	54.71	16.91	5.10	23.28	656.0

Note: Based on DANE data. Total employment by industry is from the 1964 population census except that for rubber the census figure (5,428) was adjusted (to 7,900) since it indicated a smaller employment than reported for the factory subsector alone in DANE's annual survey of manufacturing. The figure for transport equipment was correspondingly reduced on the grounds that the census reporting had probably confused repair activities in these two sectors. (DANE, *XIII Censo de Población: Resumen General*, pp. 134–36). The employment for size categories of 25+ workers was taken, without adjustment, from DANE, *Boletín Mensual de Estadística*, no. 224 (March 1970), pp. 115–17. Figures for the range 5–24 took into account the upward adjustments to the official figures shown in table 2–7. Unfortunately, although the evidence was strong that underreporting prevailed in the category 5–9 workers and to a lesser degree in the larger ones, little evidence was available with which to allocate this underreporting by industry, so our estimates are somewhat arbitrary. CS employment was then calculated as the residual between total employment and that in establishments of 5+ workers. Persons recorded as unemployed constitute 4.9 percent of the labor force and 6.8 percent of that in urban areas in the 1964 population census; many or most of those in manufacturing are likely to be captured in our estimate of CS, with a few possibly in SI. Workers in the 25–99 plant range were allocated between SI and MI according to the 1966 figures at the two-digit level and the aggregate 1964 figures. The same adjustment was made in the 1966 figures to each industry so that the true 1964 aggregate figures would be produced.

Table 2-9. *Distribution of Employment among Branches of Industry in Cottage Shop and Small, Medium, and Large Industry, 1964*
(percent)

Industry	CS	SI	MI	LI	Total
Wood furniture	16.10	3.98	0.34	0.62	9.64
Clothing and footwear	33.55	17.43	11.99	6.50	23.43
Transport equipment	13.31	6.08	4.77	4.89	9.70
Nonelectrical machinery	3.53	2.69	2.44	1.01	2.75
Leather	1.39	1.89	0.75	1.41	1.45
Wood products	2.30	3.77	0.37	1.53	2.27
Printing	1.15	5.87	1.93	3.62	2.58
Metal products (excluding machinery)	2.35	8.76	8.36	5.04	4.36
Food	8.35	22.96	10.09	9.87	11.26
Tobacco	1.25	1.34	1.90	1.28	1.30
Miscellaneous	2.22	3.33	5.28	1.68	2.44
Chemicals	1.47	5.85	7.55	7.53	3.93
Textiles	4.95	5.27	4.35	24.65	9.56
Rubber	0.25	0.88	0.91	3.75	1.21
Paper	0.11	1.06	2.17	3.41	0.86
Electrical machinery	1.74	2.60	4.33	3.44	2.41
Beverages	0.53	1.77	4.40	8.98	2.88

Note: Two industries small in terms of employment—oil and coal products, and base metals—have been excluded. In each case, the figures suggested implausibly high shares of employment in establishments of less than 5 workers. Pending independent evidence that this was the case, we assume these figures are invalid due to errors of classification in the population census. Alternatively, there may be CS production of charcoal or products of nonferrous metals in these sectors, whereas the large establishments are in oil and steel products, respectively. The result of excluding these sectors is that the figures in each column add to less than 100 percent.

Source: See table 2-8.

was strong for beverages, paper, rubber, and textiles and a little less so for electrical machinery.

Labor Productivity and Earnings

Apart from location and industrial composition, SMI differs from both CS and LI in capital intensity, skill mix, labor productivity, and earnings. The differences in labor productivity are striking; in 1975, average levels of CS and SMI labor productivity were, respectively, only 12.9 percent and 38.9 percent of the levels achieved by LI (table 2-10). Labor productivity in LI was nearly five times that of the labor force as a whole; that of SI was about 50 percent higher, and that of CS only about 60 percent as high. Earnings of cottage-shop workers from their labor inputs are probably at about the average for all employed persons in the economy.

Table 2-10. *Labor Productivity in Manufacturing by Plant Size, 1975*

Plant size	Labor productivity (thousands of pesos)	Index of labor productivity (LI = 100)
CS	28.56	12.90
SI	75.19	33.98
MI	120.10	54.27
SMI	86.56	38.94
LI	222.30	100.00
Total manufacturing	97.62	44.11
Colombian economy (all sectors)	46–48	20.7–21.6

Source: Appendix table 7, except for figures for the whole economy, which are based on a division of private income as estimated in the national accounts (the sum of remuneration of paid workers plus household income from nonincorporated businesses and other property) by the employed labor force. A range is given to allow for the uncertainty as to the size of the employed labor force.

At the two-digit level, relative labor productivity by size varied greatly from industry to industry, but the positive relationship with size was almost always present (table 2-11).[29] These gaps probably result more from greater use of skilled personnel[30] and higher capital-labor ratios[31] than from differences in levels of economic efficiency. The role of higher capital intensity is suggested by the fact that average earnings increased less with plant size than did labor productivity. Basic earnings in LI (excluding fringe benefits) were about 70 percent higher than in SMI and a little more than twice as high as those in CS.[32] When fringe benefits are included, the average in LI is more than twice that in SMI (table 2-12), a marked differential but still somewhat less than the nearly threefold gap in labor productivity.[33] At the other end of the size spectrum, available statistics indicate that independent workers earned more than paid workers in CS and probably more than paid workers in SI as well.[34]

Average remuneration for each of the occupational categories distinguished in DANE's statistics rises with plant size, but the increase is more marked for white-collar than for blue-collar workers, especially for the highest income categories of managers (directors) and technical personnel (table 2-13). Average remuneration for these two categories in plants of 200 workers or more is, respectively, 5.6 and more than 4 times as high as that in plants with 10–14 workers. For clerical white-collar workers, the comparable differential is 3.3 times, and for blue-collar workers, 2.4 times. An obvious hypothesis suggested by these relationships is that skill levels vary more widely by size of establishment in the higher-income occupational categories. Blue-collar wages vary only moderately by size of labor force in plants of all sizes up to 100–199 workers. The marked difference between wages in this size category of plant and those in plants with 200 or more workers suggests the existence of a sort of "wage cliff." (Differentials are, however, greater and more continuous through the range of sizes when establishments are ranked by output level.)

Without knowing the extent of skill differentials by size of establishment in a particular occupational category (for example, blue-collar workers), we cannot judge by how much wages differ by establishment size for persons of comparable skills. The presumption is that the differential is less than the nearly 2:1 ratio shown in table 2-12 between paid

Table 2-11. *Labor Productivity, by Industry and by Plant Size, 1975*
(absolute figure in thousands of pesos)

		Plant size			Index of labor productivity (average = 1.00)[b]		
Industry	Total	SI	MI	LI	SI	MI	LI
Food	190.3	115.0	208.5	221.0	0.60	1.10	1.16
Beverages	489.5	104.2	332.5	513.9	0.38	0.68	1.05
Tobacco	472.8	50.9	12.9[a]	533.1	0.11	0.03[a]	1.13
Textiles	134.0	64.0	75.8	146.9	0.48	0.57	1.10
Footwear and clothing	61.1	44.1	48.4	73.7	0.72	0.79	1.20
Wood	110.8	53.6	49.3	214.0	0.48	0.44	1.93
Wood furniture	59.5	43.8	48.2	91.1	0.74	0.81	1.53
Paper	232.2	83.0	125.6	315.5	0.36	0.54	1.36
Printing	123.9	61.1	94.9	155.9	0.49	0.77	1.26
Leather	85.3	49.2	47.0	101.5	0.58	0.55	1.19
Rubber	203.4	103.1	92.7	246.8	0.51	0.46	1.21
Chemicals	300.3	182.9	247.4	329.8	0.61	0.82	1.10
Industrial	400.6	339.5	503.1	399.4	0.85	1.26	1.00
Other	251.1	121.2	151.9	291.8	0.48	0.60	1.16
Oil and products							
Nonmetallic minerals	145.5	54.4	69.2	191.9	0.37	0.48	1.32
Clay	82.3	32.2	44.4	94.0	0.39	0.54	1.14
Glass	130.8	55.9	42.7	149.9	0.43	0.33	1.15
Other	167.9	56.9	78.1	219.5	0.34	0.46	1.31
Metal products	125.1	70.2	92.5	174.9	0.56	0.74	1.40
Nonelectrical machinery	126.9	80.5	141.6	150.7	0.63	1.12	1.19
Electrical machinery	148.4	84.8	146.3	168.9	0.57	0.99	1.14
Transportation	243.7	68.7	99.9	304.2	0.28	0.41	1.25
Plastic	107.9	74.7	89.0	125.9	0.69	0.82	1.17
Total	179.1	81.7	120.2	221.4	0.46	0.67	1.24

a. Based on a very small number of plants, which are clearly quite atypical, or for which the data were incorrectly reported.

b. Averages refer to the specific industry, not to all manufacturing.

Source: Unpublished DANE data from *Industria Manufacturera,* 1976. For data by more detailed classification of plant sizes, see appendix table 12.

Table 2-12. *Average Annual Earnings of Workers, by Plant Size and Type of Work, 1975*
(pesos)

Plant size and job position	Excluding fringe benefits			Including fringe benefits	
	Blue-collar	White-collar	Total	Total	(LI = 100)
Cottage-shop					
Independent workers	n.a.	n.a.	30,000	n.a.	n.a.
Paid workers	18,000	23,400	19,100	n.a.	n.a.
Factory (paid workers)					
SI	9,000	36,000	23,081	29,902	43.6
MI	22,150	53,000	28,750	39,645	57.8
LI	33,600	73,625	43,476	68,612	100.0
SMI			25,352	33,808	49.3
All factory	28,879	65,126	37,485	57,107	83.2
Owners and managers (all manufacturing)	n.a.	n.a.	70,000	n.a.	n.a.

n.a. Not available.

Sources: Based on DANE, *Industria Manufacturera*, 1975; DANE's seven-city household survey of October 1975; and other sources, including those cited in the notes to appendix table 7.

blue-collar workers in LI and in CS. In fact, evidence from household surveys suggests that for the urban economy as a whole (not just for manufacturing), earnings differentials between employees in establishments with five or fewer workers and those in establishments with six or more are relatively small after allowing for differences in such personal characteristics as age and education; the differential seems to be on the order of 20–40 percent, but tends to be at the lower end if fringe benefits are not taken into account and at the upper end if they are.[35] If fringe benefits are included in earnings, the skill-adjusted earnings differential between LI and CS in manufacturing might be in the 50–75 percent range.[36] That between LI and SMI might be 30–50 percent. The relationship between SMI and LI wages is of particular interest: as we shall see,

Table 2-13. *Index of Relative Earnings, by Occupational Category and Plant Size, 1976*
(LI = 100)

Plant size	Blue-collar apprentices	Blue-collar workers	Clerical	Technical workers		Managers
				National	Foreign	
SI	54.59	47.49	44.12	36.10	34.25	29.47
MI	58.71	58.43	63.87	50.98	60.37	52.72
SMI	56.33	51.95	52.56	42.96	43.84	37.78

Source: Appendix table 15.

SMI and especially SI experienced particularly rapid growth in the 1970s, and it may be that the wage gap provided these firms with an important cost advantage.

Within SMI, blue-collar wages vary moderately by size of plant in the metalworking and food processing industries (table 2-13). Where our surveys provide information on the skill levels of workers, average daily wages (excluding fringe benefits) show little relationship with size in any of the three manual skill categories we distinguish (apart from being lower for the smallest food processing firms of 1–7 workers), but do rise markedly for foremen or supervisors (table 2-14). When fringe benefits (social security, severance pay, and so on) are included, the differentials between smaller and larger firms within each skill category confirm the proposition that small firms usually have a labor cost advantage over larger ones (the data are presented in appendix table 17).

Earnings are not always lower for workers in small establishments, however. In the metalworking firms sampled we found that entrepreneurs frequently contracted specific jobs to skilled and semiskilled workers within the firms. Under this arrangement, the worker is allowed to use the firm's equipment and to hire other workers. Money earned in this way does not enter the firm's wage records; its inclusion could narrow or erase the earnings gap between small and large firms; although some large firms engage in this practice, those that are unionized are seldom able to do so since unions generally oppose it.

It is sometimes argued that the apparent advantage of small firms with respect to lower labor costs is offset by higher labor turnover. This is not evident from our data. Although unskilled workers appear to move from smaller to larger firms, skilled workers, whose departure is more likely to entail disruption costs, move in both directions. Furthermore, it is easier for small firms to lay off or fire workers.

Occupations and Skills

The paid white-collar worker is to some extent the hallmark of large establishments. When plants are grouped by level of output, this group constitutes less than 10 percent of the work force in the smallest plants and nearly 30 percent in the largest.[37] Paid blue-collar workers make up a fairly constant 72–79 percent of the total work force, while household or family workers (who are not paid for their labor but often perform both manual and nonmanual activities) account for more than 10 percent of employment in the smallest plants and a negligible proportion in the largest. When plants are classified by size of work force, these patterns are similar but less marked. The main observable difference between SMI as a whole and LI is the rising proportion of clerical workers with plant

Table 2-14. *Average Daily Wages (Excluding Fringe Benefits), by Skill Category of Workers in Metalworking and Food Processing Firms*

Plant size (number of workers)	Skill category				Fringe benefits as percentage of basic wages
	Supervisors and technicians	Skilled workers	Semiskilled workers	Unskilled workers	
Metalworking firms					
1–10	— (0)	174 (13)	127 (8)	75 (11)	30.8
11–20	216 (3)	179 (20)	122 (17)	90 (17)	35.5
21–40	343 (6)	220 (16)	130 (8)	86 (9)	39.6
41–60	271 (2)	190 (13)	127 (10)	92 (11)	46.0
61+	292 (2)	206 (10)	122 (8)	86 (7)	49.4
All	295 (13)	193 (72)	125 (51)	86 (55)	39.2
Food processing firms					
1–7	— (0)	130 (5)	102 (7)	89 (11)	18.5
8–15	190 (2)	154 (10)	128 (5)	108 (10)	24.4
16–29	290 (4)	157 (6)	120 (6)	98 (7)	32.5
30+	512 (3)	161 (6)	125 (6)	110 (6)	40.8
All	342 (9)	152 (27)	118 (24)	101 (34)	27.1

— Not applicable.

Note: Wages for metalworking firms are in pesos of December 1977; those of food processing firms are in pesos of January 1979. Figures in parentheses denote number of firms.

Source: Authors' surveys of metalworking and food processing firms.

size (table 2-15). No aggregate data are available on skill groupings within the blue-collar category.

The structure of labor costs by occupation varies more than the labor force structure, since white-collar earnings rise more rapidly with the size of establishment than do the earnings of blue-collar workers. For establishments ranging from the smallest plants up to those with 100–199 workers, the share of labor costs going to each of the three white-collar categories rises steadily; this trend is mirrored by a decline in the share going to blue-collar workers (table 2-15). The smallest plants (those with fewer than 10 workers) pay less than a quarter of their wage bill to white-collar workers, whereas those with 100–199 workers pay 46 percent. (The differentials are even more marked when plants are ranked by output level.) This pattern is reversed when we compare plants with 100–199 workers and those with 200 or more; the share of labor remuneration going to executives falls sharply in the latter group by comparison with the former. But this last result may be partly due to the fact that when the number of workers is the measure of size, firms that are relatively intensive in blue-collar workers rank higher in size than they would on other criteria; when plants are ranked by output, the white-collar share of labor costs rises monotonically with size.

These patterns in the composition of the labor force and labor costs by size appear to be due mainly to intra-industry differences; they are not due to an aggregation process across industries with little or no internal relationship between size and labor force composition. They support the general proposition that a large share of the income generated in large plants goes either to high-income owners of capital or to well-paid white-collar workers, whereas the income generated in small plants goes to lower-income people.

Capital Intensity and Size

Physical capital per worker (FK/L) tends to rise markedly with plant size. Data for plants reporting to DANE in 1977 show that the book value of fixed assets per worker was twice as high in LI as in SI, and energy used per worker was 3.2 times greater; inventories plus book value of fixed assets per worker were more than 2.5 times higher in 1976 (table 2-16). Although neither of these is a wholly satisfactory proxy for the FK/L ratio, together they provide an indication of the large differential by plant size.[38] If plants are classified by output, the gap becomes wider.

In none of these measures of capital intensity do the smallest firms systematically have the lowest FK/L ratios. In the case of the DANE data used here, this finding could be a spurious result of differential coverage by size of plant, although it also shows up in our samples of firms in the

Table 2-15. Distribution of the Labor Force and of Labor Cost among Occupational Categories, by Plant Size, 1976
(percent)

Plant size	Unpaid	Paid white-collar				Paid blue-collar		
		Total	Executive	Technical	Clerical	Total	Regular	Apprentice
		Labor force						
SI	5.62	19.53	3.19	1.56	14.78	74.82	73.65	1.17
MI	1.44	21.18	2.66	1.95	16.56	77.38	76.10	1.28
LI	0.21	25.89	1.58	2.38	21.92	73.91	72.25	1.65
SMI	3.95	20.19	2.98	1.72	15.49	75.84	74.63	1.22
All	1.46	23.98	2.05	2.17	19.76	74.56	73.05	1.51
		Labor costs						
SI	—	34.64	9.53	3.96	21.15	63.36	n.a.	n.a.
MI	—	40.09	10.27	5.09	24.73	59.91	n.a.	n.a.
LI	—	43.39	6.72	6.94	29.72	56.61	n.a.	n.a.
SMI	—	37.26	9.89	4.50	22.87	62.74	n.a.	n.a.
All	—	42.18	7.34	6.46	28.38	57.82	n.a.	n.a.

n.a. Not available.
— Not applicable.
Source: Appendix table 18 and unpublished DANE data.

Table 2-16. *Indicators of Capital-Labor Ratios, by Plant Size, 1976 and 1977*

Plant size (number of workers)	Book value of fixed assets per worker, 1977 (thousands of pesos)	Kilowatt-hours consumed per worker, 1977	Inventory plus book value of fixed assets, 1976 (thousands of pesos)	
			Per worker	Divided by labor costs
5–9	70.29	4,013	78.24	3.00
10–14	62.39	3,877	67.85	2.29
15–19	64.30	3,205	82.17	2.58
20–24	66.02	3,369	85.49	2.52
25–49	67.52	3,896	106.03	2.65
50–74	80.64	4,485	127.62	2.76
75–99	87.93	4,156	149.79	2.71
100–99	109.71	6,959	182.96	2.81
200+	149.10	13,323	279.10	3.02
All	117.80	9,227	208.56	2.93
SI	66.35	3,691	96.18	2.67
MI	83.78	4,338	136.88	2.74
LI	140.10	11,871	256.98	2.98
SMI	73.41	3,953	112.75	2.71

Source: DANE, *Industria Manufacturera,* 1977, and unpublished DANE data.

metalworking and food industries when plants are ranked by number of workers.[39] When our sample plants are ranked by level of capital stock, however, FK/L rises monotonically with size (see chapter 3, table 3-17).[40] One wonders how often the high reported capital intensity of very small firms has been due to the way size was measured.

With the possible exception of the smallest plants, the ratio of physical capital to number of workers clearly rises substantially with plant size; were one to treat labor skills as contributing to (human) capital, then the ratio of capital (physical and human) to number of workers would rise even faster with size. In contrast, the ratio of physical capital to labor inputs adjusted for quality rises much less with size. If we make the extreme assumption that labor costs accurately reflect the quantum of labor inputs across plant size (in other words, that after skill differences are taken into account earnings do not vary at all by size of plant), then the ratio of capital to labor would not rise much with plant size—perhaps by 10–30 percent between SI and LI.[41] The true differential, however, is probably around 60–80 percent, to judge from our earlier conclusions on the extent to which the higher wages in large plants reflect greater skills.

Although the ratio of physical capital to labor does increase systematically with size, the same cannot be said of the capital-output ratio. The ratio of book value of fixed assets to value added tends first to fall and later to rise with plant size defined by number of workers, although at the two-digit level there seems to be a variety of patterns (see appendix table 20). This ratio falls sharply and systematically, however, when size is measured by level of output (table 2-17), a pattern that reflects a tendency for plants with high total factor productivity to rank higher in output than in employment. The ratio of inventories to value added tends to rise moderately with size. When inventories are added to our estimates of the value of fixed assets (which are almost certainly too low), the relationship to employment is erratic; the highest values tend to correspond to small and large plants. When plants are ranked by output, the ratio tends to decrease monotonically.

Cost Structure and Returns to Capital

Differences in factor shares and profit rates by size of plant are not great. As of 1976, paid labor's share of value added showed no clear relationship to plant size, although when contracted professional services and imputed wages of working proprietors are included there seems to be a mildly negative relationship, falling from 35.6 percent for SI to 31.1 percent for LI (table 2-18). DANE's figures in *Industria Manufacturera* for the various years of the 1970s suggest that this differential may have been greater in some other years during the decade. Profits plus imputed wages as a share of value added were lowest in plants of 50–199 workers (in part reflecting a higher ratio of indirect taxes to value added for this group), and somewhat higher in both smaller and larger ones.[42] Rent payments were particularly important for small plants, as were interest payments for larger ones.

The average return to capital was high for all size categories of plants in 1976, the year for which our data are most detailed (although the information is still plagued by inadequate data for capital). The ratio of net pretax profits to the sum of book value of fixed assets and value of inventories was 35.2 percent for manufacturing as a whole and a little lower for MI—31.3 percent (table 2-19).[43] Even if one allows for the possibility of some overstatement in the figures for gross profits, these rates are clearly high, probably 25–30 percent or more for SI, MI, and LI.[44] Profit rates net of depreciation are probably about 5 percent lower; direct taxes leave them much smaller but still healthy. The profit rate after direct taxes may have been greater in SI than in LI if, as seems likely, those taxes impinged more heavily on larger firms.[45] At any rate, they were sizable enough to give SMI a good incentive to expand. The 1976 figures seem to be reasonably typical of the decade (see appendix table 22).

Investment Patterns and Their Implications

Like most developing countries, Colombia imports much of the machinery and equipment it needs, which in turn constitutes a high share of total manufacturing investment. Most of these imports consist of new machinery, though some overseas purchases of secondhand goods do occur. Large firms usually undertake their own foreign purchases of new or used capital goods, whereas small firms are more likely to buy these items from commercial intermediaries. Although a detailed breakdown of the relevant data is not available, larger firms also appear to account for the bulk of capital equipment imports. This reflects the fact that their technologies are relatively modern and sophisticated—and perhaps also reflects their relatively privileged access to foreign exchange with which to purchase such equipment (especially when foreign exchange is rationed). Nevertheless, middle-size and even small firms also rely quite heavily on imported equipment, especially if secondhand items that were previously imported by a larger firm are included in the total. Hence the state of the balance of payments can significantly affect the availability over time of machinery and equipment for factories of all sizes. This effect may even be more pronounced for SMI than for LI (see chapter 6).

During the early 1960s, when the balance of payments constraint was generally tight, the ratio of gross fixed investment to output was markedly higher in LI than in SMI, but in the late 1960s and the 1970s, when the

Table 2-17. Indicators of Capital-Output Ratios, by Plant Size, 1976

Plant size	Inventories ÷ value added	Book value of fixed assets ÷ value added	Inventory and book value of fixed assets ÷ value added	Consumption of energy ÷ value added[a]	Percentage of workers in category	Percentage of value added in category
Value of production (millions of pesos)						
0.2–0.4	0.298	1.554	1.852	0.078	0.19	0.02
0.4–0.6	0.307	0.988	1.295	0.052	0.41	0.05
0.6–0.9	0.353	0.781	1.134	0.048	0.80	0.18
0.9–1.5	0.308	0.866	1.174	0.041	1.99	0.36
1.5–2.0	0.320	0.784	1.104	0.049	1.64	0.33
2.0–4.0	0.305	0.634	0.939	0.035	5.94	1.46
4.0–10.0	0.372	0.615	0.987	0.032	10.43	3.59
10.0–50.0	0.458	0.593	1.051	0.033	21.50	10.47
50.0+	0.440	0.431	0.871	0.042	56.98	83.91
Total	0.437	0.461	0.897	0.041		

Number of workers						
1–4	0.432	0.646	1.078	0.039	—	—
5–9	0.305	0.746	1.051	0.047	0.99	0.34
10–14	0.377	0.619	0.996	0.038	2.56	0.94
15–19	0.307	0.605	0.912	0.034	2.78	1.08
20–24	0.225	0.428	0.653	0.028	2.74	1.54
25–49	0.405	0.491	0.896	0.029	11.04	5.61
50–74	0.461	0.537	0.998	0.034	7.90	4.35
75–99	0.358	0.395	0.753	0.044	5.52	4.73
100–99	0.459	0.384	0.843	0.024	15.28	14.26
200+	0.447	0.469	0.916	0.046	51.15	67.12
Total	0.437	0.461	0.897	0.041	100.00	100.00
SI	0.359	0.516	0.875	0.0310	20.15	9.54
MI	0.408	0.462	0.870	0.0392	13.42	9.08
LI	0.449	0.454	0.903	0.0421	66.43	81.38
SMI	0.383	0.490	0.873	0.0350	—	—

— Not applicable.
a. Kilowatt-hours per peso of value added.
Source: Unpublished DANE data.

Table 2-18. *Composition of Value Added, by Plant Size, 1976*
(percentage of value added)

Plant size	Value added (billions of pesos)	Paid labor	All labor[a]	Contracted professional services	Rent	Interest
Number of workers						
1–4	.04	13.67	18.90	1.45	4.45	8.83
5–9	0.37	32.92	39.16	1.47	5.21	3.88
10–14	1.03	34.61	38.57	1.89	4.03	4.29
15–19	1.18	35.29	38.04	1.48	3.14	4.39
20–24	1.68	25.95	27.44	1.19	1.83	3.58
25–49	6.13	33.85	34.96	1.70	2.20	6.03
50–74	4.75	36.10	36.80	1.54	1.85	6.67
75–99	5.16	27.79	28.01	1.31	1.20	6.66
100–99	15.57	30.03	30.21	1.20	1.36	8.25
200+	73.31	30.29	30.31	0.75	0.92	8.33
SI	10.42	32.01	33.92	1.66	2.54	5.21
MI	9.92	31.75	32.20	1.42	1.51	6.61
LI	88.87	30.25	30.29	0.82	1.00	8.32
SMI	20.34	32.25	33.47	1.54	2.04	5.92
All	109.21	30.62	31.07	0.96	1.19	7.87
Value of production (millions of pesos)						
0.2–0.4	0.02	78.03	n.a.	1.72	12.55	4.38
0.4–0.6	0.05	71.76	n.a.	1.20	7.44	4.87
0.6–0.9	0.13	60.19	n.a.	1.35	6.68	3.75
0.9–1.5	0.39	57.07	n.a.	1.74	5.94	3.88
1.5–2.0	0.36	56.20	n.a.	1.94	4.88	3.74
2.0–4.0	0.16	51.74	n.a.	1.98	4.22	5.09
4.0–10.0	3.59	49.60	n.a.	1.94	2.86	5.66
10.0–50.0	11.43	42.22	n.a.	1.90	1.81	8.11
50.0+	91.65	27.76	n.a.	0.78	0.95	8.02
All	109.21	30.62	31.07	0.96	1.19	7.87

n.a. Not available.

Note: DANE definition of value added includes several items that are not part of value added.

constraint was absent, the ratio for SMI rose, while the ratio for LI showed no clear trend.[46] By 1977–78, the SMI investment ratio was well above that for LI (table 2-20).[47] The near doubling of the SMI ratio from 10.27 percent in 1962–66 to 19.08 percent in 1977–78 is consistent with the rapid growth observed for those years in the firms we sampled in the food and metalworking sectors. More generally, SMI's rising investment rate supports the contention that the 1970s were years of rapid growth in this subsector, at least through 1978.[48] As we shall show in chapter 4, the rate of growth of employment in representative small plants appears to have risen relative to that in representative large plants between the mid-1960s and the 1970s, a pattern that is broadly consistent with the trends in the investment-output ratio.

Depreciation	Indirect taxes	Regalias[b]	Publicity, insurance, utilities, other	Profits and imputed wages	Profits	Plant size
						Number of workers
5.72	10.29	0.06	10.78	44.75	39.52	1–4
3.71	18.18	0.02	7.51	27.10	20.86	5–9
4.13	8.91	0.10	10.66	31.38	27.42	10–14
4.86	7.12	0.08	10.56	33.08	30.33	15–19
3.24	5.17	0.17	7.78	51.09	49.60	20–24
4.48	10.08	0.19	12.24	29.23	28.12	25–49
5.23	13.33	0.18	11.58	23.52	22.82	50–74
3.69	15.94	0.14	11.96	31.31	31.09	75–99
4.85	12.72	0.42	14.04	27.13	26.96	100–99
5.66	9.62	0.36	10.59	33.48	33.46	200+
4.27	9.13	0.16	11.00	34.02	32.11	SI
4.43	14.68	0.16	11.77	27.67	27.24	MI
5.51	10.17	0.37	11.19	32.37	32.33	LI
4.35	11.84	0.16	11.38	30.52	29.41	SMI
5.30	10.48	0.33	11.23	32.02	31.57	All
						Value of production (millions of pesos)
5.23	6.95	0.01	9.80	–18.67	n.a.	0.2–0.4
3.94	8.29	0.01	9.41	–6.92	n.a.	0.4–0.6
3.58	8.13	0.03	7.59	8.70	n.a.	0.6–0.9
5.25	8.63	0.08	8.97	8.44	n.a.	0.9–1.5
5.17	8.31	0.13	10.43	9.20	n.a.	1.5–2.0
4.35	8.83	0.10	10.54	13.15	n.a.	2.0–4.0
4.67	8.70	0.11	11.95	14.51	n.a.	4.0–10.0
5.66	9.52	0.34	13.88	16.56	n.a.	10.0–50.0
5.30	10.71	0.34	10.90	35.24	n.a.	50.0+
5.30	10.48	0.33	11.23	32.02	31.57	All

a. Including an imputation for self-employed individuals.

b. Royalty and similar payments for the right to produce patented items or use patented products.

Source: Unpublished DANE data.

The nature of investment expenditures varies. Smaller plants put a substantially higher share than larger ones do into building and transport equipment and correspondingly less into machinery (table 2-21). The extensive expenditure on buildings probably reflects the relative youth of these plants. Older (and generally larger) plants are likely to have undertaken expenditures of this kind some years ago. As noted earlier, smaller plants, many of which are young, spend more on rent than larger ones do, since a higher proportion of the former still operate in rented quarters.

The use of secondhand capital goods is particularly prevalent in smaller plants, especially among those with low levels of output, because

Table 2-19. *Indicators of Profit Rates, by Plant Size, 1976*

	Ratio of profits + imputed wages to		Profits ÷ book value + inventory
Plant size	Book value	Book value + inventory	
Number of workers			
1–4	n.a.	n.a.	n.a.
5–9	39.27	27.43	21.11
10–14	50.69	31.51	27.53
15–19	54.68	36.27	33.25
20–24	119.37	78.24	75.96
25–49	59.53	32.62	31.38
50–74	43.80	23.57	22.87
75–99	79.27	41.58	41.29
100–99	70.66	32.18	31.98
200+	71.38	36.26	36.53
SI	65.94	38.90	36.72
MI	59.89	31.08	31.30
LI	71.30	35.84	35.79
SMI	62.29	34.96	33.61
All	69.46	35.70	35.20
Value of production (millions of pesos)			
0.2–0.4	n.a.	−10.08	n.a.
0.4–0.6	n.a.	−5.34	n.a.
0.6–0.9	n.a.	7.67	n.a.
0.9–1.5	n.a.	7.19	n.a.
1.5–2.0	n.a.	8.33	n.a.
2.0–4.0	n.a.	14.00	n.a.
4.0–10.0	n.a.	14.70	n.a.
10.0–50.0	n.a.	15.76	n.a.
50.0+	n.a.	40.46	n.a.
All	69.46	37.32	36.80

n.a. Not available.
Source: Unpublished DANE data.

of their relatively limited access to capital and their desire to minimize the risks associated with a new or relatively risky enterprise. In the factory sector as a whole, purchases of secondhand items accounted for 10.7 percent of 1976 investment in fixed assets (excluding land and capital goods produced by the plant itself).[49] For firms in the largest size category by value of output (those with gross production worth more than 50 million pesos) the share was only 8 percent, whereas in plants whose output was worth less than 1.5 million pesos the proportion was nearly one-half (table 2-22). For plants with between 1.5 and 50 million pesos of output, the proportion ranged from one-fifth to one-third.[50] Secondhand purchases are naturally more common in the case of buildings (27 percent of total investment) than of other assets; for machinery and equipment the

Table 2-20. *Investment-Output Ratios, by Plant Size, 1962–78*

Plant size	1962–66 gross	1967–71 gross	1972–76 Net	1972–76 Gross[b]	1977–78[a] Net	1977–78[a] Gross[c]
SI	10.23	11.63	9.31	15.91	10.88	19.19
MI	10.33	12.75	8.84	15.10	10.75	18.96
LI	14.14	13.29	8.01	13.70	7.99	14.09
100–99	8.96	10.05	5.47[d]	9.35[d]	7.48	13.19
200+	15.90	14.33	8.53[d]	14.58[d]	8.08	14.25
SMI	10.27	12.09	8.26	14.11	10.82	19.08
All	12.91	12.95	7.87	13.45	8.15	14.37

Note: Data in the three groups of years are not comparable. Those for 1967–71 are gross of legal depreciation; the rest are net but with the additional adjustment mentioned in note a.

a. Data in 1978 include revaluation of fixed assets, whereas those in 1977 do not.

b. Based on application of the sectorwide average gross-net ratio of 1.709 to each size category.

c. Based on application of the sectorwide average gross-net ratio of 1.764 to each size category.

d. Assumes the same figure for firms with 100–99 workers and for those with 200+ in 1974, as we had only the average of these two categories for that year.

Source: DANE, *Anuario General de Estadística* for years through 1967; *III Censo Industrial* for 1970; and *Industria Manufacturera* for other years.

average was about 9 percent. Small plants resort more frequently to the secondhand market for capital goods of all kinds than do large ones, the difference being most noticeable in the case of machinery—plants with output of up to 4 million pesos bought about 60 percent of their machinery secondhand; for plants with output worth 50 million pesos or more, the comparable figure was 6.6 percent. Smaller but still marked differences are also evident in purchases of transport equipment and office machinery, while the gap is predictably smallest in the case of buildings.

In general, the largest plants, which are the main importers of capital goods, are net sellers of used machinery and fixed assets, while smaller plants are net buyers (table 2-23). Although no information is available on

Table 2-21. *Composition of Investment Expenditures, by Plant Size, 1976*
(percent)

Plant size	Buildings	Machinery and equipment	Transport equipment	Office equipment
SI	19.85	59.27	15.37	5.50
MI	16.55	68.04	10.28	5.13
LI	10.56	78.07	8.93	2.84
All	11.87	75.62	9.24	3.27

Source: Unpublished DANE data.

Table 2-22. Purchase of Used Capital Goods as a Percentage of Total Investment, by Type of Capital Goods and Plant Size, 1976

Plant size	All capital goods	Buildings	Machinery and equipment	Transport equipment	Office machinery	Percentage of all workers in size category
Value of production (millions of pesos)						
0.0–1.4	47.57	31.75	52.15	49.80	39.83	3.39
1.5–4.0	33.64	35.48	32.58	43.28	31.53	7.58
4.0–50.0	21.04	27.26	20.06	20.28	13.45	31.93
50+	8.00	18.71	6.56	7.99	7.14	56.98
Total	10.73	26.84	8.90	11.87	10.68	100.00
Number of workers						
5–49 (SI)	26.89	27.91	26.62	35.62	21.21	20.15
50–99 (MI)	19.93	28.70	18.70	20.07	15.44	13.42
100+ (LI)	8.05	18.67	6.63	7.86	7.12	66.43
5–99 (SMI)	23.30	28.28	22.27	27.92	18.33	33.57

Source: Unpublished DANE data.

Table 2-23. Purchases and Sales of Used Fixed Assets, by Plant Size, 1976
(absolute figures in millions of pesos)

Plant size (number of workers)	All fixed assets				Machinery and equipment			
	Purchases		Sales		Purchases		Sales	
	Amount	Percent	Amount	Percent	Amount	Percent	Amount	Percent
1–9	13.08	0.88	14.14	1.04	5.28	0.55	8.44	0.97
10–14	43.05	2.88	15.80	1.16	26.32	2.75	5.90	0.68
15–19	38.63	2.59	17.30	1.28	19.38	2.02	11.20	1.29
20–24	40.66	2.62	17.16	1.26	21.73	2.27	8.23	0.95
25–49	179.10	11.99	91.11	6.71	114.84	11.98	45.47	5.25
50–74	110.13	7.37	48.46	3.57	71.71	7.48	19.42	2.24
75–99	147.25	9.85	24.61	1.81	89.39	9.32	8.39	0.97
100–99	236.71	15.84	153.46	11.31	175.55	18.31	67.73	7.81
200+	685.62	45.88	974.81	71.84	434.55	45.32	691.82	79.83
Total	1494.23	100.00	1356.83	100.00	958.75	100.00	866.60	100.00
SMI	571.90	38.28	228.56	16.83	348.65	36.37	107.05	12.35
LI	921.33	61.72	1128.27	83.17	610.10	63.63	759.55	87.65

Note: It is assumed here that fixed assets sold have all been used; this may not be the case.
Source: Unpublished DANE data.

the extent to which assets sold by large plants are purchased by smaller ones this seems likely to be the normal pattern. Some used assets are imported and some come from other sectors. Some assets are not sold directly or indirectly to other manufacturing plants; some machinery, for example, is sold for scrap. Relatively large plants of 100–199 workers are heavy net buyers of used machinery and equipment (probably from still larger plants), but are net sellers of other fixed assets (see table 2-23). SMI plants are heavy net buyers of machinery and equipment and of other fixed assets as well. With respect to buildings, machinery, and equipment, plants of up to 50 workers (SI) had sales nearly half as great as their purchases, whereas in MI (plants of 50–99 workers) this ratio was only about 20 percent. The greater tendency of SI units both to buy and to sell used capital items suggests a frequent turnover of equipment or relatively frequent exits from business in this subsector.[51]

Purchases of used machinery tend to be high in most of the consumption goods industries where small producers are important—such as clothing, footwear, wood, and furniture—and in the cement and metalworking industries.[52] The ratio is low in most of the industries that use modern technology, including beverages, petroleum refining, rubber, ceramics, paper, glass, and base metals. It is also low in textiles (see appendix table 21).

Imports and Exports

Large plants are typically more closely tied to the foreign sector than small ones. They buy a higher share of their machinery abroad and their inputs as a whole are much more import-intensive. As of 1976, imports made up less than 5 percent of the raw materials used by plants with less than 2 million pesos of output, but amounted to 26 percent for those with output worth 50 million pesos or more (table 2-24). When plants are ranked by number of workers, this relationship is less extreme; nevertheless, the difference between LI (whose average is 28 percent) and SMI (15 percent) is still striking.

Manufactured exports, which reached significant levels during the late 1960s and the 1970s, appear also to be concentrated in the large firms. In 1970, twenty-four firms (ten of them foreign owned) accounted for 62 percent of manufactured exports (excluding sugar).[53] Figures for more recent years are not available. The greater tendency of large plants to import capital equipment and raw materials is a natural result of their more modern technology and greater capital intensity. Why they also export a higher share of output than smaller, more labor-intensive firms do is less clear.[54] Possible causal factors include the advantages of size for winning contracts in international markets and perhaps a tendency for

Table 2-24. *Imported Raw Materials as a Percentage of All Raw Materials, by Plant Size, 1976*

Plant size (value of production, millions of pesos)	Raw materials imported (percent)	Plant size (number of workers)	Raw materials imported (percent)
0.0–0.1	2.1	1–4	3.2
0.2–0.4	2.6	5–9	10.7
0.4–0.6	2.9	10–14	15.4
0.6–0.9	3.8	15–19	14.0
0.9–1.5	4.6	20–24	28.5
1.5–2.0	5.0	25–49	19.2
2.0–4.0	6.3	50–74	13.3
4.0–10.0	8.9	75–99	9.6
10.0–50.0	18.8	100–99	24.0
50.0+	25.6	200+	28.8
All	24.0	All	24.0
		SI	19.1
		MI	11.5
		LI	27.8
		SMI	15.5

Source: Unpublished DANE data.

firms with foreign involvement, which are also usually large, to export a higher share of output than locally controlled firms.[55]

Summary

The rapid growth of the Colombian manufacturing sector during this century has been accompanied by a marked change in its plant-size structure, improvements in technology, and increases in the capital-labor ratio, labor productivity, and labor remuneration. These changes have occurred in different degrees for plants of different sizes. As late as 1970, the cottage-shop sector (comprising establishments of fewer than 5 workers) accounted for more than half of all manufacturing employment, large factories (100 workers or more) for about one-quarter, and small and medium factories (5–99 workers) for about one-quarter. Since labor productivity increases with size, the share of LI in output was well over half; that of SMI was between 20 and 25 percent.

SMI employment is concentrated in food products, clothing and footwear, metal products, chemicals, transport equipment (mainly repairs), and textiles. Since the capital-labor ratio, labor productivity, and mean labor remuneration are all positively associated with size both for manufacturing as a whole and in the typical manufacturing subsector, SMI falls between CS on the one hand and LI on the other in all these respects. Variations between different firm-size categories are wide. The ratio of physical capital to labor is 2.5–3.0 times higher in LI than in SI, labor productivity nearly 3.0 times higher, and earnings 2.0 to 2.5 times higher. These differences may be partly due to the fact that the average level of skills is greater in larger establishments; when education and experience are allowed for, labor remuneration is probably less than 50 percent higher in LI than in SI (perhaps not more than 25 percent higher). Similarly, if labor is measured by efficiency units rather than number of workers, the labor productivity gap is much reduced, as is that of the K/L ratio. This is consistent with the fact that the rate of return to physical capital appears to differ very little between SMI and LI; as of 1976 it was quite high in both.

Over the several decades for which data are available, the share of manufacturing output and employment accounted for by LI has risen and that of CS has fallen; the share of SMI appears to have risen up to 1960 or so, then to have fallen until about 1970, only to rise again more recently. From at least the 1940s (and probably throughout this century) to about 1960, SMI was expanding its share of both output and employment at the expense of CS; during the 1960s it lost ground to LI, but began to gain once more in the 1970s, at the expense of both CS and LI. The most striking feature of this evolution is the reversal of the roles of SMI and LI in the 1970s, with the former showing the greater dynamism.

Labor productivity in manufacturing has risen rapidly during this century, averaging probably 4.0 to 4.5 percent a year. Much of this growth has been associated with the expansion of the factory sector at the expense of cottage-shop activities and with the increasing role of large industry within the factory sector. Available (though incomplete) data suggest that since 1953 labor productivity has risen especially sharply within LI and has also increased in SI but not in MI. The labor productivity of CS also appears to have risen substantially. Although no data are available, capital per worker has almost certainly risen significantly for SMI as well as LI, and probably for CS as well. During the early 1960s (and perhaps sooner, although confirmatory data are again not available), the ratio of investment to output was markedly higher in LI than in SMI; this relationship seems to have gradually reversed itself over time, however, so that by the late 1970s the opposite was true. The gross differential in remuneration of employees by size of plant appeared to be increasing in the late 1950s and the 1960s, but to be narrowing again in the 1970s.

The evidence of SMI's increasing capitalization and labor productivity, together with its ongoing contribution to the growth of manufacturing employment and output, suggests that the subsector will continue to play a significant role well into the future. Its economic use of scarce resources is well exemplified by its tendency to use fewer imported inputs than LI and to buy a larger proportion of its physical capital secondhand.

Notes

1. A few entrepreneurs set up small plants, such as soap and candle factories and a French-owned lamp and lamp oil factory, but most of them failed. See William P. McGreevey, *An Economic History of Colombia, 1845–1930* (Cambridge, Eng.: Cambridge University Press, 1971), p. 179.

2. See McGreevey, *An Economic History,* especially chap. 7; Luis Nieto A., *El Café en la Sociedad Colombiana* (Bogotá: Ediciones La Soga al Cuello, 1971); and Nieto, *Economía y Cultura en la Historia de Colombia* (Bogotá: Ediciones Tercer Mundo, 1962).

3. Albert Berry, "The Limited Role of Rural Small Scale Manufacturing for Late Comers: Some Hypotheses on the Colombian Experience," Working Paper B.4 (Toronto, Ont.: University of Toronto Development Studies Program, 1984), pp. 7–10.

4. Industrialization came later to Colombia than to countries such as Argentina, Brazil, Chile, and Mexico. In Argentina and Chile, manufacturing accounted for almost 20 percent of total production by about the turn of the century; in Mexico it made up 10–15 percent, while in Colombia the figure was probably 10–12 percent.

5. For further details on the growth rates discussed here and in the next paragraph, see Albert Berry, "A Descriptive History of Colombian Industrial Development in the Twentieth Century," in *Essays on Industrialization,* ed. Albert Berry (Tempe, Ariz.: Arizona State University Center for Latin American Studies, 1983).

6. Manufacturing's share of the nonagricultural labor force declined between 1938 (when it approached 40 percent) and 1970 (when it was probably 23–25 percent); this decline reflected the rapid growth of employment in the service sector. Since 1970, however, this share has stabilized or risen a little.

7. The range of estimates is based roughly on the two sets of assumptions under which estimates are made for June 1978 in table 2-2. See the note to that table.

8. This is not to say that the typical small firm grew less rapidly than larger ones in the 1950s and 1960s. Rapid growth by individual small firms near the upper limit of the size category moves them out of that category and contributes to a slow growth of total employment in the category.

9. The statistical problems include the probable noncomparability of some of the sources. If one assumes comparability of the 1970 and 1978 household surveys, the growth rate of total manufacturing employment over 1970–78 would be an astonishing 6.6 percent a year; even more surprising would be a growth rate of 10.4 percent a year for employment in small and medium plants (calculat-

ed as a residual), while that in large plants was increasing at 6.2 percent a year (for LI, we accept DANE's annual manufacturing survey data as accurate). Probably the true growth of manufacturing employment was less than 6.6 percent a year, but still high.

10. DANE's reporting for the factory sector (in *Industria Manufacturera*, various years) shows a continuation of the relative decline of employment in SMI. But any plausible downward adjustment to the figure for aggregate growth of manufacturing employment, taken together with data on the number of independent workers and the size distribution of establishments reported by workers in the household surveys, implies the result indicated in the text.

11. If the employment share of each industry had remained at its 1956 level but the distribution by size in each industry had moved to its 1975 level, the aggregate shares of small, medium, and large industry in 1975 would have scarcely differed from what they were. By contrast, the relative decline of cottage-shop employment over time does appear to have been associated partly with changing industrial structure.

12. The 1975 figures for two-digit industries are incomplete because of imperfect coverage in the SI size range; these qualitative conclusions would probably still hold, however, if full data were available.

13. For the set of industries in which SI's employment share fell by less than the average, and taking industry labor productivity to be equal to 1, the unweighted averages of SI, MI, and LI labor productivities were 0.90, 1.17, and 1.16, respectively; for the set of industries in which the fall in SMI's employment share was atypically rapid, the comparable figures were 0.61, 1.03, and 1.77, respectively. Although the figures are affected by the odd patterns in wood and tobacco, the differences were marked even if these two cases are excluded.

14. In interpreting trends in the labor force and labor productivity, it should be noted that the sector has undergone wholesale substitution of more highly skilled male laborers for less skilled female laborers and possibly of full-time workers for part-time ones. For further details, see Berry, "A Descriptive History."

15. Ibid., table 2-2.

16. Estimates are not available for the 1970s, since we have no manufacturing capital stock series.

17. The figures in table 2-4 give labor productivity for each size category at current prices, deflated by the national accounts deflator for the manufacturing sector as a whole. We have also calculated deflators that reflect the industry composition of SI, MI, and LI (average composition across 1956, 1966, and 1975). The results are not greatly changed by this adjustment. There is, of course, no way to be certain that the price trends for SI, MI, and LI did not vary within given industries. The only sure way to measure quantum trends is directly, but this would be difficult and time-consuming.

The increasing undercoverage of SI during the 1970s probably implies an upward bias in the figure for it. To exemplify, if the percentage coverage fell by one-half, and the average productivity of the firms covered at the beginning of the period but not at the end were 30 percent below that of those covered in both cases, a spurious increase of 15 percent would have occurred. The biasing effect of this change would have to be very large to overturn the conclusion that labor productivity rose markedly in SI. Note also that in 1956 labor productivity in MI was unusually high relative to that of SI (about 2:1) and relative to LI (about 86 percent as high). The absence of any subsequent increase in labor productivity for the MI category is probably related to this fact.

18. Given the degree of fluctuations observed, the results can vary considerably according to the first and last years chosen. The figures show a sharp increase between 1953 and 1956; although there is no specific reason to doubt that such an increase occurred, its magnitude for middle and large industry is surprising, and it could be at least in part a spurious result of some difference between the 1953 data (taken from the industrial census of that year) and the 1956 data (from the first of the annual surveys). The 1977 and 1978 figures are far above those of the mid-1970s and thus raise a similar problem of interpretation. Labor productivity trends were related (whether causally or not is another matter) to inflation patterns in the 1970s; decreases corresponded to the first half of the decade as inflation accelerated, and increases to subsequent periods of declining inflation. Even in 1978, however, inflation was well above the pre-1970 levels, so it seems plausible to assume that the growth of labor productivity calculated between a high year (1956) and a year that may or may not be above some kind of normal trend line (1978) should not seriously overestimate that growth. That the figures do overstate labor productivity growth is, however, suggested by the slower growth of calculated labor productivity when one uses the national accounts physical output index to measure output growth. The reason for the discrepancy between the sources is not clear; one factor may be that the national accounts physical quantum index, being a Laspeyres index across the two-digit sectors, does not include the productivity effects of changing composition of output.

19. See Albert Berry, "The Effects of Inflation on Income Distribution in Colombia: Some Hypotheses and a Framework for Analysis," *Economic Policy and Income Distribution in Colombia*, ed. Albert Berry and Ronald Soligo (Boulder, Colo.: Westview, 1980).

20. Assessing productivity trends in CS is very difficult since there are no reliable physical output series. The national accounts present one, but it is based more on guesswork than on data. The increase of 80 percent is based on the conservative estimate (from national accounts output figures) that between 1953 and 1975 labor productivity in the factory subsector rose by about 53 percent. We estimated the average labor productivity (in current prices) of very small establishments at 22 percent of the average for factory manufacturing in 1953 but at about 26 percent by 1975, so that real labor productivity must have risen substantially for these subfactory establishments as well, even if some of the estimated increase is due to statistical error or to price increases for the products of such establishments relative to those of the factory subsector.

21. In their study of the artisan sector (which we have called CS) Urrutia and Villalba concluded that average earnings rose by about 24 percent between 1953 and 1964. Miguel Urrutia and Clara Elsa Villalba, "El Sector Artesanal en el Desarrollo Colombiano," *Revista de Planeación y Desarrollo*, vol. 1, no. 3 (October 1969), pp. 43–78.

22. Decreases in the coverage of small plants in the late 1960s make it difficult to compare this period with the earlier years, but sensitivity analysis suggests that the cited conclusions do not result from them.

23. We may have overestimated the gains of independent workers. Our assumption was that their income in 1953 was 40 percent above that of paid workers; this percentage is apparently not out of line with the findings of Urrutia and Villalba, but perhaps the true difference was greater.

24. John C. H. Fei and Gustav Ranis, *The Labor Surplus Economy: Theory and Policy* (Homewood, Ill.: Irwin, 1964), pp. 125–34.

25. Miguel Urrutia, *Winners and Losers in Colombia's Economic Growth in the 1970s* (New York: Oxford University Press, 1985).

26. Albert Berry, "Predicting Income Distribution in Latin America During the 1980s," in *Latin American Prospects for the 1980s: Equity, Democratization and Development*, ed. David H. Pollock and A. R. M. Ritter (New York: Praeger, 1983).

27. The CS sector is made up largely of household operations, which accounted for approximately one-third of all employment in manufacturing, according to the population census of 1973. Other very small firms—here referred to as shops—accounted for 15–20 percent. An even higher share of CS workers probably worked in household activities in earlier years.

28. The oil and base metal industries should also be included in this category, as indicated in the note to table 2-9.

29. It would have been advantageous to disaggregate further (for example, to the three-digit level), but the data did not permit this.

30. As judged by occupational categories and, in lesser degree, by incomes.

31. One might speculate that observed differences in labor productivity and earnings by size of establishment might be partly due to a tendency for larger plants to be located disproportionately in larger cities—which would, for separate reasons, have relatively high wages and productivity, regardless of plant size. This does not in fact appear to be the case in Colombia, to judge from the data for 1974.

32. As with labor productivity, the earnings-size relationship varies from industry to industry, but it is systematically present, usually in much the same pattern as in the aggregate, that is, a modest increase with size within SMI but a sharp jump between SMI as a whole and LI. (For data on clothing products, see appendix table 16).

33. The differentials are larger if establishment size is defined by level of output rather than number of workers. The earnings ratio between the top half and the bottom 8.4 percent of workers, for example, is 3.52 when output is the measure of size, and 2.72 when number of workers is used. Although in some respects it might be preferable to use the definition of size that generates the largest wage differentials—since one of our objectives is to study and understand them—the time-series data on size measured by output are more sparse than those on size measured by number of workers; we therefore rely mainly on the latter.

34. Within cottage-shop activities, income levels vary widely by type of product; Urrutia and Villalba found that the lowest incomes were those of women working in *confecciones* (clothing); the highest were those of mechanics in automobile repair shops. See Urrutia and Villalba, "El Sector Artesanal."

35. See François Bourguignon, "Pobreza y Dualismo en el Sector Urbano de las Economías en Desarrollo: El Caso de Colombia," *Desarrollo y Sociedad*, no. 1 (1979), pp. 37–72; and Bernardo Kugler, Alvaro Reyes, and Martha I. de

Gutiérrez, *Educación y Mercado de Trabajo Urbano en Colombia: Una Comparación entre Sectores Modernos y no Modernos* (Bogotá: Corporación Centro Regional de Población, July 1979). In his analysis of DANE's 1974 household survey of seven cities, Bourguignon defined the modern sector as including all production units of six or more employees, plus all individuals with a university education and all government employees ("Pobreza y Dualismo," p. 708). Although the gross income differential between the modern and traditional sectors was 1.86, most of it was related to educational and other characteristics likely to affect personal productivity. If, as may be the case, the modern sector selects workers of higher ability (given the level of education, experience, and so on), then the true differential—holding ability constant—would be even less than Bourguignon's figures show. However, fringe benefits, which are higher in the modern sector, appear to be seriously underreported. It is possible that, if the modern-traditional earnings gap was indeed as low as Bourguignon estimates it to have been in 1975, it had fallen from earlier periods when it was more marked. This hypothesis remains to be tested.

36. It is a matter of debate whether basic wages or wages plus fringe benefits give a better indication of relative benefits to the worker. For those with high discount rates, the basic wage may be more relevant; this is suggested by some of the evidence from our samples of firms in the metalworking and food industries. This fringe-inclusive differential is estimated at 50–75 percent rather than the 20–40 percent cited in the text because LI is at the upper end of the size range that includes establishments of five or more workers and we suspect the earnings differentials may be larger in manufacturing than in other sectors.

Unfortunately, it remains open to question whether earnings differentials by education and age are mainly the result of productivity differentials, as the human capital model assumes, or are also significantly affected by institutionalized practices in wage and salary setting. Practices that could generate earnings differentials by level of education include the payment of high wages to highly educated people in the large-scale high-profit sector, which hires the great majority of such people. High-profit sectors have the option of not paying groups according to their marginal productivity. If institutional factors were important in these size-related earnings differentials, the true skill-adjusted productivity differentials would be larger than suggested by regressions such as those of Bourguignon ("Pobreza y Dualismo") and of Kugler and his colleagues (*Educación y Mercado de Trabajo Urbano*).

37. Grouping by level of output tends to put establishments with high capital-labor ratios, and hence high output-labor ratios, higher in the distribution than does grouping by number of workers.

38. Data on book value are presumed to be underestimates of the commercial value of fixed assets at current prices, given the severe inflation in Colombia during the 1970s, but it is not known how the degree of understatement varies with plant size.

As indicated in table 2-20, there is no strong relationship between plant size (number of workers) and the ratio of investment to value added. This fact, coupled with evidence discussed in chapter 4 that the rate of employment growth (and therefore probably the rate of output growth) did not differ greatly by plant size for establishments identified in both 1970 and 1975, suggests the possibility of similar degrees of understatement across plant size. The greater average age of larger plants might, however, imply greater understatement for them.

39. From the late 1960s onward, DANE's coverage of smaller plants was greatly reduced, with very few units employing less than ten workers still reporting. The smaller plants still covered are therefore probably atypically capital-intensive and modern. The only indicator of capital intensity by size available in the data for the late 1960s (before coverage was reduced) was installed capacity per worker, which was frequently, though not always, an increasing function of size, even among the smallest size categories; the negative relationship within the first few size classes has been most systematic from 1973 onward, when the number of small plants covered was reduced to its present level.

40. Neither the higher FK/L ratios for the smallest firms than for somewhat larger ones nor the wide gap between SMI and LI is due to aggregation across industries. The relationship of electricity consumed per worker to size does differ across industries, but the average case would probably be very similar to the aggregate figures. Data for selected industries are presented in appendix table 19.

41. When we compare the sum of the value of fixed assets and the value of inventories to labor costs, the differential in question is only 12 percent (table 2-16, column 3). Probably, however, the relative youth of smaller plants means that the ratio of book value to replacement cost or to commercial value would be higher for them than for the larger plants, so their relative capital intensity would be overstated and the differential understated. Use of output rather than employment as a measure of size would also increase the differential. Exclusion of capital other than the two types listed may also bias the results somewhat.

42. Indirect taxes rose dramatically, from 1.5 percent of value added in 1970 to 10.5 percent in 1976, and to 18.2 percent in 1978 (appendix table 22).

43. Net pretax profits are defined here as value added minus all listed costs (see table 2-18).

44. The ratio of book value of fixed assets to gross value added fell from 0.732 in 1970 to 0.390 in 1978. If the figures are corrected for inputs that are really not part of value added, the ratios for the two years are 0.826 and 0.474, respectively. The 1970 ratio was probably reasonably close to a meaningful estimate of the commercial value of fixed capital, while those for 1975 onward were seriously downwardly biased because of inadequate correction for inflation. It is interesting, however, that the fixed capital-labor ratio obtained from our sample in the metalworking sector in 1978 was quite close to that reported in DANE's book value figures for 1976. Any upward bias in the profit rate owing to underestimates of capital might be offset by downward biases resulting from the likelihood that gross profits were understated in the figures reported to DANE and the possibility that the plant's own capital is less than the capital it uses. In principle, the profits earned by the plant should be related to the capital it owns, and the capital income generated by it (that is, all nonwage income, including rent and interest paid to others) should be related to the total capital it uses. In each case capital should include financial working capital, on which we have no data for manufacturing as a whole.

Although profit rates show no systematic variation by size of plant defined by number of workers, they bear a strongly positive association with level of output (see table 2-19). The rate of return is more than twice as high for plants in the largest size category (output in excess of 50 million pesos; 84 percent of total output was in this category) as for all small plants taken together. But when plants are classified by output, the ratio of investment to value added is much higher for small plants; this suggests that their capital is on the average newer and that its value is therefore underreported by a smaller proportion than is that of the plants with high output levels.

45. As suggested by some other calculations (not, however, referring to the late 1970s). See Berry, "A Descriptive History," table A.80.

46. Some of the increase for SMI is probably a spurious result of the decrease in DANE's coverage in the SI sector (in particular, in the coverage of plants with fewer than ten workers) from 1969 onward, but it seems unlikely that this could significantly bias the trend. Up to 1968 the two smallest size categories always had investment ratios well below the manufacturing average; when the samples became highly biased from 1969 onward, this was no longer the case. The investment ratio for plants of 10–14 workers also rose sharply in 1969, but was still typically below the sectoral average in subsequent years.

47. Within LI, plants of 100–199 workers seem systematically to have had a lower ratio than plants of 200 or more workers. The figure for the latter category is pushed up by the presence of a number of public companies with extremely high investment ratios. As of 1966, the most recent year for which data are available, the gross investment rate of plants with 200 workers or more was 19.48 percent; excluding public companies it was only 12.94 percent. At that time, investment-output ratios among proprietorships had a much stronger positive association with size than was true for all establishments taken together. This is unlikely to have been true during the 1970s, to judge from the other evidence available.

48. Since 1978 SMI has probably suffered along with the rest of the manufacturing sector. Note that an above-average investment ratio might not imply above-average output growth if the plants in question had a high fixed capital-output ratio, but the data of table 2-17 suggest little difference between SMI and LI. If, as seems plausible, secondhand machinery or other capital goods provide, at least in the short run, more productive capacity per peso of outlay than new machinery, its greater use by small firms would also be consistent with faster growth rates for them. Relating investment-output ratios to growth may be complicated, especially if SMI firms make a single large initial investment, which is not picked up by DANE, and then make few changes for a long period.

49. This figure is close to the average for 1975–78 (11.0 percent), but well below the 1967–73 average of 16.39 percent.

50. There is a weaker but still striking negative relationship when plants are ranked by number of workers. Firms in the smallest category by this definition buy 33 percent of their fixed capital secondhand.

Some of the plants with very low output levels may be new (and thus were operational for only part of the reference year) or ones undergoing major reorganization, so that their "normal" output level is not low at all. This is evident from a look at the ratios of investment to value added—88 percent for the smallest category of plants, 54 percent for the second, and 38 percent for the third. Only for the fourth (11 percent) does the ratio reach a level that would be consistent with the presence of only a few such plants.

51. These data are available for only one year, so we cannot judge the robustness of the results over the longer term.

52. Based on the weighted averages of the share of machinery and equipment purchases of used items in 1970, 1972, 1973, 1975, and 1976. The average for industrial chemicals was also high, but it reflected very high purchases in one year and may not be typical.

53. Albert Berry and Carlos Díaz-Alejandro, "The New Colombian Exports: Possible Effects on the Distribution of Income," in *Economic Policy*, ed. Berry and Soligo, p. 156.

54. Especially in view of the fact that on the average exports appear to be more labor-intensive than import-competing goods. Francisco Thoumi, "Estrategias de Industrialización, Empleo y Distribución del Ingreso en Colombia," *Coyuntura Económica*, vol. 9, no. 1 (April 1979), pp. 119–42.

55. There is only limited evidence on this last point. Using 1974 data, Silva found that firms with some foreign investment accounted for 43 percent of production but 50 percent of exports, giving them an export-output ratio about 30 percent higher than that of firms with only domestic investment. There appeared to be no simple explanation for this difference in the industrial composition of output of foreign and domestic firms at the three-digit level. Jaime Silva, "Direct Foreign Investment in the Manufacturing Sector of Colombia," Ph.D. diss., Northwestern University, 1976.

3

Economic Performance and Technical Efficiency

This chapter shows how we used benefit-cost ratios and technical efficiency indices to assess the economic performance of SMIs in the metalworking and food processing sectors of the Colombian economy. It discusses variations in performance levels by size of firm *within* SMI and identifies some of the variables that affect SMI performance. In chapter 4 we shall see how the static efficiency assessments of this chapter can be augmented to allow for firm dynamics.

Metalworking and food processing were selected because they appear to share a number of relevant characteristics with various other SMI activities. The metalworking industry manufactures consumer durables and capital goods for other industries, while food processing firms specialize in the manufacture of nondurable consumer products. The metalworking firms in our sample make three types of products: agricultural implements and sprayers; pumps and other agricultural capital goods; and oil stoves, bakery ovens, and integrated kitchens. The food processing firms produce various kinds of cheese, guava paste, and potato chips. There are no multiplant firms in the sample, so firm size is the same as plant size. Because all the firms surveyed are managed by their owners, it is easy to analyze managerial efficiency—its sources and its effects on the economic performance of firms. Summary statistics on some basic features of the sample are given in table 3-1; the procedures used for collecting and analyzing the data are described in the methodological appendix.

Economic Performance of Small and Medium Firms

Our main interest in this study, and one of the central issues in the literature on small enterprises, is the actual and potential efficiency of SMI. In analyzing the relative efficiency of firms by size, we wish to distinguish:

- The direct effects of size per se on efficiency—for example, where economies of scale result from the nature of the technology itself
- The indirect effects of size on private and social efficiency—for example, where size implies or creates better-than-average terms in

Table 3-1. Selected Statistics on Metalworking and Food Processing Firms Sampled

Item	Metalworking firms[a]				Food processing firms[b]			
	Mean	Standard deviation	Minimum	Maximum	Mean	Standard deviation	Minimum	Maximum
Number of workers	33	29	3	150	16	14	2	56
Unskilled equivalent man-days[c]	20,985	18,684	2,354	92,920	8,969	8,912	511	45,984
Annual sales	10,123	17,197	400	120,000	12,560	17,797	144	84,000
Value added	4,861	6,776	244	39,600	3,787	4,409	45	17,078
Value of plant and equipment[d]	2,652	3,506	80	23,190	2,833	5,760	48	24,209
Working capital	2,620	4,713	10	25,530	886	9	0	3,090
Total capital stock	5,273	7,541	100	40,596	3,719	5,756	201	26,806
Flow of total capital services	287	390	8	2,017	410	741	7	3,795
Capital (stock) per unit of labor[e]	236	158	19	793	412	379	47	2,108
Capital (flow) per unit of labor[e]	14	10	1	41	44	56	3	298
Value added per unit of labor[e]	208	115	48	650	396	44	86	1,054
Value added per unit of capital								
Stock	1.2	1.1	0.2	6.0	1.4	1.1	0.2	4.1
Flow	23.1	19.7	2.5	81.4	17.3	19.2	1.1	11.0
Age of enterprise (years)	14.2	11.3	1.0	53.0	11.7	9.8	1.0	36.0

Note: Stock figures refer to the time of the sample. Flow figures refer to the annual rate of capital services at that time. Averages (means) of ratios are unweighted. As a result, the (unweighted) figure given for capital stock per unskilled equivalent man-day (236), for example, is not equal to the ratio of mean capital stock to mean unskilled equivalent man-days. Dividing 5,273,000 by 20,985 gives the (weighted) average of 25 percent.

a. All monetary data are in thousands of mid-1977 Colombian pesos.

b. All monetary data are in thousands of January 1979 Colombian pesos.

c. For the way unskilled equivalent man-days were estimated, see the methodological appendix, note 26.

d. Commercial value of plant and equipment. In the food sector it includes transportation equipment.

e. That is, per unskilled equivalent man-day.

Source: In all the tables that follow, if no source is specified the statistical material is from the author's surveys of metalworking and food processing firms in 1978 and 1979.

the capital market but invites labor to press for above-average wages (When examining indirect effects, it is important to distinguish those that can be modified by policy from those that cannot.)

- The effects of efficiency on size—for example, where differences in entrepreneurial ability lead to differences in growth and hence in size
- The (spurious) associations between size and efficiency that can arise when both are causally linked to some third factor—for example, lack of access to credit may be related to a firm's young age (and therefore lack of personal contacts), but it will appear to be related to size if most young firms are also small.

The analysis that follows is based mainly on data collected from our metal products and food processing samples. Four factors were considered to be useful indicators of performance:

- The social benefit-cost ratio (SBC), which relates the value of a given firm's (or an industry's) total output to the costs of all the inputs it uses (both output and inputs are valued at social prices, or social opportunity costs). The SBC is thus a measure of the average payoff, from the point of view of the economy as a whole, to the use of factors (resources) by the firm.
- The private benefit-cost ratio (PBC), which also relates output to all inputs, but values both at their market prices. The PBC thus measures the average payoff, from the point of view of the owners of resources used by the firm, to the use of those resources by the firm.
- The entrepreneurial benefit-cost ratio (EBC), which relates the market value of output less the cost of inputs purchased by the entrepreneur to the market value of the entrepreneur's own inputs. The EBC thus measures the average payoff to those resources owned by the entrepreneur and used by the firm.
- The technical-efficiency index (TEI), which measures the relative ability of different firms in an industry to achieve a high quantum (rather than value) of output from given quanta of inputs.

Differences between a firm's (or industry's) SBC and its PBC reflect the extent to which the market prices of its inputs or outputs differ from their true opportunity costs and hence indicate whether the firm is failing to combine inputs efficiently from the point of view of the economy as a whole. Differences in the TEIs of firms reflect the extent to which firms differ in the amount of output they obtain from a given level of inputs and hence indicate whether one firm is able to utilize those inputs more efficiently than another. (The methodological appendix explains the varying informational inputs and analytical uses of these indicators and describes some of the methodological and measurement problems related to their use in this study.)

Table 3-2. *Benchmark Estimates of Average Benefit-Cost Ratio and Technical Efficiency Index for Metalworking and Food Processing Firms, by Firm Size*

Firm size (number of workers)	Number of firms	Benefit-cost ratio			Technical efficiency index[a]
		Private	Social	Entrepreneurial	
Metalworking firms					
1–10	13	1.47 (0.63)	1.22 (0.52)	2.35 (2.20)	0.38 (0.19)
11–20	17	1.76 (0.93)	1.41 (0.68)	4.14 (4.03)	0.55 (0.28)
21–40	15	1.55 (0.75)	1.43 (0.63)	3.97 (4.07)	0.52 (0.25)
41–60	12	1.90 (0.96)	1.72 (0.81)	7.26 (6.97)	0.69 (0.27)
61+	8	2.07 (1.36)	1.73 (1.07)	7.74 (9.50)	0.72 (0.38)
All	65	1.72 (0.91)	1.47 (0.73)	4.76 (5.53)	0.56 (0.29)
Food processing firms					
1–7	11	2.11 (1.11)	1.72 (0.90)	3.58 (2.56)	0.53 (0.31)
8–15	11	2.62 (1.90)	2.24 (1.73)	7.41 (7.51)	0.66 (0.23)
16–29	8	2.87 (2.00)	2.58 (1.76)	8.94 (7.50)	0.69 (0.29)
30+	6	3.08 (1.78)	2.85 (1.63)	19.20 (17.27)	0.34 (0.19)
All	36	2.60 (1.66)	2.26 (1.50)	8.54 (9.98)	0.58 (0.24)

Note: Figures are unweighted averages across firms in a given size category. Standard deviations are in parentheses.

a. Calculated using the linear programming method described in the methodological appendix. It was possible to calculate this index for only 26 food processing firms corresponding to the cheese and guava paste product groups. They were distributed as follows by size category: 9, 10, 4, 3. Hence the BC and TEI figures shown in this table are not comparable in the food processing case.

We also briefly describe an earlier study on Colombia that permits some comparisons between SMI and large firms. (Our own samples included only two makers of metal products that had 100 or more workers.) We have used this study together with the results described in chapter 2 to extend the discussion to other industries. We begin by looking at the evidence from our own samples.

Table 3-2 gives some basic performance data for the 65 metalworking and 36 food processing firms in our sample that provided us with enough information to calculate values for the indicators described above. These data are subdivided by firm size within the SMI category. Average benefit-cost ratios (BCs) are high; the PBC averages 1.7 in the metal products industry and 2.6 in food processing, while their SBCs average 1.5 and 2.3, respectively.[1] In both industries, smaller firms have lower average BCs than larger ones, but the BCs vary greatly across firms. Errors of measurement may have contributed to this last finding, but the variance of the true BCs also appears to be high.[2]

The finding that average BCs are high does not appear to be sensitive to plausible modifications in our assumptions. When the replacement value of fixed capital in the metalworking sample is used, the average SBC drops from the benchmark figure of 1.47 to 1.29, and the average for the smallest size category approaches unity (table 3-3).[3] We lack data on replacement capital in the food sector, but SBCs would remain high were we to use it. And although at times the social opportunity cost of capital in Colombia may have exceeded 12 percent (our benchmark assumption in the SBC calculations), this figure would more likely be biased upward than downward.[4] Column 3 of table 3-3 shows the effects of assuming a rate of 8 percent instead of our benchmark 12 percent.

The apparently positive relation between the SBC and firm size in the metalworking sector may be partly because different firms charge differ-

Table 3-3. *Sensitivity of Average Social Benefit-Cost Ratio to Assumptions on Capital Stock, Opportunity Cost of Capital and of Entrepreneur's Time, and Differences in Product Prices: Metalworking and Food Processing Firms*

Firm size (number of workers)	Basic estimate[a] (1)	Adjustment to basic estimate			
		Replacement value instead of commercial value of capital (2)	Capital costed at 8 percent (3)	Opportunity cost of entrepreneur set equal to earnings of a skilled mechanic (4)	Product prices adjusted[b] (5)
Metalworking firms					
1–10	1.22	1.02	1.28	1.18	1.40
11–20	1.41	1.19	1.49	1.44	1.38
21–40	1.43	1.28	1.49	1.47	1.38
41–60	1.72	1.58	1.82	1.80	1.65
61+	1.73	1.53	1.88	1.77	1.68
All	1.47	1.29	1.56	1.50	1.47
Food processing firms					
1–7	1.72	n.a.	1.83	1.56	n.a.
8–15	2.24	n.a.	2.39	2.10	n.a.
16–29	2.58	n.a.	2.71	2.09	n.a.
30+	2.86	n.a.	3.05	2.76	n.a.
All	2.26	n.a.	2.40	2.04	n.a.

n.a. Not available.

a. Assumes real opportunity cost of capital is 12 percent for all capital; capital is measured by its reported commercial value; entrepreneur's opportunity cost is based on the income-generating function estimated by Mohan for Bogotá in 1978 (Rakesh Mohan, *The Determinants of Labor Earnings in Developing Metropolises: Estimates from Bogotá and Cali, Colombia*, World Bank Staff Working Paper 498 [Washington, D.C., October 1981], pp. 28–34), and no adjustment is made to value added to allow for differences in product prices across firms.

b. When the respondent indicated his prices were lower (higher) than his competitor's, his firm's value added was raised (lowered) by 25 percent.

ent prices for what is essentially the same product. Our benchmark estimate was not adjusted to the value-added figures reported by the firms, and thus the implicit assumption is that each firm charges the same price for a given quality of product. Price differences do exist, however, and although they may partly reflect quality differences, in some cases small firms charge low prices to break into a market even when their product is better than that of their competitors (see the section below "Factors that Affect a Firm's Economic Performance"). Our best guess is that if we were to assign social prices whose differences across firms reflected only quality differences, the average SBC of firms with 10 workers or less would still fall below that of firms with more than 60 workers, although perhaps by as little as 10 percent. The figures in column 5 of table 3-3 reflect an upward adjustment of 25 percent to the value added of firms whose prices were lower than those of their competitors; a corresponding downward adjustment was made for firms whose prices were higher. Entrepreneurs could provide only an informal estimate of the extent of price differences after quality was taken into account. We believe, however, that the correct adjustments would probably be less than those made for column 5 of table 3-3, although the opposite possibility cannot be ruled out.[5]

Product prices do not appear to vary significantly in the food industry; small firms do pay higher average prices for raw materials than larger ones, but regression analysis suggests that this tendency has relatively little effect on PBC. The true SBC for the smallest size category in the metal products sector is likely to be 70–90 percent of that of the largest; comparable figures for the food sector would be 60–75 percent.[6] Whereas the average SBC for the smallest category of metalworking firms may not be much above 1 (as in table 3-3, column 2), the average PBC is comfortably so; in food processing SBC in all likelihood exceeds 1.5, and PBC is about 2.

Lack of information on failure rates and the economic implications of a firm's closing prevented us from taking this phenomenon into account in the BC estimates. Since failure rates are higher in smaller firms, there is an upward bias of unknown degree in the absolute and relative BCs for these firms.

The PBC estimates given in our tables are systematically higher than the SBCs because we have assumed that the social opportunity cost of capital exceeds the average private cost, which is kept down mainly by the low cost assumed for self-financed investment.[7] The gap between PBC and SBC varies across size categories from a little less than 10 percent to about 25 percent.

The data also indicate that food firms are more profitable than metalworking firms. This reflects a strong growth in the demand for the food products we studied as well as the advantages created by the following operational features: (1) the unskilled workers in food processing firms earn less than those in metalworking firms; (2) food processing firms use very simple equipment, which is produced locally according to the user firm's specifications; and (3) they do not have to provide as much credit for clients as metalworking firms do. In an industry where entry is relatively easy, competitive pressures may eventually drive these profits down, but the supply response was still lagging behind the growth of demand during our survey.

The great variation in performance levels is not confined to the smallest firms in either industry; the ratio of the standard deviation of SBC or PBC to its mean is high for all firm sizes within the SMI category as a whole. However, the incidence of SBC ratios of less than 1 (using our benchmark figures) is greater among the smaller firms. Of the 65 firms in the metalworking sample, 20 fall below this line (including 5 with SBCs between 0.9 and 1.0), and 16 of the 20 come from the 45 firms with 40 workers or less (table 3-4). Of the 36 firms in the food processing sample, 6 had SBCs lower than 1, and 5 of these had 15 or fewer workers. If our rather stringent assumption of a 12 percent social cost of capital is correct, new investment in such firms would not be warranted unless their typical performance exceeded that of the sample year. Somewhat fewer firms had PBCs and EBCs lower than 1—11 in metal products and 5 in food processing. For these 16 firms, the average PBC was 0.76, although 10 of the 16 had values of about 0.80.

What explains the existence of firms with these low returns? Nine of the 16 firms with PBCs (and EBCs) less than 1 were nevertheless covering their variable costs.[8] These 9 included 6 of the 10 firms in the two smallest size classes of the two industries. One might guess that a disproportionate share of firms with PBCs below 1 are young, but only 3 of the 11 such firms in the metal products sector were five years old or younger.[9] In the food sector, 3 of the 5 firms with low PBCs were two years old or younger.

No doubt some firms whose performance was unsatisfactory in the sample year expected to do better in the future. Others may have done better over the past several years than in the year of our surveys. Consistent with such an interpretation or with our having underestimated PBCs and EBCs for some firms is the preponderance of owners who indicated that they were better off since having their own business (60 of 65 mechanical firms and 31 of 35 food processing firms); moreover, this view was only weakly associated with a firm's having a PBC greater than 1. (Of course respondents could have been biased toward saying that their businesses have helped their situation.) Of the 15 firms with PBCs and EBCs of less than 1 who also answered this question, 13 indicated that their position had been improved by their present business. In some of

Table 3-4. *Distribution of Metalworking and Food Processing Firms, by Benefit-Cost Ratios and Size*
(number of firms)

Benefit-cost ratios	Firm size (number of workers)					
	1–10	*11–20*	*21–40*	*41–60*	*61+*	*All*
Metalworking Firms						
Private						
Less than 1	3	3	3	1	1	11
1–1.5	5	6	6	5	3	25
1.5+	5	8	6	6	4	29
All	13	17	15	12	8	65
Entrepreneurial						
Less than 1	3	3	3	1	1	11
1–1.5	2	3	2	1	0	8
1.5+	8	11	10	10	7	46
All	13	17	15	12	8	65
Social						
Less than 1	6	6	4	1	3	20
1–1.5	2	3	6	5	1	17
1.5+	5	8	5	6	4	28
All	13	17	15	12	8	65
Short-term private						
Less than 1	1	0	2	0	1	4
1–1.5	6	8	7	6	2	29
1.5+	6	9	6	6	5	32
All	13	17	15	12	8	65

	Firm size (number of workers)				
	1–7	*8–15*	*16–29*	*30+*	*All*
Food processing firms					
Private					
Less than 1	2	2	0	1	5
1–1.5	1	1	2	0	4
1.5+	8	8	6	5	27
All	11	11	8	6	36
Entrepreneurial					
Less than 1	2	2	0	1	5
1+	9	9	8	5	31
All	11	11	8	6	36
Social					
Less than 1	2	3	0	1	6
1–1.5	2	2	4	0	8
1.5+	7	6	4	5	22
All	11	11	8	6	36
Short-term private					
Less than 1	2	1	0	0	3
1–1.5	0	1	1	1	3
1.5+	9	9	7	5	30
All	11	11	8	6	36

these cases we have probably overestimated the opportunity cost of the entrepreneur's labor or capital.[10] (Our estimates of these opportunity costs are based on averages for persons with characteristics similar to those of the entrepreneurs and for capital derived from similar sources; see the methodological appendix for details).

It might be that better information would yield PBC and EBC ratios greater than 1. Our EBC estimates ask the question, "Would an entrepreneur whose labor market opportunities were those we have estimated to be typical for a person with his education and experience, and whose opportunities for investment of his own capital and costs of borrowed capital were as we have estimated, be better or worse off having the business he has, if he always operated as he does at present?" When an entrepreneur with an apparently low EBC or PBC ratio continues in business, we must consider the possibility that some opportunity cost has been overestimated.

Some entrepreneurs, however, may underestimate the opportunity cost of their resources, especially the cost of their own time. The main aspiration of several entrepreneurs in the metalworking firms was to be independent and receive an income equal to or above the wage they had received as skilled workers. When asked if their enterprise was successful, most judged the improvement in their standard of living since they left their previous occupation to be the main sign of success. This type of entrepreneur commonly performs a number of tasks (administration, sales, and production control) that would be performed by hired personnel in larger firms. Few small entrepreneurs think that these activities deserve additional remuneration over and above entrepreneurial profits, and this attitude affects their perception of their firm's success.

An important point to note here is that we are defining success on the basis of the BC ratios, not the absolute income of the entrepreneur. Many owners whose earnings are low compared to those of entrepreneurs as a group might nevertheless carry on because of their limited opportunities and expectations—which in turn usually stem from their comparative lack of education and relatively humble social origins. The major assets of the owner of a small enterprise are his managerial ability, technical knowledge, and equipment. Entrepreneurs who have previously been manual workers acquire management training on the job and work primarily with secondhand equipment; they may find the malleability and mobility of their assets rather limited. Their managerial abilities are not recognized by large firms, which prefer to hire college graduates, and their technical knowledge is more useful in the specific sector and perhaps when applied to the particular vintage of equipment with which they are familiar. Hence we assumed that the opportunity costs of these entrepreneurs are not much higher than the wages of skilled workers (see the following discussion and the methodological appendix). Furthermore, their secondhand equipment, when accepted as collateral, is usually valued by lenders at one-third of its commercial value or less. In view of these considerations, it is hardly surprising that small entrepreneurs do not easily exit from the market.

The above comments pertain to firms that are in difficulty. The average entrepreneur in these two industries was doing very well as of 1977–79. Under any reasonable assumption about the opportunity cost of his capital, he was earning far more than he could in likely job alternatives. It is not possible to determine the extent to which this success may have been related to the unusually rapid growth of the Colombian economy in the 1970s. Column 3 of table 3-5 shows the average reported labor income of persons with an entrepreneur's education and labor market experience in Bogotá as of 1978. These figures may be underestimates of the wage-earning capacity of the individuals who become entrepreneurs;[11] nevertheless, it seems reasonable to conclude that their average entrepreneurial earnings are much greater than their true opportunity costs and thus (even for the very smallest firms) are considerably above what the owner could earn elsewhere. Estimates for the food sector are less precise, but the average net gains from entrepreneurship appear to be greater still. Thus, although SMI entrepreneurship in these two industries involves risks, the average payoff is good and the gains accruing to the big winners are very large indeed. These results cannot be generalized to SMI as a whole, since both of the industries under discussion experienced above-average growth of demand in the few years prior to our survey. But there were probably several other manufacturing industries with payoffs similar to those of SMI entrepreneurship.

The opportunity cost of entrepreneurs' labor that we used in our calculations—which is probably downward biased—translates into an average internal rate of return (IRR) to capital of 51 percent for all metalworking firms and 29 percent for the smallest firms with 1–10 workers (table 3-6). We have calculated a floor level for the IRR by using the (higher) replacement value of capital, instead of its commercial value, and an opportunity cost of the entrepreneur's time that is double the figure shown in table 3-5. The average entrepreneur would then be earning 34 percent on his own capital. If his firm was very small (1–10 workers), his return would drop to 17 percent, which is not much different from the rate that moneylenders obtain in Colombia and represents a good return for ex-production workers, most of whom lack either the resources or the inclination to become moneylenders themselves.

It must be borne in mind that our data provide an upward bias to the economic and financial success of SMI because they do not take into account firms that have failed (although we do have some data on disappearance rates).

Table 3-5. *Average Monthly Return to Entrepreneur's Labor in Metalworking Firms, by Firm Size, Private Benefit-Cost Ratio, and Age and by Entrepreneur's Education*
(thousands of 1977 pesos)

Category	Return when other inputs valued at		Estimated opportunity cost of entrepreneur's time[a]	Number of firms
	Market prices (1)	Social prices (2)	(3)	
Firm size (number of workers)				
1–10	25.4	18.0	8.0	13
11–20	55.0	40.6	11.2	17
21–40	68.5	57.1	11.4	15
41–60	159.2	143.6	13.4	12
61+	416.1	356.2	16.2	8
All	115.8	97.8	11.6	65
Firm's private benefit-cost ratio				
Less than 1	−11.4	−19.6	9.1	11
1–1.5	36.7	20.9	12.6	25
1.5+	232.3	208.6	11.8	29
All	115.8	97.8	11.6	65
Firm's age (years)				
1–5	73.7	62.3	11.4	17
6–10	198.2	172.8	11.6	14
11–15	181.9	152.9	11.2	9
16–25	61.4	48.6	13.3	16
26+	98.0	80.2	9.5	9
All	115.8	97.8	11.6	65
Entrepreneur's education				
Primary	57.5	46.1	7.6	19
Secondary	28.2	14.3	8.9	19
University or technical	218.5	192.8	16.4	27
All	115.8	97.8	11.6	65

Note: The return to entrepreneur's labor is calculated using our standard assumptions on the cost of capital from various sources (see the methodological appendix).

a. Calculated from data presented in Rakesh Mohan, *The Determinants of Labour Earnings in Developing Metropolises: Estimates from Bogotá and Cali, Colombia,* World Bank Staff Working Paper 498 (Washington, D.C., October 1981).

Other Evidence on Economic Performance by Firm Size

The firms sampled in this study provide the most detailed information to date on the relation between economic performance and firm size in Colombia. They do not include large firms, however, and are restricted to the metalworking and food processing industries. From aggregate data for all manufacturing industries over the period 1957–66, Todd has concluded that the net social benefit per unit of capital was lower in large

Table 3-6. *Average Rate of Return to Capital in Metalworking Firms, by Firm Size, Private Benefit-Cost Ratio, and Age and by Entrepreneur's Education*
(percent)

Category	Rate of return when borrowed capital valued at[a]		Rate of return to total capital employed by firm[b]	Number of firms
	Market prices	Social prices		
Firm size (number of workers)				
1–10	0.33	0.33	0.29	13
11–20	0.97	0.96	0.47	17
21–40	1.05	1.04	0.62	15
41–60	0.97	0.93	0.68	12
61+	0.46	0.43	0.48	8
All	0.80	0.78	0.51	65
Firm's private benefit-cost ratio				
Less than 1	−0.28	−0.29	−0.08	11
1–1.5	0.28	0.27	0.26	25
1.5+	1.66	1.63	0.94	29
All	0.80	0.78	0.51	65
Firm's age (years)				
1–5	1.11	1.09	0.58	17
6–10	0.39	0.37	0.38	14
11–15	1.78	1.74	0.87	9
16–25	0.41	0.40	0.38	16
26+	0.58	0.55	0.45	9
All	0.80	0.78	0.51	65
Entrepreneur's education				
Primary	0.98	0.95	0.53	19
Secondary	0.27	0.26	0.17	19
University or technical	1.05	1.03	0.73	27
All	0.80	0.78	0.51	65

Note: The entrepreneur's labor input is costed as in our BC estimates. Capital is measured at its commercial value.

a. Total capital consists of the entrepreneur's investment plus borrowed capital. Firm revenues minus all costs other than that of the entrepreneur's own capital investment divided by that capital, minus 1.

b. Firm's revenues minus all noncapital costs divided by the total capital in use, minus 1.

plants of 200 or more workers than in smaller ones.[12] In the three smaller categories he used, relative performance depended on the assumptions made (see the estimates based on past investment in table 3-7; estimates based on installed horsepower are presented for completeness, but Todd has argued persuasively that this is a poor proxy for fixed capital).

The lower ranking of plants with more than 200 workers is of particular interest. If such a result was valid and applicable to industry in general, our mechanical and food industry samples would appear to in-

Table 3-7. *Todd's Estimates of Net Social Benefit per Unit of Fixed Capital under Varying Assumptions, by Plant Size, 1956–67 Average*

Basis of estimates	Plant size (number of workers)			
	1–14[a]	15–49	50–199	200+
Fixed capital estimated from accumulated past investment				
VA/K	1.01 (1.17)	1.06	0.83	0.48
(VA − wage bill[b])/K	0.60 (0.68)	0.66	0.59	0.32
(VA − adjusted wage bill[c])/K	0.60 (0.68)	0.80	0.72	0.42
Fixed capital estimated from installed horsepower				
VA/K	2.63 (3.06)	2.97	4.33	2.69
(VA − wage bill[b])/K	1.56 (1.79)	1.87	3.09	1.80
(VA − adjusted wage bill[c])/K	1.56 (1.79)	2.24	3.75	2.35

Note: VA denotes value added; *K*, total capital. Figures in parentheses include an adjustment to DANE figures to allow for the understating of small plant data in certain years.

a. Plants of less than 5 workers are included in principle only if output exceeds 24,000 pesos.

b. Includes an imputation for unpaid family workers equal to the average earnings of paid workers.

c. Wage bill calculated as the labor force times the average wage of workers in the smallest size class distinguished (1–14 workers).

Source: John Todd, "Plant Size, Factor Proportions, and Efficiency in Colombian Industry," in *Essays on Industrialization in Colombia,* ed. Albert Berry (Tempe, Ariz.: Arizona State University, Center for Latin American Studies, 1983), table 6-15; for details of the estimates based on past investment, see pp. 202–05.

clude firms from the most efficient size range, and we could conclude that the best of them are efficient in an absolute sense in the Colombian context. Also relevant from Todd's study, based on assumptions close to those we used in estimating SBC, is the suggestion that there is a gap in efficiency between the smallest category of plants (less than 15 workers) and the next size up (15–49 workers; see table 3-7). His finding tends to confirm the gap we report in table 3-2 for the metalworking and food processing industries.

Our aggregate figures for factor productivity in all manufacturing for 1976 (see tables 2-17 and 2-19) also suggest that any rate of return or benefit-cost advantage of plants having 100 workers or more is unlikely to be very great. Plants with 20–99 workers have a higher average level of capital productivity than smaller or larger ones.[13] When differences in labor quality and composition are taken into account, their labor productivity is probably not more than 20–30 percent below that of plants with 200 workers or more (see the discussion on SMI and other manufacturing in chapter 2). Thus total factor productivity is unlikely to be more than a few percentage points higher in LI than in this segment of SMI, as is suggested by the similar profit rates for the two size categories.[14] Therefore, neither these data nor Todd's study suggests that total factor productivity in LI is significantly higher than in SMI as a whole.[15]

Our productivity estimates (see tables 2-17 and 2-19) suggest that the efficiency differential between medium and small plants in the aggregate is broadly similar to what we have found in the metalworking and food processing samples.[16] These two sectors may thus be reasonably typical of Colombian manufacturing in this respect. According to DANE's 1975 figures, gross labor productivity differentials between SI and MI firms in the metal products industry were reasonably typical of those in manufacturing in general, while in food processing (a very heterogeneous sector, many of whose products were not included in our sample), the differential was well above average.[17] In the metal products sector, capital productivity was higher in MI than in SI, but no significant difference showed up for manufacturing as a whole. This suggests that the relative efficiency of SI is not atypically high in metalworking or food processing.

In summary, our aggregate data on Colombian manufacturing suggest that middle-size and large plants are roughly comparable in efficiency. If the same tends to be true in the metalworking and food processing industries (it may, of course, vary across branches within these industries), the most efficient firms in our samples are likely to be about as efficient as any in their respective sectors. The aggregate data also suggest that the relative performance of SI and MI in our samples is similar to the relative performance of SI and MI within manufacturing as a whole.

Factors That Affect Economic Performance

Many factors affect a firm's economic performance, including the quality and aims of the entrepreneurs, the quality and cost of labor, the cost of investment funds and access to them, the quality and cost of raw materials and other nonlabor inputs, access to information about such matters as product market conditions, market intermediaries, and production techniques. Performance may also be related to a firm's size, age, location, and other quantifiable variables. Furthermore, these variables may be interrelated in many ways. Consequently, a comprehensive picture of all the elements underlying a firm's economic performance would require a simultaneous equation model far beyond anything that our data can support. The analysis in this section has the more limited objective of probing the factors underlying the already noted relations between BC ratios and firm size.

The effect of many of the factors cited above may depend on the size of the firm. For example, small firms in developing countries usually have relatively low labor costs because few of them are required to pay minimum wages or social security; at the same time, they are discriminated against in capital markets. Thus they may favor production techniques that are more labor-intensive than those used by larger firms. Broadly speaking, our aim is to use the available data to study the statistical associations between the measures and possible determinants of efficiency and to develop hypotheses about the relative importance of different factors in improving performance.

We begin by considering to what extent the PBC ratios of firms vary with differences in allocative (or price) efficiency, technical efficiency, and absolute factor and product prices. At first glance, our data suggest that differences in technical efficiency strongly affect PBC ratios in the metalworking sector and play a smaller but still prominent role in the two product groups of the food sector where it was possible to calculate TEIs.[18] The simple correlation between observed PBCs and TEIs is 0.79 for the metalworking firms and 0.52 for the food processing firms; thus TEI "explains" 62 percent and 27 percent of the variance of PBC in these respective industries. The poor quality of the data on firm-specific prices, in contrast to the information on technical efficiency, probably accounts in part for the finding that technical efficiency is a dominating influence on PBC variance in the metalworking industry. Only wage differences for given categories of workers and differences in the price of capital by source enter the PBC estimates; the latter are of doubtful accuracy, however, owing to the difficulty of attaching a realistic price to self-financing, which is a significant factor here. Product price differences cannot be introduced formally into the estimates because of the problems in quantifying them. These gaps in the data make it impossible to determine the extent to which differences in PBC ratios are caused by absolute price differences or differences in allocative efficiency. Less obviously, they may exaggerate differences in technical efficiency; a high product price (for the same quality of product provided by another firm) would tend to be reflected (incorrectly) in our estimates as a high level of technical efficiency and (correctly) as a high PBC. But our impression is that product price differentials are not large enough to cause a serious upward bias in our estimates of the variance of TEI or to suggest that absolute price differences play a major part in explaining variances in true PBCs.[19] The rather limited range of capital-labor ratios leads us to believe that allocative inefficiency is likewise not great (scattergrams supporting this point are not reproduced here, but are available from the authors upon request). We thus tentatively conclude that much, probably most, of the observed interfirm variations in true PBCs is associated with differences in technical efficiency.

In the branches of food processing for which we could calculate TEIs with reasonable accuracy, we used quantity produced (rather than value

Table 3-8. *The Relations between Technological Sophistication, the Technical Efficiency Index, and Private Benefit-Cost Ratio among Metalworking and Food Processing Firms*

	Metalworking firms					Food processing firms			
Item	Number of firms	Average PBC	Average TEI	Average index of technological sophistication[a]	Item	Number of firms	Average PBC	Average TEI	Average index of technological sophistication[a]
PBC					PBC				
Less than 1	10	0.80	0.26	2.20	Less than 1	5	0.68	0.34	2.00
1–1.5	24	1.18	0.43	2.00	1–1.5	4	1.29	0.59	2.00
1.5–2.0	8	1.80	0.70	2.00	1.5–2.0	7	1.67	0.40	2.00
2.0+	21	2.81	0.80	2.00	2.0–2.5	4	2.20	0.52	1.75
					2.5+	16	4.02	0.69	2.00
Firm size (number of workers)					*Firm size (number of workers)*				
1–10	13	1.47	0.38	1.38	1–7	11	2.11	0.53	1.58
11–20	16	1.82	0.55	1.56	8–15	11	2.62	0.66	2.27
21–40	15	1.55	0.52	2.40	16–29	8	2.87	0.69	1.60
41–60	11	1.96	0.69	2.45	30+	6	3.08	0.34	2.67
61+	8	2.07	0.72	2.75	All	36	2.60	0.58	2.17
All	63	1.74	0.56	2.03					

a. The index is calculated by allocating one point for simple, two points for intermediate, and three points for more sophisticated technology.

added) as the measure of output (see note 18); this lack of definitional symmetry with PBCs may partly explain why the correlation between the two variables is lower in food processing than in metalworking. In addition, because the quantity of production is unadjusted for quality, there is a downward bias in the TEI figures for the more technologically sophisticated and usually larger firms in comparison with the smaller ones. This bias in turn has probably produced a downward bias in the estimate of the correlation between PBC and TEI.

In any case, the relation between technical efficiency and PBCs probably does differ between the two industries. In the metal products sector, low technical efficiency contributes significantly to the weak performance of firms whose PBC ratios are less than unity (table 3-8); both PBC and TEI are about 55 percent below the sample average. The ratio of TEI to PBC tends to rise with PBC except among the firms with the highest PBCs. Thus, TEI seems to be more important in distinguishing good performers (those with PBC ratios between 1 and 2) from poor ones than in distinguishing the best from the good. The relation of TEIs to PBCs in different firm-size categories reflects this pattern, especially among the smallest firms of 10 workers or less, whose low TEIs are important determinants of their low average PBCs. Among food processing firms, by contrast, the ratio of TEIs to PBCs is lower for firms with PBCs above 1.5 than for those with PCBs below 1.5 and does not seem to be related to firm size, except that it is unusually low for the three firms with 30 workers or more.[20] It is clear that technical efficiency plays a more limited role as a source of PBC variation in this industry. The TEI is considerably higher (about 50 percent) for the firms with PBCs above 2.5 than for the rest—but the PBC ratio is 150 percent higher.

Several entrepreneurial and technological variables seem to be strongly associated both with the technical efficiency of firms and their benefit-cost ratios. These variables, which include the entrepreneur's educational attainments and the nature of his main skills, could account for the high share of PBC variance that appears to be associated with TEI variance. Other variables that may be important in explaining PBC ratios and TEIs (see table 3-9 for metal products and table 3-10 for food processing) reflect price differences across firms (including the firm's output prices compared with those of its competitors), the individual firm's main source of finance, and its labor costs relative to those of other firms. Size of firm (number of workers) does *not* have a statistically significant association with PBCs or TEIs when these other variables are present.[21] This suggests that most or all of the advantages of larger firms within the SMI range are the result of factors other than technical economies of scale. A size-related variable that has considerable explanatory power is "sophistication of technology." But, as discussed below, its effect on the BC ratios appears to be quadratic rather than linear with a positive sign.

Table 3-9. Results of Linear Regressions to Explain Variation in Benefit-Cost Ratio and Technical Efficiency Index among Small and Medium Metalworking Firms

Item	PBC		EBC		SBC		TEI	
	Coefficient	t statistic	Coefficient	t statistic	Coefficient	t statistic	Coefficient	t statistic
Constant	3.973		18.173		2.594		1.067	
Relative wages	-1.650	-2.78[a]	-7.624	-2.14[b]	-0.648	-1.32	-0.269	-1.26
Percentage of workers in courses	0.015	2.41[b]	0.102	2.83	0.012	2.50[a]	0.002	0.98
Percentage of equipment secondhand	0.004	1.01	0.024	1.04[a]	0.004	1.32	0.001	0.96
Entrepreneur's education[c]								
Primary	0.788	2.96[a]	4.088	2.66[a]	0.563	2.65[a]	0.151	1.64
University or technical	0.565	2.24[b]	2.443	1.68[b]	0.404	2.01[b]	0.229	2.63
Entrepreneur's main skills[d]								
Production only	-0.663	-2.52[a]	-5.291	-3.48[a]	-0.554	-2.64[a]	-0.134	-1.47
Administration and production	0.140	0.35	0.177	0.08	0.173	0.54	0.132	0.95
Sales and administration	-0.276	-0.62	-4.309	-1.69	-0.260	-0.74	-0.084	-0.55
Sources of finance[e]								
Private banks	0.270	0.89	0.572	0.33	0.231	0.97	0.032	0.31
Public banks	-0.317	-1.33	-2.303	-1.68[b]	-0.260	-1.37	-0.041	0.50
Moneylenders	-0.598	-2.29[b]	-4.262	-2.83[a]	-0.421	-2.02[b]	-0.169	1.88

Firms' prices compared with those of competitors[f]

	(1)		(2)		(3)		(4)	
Higher	0.333	1.23	2.789	1.79[g]	0.294	1.36	0.120	1.29[b]
Lower	-0.594	-2.49[a]	-3.810	-2.77[a]	-0.520	-2.74[a]	-0.202	-2.46[b]
Type of technology[h]								
Simple	-0.612	-2.35[b]	-4.338	-2.88[a]	-0.511	-2.46[a]	-0.220	-2.46[b]
More Sophisticated	-0.517	-2.13[b]	-3.114	-2.22[b]	-0.476	-2.46[a]	-0.235	-2.81[b]
Labor mobility[i]								
High	0.005	0.03	-0.226	-0.18	0.004	0.03	0.043	0.59
Low	0.707	2.09[b]	3.873	1.98[b]	0.534	1.98[b]	0.084	0.72
Product group[j]								
Agricultural implements	-0.498	-1.96[b]	-3.128	-2.14[b]	-0.331	-1.64[g]	-0.175	-2.00
Ovens, stoves, kitchens	-0.369	-1.37	-2.343	-1.51	-0.224	-1.05	-0.264	-2.84[b]
R^2	0.61		0.66		0.60		0.53	
R^2 (adjusted)	0.44		0.51		0.44		0.33	
Degrees of freedom (DOF)	43		43		43		43	
F	3.59[a]		4.33[a]		3.56[a]		2.60[a]	

a. Significant at the 0.01 level or less.
b. Significant at ≥ 0.01 to ≤ 0.05.
c. In the base, secondary education.
d. In the base, administration only.
e. In the base, self-financing only.
f. In the base, same prices as competitors.
g. Significant at ≥ 0.05 to ≤ 0.1.
h. In the base, moderate technology.
i. In the base, moderate labor mobility.
j. In the base, pumps and agricultural capital goods.

Table 3-10. Results of Linear Regressions to Explain Variation in Benefit-Cost Ratio and Technical Efficiency Index among Small and Medium Food Processing Firms

Item	PBC Coefficient	PBC t statistic	EBC Coefficient	EBC t statistic	SBC Coefficient	SBC t statistic	TEI Coefficient	TEI t statistic
Constant	3.438		13.644		3.034		0.937	
Percentage of equipment secondhand	-0.012	-1.13	-0.083	-1.28	-0.010	-1.14	-0.006	1.35
Entrepreneur's education[a]								
Primary	-0.967	-1.49	-4.380	-1.06	-1.030	-1.77[b]	-0.339	-3.35[c]
University or technical	-0.783	-1.22	-4.410	-1.07	-0.717	-1.24	-0.052	-0.41
Entrepreneur's skills[d]								
Only administration	-0.296	-0.34	-4.923	-0.89	-0.351	-0.45		
Administration and sales	-0.251	-0.32[b]	-2.686	-0.53	-0.128	-0.18		
Only production	2.028	1.93	3.980	0.59	1.893	2.01[e]		
Type of technology[f]								
Simple	-1.154	-1.62	-8.516	1.88[e]	-1.034	-1.62	-0.341	-3.21[c]
More sophisticated	-2.222	-3.11[c]	-10.761	2.36[b]	-1.807	-2.82[c]	-0.238	-1.84[e]
Sources of finance[g]								
Private banks	2.027	2.99[c]	11.531	2.67[e]	1.742	2.87[c]		
Public banks	0.199	0.10	9.047	1.61[b]	0.133	0.17		
Moneylenders and suppliers	1.840	1.70[b]	6.989	1.01	1.956	2.01[e]		
R^2	0.55		0.49		0.56		0.52	
R^2 (adjusted)	0.34		0.25		0.35		0.40	
DOF	23		23		23		20	
F	2.59[e]		2.03[b]		2.62[e]		4.33[c]	

a. In the base, secondary education.
b. Significant at > 0.05 to ≤ 0.1 level.
c. Significant at the 0.010 level or less.
d. In the base, administration, production, sales.

e. Significant at > 0.01 to ≤ 0.05 level.
f. In the base, moderate technology.
g. In the base, self-finance only.

The following subsections discuss the results of a series of multiple linear regressions that we have used to analyze the relative importance of different determinants of BC ratios and TEIs. We turn first to characteristics of the entrepreneur, partly because they are among the more unambiguously exogenous variables we have and partly because their association with firms' BC ratios is strong.[22]

Entrepreneur's Education, Skills, and Background

The success of the firm, as defined by the PBC, is significantly related to the entrepreneur's education and skills. These endowments have important explanatory power in our multiple regressions. Further, some of the less direct effects of these entrepreneurial characteristics may be picked up by other variables included in the regression, so that their total effects could be somewhat greater than those suggested by the multiple regression coefficients.[23]

If differences in entrepreneurial income (net of a normal return to capital) can be attributed to differences in the education and experience of the entrepreneur, one could conclude that, compared with primary education, postsecondary education pays off in better economic performance and in higher entrepreneurial income in both sectors.[24] In the metalworking sample, our estimate of the return to entrepreneur's labor inputs (after subtracting the opportunity cost of his capital from his total income) implies a ratio of 4:1 between these two groups (table 3-5).[25] Thus the difference between the returns to higher and to primary education appears to be greater in entrepreneurial activities than in most other activities typical of people at these educational levels.[26] With the exception of PBCs in the food processing sector, BC ratios and TEIs are generally higher for university graduates (tables 3-11 and 3-12).

That the relation between educational attainment and success in small industry is not a simple one is suggested by a sharp difference between the two sectors in the relative success of entrepreneurs with secondary education. In metalworking, their performance is below average according to any relevant indicator; labor income for entrepreneurs with secondary schooling is lower in absolute terms than that for entrepreneurs with only primary schooling (table 3-5). As table 3-11 shows, PBC averages 1.96 for entrepreneurs with university or technical training and 1.84 for those with primary, but only 1.25 for those with secondary; TEI values present a similar picture. In food processing, by contrast, entrepreneurs with secondary education achieve the highest average performance levels (PBC, 3.2; TEI, 0.66); the values for those with primary schooling are much lower (PBC, 2.17; TEI, 0.45), as they are for those with university education (PBC, 1.95; TEI, 0.62).[27] These differences between

Table 3-11. *Average Benefit-Cost Ratio and Technical Efficiency Index of Small and Medium Metalworking Firms, by Entrepreneurial Characteristics*

Entrepreneurial characteristics	Number of firms	PBC	EBC	SBC	TEI
Entrepreneur's main skills					
Production	40	1.52	3.28	1.29	0.51
Administration	12	2.09	8.48	1.87	0.67
Production and administration	5	2.12	7.29	1.90	0.68
Administration and sales	4	2.05	5.16	1.65	0.62
Entrepreneur's previous job					
First job	4	2.29	9.35	1.91	0.86
Father's firm	5	2.09	6.34	1.73	0.74
Mechanic or technician	30	1.49	2.94	1.24	0.45
Independent professional	5	1.71	4.11	1.72	0.66
Sales or management	12	1.80	6.91	1.56	0.56
Owner of enterprise	9	1.91	5.43	1.65	0.61
Entrepreneur's education					
Primary	19	1.84	4.86	1.50	0.52
Secondary	19	1.25	2.46	1.08	0.42
University or technical	27	1.96	6.30	1.73	0.67
Way firm was acquired					
Founded by present owner	9	2.07	6.70	1.71	0.66
Bought	56	1.66	4.45	1.43	0.54
Sources of entrepreneur's skills					
Work in large firms	9	1.69	4.33	1.38	0.44
Work in small and medium firms	13	1.51	2.85	1.25	0.46
Training institutions	13	1.46	3.56	1.28	0.47
University	17	1.83	5.28	1.66	0.70
All firms	65	1.72	4.76	1.47	0.56

the two sectors may reflect the importance of technical expertise in metalworking firms—either the hands-on experience that often typifies entrepreneurs with primary schooling only or the more abstract knowledge of university graduates. In food processing, technical expertise is not common among entrepreneurs, and other skills seem to be more important. By contrast, most entrepreneurs in metalworking do have technical expertise; their deficiencies are often in the areas of administration or sales.

Our skill variables themselves reveal this difference. Higher-than-average PBCs and TEIs are registered by food processing firms whose entrepreneurs have production skills and also, in some cases, administrative ability.[28] In the metalworking industry, however, firms tend to have relatively low PBCs and TEIs if their entrepreneurs are experienced only in

Table 3-12. *Average Benefit-Cost Ratio and Technical Efficiency Index of Small and Medium Food Processing Firms, by Entrepreneurial Characteristics*

Entrepreneurial characteristics	Number of firms[a]	PBC	EBC	SBC	TEI
Entrepreneur's main activities					
Administration	4	3.09	11.22	2.66	0.57
Administration or sales	5	1.91	6.93	1.72	0.54
Administration, production, or production control	25	2.53	6.77	2.18	0.57
Entrepreneur's previous job					
Skilled worker	5	2.65	5.47	2.33	0.42
Salesman	9	2.33	8.05	2.03	0.49
Management or Professional	10	2.73	11.73	2.43	0.71
Firm owner	4	3.15	9.33	2.68	0.71
First job	4	2.57	7.04	2.14	0.36
Entrepreneur's education					
Primary	12	2.17	5.14	1.69	0.45
Secondary	16	3.24	12.51	2.90	0.66
University or technical	8	1.95	5.70	1.77	0.62
Way firm was acquired					
Founded by present owner	22	2.92	6.79	2.51	0.58
Bought	12	2.21	8.17	1.98	0.57
Sources of entrepreneur's skills					
Self-taught	14	2.68	8.13	2.32	0.54
Previous job	9	2.01	6.29	1.73	0.53
Previous jobs and courses	3	3.51	10.41	3.21	0.62
Self-taught, courses, or assistance	7	2.36	6.21	1.98	0.62
All firms	36	2.60	8.54	2.26	0.58

a. Refers to the number of firms for which BC ratios were calculated. For TEI, only twenty-six firms are included.

production and lack administrative skills.[29] Although these entrepreneurs often find it hard to organize such crucial aspects of their businesses as product marketing and procurement of inputs, they are nevertheless obliged to undertake administration and sales functions— often with unfortunate results for efficiency, especially in larger firms. Entrepreneurs who possess only production skills are most commonly found in very small firms of 10 or less workers: in our sample, 9 of 13 such small-firm entrepreneurs fall into this category, but only 1 works exclusively in production control; the rest are responsible for administration and sales as well as for production. Interestingly, the PBCs of these firms are only a little lower than those of other very small firms. It is only in firms with 40 workers or more that entrepreneurs' lack of nonproduction skills becomes associated with a much lower than average PBC (table 3-13). These firms do achieve somewhat higher TEIs than smaller ones that are also run by former production workers, but the weakness that shows up in their low PBCs evidently lies in the nontechnical aspects of operating the firm.

In the metalworking sector, an entrepreneur's main skills are related to his previous job and to his education. Although the previous job is associated with indicators of economic success (table 3-11), this variable adds little explanatory power to the equation.[30] Firms whose entrepreneurs were previously production workers or even technicians have, on the average, lower TEIs than firms whose entrepreneurs had previously held managerial positions or had run another business (table 3-11). High TEIs are also registered by firms whose entrepreneurs have succeeded their fathers as owner-managers of family businesses. The founders of such firms generally send their children to college to acquire technical or managerial skills for later use in the family business. When the management of the firm passes to the second generation, there is usually a noticeable improvement in the way the firm is run.[31] Firms whose entrepreneurs are currently in their first jobs also tend to have high TEIs. These first-generation entrepreneurs are usually highly educated and may share some of the characteristics of the second-generation entrepreneurs in family businesses.

In contrast to the metalworking sector, few entrepreneurs in food processing firms have acquired production skills through training institutions or previous work in other food processing firms. Most entre-

Table 3-13. *Average Private Benefit-Cost Ratio and Technical Efficiency Index of Small and Medium Metalworking Firms, by Entrepreneur's Main Skills and Firm Size*

Entrepreneur's main skills	Size of firm (number of workers)			
	1–10	*11–40*	*41+*	*All*
Production only				
PBC	1.43	1.64	1.22	1.52
TEI	0.34	0.55	0.57	0.51
Number of firms	9	24	7	40
Administration[a]				
PBC	1.65	1.99	2.25	2.09
TEI	0.52	0.58	0.76	0.67
Number of firms	3	6	12	21
All firms				
PBC	1.49	1.72	1.87	1.72
TEI	0.39	0.56	0.68	0.56
Number of firms	12	30	19	61

a. Administration only, production and administration, or administration and sales.

preneurs have to hire a technician or, in the smallest firms, a skilled worker who knows the production process. Perhaps as a result of this, entrepreneurs with secondary education are able to achieve high TEIs (about the same as those for persons with university education); but since the higher opportunity cost of the university-trained entrepreneur is not matched by higher firm productivity, average PBC ratios in firms managed by university graduates are well below those of firms whose entrepreneurs have a secondary education. The specific nature of previous work experience seems to be of little significance: entrepreneurs who had formerly worked in management or in independent professional activities performed as well (especially with respect to TEIs) as persons who had previously run a business.

How is efficiency affected by entrepreneurs' education, experience, and skills? Some of the consequences have to do with the way these factors affect choice of technology—because, as will be shown below, the level of technological sophistication is a significant determinant of PBCs and TEIs, especially in food processing. Both the entrepreneur's education and his previous occupation are associated with types of technology chosen. University-educated entrepreneurs employ a wide range of techniques (generally with success), whereas entrepreneurs with only elementary education tend to choose the simplest techniques (table 3-14). Entrepreneurs in the metal products sector who have previously

Table 3-14. *Average Private Benefit-Cost Ratio and Technical Efficiency Index of Small and Medium Metalworking Firms, by Level of Entrepreneur's Education and Type of Technology*

Level of entrepreneur's education	Type of technology			
	Simple	Intermediate	Sophisticated	All
Primary				
PBC	1.63	2.00	2.07	1.84
TEI	0.41	0.62	0.53	0.50
Number of firms	9	6	4	19
Secondary				
PBC	1.52	1.25	0.96	1.27
TEI	0.49	0.56	0.29	0.44
Number of firms	8	4	6	18
University or technical				
PBC	1.76	1.90	2.05	1.96
TEI	0.67	0.70	0.69	0.69
Number of firms	4	8	14	26
All firms				
PBC	1.61	1.79	1.78	1.73
TEI	0.49	0.64	0.56	0.56
Number of firms	21	18	24	63

Table 3-15. *Average Private Benefit-Cost Ratio and Technical Efficiency Index for Metalworking and Food Processing Firms, by Firm Size and Type of Technology*

Firm size (number of workers)	PBC by type of technology				TEI by type of technology			
	Simple	Intermediate	Sophisticated	All	Simple	Intermediate	Sophisticated	All
Metalworking firms								
1–10	1.60	0.91	2.0	1.47	0.42	0.24	0.44	0.38
	(9)	(3)	(1)	(13)	(9)	(3)	(1)	(13)
11–20	1.66	1.96	1.86	1.80	0.55	0.64	0.48	0.57
	(7)	(6)	(2)	(15)	(7)	(6)	(2)	(15)
21–40	1.59	2.11	1.35	1.55	0.55	0.80	0.42	0.52
	(3)	(3)	(9)	(15)	(3)	(3)	(9)	(15)
41–60	1.54	2.42	1.68	1.90	0.53	0.87	0.62	0.69
	(2)	(4)	(6)	(12)	(2)	(4)	(6)	(12)
61+	—	0.89	2.47	2.07	—	0.55	0.78	0.72
	(0)	(2)	(6)	(8)	(0)	(2)	(6)	(8)
All	1.61	1.79	1.78	1.73	0.49	0.64	0.56	0.56
	(21)	(18)	(24)	(63)	(21)	(18)	(24)	(63)
Standard deviation	0.61	1.18	0.93	0.91	0.23	0.33	0.30	0.29
Food processing firms								
1–7	1.91	2.43	1.53	2.11	0.40	0.62	—	0.53
	(5)	(5)	(1)	(11)	(4)	(5)	(0)	(9)
8–15	1.98	3.30	1.76	2.62	—	0.71	0.59	0.66
	(1)	(6)	(4)	(11)	(0)	(6)	(4)	(10)
16+	2.71	3.18	2.94	2.96	0.45	0.93	0.34	0.54
	(4)	(5)	(5)	(14)	(2)	(2)	(3)	(7)
All	2.24	2.99	2.33	2.60	0.42	0.71	0.48	0.58
	(10)	(16)	(10)	(36)	(6)	(13)	(7)	(26)
Standard deviation	1.51	1.78	1.63	1.66	0.24	0.28	0.18	0.27

— Not applicable.
Note: Figures in parentheses are the number of firms.

been production workers and who usually have relatively low levels of education use mainly simple technologies—those who do use more sophisticated techniques have relatively low technical efficiency levels. Entrepreneurs with sales and administrative skills, however, tend to use more sophisticated technologies, possibly because of preference or affordability or because these technologies help to release the entrepreneur from production control so he can better utilize his sales and administrative skills.

Production Technology and Capital Intensity

Of the various features of firm technology on which we have obtained information, only the level of sophistication bears a strong relation to PBCs and TEIs when other explanatory factors are also taken into account. In both sectors the criterion used to distinguish technologies in this way is the degree of equipment sophistication in the firm's main stages or shops.[32] In the food sector, intermediate technologies give the best results in all size categories for which data are available (there are few medium and no large firms in this sample), although the advantage is more marked for the smaller firms (table 3-15). In the metalworking sector, the pattern is more complicated; the optimal technology is more sophisticated the larger the firm. Thus the smallest firms (1–10 workers) do best with the simple technologies, firms with 11–60 workers do best with intermediate technologies, and firms with 60 workers or more do best with relatively sophisticated technologies (though comparisons are difficult in this last case because only two firms use anything other than sophisticated techniques). None of the large firms in this sample use the simplest techniques and none of the very small firms use the most sophisticated techniques, but table 3-15 does suggest that some firms in each size group use an inappropriate technology for their size, with the errors lying in both directions. The standard deviation of PBC is least for firms using simple technologies, with the result that although their average PBC is a little lower than for the other two groups, only one of the firms with PBCs of less than 1 uses simple technology; most (six) use intermediate technologies and a few (three) use sophisticated ones. In the food sector, moreover, sophisticated technology does not seem to be a passport to high technical efficiency or to high PBCs.[33] The advantages of intermediate technologies in both sectors are confirmed by our PBC and TEI multiple regressions; the coefficients indicate that technology choice makes a significant difference.

Many small firms seem to have relatively high capital-labor (K/L) ratios, which may partly reflect excessively sophisticated technology. Among small metal products firms (up to 20 workers) K/L is about 25 percent higher in firms that use sophisticated techniques than it is in ones using simple technology (table 3-16); for small food processing firms having up to 15 workers, the differential is 50 percent or more. Among some of the less successful firms (for example, those with PBCs less than 1), there does appear to be a mismatch between size and the capital-labor ratio.[34]

These findings are of some general interest, since it is often suggested that smaller firms are economical users of capital. Although this generalization holds when SMI is compared with LI (see chapter 2), it is not obviously true for very small firms relative to larger ones within the SMI size group. Neither of our industry groups showed a K/L ratio that rose with firm size, as measured by number of workers employed. Could technological indivisibilities explain the rather unexpectedly high K/L ratios of small firms? If such indivisibilities were important, one would expect to see few firms in the very small size range (but that is obviously not the case) or to find that such firms are typically inefficient or have K/L ratios higher than those of somewhat larger firms. It is true that the ratio is on the average lower for firms of 21–40 workers in metalworking or 16–29 workers in food processing than in the smaller categories, but in neither case does the small category with high K/L have a relatively low PBC or TEI. Moreover, when size is defined by total capital stock rather than employment, the K/L ratio does in fact increase monotonically with size (table 3-17), and the smallest firms are at less of a disadvantage with regard to efficiency than are firms with the fewest workers. Thus, neither low total capital nor a low capital-labor ratio precludes an acceptable level of efficiency. In short, indivisibilities related to the size of capital stock, while no doubt a problem for some small firms, are not too serious an overall barrier. The K/L ratio is more systematically related to the level of technological sophistication than to firm size (table 3-16); choice of certain techniques clearly does present a firm with ex post indivisibilities. Age of firm may also bear some relation to the K/L ratio, although the latter is noticeably and systematically higher only for firms that are more than fifteen years old (table 3-18).

A number of firms did indicate in our interview that their K/L ratios were initially relatively high because of equipment indivisibilities.[35] As these firms consolidated their market positions over time and added more labor without expanding their capital, their K/L ratios began to fall. This process may explain why in our cross section of metalworking firms low K/L ratios were found among firms five years old or younger that were nevertheless large enough to spread fixed costs over a relatively sizable work force (21–60 workers; see table 3-18).[36] Smaller but older firms—those that have 20 or fewer workers and are six to fifteen years old—were the other group with very low K/L; they, too, had typically

Table 3-16. *Average Capital-Labor Ratio, by Type of Technology and Firm Size in Metalworking and Food Processing Firms*
(thousands of pesos)

Firm size (number of workers)	Ratio	Type of technology			
		Simple	Moderate	More sophisticated	All
Metalworking firms					
1–20	FK/L	140	137	206	146
	WK/L	66	102	66	78
	K/L	206	239	272	224
	No. of firms	16	9	3	28
21–60	FK/L	82	95	104	98
	WK/L	88	96	113	104
	K/L	170	191	217	202
	No. of firms	5	7	15	27
61+	FK/L	—	28	231	181
	WK/L	—	87	226	191
	K/L	—	115	457	372
	No. of firms	0	2	6	8
All	FK/L	126	108	149	130
	WK/L	72	99	135	103
	K/L	198	207	284	233
	No. of firms	21	18	24	63
Food processing firms					
1–15	FK/L	188	213	391	247
	WK/L	100	173	191	157
	K/L	288	386	582	404
	No. of firms	6	11	5	22
16–29	FK/L	145	230	170	180
	WK/L	46	118	10	68
	K/L	191	348	180	248
	No. of firms	4	3	1	8
30+	FK/L	—	358	645	549
	WK/L	—	110	108	109
	K/L	—	468	753	658
	No. of firms	0	2	4	6
All	FK/L	171	234	471	282
	WK/L	78	155	139	130
	K/L	249	389	610	412
	No. of firms	10	16	10	36

— Not applicable.

Note: FK/L denotes fixed capital stock per unskilled equivalent man-days per year; WK/L, working capital per unskilled equivalent man-days per year; and K/L, total capital stock per unskilled equivalent man-days per year.

Table 3-17. *Average Capital-Labor and Capital-Output Ratios of Metalworking and Food Processing Firms, by Size*
(thousands of pesos)

Firm size	Number of firms	K/L	VA/L	$\frac{VA}{Labor\ cost}$	VA/K	$\frac{VA}{Capital\ cost}$	PBC	TEI
Number of workers								
Metalworking firms								
1–10	13	209	159	1.68	0.91	16.8	1.47	0.38 (13)
11–20	17	246	200	2.02	1.06	21.6	1.76	0.55 (17)
21–40	15	202	193	1.69	1.46	23.3	1.55	0.52 (15)
41–60	12	202	239	2.08	1.71	30.0	1.90	0.69 (12)
61+	8	372	281	2.42	0.95	25.5	2.07	0.72 (8)
All	65	236	208	1.94	1.23	23.0	1.72	0.56 (65)
Food processing firms								
1-7	11	341	307	2.72	0.99	20.9	2.11	0.53 (9)
8–15	11	467	431	3.52	1.39	13.7	2.62	0.66 (10)
16–29	8	248	356	3.54	1.85	18.7	2.87	0.69 (4)
30+	6	658	549	4.20	1.53	15.3	3.08	0.34 (3)
All	36	412	396	3.39	1.39	17.3	2.60	0.58 (26)
Capital stock (thousands of 1977 pesos)								
Metalworking firms								
Less than 1,000	12	122	165	1.80	0.93	30.2	1.75	0.52 (12)
1,001–2,000	14	196	165	1.72	1.13	22.2	1.51	0.43 (14)
2,001–3,000	10	217	207	1.86	1.45	21.3	1.67	0.58 (10)
3,001–5,000	12	230	216	1.91	1.45	20.6	1.69	0.54 (12)
5,001+	17	263	266	2.27	1.46	21.5	1.98	0.68 (17)
All	65	236	208	1.94	1.23	23.0	1.72	0.56 (65)
Food processing firms								
Less than 1,000	11	217	253	2.33	1.56	25.8	2.04	0.44 (9)
1,001–2,000	6	310	455	3.93	1.70	18.1	3.14	0.77 (5)
2,001–3,000	6	348	366	3.54	1.00	11.3	2.61	0.66 (5)
3,001–5,000	7	478	497	4.07	1.59	15.4	2.97	0.62 (5)
5,001+	6	658	512	3.86	0.95	8.9	2.63	0.42 (2)
All	36	412	396	3.39	1.39	17.3	2.60	0.58 (26)

Note: K denotes total capital; L, unskilled equivalent man-days per year; and VA, value added. Labor cost includes paid wages plus the imputed cost of the entrepreneur's time. Capital cost is the private cost of capital, including an imputation of 1 percent for the entrepreneur's own capital.

Figures are unweighted averages across the values for the firms in a given cell. As a result, relations that are tautologies for individual firms (for example, $VA/L \div VA/K = K/L$) do not hold for aggregate data. The weighted average figures tell essentially the same story with respect to the issues of interest here.

Figures in parentheses denote the number of firms for which TEI was calculated. As noted earlier, it could be calculated for only two of the three food processing product groups.

Table 3-18. *Average Capital-Labor Ratios of Metalworking and Food Processing Firms, by Age and Size*
(thousands of pesos)

Firm size (number of workers)	Ratio	Firm's age (years)			
		1–5	6–15	16+	All
Metalworking firms					
1–20	FK/L	143	69	225	154
	WK/L	88	49	88	76
	K/L	231	118	313	230
	No. of firms	9	9	12	30
21–60	FK/L	76	100	110	98
	WK/L	61	134	107	104
	K/L	137	234	217	202
	No. of firms	7	9	11	27
61+	FK/L	106	200	170	181
	WK/L	160	170	256	191
	K/L	266	370	427	372
	No. of firms	1	5	2	8
All	FK/L	114	109	171	134
	WK/L	80	109	109	102
	K/L	194	218	280	236
	No. of firms	17	23	25	65
Food processing firms					
1–15	FK/L	294	163	276	247
	WK/L	71	150	264	157
	K/L	365	313	540	404
	No. of firms	8	7	7	22
16+	FK/L	154	246	1,076	338
	WK/L	60	68	208	86
	K/L	214	314	1,284	424
	No. of firms	4	8	2	14
All	FK/L	248	207	454	282
	WK/L	67	106	251	130
	K/L	315	313	705	412
	No. of firms	12	15	9	36

Note: FK/L denotes fixed capital per man-days per year; WK/L, working capital per unskilled equivalent man-days per year; and K/L, total capital per man-days per year.

added workers since their founding. Older firms that still have low employment have higher K/L ratios because new and more modern machines are added over time. The highest K/L ratios are found among the largest and oldest firms in the sample. In the food sector also, firms six to fifteen years old with small work forces (1–15 workers) tend to have

Table 3-19. *Average Capital-Labor Ratios of Metalworking Firms,*
by Source of Finance and Size
(thousands of pesos)

Source of finance	Firm size (number of workers)					
	1–10	*11–20*	*21–40*	*41–60*	*61+*	*All*
Self-finance only						
FK/L	173	172	169	145	171	168
WK/L	68	84	82	134	166	103
K/L	241	256	251	279	337	271
Number of firms	5	8	4	4	5	26
Main external source						
Public banks						
FK/L	148	133	73	84	145	109
WK/L	23	110	137	116	101	104
K/L	171	243	210	200	246	213
Number of firms	3	4	6	3	2	18
Moneylenders and suppliers						
FK/L	96	161	80	75	—	99
WK/L	105	61	43	51	—	161
K/L	201	222	123	126	—	173
Number of firms	5	2	2	3	0	12
Private banks						
FK/L	—	194	60	64	299	132
WK/L	—	62	111	102	494	129
K/L	—	256	171	166	793	261
Number of firms	0	3	3	2	1	9
All firms						
FK/L	138	166	97	98	181	134
WK/L	71	79	105	104	191	102
KL	209	245	202	202	372	236
Number of firms	13	17	15	12	8	65

— Not applicable.

Note: FK/L denotes fixed capital per unskilled equivalent man-days per year; WK/L,
working capital per unskilled equivalent man-days per year; and K/L, total capital per unskilled equivalent man-days per year.

low K/L ratios; among larger firms, however, K/L is a monotonically positive function of age (table 3-18).

In the metalworking sector, K/L ratios seem to be about 35 percent
lower among firms that make use of external funds than among self-
financed firms (see table 3-19 and the regression results of table 3-20). In
the food sector, average K/L does not seem to be higher for firms that are
exclusively self-financed. When other determinants of K/L are allowed
for, however, firms whose main sources of outside funds are private
banks or moneylenders and suppliers do seem to have a K/L ratio below
that of self-financed firms (table 3-20)—although the small size of our

Table 3-20. *Logarithmic Regression Results to Explain the Fixed Capital-Labor Ratio of Small and Medium Metalworking and Food Processing Firms*

Independent variables	Metalworking		Food processing	
	Coefficient	t statistic	Coefficient	t statistic
Constant	4.916		3.827	
Firm size (number of workers)	−0.199	−1.61	−0.111	0.44
Firm age (years)	0.300	2.73[a]	0.435	1.81
Entrepreneur's experience	...		0.475	2.29[b]
Entrepreneur's skills[c]				
Production only	0.357	1.56	0.145	0.28
Administration and production	0.138	0.39	−0.507	1.39
Sales and administration	−0.644	−1.67	0.203	0.36
Entrepreneur's education[d]				
University or technical	0.139	0.61	1.264	2.68[b]
Primary	−0.212	−0.87	−0.728	2.46[b]
Sources of finance[e]				
Private banks	−0.230	−0.87	−0.120	0.31
Public banks	−0.457	−2.21[b]	0.569	1.23
Moneylenders and suppliers	−0.493	−2.06[b]	0.148	0.26
Product groups[f]				
Agricultural implements	−0.233	−1.04	—	—
Ovens, stoves, kitchens	−0.743	−3.10[a]	—	—
Guava paste	—	—	−0.592	1.47
Cheese	—	—	−0.540	1.15
R^2	0.43		0.75	
R^2 (adjusted)	0.29		0.54	
DOF	51		16	
F	3.15[a]		3.67[a]	

... Not significant.
— Not applicable.
a. Significant at the 0.01 level or less.
b. Significant at >0.01 to ≤0.05.
c. In the base, administration only.
d. In the base, secondary.
e. In the base, self-financing only.
f. In the base, pumps and agricultural capital goods.

sample and the low statistical significance of the results make this finding no more than suggestive. In both sectors, the results are consistent with a fairly tight credit market in which firms that borrow do not overcapitalize themselves, but some of those that have adequate capital of their own indulge in somewhat higher capital intensities. This in turn suggests that Colombian SMI is not prone to that bugaboo of the literature—excessive use of capital due to overly cheap and accessible credit. Such a condition would, of course, be more likely to characterize LI. But if there is a capital market imperfection that might lead to excessive capital intensity in some cases, it takes the form of a shortage of financial outlets in which the small entrepreneur can invest at a good rate of return.

In the food sector, K/L is positively associated with the level of the entrepreneur's education; in the metalworking sector, no significant difference of this sort emerges. We were unable to detect any effect of the wage rate on the fixed capital per man-days per year (FK/L) so it is not included in table 3-20; this finding is probably not surprising in the light of the quite moderate differences that we observed between size categories (see table 2-14) and more generally between individual firms. This result does not imply that the wage rate would be an unimportant determinant of FK/L differences between LI and SMI since wage differences are considerably greater in that instance.

Secondhand Equipment

The amount of fixed capital a small business needs depends significantly on whether it can buy secondhand equipment. In both our samples, about one-quarter of all equipment had been bought secondhand, either in the local market (by smaller firms) or directly from dealers in the United States and Western Europe (by larger ones).[37] The availability of secondhand equipment at one-third to one-quarter of the price of new equipment frequently determines whether skilled workers with some savings can try to become independent producers; its low initial fixed cost may be offset, however, by higher variable costs related to the maintenance and repair needs or the low technical efficiency of such equipment. Past studies of the use of secondhand equipment in developed countries have been unable to shed much light on this issue.

Our regression analyses reveal that the proportion of equipment bought secondhand is negatively related to measured PBC in the food sector, but that the coefficient is not statistically significant and the predicted effect is quantitatively unimportant. For metalworking firms, the coefficient is positive but insignificant. Thus, private returns (which are calculated on the basis of the commercial or market value of equipment) seem to be virtually unrelated to whether capital is bought new or secondhand. Any positive or negative effects of the use of secondhand equipment might also be expected to show up in the levels of technical efficiency. In neither sector, however, do our regressions detect any more significant effects than those noted for PBCs.[38] Given these results, one would expect the use of secondhand equipment to be reflected in a higher PBC if the purchase price of capital rather than its commercial value were incorporated into the PBC formula. If the replacement or commercial value of the equipment was used, the results would not reflect the many cases in which firms are able to take advantage of especially favorable offers in the secondhand market or those in which the firm itself has done much of the reconstruction work at lower-than-market prices. These situations are probably more common in the metalworking sector than in food processing.

A relatively positive effect of secondhand equipment in the metalworking sector could be due to the particular characteristics of the equipment and labor force used there. Metalworking firms use machine tools and various types of cutting, folding, and welding equipment, some of which have long working lives if properly maintained. Skilled workers in this sector know how to operate and maintain this equipment; in many cases they can even make spare parts that would otherwise be difficult to obtain. In the food sector, however, production workers have relatively low mechanical skills and are not usually able to repair their own equipment; as a result, when old equipment breaks down, time is lost while a mechanic from outside repairs it.

The tradition of using secondhand equipment in Colombia derives in part from the country's chronic shortage of foreign exchange. A network of local traders has developed to supply SMI entrepreneurs who cannot travel abroad to acquire secondhand equipment directly, and these traders usually provide credit and performance guarantees to their customers. Between 1974 and the early 1980s the country's buoyant balance of payments situation encouraged large firms to reequip their plants. Their sales of old equipment in turn expanded the local secondhand market so that some firms were able to obtain used equipment at bargain prices. To what extent these lower prices have been reflected in entrepreneurs' estimates of the commercial value of their fixed capital is unclear.

Characteristics of the individual firm, such as its age, help to determine the amount of secondhand equipment it uses. Firms that are 5 years old or younger have nearly twice as high a share of secondhand equipment as older ones (table 3-21); this pattern is apparent for nearly all sizes of firms and levels of technological sophistication in both our industry samples. As firms become more firmly established in the market, however, most of them expand output with newer machines, although they usually keep the older ones for auxiliary work.[39] The tendency to acquire more modern machines is also reflected in the large number of firms that have increased the mechanization of their main production processes. But the older firms in our samples (those more than 10 years old) seem to rely more on secondhand machinery. The reasons for this are not immediately apparent, but it may be that older firms are owned by older entre-

Table 3-21. *Average Proportion of Secondhand Equipment among Metalworking and Food Processing Firms, by Size, Type of Technology, and Age*

Firm size and type of technology	Firm's age (years)			
	1–5	6–10	11+	All
Metalworking firms				
Firm size (number of workers)				
1–10	0.32	0.18	0.10	0.19
	(4)	(4)	(5)	(13)
11–20	0.26	0.08	0.22	0.21
	(5)	(3)	(9)	(17)
21–40	0.50	0.07	0.37	0.38
	(6)	(2)	(7)	(15)
41+	0.32	0.17	0.21	0.21
	(2)	(5)	(13)	(20)
All	0.37	0.14	0.22	0.25
	(17)	(14)	(34)	(65)
Type of technology				
Simple	0.36	0.12	0.20	0.22
	(5)	(6)	(10)	(21)
Intermediate	0.30	0.10	0.17	0.19
	(4)	(4)	(10)	(18)
Sophisticated	0.42	0.21	0.29	0.31
	(6)	(4)	(14)	(24)

	Firm's age (years)			
	1–5	6–15	16+	All
Food processing firms				
Firm size (number of workers)				
1–7	0.07	0.25	0.43	0.23
	(4)	(4)	(3)	(11)
8–15	0.84	0.32	0.30	0.50
	(4)	(3)	(4)	(11)
16+	0.27	0.10	0.10	0.15
	(4)	(8)	(2)	(14)
All	0.40	0.18	0.30	0.28
	(12)	(15)	(9)	(36)
Type of technology				
Simple	0.02	0.03	—	0.02
	(5)	(5)	(0)	(10)
Intermediate	0.74	0.24	0.31	0.18
	(4)	(5)	(7)	(15)
Sophisticated	0.56	0.28	0.25	0.30
	(3)	(5)	(2)	(9)

— Not applicable.

Note: The number of firms is in parentheses.

preneurs who may not wish to invest too heavily in new machinery. In some cases, however, it is simply that the firm is in the size range where it can tap the foreign secondhand market.

Having the opportunity to buy secondhand equipment clearly helps many small firms to get started. Less obviously, it seems to give some of them access to relatively sophisticated production systems—a conclusion suggested by the greater prominence of such equipment in firms that use relatively modern technology. This seems to be especially true for the food processing sector. The firms in our sample that used the simplest technology had almost no secondhand equipment, whereas in firms employing more sophisticated technology 30 percent of the equipment was secondhand (table 3-21). In metalworking, too, the firms with the more advanced technology had the highest propensity to use secondhand equipment, although those with simple and intermediate production technologies made considerable use of it as well. In neither industry did the smallest firms (measured by number of workers) make the greatest use of secondhand equipment, though this is the case for manufacturing as a whole, as reported in table 3-21.

In both sectors, entrepreneurs with primary school or college education use more secondhand equipment than those with high school education, given the other variables taken into account in the regressions reported in table 3-22. Most of the entrepreneurs with only a primary education are former production workers who may buy secondhand equipment for a number of reasons—their resources may be limited, their skills may be confined to a particular type or vintage of equipment, or they may be skilled enough in repair and maintenance to get good performance out of even an elderly plant. Entrepreneurs with a high school education tend to have more resources and may regard new equipment as a status symbol. College graduates, however, may be better able to calculate production costs accurately and may therefore rationally choose secondhand equipment when they find that the unit costs of production are lower. Also, many of them speak English and can consequently tap the large U.S. secondhand market directly.

Input Costs, Output Prices, and Market Access

A firm's private profits are affected not only by the technical efficiency with which it converts inputs to outputs and its ability to choose the cheapest set of inputs available, but also by the absolute levels of its input and output prices. We have qualitative information on the output prices of firms in the metalworking sample and those of their competitors. The price variations in this industry, by the way, are wider than in the more

Table 3-22. *Results of Linear and Logarithmic Regressions to Explain the Proportion of Secondhand Equipment in Metalworking and Food Processing Firms*

Independent variables	Simple linear regression		Log regression	
	Coefficient	t statistic	Coefficient	t statistic
Metalworking firms				
Constant	−9.062		−0.564	
Fixed capital	0.015	3.10[a]	0.469	1.83
Proportion self-financing	25.091	1.64	0.383	0.62
Age of the firm (years)	−0.772	−2.18	−0.870	−3.09[a]
Entrepreneur's experience	0.295	0.72	0.174	0.42
Entrepreneur's education[b]				
Primary	22.724	2.34[c]	1.497	2.57
University or technical	10.209	1.18	0.403	0.74
Type of technology[d]				
Simple	−2.855	0.33	−0.091	−0.17
More sophisticated	−0.113	−0.01	−0.032	−0.06
R^2	0.31		0.23	
R^2 (adjusted)	0.21		0.12	
DOF	56		55	
F	3.09[a]		2.05[e]	
Food processing firms				
Constant	−5.815			0.52
Fixed capital	0.00007	0.05	−0.299	1.30
Proportion self-financing	16.333	0.89	0.037	0.09
Age of the firm (years)	−1.779	−2.86[a]	−0.291	0.90
Entrepreneur's experience	1.315	2.32	1.196	3.65[a]
Entrepreneur's education[b]				
Primary	17.064	1.29	0.580	0.67
University or technical	18.230	1.50	0.080	0.14
Type of technology[d]				
Simple	−38.941	−3.73[a]	−1.540	−2.55
More sophisticated	−6.433	−0.52	0.460	0.77
Type of product[f]				
Guava paste	27.767	2.54	1.419	2.59[c]
Cheese	10.937	0.90	1.325	2.08
R^2	0.68		0.73	
R^2 (adjusted)	0.55		0.59	
DOF	24		19	
F	5.11[a]		5.25[a]	

a. Significant at the 0.01 level or less.
b. In the base, secondary education.
c. Significant at the level of >0.01 to ≤ 0.05.
d. In the base, intermediate technology.
e. Significant at the level of >0.05 to ≤ 0.1.
f. In the base, potato chips.

Table 3-23. *Average Benefit-Cost Ratio and Technical Efficiency Index of Metalworking and Food Processing Firms, by Market Characteristic*

Market characteristic	Number of firms	PBC	EBC	SBC	TEI	
Metalworking firms						
Firm's prices compared with those of competitors						
Higher	19	2.04	7.55	1.73	0.62	
Same	26	1.73	4.51	1.49	0.58	
Lower	19	1.39	2.39	1.16	0.46	
Product quality compared with that of competitors						
Higher	22	1.71	5.27	1.52	0.53	
Same	30	1.77	4.39	1.41	0.53	
Lower	3	1.36	2.70	1.41	0.63	
Sales fluctuation						
Yes	19	1.54	4.12	1.32	0.44	
No	23	1.83	5.65	1.57	0.61	
Channels of distribution						
Final consumers	39	1.53	3.40	1.30	0.47	
Distributors	26	2.00	6.85	1.73	0.69	
Sources of finance						
Self-finance only	26	1.72	5.06	1.42	0.55	
Public banks	18	1.65	4.21	1.36	0.57	
Private banks	9	2.39	8.59	2.00	0.70	
Suppliers and moneylenders	12	1.31	2.07	1.23	0.43	
Food processing firms						
Firm's prices compared with those of competitors						
Higher	10	1.77	5.97	1.60	0.67	(6)
Same	14	3.19	10.36	2.75	0.58	(11)
Lower	9	2.73	9.44	2.33	0.51	(6)
Product quality compared with that of competitors						
Higher	14	2.88	9.86	2.55	0.62	(8)
Same	16	2.48	8.97	2.19	0.56	(13)
Lower	5	2.29	4.40	1.79	0.57	(5)
Materials prices compared with those of competitors						
Higher	9	2.47	10.16	2.13	0.55	(6)
Same	18	2.78	8.31	2.45	0.58	(13)
Lower	6	2.34	7.50	1.93	0.62	(5)
Sources of finance						
Self-finance only	17	1.92	3.59	1.61	0.55	(12)
Public banks	5	2.42	14.51	2.13	0.55	(4)
Private banks	12	3.37	12.24	2.96	0.62	(8)
Suppliers and moneylenders	2	4.11	13.52	3.86	0.68	(2)

Note: The number of food processing firms for which TEI has been calculated is in parentheses.

competitive food processing industry. There is a significant positive association between a firm's PBC ratio and its output prices relative to those of its competitors (tables 3-23 and 3-9). The prices charged by most very small firms are lower than those of their competitors, while the prices charged by one-third to one-half of the larger firms are higher than those of their competitors. The variation in product price by size of firm could have a number of explanations. For example, the clientele of small firms may differ from that of larger ones, the products of small firms may be lower in quality, or new small firms may undersell larger, more established ones to get a foothold in the market. On the whole, we found that although small and large firms do compete in the market for supplying low-income customers, small producers usually concentrate on this customer group whereas large firms produce for both low- and high-income markets.

Small firms charge low prices and adapt their products to clients' needs to break into markets previously held by larger firms. A case in point is that of seven small producers of agricultural implements founded in the Cali-Palmira region in the 1970s. From the start these firms had to compete with the largest producers of heavy plows, who dominated the Colombian market. The first light plows produced in Palmira in 1972 sold for about 60,000 pesos, while those of the main regional distributor for a large firm sold for 80,000–85,000 pesos. In 1973 heavy plows made by the traditional producers sold in Cali for about 150,000 pesos; the locally produced ones cost about 140,000. In 1974, the largest firm's distributor lowered its price to 126,000 pesos, trying to retain the market; at the beginning of 1975, local producers were able to sell similar plows for 108,000 pesos. As a result, the distributor had to abandon selling this line of products in the Valle region. Competition subsequently continued among the small producers with further price cuts. In 1976 the same type of heavy plow was being sold in Palmira for about 100,000 pesos despite the severe inflation of the previous three or four years.

In the case of stoves and cookers, large firms produce both the most expensive, sophisticated units and small cheap units fueled by petroleum or gas. Small firms compete with larger ones in the production of the cheaper units, which are bought mostly by low-income groups.

In the market for food products, larger firms tend to sell at higher prices that reflect (but in our judgment understate) quality differences. The more technologically sophisticated and usually larger producers of both cheese and guava paste operate more hygienically (for example, they use pasteurized milk to make cheese) and have better quality control, with the result that they have a better and safer product. Small and large producers alike sell mainly through supermarkets that do not seem particularly concerned with quality, however, or may prefer not to complicate the price structure they present to the consumer. Whatever the reason, the extent to which large producers' prices (at point of sale to the supermarket) exceed the prices charged by small firms appears to understate their quality advantage; the competitiveness of the small producers seems to be abetted by the market's failure to reward higher quality.[40] This situation is in sharp contrast to the case of agricultural implements, where small producers have often competed on the basis of product superiority, and illustrates the impossibility of generalizing across industries on a matter such as the relation between firm size and product quality. In the market for agricultural implements, the buyer usually knows what he wants and can make skillful quality comparisons; in the case of food products such as cheese and guava paste, either the consumer is not similarly interested and informed, or the intermediary (the supermarket) keeps quality-related price differentials small for reasons of its own.

Price differences adjusted for quality are hard to measure. If the entire statistical impact of product price differences in our PBC regressions for the metal products sector were due to real price differences (in other words, if neither quality differences nor other factors associated with both low PBCs and low output prices were involved), those price differences would be on the order of 15 percent in each direction from the base.[41] Some of the conclusions discussed above could be affected if such a price gap exists; it was noted earlier that the gap in SBC and TEI by firm size in the metalworking sector may for this reason be substantially exaggerated in our benchmark figures (see table 3-3).

Although we do not have precise information on the quality of each firm's work force, we believe that the moderate wage differences between smaller and larger firms in the metal products sector are unlikely to be associated with large quality differences. This proposition is supported by the lack of a statistically significant relation between wage differentials and technical efficiency. Higher-than-average wages are negatively and statistically significantly related to PBC (see table 3-9), as one would expect in the absence of an association between wages and technical efficiency. Since the variance in wages is not very great, however, it does not explain much of the variance in PBC. A low rate of labor turnover could imply a relatively high accumulation of firm-specific skills and hence high productivity, but we could find no statistical relation between TEI and a proxy for labor turnover, although again there was an association with the BC ratios—low turnover being associated with high PBCs (table 3-9).[42] In the metal products sector, the proportion of workers attending practical courses (given by SENA or by the firm itself with its own equipment) during the year before the interviews might be expected to be reflected in labor quality. We found that this proportion was indeed positively correlated with TEI, and its coefficient in our multiple regression to explain TEI is positive but not significant (table 3-9); its coefficient in the regressions to explain the BC ratios is also quite significant, although the causation could be going from profitability to placement of workers in courses.

Variations in prices of raw materials seem to be larger in food processing than in the metal products sector, probably because of the varying ability of different food firms to buy and preserve stocks at harvesttime when prices are lower and to hold them until they are scarce in the market. Firms that pay higher-than-average prices for their raw materials tend to have lower BCs than ones that pay average or below-average prices. Our conclusions about the main factors explaining interfirm differences in SBCs would not be significantly affected by an adjustment of this kind in our value added figures.

Sources and Availability of Investment Funds

The unavailability or high cost of credit is usually seen as a major constraint on small firms. We might therefore expect differences in capital costs to explain some of the interfirm variations in PBCs. In fact, however, the firms in our two samples are largely self-financed; consequently, the cost of borrowed capital has little effect on either the average cost of capital or firms' PBCs. In this context, the key question may be whether a firm is able to obtain credit when extra resources are needed to complement its own investment funds, even if such loans do not loom large in its total investment capital. For this reason, and because of inadequate data on the cost of borrowed capital, we have chosen as explanatory variables in our PBC regression calculations the main sources of finance that firms use other than reinvestment (rather than the cost of capital).[43]

These external sources of finance are divided into three groups: public banks, private banks, and moneylenders and suppliers. Public banks are the main sources of external finance for our sample of metalworking firms (used by 28 percent of the sample); in the food sector private banks predominate (used by 34 percent of the firms). The greater involvement of private banks in the food sector may be a consequence of the much higher profitability of food firms.

It is particularly difficult to judge from our information how access to sources of finance affects economic performance, since one must assume that the causation also runs in the opposite direction—performance itself helps to determine the sources of finance to which a firm has access. A portion of the statistical association that shows up in our regressions thus probably reflects this latter causal relationship. In both sectors, firms with access to credit from private banks tend to have higher PBCs than ones that use only their own resources (table 3-24), even though external financing presumably raises the average cost of capital and hence has a direct negative effect on PBCs. The relation between external financing and PBCs is stronger in the food sector than in metalworking, perhaps because most of the latter are fully self-financed. In the metal sector, smaller firms (those with less than 20 workers) that rely completely on self-financing have lower PBCs than those that use outside funds, whereas larger firms that are exclusively self-financed have relatively high PBCs. In the food sector, firms of all sizes have below-average PBCs when they are totally self-financed; no firm with more than 30 workers is in this position.

The particular external source of financing used by individual firms also seems to be related to their PBC ratios. Firms whose main sources of loans are private banks tend to have substantially higher PBCs than those

Table 3-24. *Average Private Benefit-Cost Ratio of Metalworking and Food Processing Firms, by Size and Main Source of Finance*

Firm size (number of workers)	Only reinvestment	Public banks	Private banks	Suppliers and moneylenders	All
Metalworking firms					
1–10	1.37	1.36	—	1.62	1.47
	(5)	(3)	(0)	(5)	(13)
11–20	1.61	2.12	2.05	1.20	1.76
	(8)	(4)	(3)	(2)	(17)
21–40	1.58	1.70	1.58	0.99	1.55
	(4)	(6)	(3)	(2)	(15)
41–60	1.85	1.83	3.37	1.06	1.90
	(4)	(3)	(2)	(3)	(12)
61+	2.25	0.72	3.91	—	2.07
	(5)	(2)	(1)	(0)	(8)
All	1.72	1.65	2.30	1.31	1.72
	(26)	(18)	(9)	(12)	(65)
Food processing firms					
1–7	1.89	—	4.30	—	2.11
	(10)	(0)	(1)	(0)	(11)
8–15	2.32	1.59	2.43	4.11	2.62
	(4)	(1)	(4)	(2)	(11)
16–29	1.5	2.06	4.75	—	2.87
	(3)	(2)	(3)	(0)	(8)
30+	—	3.17	3.03	—	3.08
	(0)	(2)	(4)	(0)	(6)
All	1.92	2.42	3.37	4.11	2.60
	(17)	(5)	(12)	(2)	(36)

— Not applicable.
Note: The number of firms is in parentheses.

that rely on public banks. A firm's access to a particular source of finance is probably as much a consequence as a cause of its success; the banks, especially private ones, will be likely to lend mainly to already successful firms whose need for credit is a relatively minor consideration. Presumably the availability of credit also helps to raise a firm's PBC ratio, but it is hard to say which effect dominates. In the metalworking sector, the firms that rely on moneylenders or suppliers for credit tend to be considerably less successful than those that have recourse to bank credit. The ways in which moneylenders evaluate success are probably less formal than the procedures used by banks, although the methods may be equally effective. Moneylenders tend to have more personal contacts with entrepreneurs; their role as financers of firms that are profitable, but not the most profitable, could be quite beneficial, especially if they are the only available source of the external credit that such firms need. We have no evidence on this point, however. One might speculate that in the metalworking sector, where recourse to public banks and moneylenders and suppliers is associated with considerably lower K/L (table 3-19) and lower BCs (table 3-9), these firms are suffering from a capital shortage. It is possible that self-financed firms (which have the highest average K/L ratios) have more funds than they need and thus somewhat lower BCs than firms that use private bank credit. In the food sector the availability of additional capital may be so important—either to let the firm expand all inputs or to raise the K/L ratio—that it is associated with higher profits under a wide range of circumstances.

The level of self-financing is relatively high—about 75 percent—for each sample.[44] In the food sector, the degree of self-financing falls with firm size and age (see table 3-25).[45] The heavy reliance of small, young firms on self-financing is probably attributable to their lack of access to external sources of funds and perhaps also in some cases to a preference for not accumulating debts when the business is not yet clearly on a sound footing. In the metal sector, although there is something of a negative relation between size of firm and degree of self-financing, there is no such correlation with age of firm, and self-financing is high for all age categories.[46] Even large firms that would not be expected to have a problem obtaining bank loans seem to rely primarily on reinvestment—a phenomenon that may reflect no more than the fact that these firms have enough funds available from their past profits to limit their need for borrowing. Larger food firms may rely more on external financing than their counterparts in the metal sector because of the trade background of many entrepreneurs in the food sector. Moreover, the profitability record of food firms (which tends to be higher than that of metalworking firms) may have given them easier access to external sources of finance. Moreover, many of the food processors may have been growing rapidly, with

Table 3-25. *Average Proportion of Investment That Is Self-Financed among Small and Medium Metalworking and Food Processing Firms, by Size and Age*

Firm size (number of workers)	Age of firm (years)			
	1–5	*6–15*	*16+*	*All*
Metalworking firms				
1–10	0.84	0.95	0.73	0.84
	(4)	(5)	(4)	(13)
11–40	0.77	0.80	0.85	0.80
	(11)	(10)	(11)	(32)
41+	0.65	0.61	0.73	0.68
	(2)	(8)	(10)	(20)
All	0.78	0.76	0.78	0.77
	(17)	(23)	(25)	(65)
Food processing firms				
1–7	0.99	0.97	0.83	0.94
	(4)	(4)	(3)	(11)
8–15	0.89	0.73	0.57	0.73
	(4)	(3)	(4)	(11)
16–29	0.66	0.73	0.99	0.73
	(4)	(3)	(1)	(8)
30+	—	0.46	0.20	0.42
	(0)	(5)	(1)	(6)
All	0.85	0.70	0.66	0.74
	(12)	(15)	(9)	(36)

— Not applicable.

Note: The number of firms is in parentheses. Figures presented are unweighted averages of the percentage of investment that is self-financed for the firms in the cell.

the result that their need for funds has outstripped their own savings capacity. As we shall see in chapter 4, smaller firms in the metalworking sector tend on the average to grow faster than larger ones; we do not have data on this point for the food processing sample.

Fully 58 percent of the metalworking firms and 51 percent of the food processing firms in our samples have had no loans from any bank, public or private. Of these, 31 metalworking and 21 food processing firms gave some explanation for not having such loans. Although about one-third of the metalworking firms (11) have had their applications rejected, primarily because of difficulties in providing collateral, others have not applied for loans because of excessive paperwork (5 firms) or because they do not like to have debts (5 firms). Among the sample of food firms, 5 have had difficulty in providing collateral, and 7 have never applied for bank loans. For some small firms, the lack of collateral is related to the underevaluation of assets that they have acquired secondhand. Secondhand equipment is often sold without invoices or at understated prices because the sellers are trying to evade taxes. This equipment has little value as collateral because the banks recognize only 30 or 40 percent of the (already undervalued) book value.

The paperwork in a loan is a problem for small entrepreneurs. Many of them do not have the income statements, balance sheets, proofs of ownership of assets that banks require. A large number also lack the tax clearance that public banks require. Further, the entrepreneurs in our survey indicated that paperwork had a high opportunity cost in terms of their time spent from their enterprises. It is quicker to arrange a loan with a commercial bank than with a development finance institution, provided that the entrepreneur has maintained a current account with the former for some time or is otherwise known to it. Moneylenders are more willing to lend at short notice than either kind of bank, but they also charge higher interest rates. Some entrepreneurs with blue-collar backgrounds do not go to banks because they feel uncomfortable in dealing with middle-class bank officials; they prefer to go to local moneylenders whom they know, even though they have to pay more for their money.

Summary

Aggregate data for 1976 on SMI as a whole along with more detailed information from our metalworking and food processing subsectoral samples present a picture of relatively high returns on resources employed. At the same time, returns for the year of our survey data varied widely across firms in the two industries sampled. We suspect that this variance would have been somewhat lower, though still significant, if the reference period had been longer. For both of the industries surveyed and, as far as we could judge, for SMI as a whole, total factor productivity as measured by BC ratios was higher in medium-size firms than in small ones. The social SBC in the smallest metal products firms appeared to be 70–90 percent of that of the largest included in the sample (primarily units with 60–100 workers); in food processing, the corresponding ratio appeared to be 60–75 percent.

Much of the variance of observed PBCs across metalworking firms is associated with differences in technical efficiency. Although measurement problems preclude definitive conclusions, we believe that differences in price or allocative efficiency and in prices of inputs and outputs are less important as sources of variance of PBCs. In food processing, technical efficiency explains a smaller share of the interfirm variance in PBCs. This could be the result of a definitional asymmetry between the two variables in this case or may be related to the greater role played by differences in price efficiency or in the absolute levels of input and output prices.

In the metalworking sector, entrepreneurs with primary education (many of whom had previously been production workers) and those with university training do better than those with secondary education. The latter seem to be successful only when they use simple technologies. In the food processing firms, however, entrepreneurs with secondary education were the most successful. In the metalworking sector, entrepreneurs whose skills are limited to production tend to do rather poorly because they find it hard to organize other aspects of the business. Few food processing entrepreneurs have this kind of background—in fact, most of them have to hire a technician or skilled worker to run the production side of the business.

Intermediate technologies tend to yield the highest PBCs in both sectors, although among metalworking firms these ratios vary much more widely for intermediate than for simple technologies. The simplest technologies are associated with relatively higher PBCs among the smallest firms than among larger ones in both sectors. When firm size is defined by number of workers, the K/L ratio tends to fall with size initially and then to rise; when size is measured by amount of capital stock, the K/L ratio rises monotonically with it. As one might expect, the K/L ratio rises with a firm's level of technological sophistication and its age. Firms with few capital resources do not on the average suffer from low PBCs or TEIs, especially if they avoid the more sophisticated technologies. The use of borrowed funds tends to be associated with less-than-average K/L. In food processing, input prices are higher for the smaller establishments but product quality seems to vary less than in metalworking.

When factors such as the education and skills of entrepreneurs and types of technology used are included as determinants of PBCs in a multiple regression, size of firm has no significant effect even though, as just noted, average PBC does increase with size. If economies of scale of any importance exist, their effects must have become confounded statistically with other variables (perhaps technological sophistication); even so, the results suggest that such economies are not very important in these two industries.[47] The use of secondhand machinery may help firms to reduce the costs associated with indivisibilities; heavy reliance on used equipment is certainly a prominent feature of SMI. Markets for such equipment are now well developed in Colombia and appear to have been of special help to firms that were initially small and lacking in financial resources. In the two sectors we studied, this included the majority of firms, some of which are now quite large.

About three-quarters of the investment in each sector is self-financed; this feature is especially prominent among smaller and younger firms. The effect of external financing on BC is hard to evaluate since profitability is likely to make it easier to get credit. In both sectors, firms whose main external sources of funds are private banks have PBCs that are well above the sectoral average. The picture is less clear with respect to public banks and suppliers or moneylenders. Although the data give us no reason to doubt SMI firms' need for credit, the most striking feature of the industries we examined is their high rate of self-financing.

This chapter has examined SMI's static efficiency and returns to entrepreneurship. In chapter 4, we focus on the striking dynamism exhibited during the 1970s by firms in the SMI category; the overall picture is one of impressive achievement and great potential.

Notes

1. These figures should be taken as indicative only. The PBC figures assume a very low private opportunity cost of the entrepreneur's own capital, so they could be too high. If, however, these low rates were to reflect not only the private but also the social opportunity cost of the individual entrepreneur's capital (a possible situation if the capital involved would not be invested at all in the absence of the present opportunity) then the true SBC could be close to the estimated PBC.

2. For reasons discussed in the methodological appendix, we place less credence on EBC than on PBC or SBC. Its very high average values reflect our probable underestimation (at least relative to the longer-run average value) of the private opportunity cost of own capital. Its wide variance may reflect errors of measurement of the cost of own capital (apart from the general downward bias just cited) and of own labor inputs.

3. Since the figures under discussion are unweighted averages across firms, their value is sensitive to the distribution of firms across size categories. Were we to weight BCs by firm output, the average BCs would be higher.

4. As noted elsewhere, the alternative uses of much of the entrepreneur's own capital investment in SMI do not appear to be too remunerative, although the social payoff could be considerably higher than the private payoff. Since our information does not allow us to assess precisely the social opportunity cost of the capital used by different groups of SMI firms, we have opted simply for a rate that we believe is close to the average return to capital in the economy.

5. Our information pertains to whether a firm's prices are above, the same as, or below those of competitors. Although we also know something about the size of the competitors, we are not able to deduce in general whether a small firm's price is below that of competing large firms, for example, or indeed how great the difference is. Responses may not be too accurate on price differences in any case.

In the regression analysis presented later in the chapter, the BC of a firm whose product prices are above those of its competitors is predicted to be higher than that of a firm whose prices are below those of its competitors. In making this calculation we assumed the former's product price was 1.15/0.85 greater than that of the latter; that is, we made a 15 percent adjustment either way from the base.

6. The differential of 30 percent shown in the benchmark figure (table 3-2) may be biased downward by the use of commercial value of capital rather than

replacement value, but it is almost certain to be biased upward by the failure to allow for price differences. The 17 percent differential of table 3-3, column 5, could still be too great, but we doubt that the true gap would be less than 10 percent. In the case of food processing, the benchmark figure is thought to give an upper limit to the size of the gap.

7. The difference between the wages paid by a firm and our estimate of the social opportunity cost of its labor tends to be small; since private and social output and material input prices are assumed to be the same, the difference between the private and social prices of capital is the critical factor in producing the difference between PBC and SBC estimates. About 70 percent of capital is self-financed by the representative firm in each industry.

8. That is to say, although the PBC (EBC) was less than 1, value added did exceed the cost of working capital and labor (including the entrepreneur's own labor input, which should be treated as a variable factor as long as the entrepreneur is able in principle to move to another job).

9. In the metalworking sector, older firms do not on the average have a high PBC; if anything, the opposite is the case. It is true, however, that the 4 firms that are both young and small have a low average PBC of 1.12. Among the food processing firms, those that had been in existence for five years or less had a below-average PBC, but it was still high (1.69 for the 8 firms with 15 or fewer workers).

10. An example would be cases in which the entrepreneur bought his equipment at a bargain price and also had a low opportunity cost for his own capital. In using reported commercial value of capital as the measure of fixed capital and the low interest rate charged on own capital we may have underestimated the cost of capital inputs on the average, but for some firms the bias would nevertheless go the other way.

11. That they are entrepreneurs suggests they are not typical of their education and experience group. Furthermore, some underreporting always occurs in the type of survey on which these figures are based, a fact that provides another reason for adjusting them upward in trying to estimate the opportunity cost of these entrepreneurs' time.

12. John Todd, "Plant Size, Factor Proportions, and Efficiency in Colombian Industry," in *Essays on Industrialization in Colombia*, ed. Albert Berry (Tempe, Ariz.: Arizona State University, Center for Latin American Studies, 1983).

13. The data in tables 2-17 and 2-19 may be overestimates because of underevaluation of the book value of fixed capital and exclusion of some working capital; nevertheless, they probably give fairly valid figures by plant size.

14. If the social cost of labor was equal to that of capital in LI (we cannot know this breakdown precisely since the aggregate data on capital are not ideal) and if labor productivity were 30 percent higher in LI and capital productivity were 5 percent lower (see table 2-17), then total factor productivity would be 12.5 percent higher in LI. LI could be markedly more efficient than SMI only if its quality-adjusted labor productivity were much higher, as would be consistent with the available data only if the wages paid for a given skill were also much higher. The evidence reviewed in chapter 2 suggests a considerable wage differential of this sort, but one not large enough to generate a large gap in total factor productivity in favor of large plants.

15. Indeed, Todd's results suggest the opposite. There are several possible reasons for the difference, most of which imply that Todd's results are either likely to be less valid in general than ours or less valid for the late 1970s. First, the relative position of plants of 200 workers or more appears to have improved since the period to which his data refer. Second, he considers only fixed capital; his measure of it could be better than or inferior to book value (used in tables 2-17 and 2-19); his adjustment to installed horsepower figures to obtain total fixed capital may have overstated the fixed capital of large plants relative to small ones. His exclusion of working capital is a problem, although it would be expected to bias his estimates in favor of larger plants since their ratio of working capital to total capital tends to be higher than those of SMI. Furthermore, he did not have data on costs other than labor (for example, rent, interest, professional services, and the like); these should be subtracted from value added to provide a return to capital figure.

The difference between total factor productivity in LI and SMI could be larger within a representative industry, of course, if large plants dominate the industries where total factor productivity is low and small plants dominate where it is high, so that aggregation tends to make SMI look more efficient relative to LI. A comparison of estimates of total factor productivity by industrial branch in 1969 with the data in table 2-9 on the sector composition of SMI and LI employment suggests that the aggregation effect is not large. For the 1969 estimates, see Albert Berry, "A Descriptive History of Industrialization in Colombia," in *Essays on Industrialization in Colombia.*

16. As discussed in the previous section, the true differential may be small in our samples if product or input price differentials create a downward bias in our SBC estimates for small firms in comparison with large firms. But this same bias would probably also appear in the aggregate data.

17. These differentials make no allowance for the composition of the labor force; we do not have such information on an industry-by-industry basis.

18. As described in the methodological appendix, TEIs in the metal products sector were calculated with value added as output and labor and capital as inputs. In the food sector, two calculations were made, one using value added to measure output and the other using physical production. The latter is used in the analysis of this section, but since data on physical output were not available for potato chip purchases, the analysis is restricted to cheese and guava paste. Differences in input prices across firms (which, however, we could not measure well enough to incorporate in our methodology) seem to have distorted the value added figures to such an extent that the regression results were implausible. In using physical production as the measure of output, it would have been desirable to have materials in addition to labor and capital as inputs in the calculation of TEIs. But we do not have accurate measures of material inputs and so have used only labor and capital. We believe that the ratio of material inputs to output is quite stable across firms, however, so the failure to include them explicitly may not have affected the results much.

19. The ratio of the standard deviation of observed TEI to its mean is 0.48 for agricultural implements and sprayers; 0.63 for stoves, ovens, and integrated kitchens; and 0.42 for other agricultural capital goods. In the food processing sample, it is 0.42 for guava paste and 0.56 for cheese.

20. Since quantity of production rather than value added was the output variable in this industry, TEI may be less well measured than in the metalworking industry, and its role in explaining the variance of PBC may be understated here.

21. The above observations hold without serious modification for EBC and SBC as well as for PBC.

22. More unambiguously exogenous in the sense that there is relatively little chance that any statistical relation with the BC ratios would involve causation from the ratios to the entrepreneurial characteristics.

23. The type of technology selected is, as we see below, related to the entrepreneur's level of education; sources of finance may be related to it as well. In addition, effects may be missed by the lack of interactive terms in our regressions. When PBC is regressed only on entrepreneurial variables, however, their coefficients and levels of significance tend not to differ much from those in our full regressions of tables 3-9 and 3-10; thus such "indirect" effects may not be very important. As noted earlier, because of the small size of our samples and some measurement problems, we could not test a simultaneous equations model of the kind that one would expect to be relevant in this context.

24. That is, if one were to accept the early version of the human capital model, as expounded, for example, by Gary S. Becker in *Human Capital* (New York: Columbia University Press, 1964).

25. If Mohan's recent income-generating function is used, it appears that in the Bogotá labor market in general (that is, all occupations), a person with university training (and years of experience equal to the average for entrepreneurs with university training in the sample) would earn 2.2 times that of a person with primary education and with years of experience equal to the average for entrepreneurs with primary education in the sample. (For persons with primary schooling, we impose the condition that their predicted income could not be less than that of a number of the entrepreneurs with primary education who were previously skilled workers; it seemed implausible that they should earn less than this.) Since the number of years of experience tends to be higher for entrepreneurs with primary schooling than for those with university education, the differential is smaller than the average gap in the earnings of persons with the two levels of education. If Mohan's specification is inaccurate, a better estimate might be on the order of 3:1. (See Rakesh Mohan, *The Determinants of Labor Earnings in Developing Metropolises: Estimates from Bogotá and Cali, Colombia*, World Bank Staff Working Paper 498 [Washington, D.C., 1981].)

26. Even if our implicit assumption (used in our benchmark estimates of returns to entrepreneurial labor inputs) that entrepreneurs are typical of their education and experience groups in the population is substantially wide of the mark, this result would be unlikely to change. The coefficient for "university" in the sector regression for metalworking (table 3-9) is below that for "primary schooling," but that regression holds constant such things as skills, which are affected by the level of education.

27. These associations between education of entrepreneurs and measures of economic success (PBC and TEI) show up in essentially the same way in our regressions where a number of other variables are held constant. In the regressions for the metalworking industry, the coefficients of the dummies for primary and university education are positive and significant (the base is secondary educa-

tion); where PBC is the dependent variable, they are 0.788 and 0.565, respectively. In our calculation of the BCs, the entrepreneur's time is costed differently by level of education, in accordance with the predictions of Mohan's income-generating function. Thus, if education and years of experience paid off exactly as much when applied to the task of entrepreneurship as when applied to all activities in general, and if their effects were picked up in the coefficients of the education dummies (and not in the coefficients of other possibly related variables such as the entrepreneur's skills), the coefficients of the primary- and university-education dummies would be zero. Under the assumptions just mentioned, positive dummies signify that these two levels are associated with higher BCs than is secondary education, after the different "opportunity costs" of persons with these various levels of education are taken into account.

Neither the figures presented in table 3-5 nor the regressions constitute a test of the rate of return to education for entrepreneurs or for persons who might become entrepreneurs. It is evident that entrepreneurs with all three levels of education earn more than other persons with similar education and experience (table 3-5). The figures in table 3-5 and the regression results suggest that secondary schooling pays off well in food processing but not at all in metalworking; university education pays off well in metalworking but does so in food processing only if primary rather than secondary education is the alternative. One cannot do more than indicate these possibilities without more intensive analysis than we have been able to do. It is probable that some of the income differences associated with education (table 3-5) are due to related factors, such as good contacts or native ability. Our equations include other variables (for example, entrepreneur's skills and type of technology) through which level of education may be working, but the present study has not been designed primarily to measure the returns to education for entrepreneurs, and our data could not support the analytical effort that would be required.

28. The two firms with entrepreneurs whose main skill is only in production have the highest indicators; although this contrasts with the situation in the metalworking sector, the small size of the sample precludes drawing any inferences.

29. In each industry entrepreneurs with a combination of production and administrative skills do a little better, according to the regression, than those with administrative skills only, but the difference is not statistically significant.

30. This is also the case for the way in which skills were attained. Among small metalworking firms, entrepreneurs who acquired their skills working in other firms had on the average lower TEIs and BCs than those who went to a training institution or to a university. Among larger firms there is no significant difference by source of the entrepreneur's skills. Large firms tend to be older, so the owners are survivors who have had a chance to overcome many initial difficulties by learning on the job.

31. Interviews with people at a number of Argentinian firms that have gone through similar generational changes also showed significant improvements in the organization of the firm when the better-educated second generation reached management positions. See Mariluz Cortes, "Argentina: Technical Development and Technology Exports to Other LDCs," World Bank, Development Economics Department, Washington, D.C., March 1978; processed.

32. Other technological variables are associated with PBC and TEI when analyzed in isolation but lack explanatory power when included in the regressions with other independent variables. For example, although mechanical firms that produce in series have a higher average TEI (0.66) than firms that produce in batches or units (0.51), when we include this variable in the regressions together with level of technological sophistication and other explanatory variables, its coefficient becomes insignificant. Similarly, firms with low or high process diversification (that is, few or many stages of production, here defined as 1 to 3 stages and 7 to 9 stages, respectively) have a lower average TEI (0.47 and 0.52, respectively) than those ranking in the middle in this respect (0.64). Firms producing to order have lower TEIs (0.47) than those that produce for stocks (0.74). Although most firms that have casting facilities complain of low utilization rates, the average TEI of these firms is slightly above the average of firms without casting facilities. Among food firms, those with low product diversification have higher average TEIs (0.62 on the average) than firms with high product diversification (0.42).

33. Firms with higher PBCs do not on the average use more sophisticated technology (table 3-8). Higher technical efficiency *is* associated with higher technical sophistication in the food processing sector, except among the highest TEI firms. In the metalworking sector the pattern is less clear.

34. Our multiple regression analysis detected no relation (either linear or quadratic) between the capital-labor ratio and the measures of economic success. But one would have to use more complicated specifications, including interactive terms, to test its effects properly. Our sample sizes were too small to permit such analysis.

35. The ratio of working capital to total capital, which is 0.43 for the mechanical sample as a whole, is only 0.34 for firms with less than 10 workers and rises beyond 0.50 for the largest categories (table 3-19). The pattern is the opposite in food processing.

36. Our interview data revealed this pattern for some firms; our cross-sectional data, while consistent with the pattern, do not prove that it is the sequence followed in the *typical* firm. The lower K/L of firms 6–15 years old in comparison with younger firms could be due to a "cohort effect." Capital was scarcer when they started, and this could explain the fact that they are still less capital-intensive than other firms. Furthermore, it is true (table 3-17) that firms with the least capital also tend to have low K/L ratios.

37. For a detailed account of how the market for secondhand equipment works in Colombia, see Mariluz Cortes and Ashfaq Ishaq, "The Market of Secondhand Equipment in Colombia," World Bank, Development Economics Department, Washington, D.C., 1979; processed.

38. The simple correlation between the percentage of equipment that is secondhand and PBC was +0.01 in the mechanical sector and −0.17 in the food sector. The corresponding correlations with TEI were +0.05 and +0.01, respectively.

39. The cross-sectional data of table 3-23 and the regression results of table 3-24 do not prove that the typical cohort of firms follows this sequence. The high share for firms 1–5 years old could be supply-related—as a result of the large amounts of secondhand equipment on the market rather than the high demand

of young firms. But our interviews pointed to extensive recourse of new firms to this market as a general phenomenon, not a peculiarity of the past few years.

40. It could, of course, be argued that the small price differentials associated with quality accurately reflect consumer preferences, which put little weight on health risks that are not generally understood.

41. The coefficients of the dummy for price lower than that of competitors and that for price higher than that of competitors sum to about 0.8–1.0 in most of the regressions tried. This means that between these two conditions value added is predicted to change by about 50–60 percent (mean value added is about 1.7). Since a 1 percent change in product price implies a roughly 0.6 percent change in value added, the underlying product price change between these two cases would be about 15 percent.

42. The absence of a statistical relation between TEI and labor turnover may reflect a problem in our proxy, which was based on the share of workers having been with the firm for various periods of time (see the glossary). The measure would tend to produce an upward bias in the turnover for firms whose labor forces had risen quickly since many of them could not have been with the firm for long.

43. Our figures for the cost of borrowed funds are approximations that do not adequately reflect differences across firms. (Although firms provided illustrative data on interest rates, these were not full enough to indicate accurate firm-specific costs of borrowed capital.) We have costed all borrowed funds of a given firm at the estimated average interest rate of that firm's main source of borrowed funds. These rates were 12 percent for moneylenders and suppliers, 8 percent for private banks, 4 percent for public banks, and 1 percent for self-finance. For these calculations we also assumed that the composition of funds by source over the previous three to four years is the same as the composition of the stock of capital. The difficulties of measuring average capital cost in the conceptually desirable way may contribute to its lack of statistical association with PBC.

We did experiment with the average cost of capital but, perhaps not surprisingly in view of the associated measurement problems and the fact that marginal cost may be more relevant than average cost, it had little explanatory power, particularly for the food firms. In fact, the PBC is positively associated with the cost of the credit, just as it is among firms that rely on private bank credit (the most expensive source except for moneylenders), public bank credit (intermediate cost), and own funds exclusively (the cheapest).

44. Our estimates of this share are based on sources of funds over the three or four years prior to our surveys. Since loans are even less important at the start, our figures are likely to underestimate slightly the share of self-financed capital in the total capital stock.

45. The simple correlation of the share of investment that is self-financed and firm size is −0.525 (significant at the 0.001 confidence level) and that with firm age is −0.298 (significant at the 0.041 level).

46. The simple correlation of the share of investment that is self-financed and firm size is −0.154 (significant at 0.111); that with age is a statistically insignificant 0.094.

47. This result cannot be generalized to other industrial sectors with quite different technologies.

4

The Creation and Growth of Small and Medium Establishments

The rapid growth of SMI production and employment in Colombia during the late 1960s and the 1970s reflects the high returns to SMI that we documented in chapter 2 for the sector as a whole and in chapter 3 for the metalworking and food processing industries. In this chapter we turn to the growth process of SMI, examining features of the evolution of firms and plants—such as their growth or decline and changes in technologies and products—and the relation of the development of SMI to the dynamics of manufacturing as a whole.

The contribution of small firms to the industrialization process cannot be properly evaluated without some knowledge of the way in which these firms grow, especially since they are sometimes thought to suffer from efficiency disadvantages by comparison with larger ones.[1] The capacity to grow may signal an ability to compete successfully; alternatively, it may suggest that efficiency, although not yet very high, will increase in time. If large firms tended to become less dynamic or were less inclined to expand employment over time, a vigorous SMI sector would be all the more important. It could create desirable competition for large firms, contribute to output and employment, and lay the foundations for the large firms of the future.

Later sections of this chapter discuss the dynamics of SMI plants in the metalworking and food processing industries together with more general quantitative evidence on the growth and retrenchment of manufacturing plants in Colombia. First, however, we examine the central player in the SMI drama, the emerging entrepreneur.

The SMI Entrepreneur

The classic entrepreneur of the conventional theory of the firm is a risk-taker and innovator who organizes the various factors of production in pursuit of profits. This picture fits the SMI entrepreneur in Colombia rather well. Small firms do not have the many layers of authority found in large industry. The entrepreneur is sometimes a worker himself and is usually in close touch with the production process. In short, he is at the center of the economic activity carried out by the small or medium enterprise.

Unlike their counterparts in LI, entrepreneurs in SMI firms tend to handle all aspects of their businesses—providing capital, overseeing operations, and often participating in the production process. A 1972 survey by the Corporación Financiera Popular (CFP) reported that entrepreneurs owned more than half of the capital in about two-thirds of the SMI firms surveyed and exercised tight control over day-to-day operations and strategic decisions.[2] In our surveys of metalworking and food processing firms, more than one-third of the former and nearly half of the latter had only one owner (although some firms had nonworking partners; see table 4-1). Half of the metalworking units surveyed and two-thirds of the food firms were run by only one partner. This tendency was most marked among the smaller firms, more than 70 percent of which were run by one person. SMI entrepreneurs thus tend to be directly involved in all aspects of the business: in the smaller firms, the owners not only control the business but are also directly involved in production activities (see table 4-2).

The rapid expansion of SMI in Colombia, especially during the 1970s, implies a correspondingly rapid increase in the number of entrepreneurs. The roughly 20,000–25,000 small and medium manufacturing enterprises in existence in 1978 represented an increase of several thousand over the total a decade earlier. Among the phenomena helping to explain the recent dynamism of small industry is an expanding supply of entrepreneurial talent. It is interesting to speculate whether the observed expansion in the number of entrepreneurs was due mainly to an increase in the supply of entrepreneurial skills in general or to a higher payoff to the exercise of given entrepreneurial skills. We shall return to this point

Table 4-1. *Ownership of Small and Medium Metalworking and Food Processing Firms, by Size*
(percent)

Firm size (number of workers)	One owner	More than one owner	Family partners	Working partners[a]	Number of firms
Metalworking firms					
1–10	69.2	30.8	30.8	23.1	13
11–20	47.1	52.9	52.9	47.1	17
21+	20.8	79.2	64.6	58.3	48
All	34.6	65.4	56.4	50.0	78
Food processing firms					
1–15	77.3	22.7	22.7	22.7	22
16+	15.8	84.2	68.4	47.4	19
All	48.8	51.2	43.9	34.1	41

a. That is, someone other than the respondent was also working in the business.

Table 4-2. *Entrepreneur's Main Tasks in Small and Medium Metalworking and Food Processing Firms, by Size*
(percent)

Entrepreneur's main tasks	Size of metalworking firms (number of workers)				Size of food processing firms (number of workers)		
	1–10	11–20	21+	All	1–15	16+	All
Administration and sales	7.7	36.3	39.6	33.3	23.8	50.0	35.9
Production control	0	11.8	4.2	5.1	4.8	11.1	7.7
Administration, production control, and design	38.5	11.8	35.4	30.8	0	0	0
Administration, production control, and sales	53.8	41.2	16.7	28.2	38.1	33.3	35.9
Production control and sales	0	0	4.2	2.6	33.3	5.6	20.5
Number of firms	13	17	48	78	21	18	39

later; the rest of this section discusses some of the characteristics of SMI entrepreneurs in Colombia.

Small and medium firms act as a channel for new entrants into the entrepreneurial class in Colombia, mobilizing talents that might otherwise have relatively little chance to emerge.[3] Some of these entrepreneurs eventually contribute to the large-scale sector if their firms grow or if—as is less likely—they later manage a large establishment. Unlike the leaders of large industrial and commercial concerns, many of whom are groomed and educated for their roles, those who run SMI businesses usually have to prove themselves in the competitive context of the market before their position is secure. If the metal and food sectors are representative, in recent years new SMI entrepreneurs have tended to come from more humble social strata than the traditional sources of such individuals. The Colombian experience thus bears out the proposition, noted in chapter 1, that small enterprises expand the entrepreneurial class and enhance the management skills of the population.

Entrepreneurs in small-scale industry typically come from middle-income backgrounds; a few have low-income origins and a larger minority come from well-to-do families. Entrepreneurs in medium industry are relatively high on the income and education scale, while entrepreneurs in large industry are, of course, at the top of it. In CFP's 1972 survey, more than one-quarter of the firms with fewer than 20 workers were run by entrepreneurs who had previously been either self-employed or blue-collar workers in manufacturing; in firms with more than 50 workers, this share was about 9 percent. Fifteen and 32 percent, respectively, of the entrepreneurs running firms in these two size groups had owned businesses previously; less than 10 and more than 20 percent, respectively, had previously worked as professionals (table 4-3; figures cited in the text exclude firms whose entrepreneurs had no previous job or their previous job was unknown). The metal products sector appears to be particularly accessible to former blue-collar workers; in our 1977 sample, nearly two-thirds of the owners of firms with less than 20 workers had previously been production workers (table 4-4); only 8 percent of entrepreneurs with firms of 40 workers or more had this kind of experience, and none of those with firms of 60 or more workers had it.

Entrepreneurs in middle-size metalworking firms, as in other industries, come from diverse backgrounds: some had previously been owners of firms; others had been managers and administrators or independent professionals or had previously worked in their fathers' firms. Relatively few owners of small food processing firms are former production workers (17 percent); higher proportions had previously been farmers or salesmen of agricultural products (22 and 39 percent, respectively, in firms with 15 workers or less). As in the metalworking sector, several owners of larger food processing firms had previously been managers or administrators. The two sectors differ sharply in the degree to which

Table 4-3. *Previous Occupation of Entrepreneurs*
in 195 CFP Client Firms, by Size
(percent)

Entrepreneur's previous occupation	Size of firm (number of workers)				
	1–9	10–19	20–49	50+[a]	All
Employee in industry					
White collar	6.3	15.6	17.7	12.5	13.3
Blue collar	12.5	2.2	3.2	0.0	4.6
Independent worker					
in industry	20.8	11.1	11.3	7.5	12.8
Entrepreneur	14.6	11.1	16.1	27.5	16.9
Employee or self-					
employed in commerce	14.6	26.7	16.1	15.0	17.9
Public sector employee					
(nonprofessional)	6.2	4.4	3.2	0.0	3.6
Professional[b]					
Employed	4.2	6.7	12.9	12.5	9.7
Independent	2.1	4.4	6.5	5.0	4.6
Other	6.2	6.7	4.8	0.0	4.6
First job or no information	12.5	11.1	8.1	15.0	12.3
Number of firms	48	45	62	40	195

a. Of these 40 firms, 27 had less than 100 workers.

b. It is unclear from the source whether some of these individuals were in the manufacturing sector.

Source: CFP, *Diagnóstico de la Pequeña y Mediana Industria y Bases para una Política de Fomento y Desarrollo en Colombia* (Bogotá, 1972), p. 31.

Table 4-4. *Previous Occupation of Entrepreneurs in Small and Medium Metalworking Firms, by Size*
(percent)

Entrepreneur's previous occupation	Firm size (number of workers)				
	1–10	*11–20*	*21–40*	*41+*	*All*
Production worker					
Engineer or technician	0	0	22.7	12	10.5
Skilled worker	69.2	56.2	36.4	8	36.8
Owner of enterprise					
Production and repair	16.4	6.2	13.6	16	13.2
Commercial firm	0	6.2	9.1	16	9.2
Worked in father's firm					
or this is first occupation	7.7	6.2	9.1	16	10.5
Manager, administrator, or					
salesman	7.7	18.7	4.5	28	15.8
Independent professional		6.2	4.5	4	3.9
Number of firms	13	16	22	25	76

skills acquired in earlier jobs in larger firms are put to work by SMI entrepreneurs. This suggests that the argument in favor of protecting infant industry (on the grounds that generating skills in this way is important) may be more valid for one industry than for another.

The occupation of the entrepreneur's father is another indicator of the different social origins of owners of small and large enterprises. In the metalworking sector, the blue-collar background of many owners of small enterprises might lead one to think that a large proportion of them had come from working-class urban families or from small farms and rural tenant families. Apart from very small firms of less than 10 workers, however, in which at least 3 of 12 entrepreneurs did have fathers who were workers or employees, few fathers appear to have been employed solely in the urban wage labor force (although some might have been thus employed at some time). Nearly one-quarter of the fathers were engaged in agriculture; given the high level of education of entrepreneurs in larger firms of more than 40 workers (table 4-5), the fathers of such entrepreneurs who are described as "farmers" can be expected to be fairly affluent landowners, whereas the fathers of some smaller-scale entrepreneurs may be small farmers or tenants. Another quarter of the fathers were engaged in commerce. The fathers of still another quarter of these metalworking industry entrepreneurs were themselves owners of enterprises, more than half of which were metalworking firms. A low proportion of fathers were employees of any sort (9 percent); the rest were self-employed in commerce, agriculture (some possibly as paid laborers at some time), and other sectors.

Table 4-5. *Formal Education of Entrepreneurs in Small
and Medium Metalworking Firms, by Size*
(percent)

Level of education	Firm size (number of workers)					
	1–10	*11–20*	*21–40*	*41–60*	*61+*	*All*
Primary						
Incomplete	15.4	17.6	9.1	0	0	9.1
Complete	38.5	23.5	27.3	7.1	0	20.8
Secondary						
Incomplete	15.4	5.9	9.1	7.1	9.1	9.1
Complete	23.1	17.6	22.7	14.3	27.3	20.8
University	0	23.5	31.8	64.3	63.6	35.1
Technical	7.7	11.8	0	7.1	0	5.2
Number of firms	13	17	22	14	11	77

Fewer entrepreneurs in the food sector have fathers who were, or are, entrepreneurs themselves.[4] There is no clear relation between a father's occupation and current firm size, although it is true that the entrepreneurs of 4 of the 9 metalworking firms with more than 60 workers had fathers who were themselves manufacturing entrepreneurs. In the food sector, where nearly 70 percent of all entrepreneurs' fathers were in agriculture, this proportion approached 90 percent for the fathers of small entrepreneurs with firms of up to 15 workers; in the case of larger firms, the figure fell to 40–50 percent.

The relatively high economic status of entrepreneurs is also evident from the fact that about one-third of those sampled had other businesses. In the metalworking sector, 25 percent of the owners of firms with 1–20 workers and two-thirds of those with more than 60 workers had other businesses. The high proportion among owners of larger firms may indicate that they come from families with entrepreneurial traditions or that they believe in spreading their risks.

Consistent with the different social origins of entrepreneurs in smaller and larger firms, their levels of formal education increase markedly with firm size. In CFP's 1972 sample, the share of entrepreneurs with no more than primary education fell from 23 percent in establishments with less than 10 workers to 3.7 percent in those of 50–99 workers, while the share with at least some university education rose from 16.7 percent to 40.7 percent. In our sample of metalworking firms, 47 percent of owners of firms with less than 20 workers had only primary schooling, whereas nearly all of those who owned firms with 40 workers or more had at least attended high school, and nearly two-thirds had been to university (table 4-5). The pattern is similar in the food sector.[5] Although entrepreneurs in medium-size establishments in our sample are relatively well educated, they are distinctly less so than those in large industry. In Lipman's 1962 survey of 61 Bogotá industrialists affiliated with the Asociación Nacional de Industriales (ANDI), 52 percent had university training, 46 percent secondary, and only 2 percent primary.[6]

In the case of metalworking, the changes in the origins and characteristics of entrepreneurs over time may reflect the historical evolution of the sector and the policies followed by the Colombian government. The oldest firms in the sample (twelve units were established before 1952) were created when this industry was still very underdeveloped in Colombia; half of them were set up by workers who had acquired their skills by repairing imported products. Following this initial period, the skilled blue-collar group seems to have played a relatively minor role in the founding of firms until the late 1960s. At that time there was a new upsurge in the establishment of small firms by skilled workers—firms that are today successfully competing with larger and older entities. Several factors seem to have contributed to this development, most of them consequences of the relative maturity achieved by the sector fifteen to twenty years after its inception. The most important of these causal factors are the accumulation of personal savings and severance payments (*cesantías*), which could be used as start-up capital by workers; the accumulation of skills in the labor force through the work of the Servicio Nacional de Aprendizaje (SENA) and on-the-job training; the development of a local secondhand equipment market; falling real wages that led workers to seek higher earnings as independent producers; and the expansion of the market for some products, an expansion that was itself a consequence of the mechanization of agriculture and the growth of construction activity.[7]

The Founding of Small Enterprises

Our findings for metalworking and food processing strongly suggest that the creation of small manufacturing firms in these two industries has been essentially a result of entrepreneurial effort and resource mobilization; neither the credit system nor government programs appear to have played a significant role. In this sense the Colombian experience appears to be quite typical of developing countries, as noted in chapter 1.

The initial capital for most Colombian SMIs comes from personal savings (listed as sources by 80–90 percent of firms in the CFP sample and our own). The relative unimportance of bank loans is striking; less than 14 percent of firms included in the CFP sample and less than 10 percent of those in our two samples made use of them. Accumulated severance pay is important, especially in enterprises established by production workers;

it was a source of initial capital for nearly 80 percent of such cases in our samples. The significance of these payments for capital accumulation stems from the fact that (other than some housing credits) workers cannot collect them until they leave their jobs. In fact, nearly two-thirds of the metalworking firms that started with fewer than 8 workers were set up with the help of severance payments, usually supplemented by savings and sometimes by family loans or supplier or bank credits (see table 4-6); by contrast, only 2 out of 12 firms that started with more than 20 workers used severance payments as part of their initial capital.

Although skilled workers rely especially heavily on severance payments for initial capital, some managers also do so, as do some persons who had previously combined management of their own manufacturing or commercial enterprises with a job in a larger firm. In the food sector, where fewer entrepreneurs have previously been blue-collar workers, severance payments are a relatively unimportant source of initial investment (only 3 of 27 firms used them); two-thirds of the firms in our sample had been set up using a combination of personal savings and family loans.

To judge from our sample of metalworking firms, starting a small enterprise requires relatively little capital. The 41 firms for which data on initial capital stock were available had an average of 35 workers and a capital of 8 million 1977 pesos at the time of the survey. These firms had

Table 4-6. *Main Sources of Initial Investment for Small and Medium Metalworking Firms, by Size*
(percent)

Main sources of initial investment	Initial size of firm (number of workers)			
	1–7	8–20	21+	All
Previous business				
Sale of business	16.7	12.0	8.3	13.2
Inheritance	3.2	16.0	8.3	8.8
Savings and transfer of assets[a]	0	4.0	8.3	2.9
Own resources				
Savings and family loans	19.4	28.0	58.3	29.4
Severance and savings	38.7	32.0	0	29.4
Own resources and credit				
Suppliers, savings, and severance	12.9	8.0	16.7	11.8
Institutional credit, savings, and severance	9.7	0	0	4.4
Number of firms	31	25	12	68

a. Transfer of resources from another firm owned by the entrepreneur.

started out with an average of 14 workers (median, 8–9 workers) and 2.6 million pesos of capital (median, 0.55 million pesos). Firms starting with 7 workers or less (60 percent of all firms) had an average initial investment of only half a million 1977 pesos (about US$13,500 at the official exchange rate for 1977). Those starting with 8 to 20 workers had an initial investment eight times higher. Former skilled workers started their businesses with a lower average initial investment (336,000 pesos; see table 4-7) than did other groups. These relatively modest initial investments are within the reach of skilled workers who earn the equivalent of 250–350 1977 pesos a day and have accumulated severance payments for five to ten years.

Former technicians and persons who had previously run other enterprises also started with low average investment levels. Many of these entrepreneurs had also originally been blue-collar workers, but had previously run a small enterprise that they sold or that went bankrupt before they formed their present firm. As might be expected, the initial investment was much higher in firms whose entrepreneur had a managerial, professional, or trade background—the average was in fact fifteen times that of firms started by former skilled workers. The highest initial investment was undertaken by three firms whose owners had not worked before but who were college graduates with substantial family resources. Education (which reflects family income relatively accurately) bears a close relation to the level of initial investment. The seventeen entrepreneurs with a college education had an average initial investment of 5.2 million pesos; the figure for entrepreneurs with secondary schooling was 550,000 pesos; and for those with primary education, only 316,000 pesos.[8] There is some tendency for persons of a given educational level to invest more if they acquire a firm when they are relatively old. This tendency does not hold for entrepreneurs who have completed college, perhaps because in their case the capital market (or parental wealth) makes the process of accumulation through personal saving less relevant.

Entrepreneurs who set up firms with relatively meager assets (for example, former blue-collar workers) tend also to have relatively few workers and relatively low sales (table 4-7), but the modesty of their initial efforts is most evident in their limited capital investment. Entrepreneurs with sales, management, or professional backgrounds started with an average of about 17 workers, compared with 10 in the case of those who had formerly been blue-collar workers; by contrast, the former group's reported capital was fifteen times higher than that of the latter. These differences suggest that, even when a binding capital constraint exists, a small business can be established with a strikingly low level of capital coupled with a high labor-capital ratio, but that when capital is available a substantially more capital-intensive enterprise will result.

Table 4-7. *Average Initial Investment, Employment, and Sales of Small and Medium Metalworking Firms, by Entrepreneur's Previous Job*
(monetary amounts in thousands of 1977 pesos)

Entrepreneur's previous job	Average initial investment				Average initial level of employment		Average initial sales	
	Total investment	Fixed assets	Working capital	Number of firms	Number of workers	Number of firms	Sales	Number of firms
None	10,256	2,036	8,220	3	13	4	6,678	4
Father's firm	3,452	1,051	2,162	2	30	5	23,803	5
Mechanic	336	244	92	16	10	26	3,414	27
Independent professional	4,238	2,418	1,819	5	14	6	9,675	6
Technician	783	370	412	4	9	6	3,327	6
Sales, management	6,106	3,044	3,182	6	19	16	8,312	17
Owner of an enterprise	442	238	204	5	9	8	3,650	9
All	2,591	1,101	1,495	41	14	71	6,627	74

Note: Initial labor, initial capital, and initial sales do not necessarily correspond to the first year of the firm's existence, since in a few cases the present owner bought the firm and reported values for the time of purchase.

The severance payments and family savings that form the initial investment in most small metalworking enterprises are used to acquire some basic equipment (for instance, a welding machine or a secondhand lathe) and some working capital. In firms with little initial capital (less than 1 million 1977 pesos, that is, about US$27,000) about one-third of this investment was in the form of working capital (table 4-8). In firms starting with larger initial investments, working capital equaled or exceeded fixed capital. This seems to indicate that fixed capital indivisibilities (albeit at low dollar levels) force many small firms to start with the barest minimum of working capital.

The use of secondhand equipment can be especially helpful for a small firm starting out with a low initial investment, but its use is not limited to this group. Partly because of the chronic scarcity of foreign exchange until the 1970s, firms of all sizes typically acquired a large proportion of their equipment secondhand. In each of our SMI samples taken in the late 1970s, this proportion amounted to about one-quarter of the firms' equipment.[9] Metalworking and food processing firms that were five years old or less started out with high average proportions of secondhand equipment (37 percent and 40 percent, respectively), some of which would be replaced by new equipment as the firms grew over time. This extensive use of secondhand equipment among the newer SMI firms in our samples may reflect an increase in the number of traders in secondhand equipment over the previous five years or so. Nearly 80 percent of the twenty-four traders in secondhand equipment we interviewed had been established only since 1970. As the local market for secondhand equipment grew, the risks and costs associated with importing and using such equipment could be expected to fall. Colombian reconstructors of secondhand equipment provide credits and guarantees not provided by dealers in this kind of equipment in developed countries.

The increasing availability of skilled *mecánicos* (machine operators) at relatively low wages has also contributed to the establishment of local importers and reconstructors of used equipment—a development that

Table 4-8. *Average Total, Fixed, and Working Capital of Small and Medium Metalworking Firms, by Initial Capital Stock*
(thousands of 1977 pesos)

Initial capital stock	Total capital	Fixed capital	Working capital	Number of firms
Less than 200	119	73	46	7
201–500	329	199	130	7
501–1,000	738	500	239	6
1,001–5,000	3,359	1,676	1,683	6
5,001+	13,939	4,857	9,082	4
All	2,783	1,146	1,636	30

has in turn lowered the risks and costs associated with the maintenance, repair, and reconstruction of such equipment. Larger firms naturally benefit less from these developments, since they can purchase machinery directly from dealers in the United States or Europe. When they replace their existing machinery with equipment of more modern vintage, however, their old machinery may be bought up by smaller firms. This segment of the secondhand market was also growing in the years immediately before we undertook our survey, as a result of the stimulus to equipment replacement provided by an appreciating exchange rate and falling import tariffs on capital goods.

Both the rising savings potential of the Colombian economy during the 1960s and 1970s and the availability of secondhand machinery, which lowers the costs of initial investment, have made it possible for more and more entrepreneurs to set up their own firms. Another factor that may well have prompted production workers and others to take this step was the stagnation or decline of real wages between the late 1960s and the late 1970s. Between 1971 and 1977, the real wages of blue-collar workers in manufacturing fell by 20 percent and those of white-collar workers by 22 percent—in part because wage adjustments lagged behind the accelerating rate of inflation.[10] Entrepreneurs in our metalworking sample reported that the desire for a higher standard of living (mentioned by 83 percent) and the wish to be one's own boss (mentioned by 47 percent) were the two main reasons for establishing their own firms.

The creation since the late 1960s of a number of small metalworking firms owned by skilled workers is a sign of the maturity of the sector, and more specifically of the acquisition of skills that accompany growth in an industry where knowledge about production techniques, product design, and basic management can be acquired in training institutions or through on-the-job experience. In the metalworking sector, the knowledge of operational technology usually promotes understanding of the basic processes and the design technology used.[11] Workers who obtained training from SENA and gained experience working in older firms were later able to start their own businesses by repairing or copying the same items that they were accustomed to producing.[12] Among the metalworking sector entrepreneurs in our sample, the number mentioning previous experience in small or medium firms as a source of skills was nearly twice as large as the number mentioning such experience in large firms. Work in small or medium firms was a particularly important source of skills for persons with primary education, while working in larger firms was relatively important for those with secondary schooling (table 4-9). Persons with primary or secondary schooling are much more likely to describe themselves as self-taught than those with university education.

Table 4-9. *Source of Entrepreneur's Skills, Small and Medium Metalworking Firms, by Entrepreneur's Education*
(percentage reporting each skill)

| Source of entrepreneur's skills | Level of entrepreneur's education | | | | | | |
| | Primary | | | | | | |
	Incomplete	Complete	Both	Secondary	Higher	Technical	All
Working in small or medium firms	100.0	41.2	54.5	42.3	20.0	40.0	38.4
Working in large firms	0	23.5	18.2	38.5	8.0	20.0	21.8
Apprentice in a training institution	20.0	5.9	9.1	28.0	0	100.0	17.9
Self-taught	80.0	76.7	77.3	60.0	12.0	20.0	46.1
Number of firms	5	17	22	26	25	5	78

Note: Some entrepreneurs indicate more than one source.

The relative importance of different sources of entrepreneurial skills may have changed over time. Most of the twelve entrepreneurs in the oldest metalworking firms (those that had been in existence for twenty-six years and more) had acquired their skills in small and medium enterprises (probably through repair activities); members of the group also described themselves as self-taught. For enterprises founded between 1953 and 1973, these two sources of skills seemed to be much less important; university courses were apparently much more relevant. For the eleven entrepreneurs with firms that were five years old or less, however, experience in small and medium firms once again seemed to be a major source of skills (table 4-10). This could be a simple consequence of the growing stock of SMI firms in the ten to fifteen years prior to the survey. Furthermore, workers in smaller firms may now find it easier to become familiar with all kinds of production processes, to participate in activities such as the procurement of raw materials and equipment, and to deal directly with clients and suppliers. Information from our surveys suggested that these experiences are useful to workers who become independent entrepreneurs. We found that many workers from medium and small firms who set up their own shops had found clients among customers of their former employers and also obtained suppliers' credits from suppliers whom they had known in their previous jobs.

The competitive and growing market in Colombia has favored the successful establishment of small metalworking firms in the ten years prior to the survey. Demand for most of the products included in our sample grew substantially during this period. The mechanization of the agricultural sector stimulated the demand for agricultural implements, sprayers, and pumps, while growth in the construction sector expanded the mar-

Table 4-10. *Source of Entrepreneur's Skills, Small and Medium Metalworking Firms, by Size and by Age*
(percentage reporting each skill)

Source of entrepreneur's skills	Firm size (number of workers)			Age of firm			All firms
	1–10	11–40	41+	1–5	6–25	26+	
Work in small or medium firms	46.1	51.3	16.0	63.6	25.5	75.0	39.0
Work in large firms	46.1	24.1	8.0	27.3	18.2	33.3	22.1
Apprentice in training institution	23.1	27.5	4.0	18.2	16.4	25.0	18.2
Self-taught	76.9	41.0	36.0	45.4	36.4	91.7	45.4
University		17.9	48.0	9.1	32.7	0	24.7
Same firm	7.7	15.6	4.0	9.1	7.3	25.0	10.4
Correspondence or seminars	30.8	16.1	4.0	18.2	12.7	16.7	14.3
Previous business, friends, and family		12.0		0	3.6	8.3	3.9
Number of firms	13	39	25	11	55	12	77

Note: Some entrepreneurs indicate more than one source.

ket for integrated kitchens. The advertising and distribution efforts of firms established during the 1950s and 1960s also helped to promote demand. By the early 1970s, new small firms were entering markets in which buyers were already familiar with domestically manufactured products. In turn, these small producers were familiar (through their repair activities) with user preferences and needs.

Many of these developments can be illustrated by the evolution of small and medium producers of agricultural implements in the Cali-Palmira region of the Cauca Valley. Until the beginning of the 1970s the market for domestically produced agricultural implements was divided among the four biggest firms, none of which was located in the Cauca Valley: Firm A, established in 1924, had 1,700 workers in 1978; Firm B, established in 1964, had 188 workers in 1978; Firm C, established in 1952, had 83 workers in 1978; and Firm D, established in 1961, had 53 workers in 1978. Each produced a wide range of implements. Competition from small firms started in the early 1970s when several new units established themselves in the Cali-Palmira region—apparently as a result of the decision of an enterprising metal artisan and his brother to produce copies of light tractor-pulled implements similar to those manufactured by Firm A. In the course of four or five years both brothers entered into successive associations with several small repair shops for the production of agricultural implements. For different reasons each association proved to be unstable, but each lasted long enough to create a

group of workers familiar with the production of agricultural implements. At present all the Cali-Palmira producers of agricultural
implements are either former associates of these two brothers or enterprises formed by workers trained by them and some of the former
associates.

Many new small firms have also emerged in the food processing sector
during the past ten years. The original producers of cheese and guava
paste had begun as little more than household operations based on traditional techniques and offering a limited range of products. Industrial
production of cheese was started twenty years ago by European immi-
grants who established the two largest dairy plants in Colombia (which
are not included in our sample). By the early 1970s, newcomers were attracted by the high profits they could obtain by processing a subsidized
raw material, milk. Their entry into the market was facilitated by the previous efforts of the two large firms to develop a market for their products
(cheese, yogurt, and ice cream) and by improved access to technical advice through SENA and the National University.

The fact that the maturing of an industry can create the conditions for
increasing domestic competition even in a highly protected market is
often ignored by analysts of import substitution industrialization. The
factors that permitted the small firms in our samples not only to establish
themselves but also to grow and compete successfully with larger firms
need further examination. One explanation is that the export promotion
measures of 1967 (Decree 444), by encouraging larger firms to shift to
foreign markets to compensate for lost local markets, reduced their incentive to drive small competitors out of the market.[13]

We can only speculate whether industries other than food processing
and metalworking have undergone similar growth processes. The rapid
overall growth of SMI during the 1970s implies that many firms have
been created in a wide variety of manufacturing industries. Since most of
the factors discussed in this section are common to manufacturing as a
whole, it is not unreasonable to hypothesize that they were also important in sectors other than the ones examined in detail here.

The Development of SMI and Its Role in the Growth of Manufacturing

Large numbers of SMI firms have been created since the beginning of the
sector's boom period in the late 1960s. Meanwhile existing SMI firms
have tended to grow quickly, probably at a somewhat more rapid rate
than larger ones. Both of these phenomena have contributed greatly to
aggregate output and employment growth in factory manufacturing.

Available evidence for 1953–78 implies that the typical plant or firm that survives will grow over time, whether growth is measured by output, employment, or capital stock. DANE's factory manufacturing employment index, which is based on monthly reporting from the same sample of plants, registered average annual growth rates of 2.5 percent for existing plants during these years. Total factory employment probably rose by more than 5 percent a year (DANE's downward-biased figure is 4.3 percent); it thus seems likely that a healthy share—probably about half—of employment growth resulted from the creation of plants.[14]

DANE's figures suggest that the growth of existing plants can be separated into four fairly distinct phases: rapid growth (averaging 3.7 percent a year) between 1953 and 1960; very slow growth (on the average, 0.76 percent a year) between 1960 and 1968; an upward swing between 1968 and 1974 (with an annual average growth rate of 4.2 percent); and a slowing down between 1974 and 1978 (to an average rate of 1.7 percent a year; see table 4-11). The latter two periods roughly correspond to the years in which SMI expanded most rapidly. DANE's figures for the total growth in factory employment (which take into account the effects of the

Table 4-11. *Annual Growth Rates of Employment in Existing Plants and in Total Factory Manufacturing, 1953-78*
(percent)

Item	1953–60	1960–68	1968–74	1974–78	1953–78
Employment in fixed set of plants covered by DANE's monthly survey					
1. Total	3.68	0.76	4.24	1.70	2.55
2. Blue collar	2.90	0.42	4.02	1.43	2.13
3. White collar	7.75	2.09	5.16	2.45	4.44
Employment in all factory manufacturing					
4. DANE's Annual Survey of Manufactures	4.95	2.10	7.49	2.91	4.33
5. Our estimate	5.68	2.90	7.85[c]	7.62–9.09[c]	5.21–5.44
Estimated employment growth from creation of new plants[a]					
6. Row 4 minus row 1	1.27	1.34	3.25	1.21	1.78
7. Row 5 minus row 1	2.00	2.14	3.61	5.92–7.39	2.66–2.89
Annual growth					
8. GDP[b]	4.42	4.89	6.63	5.53	5.28
9. National income	3.00	5.29	7.96	6.10	5.40

a. Less employment loss because of closings.

b. At market prices.

c. Assumes growth of 8 percent in 1974, from the 1973 figure of table 2-2.

Sources: For rows 1–4, appendix table 23, although for the 1968–74 and 1974–78 estimates in row 4 we raised the 1974 figure by 1,800 workers and the 1978 figure by 23,000 workers to provide a conservative estimate of the effects of the deliberate change in the lower limit of the size range from 5 workers to 10. Row 5 is based on our adjustments to DANE's factory employment figures as presented in Berry, "A Descriptive History," statistical app. table A-130, and table 2-2 of this study.

creation and disappearance of firms) show the same cycles, but our revised estimates (table 4-11, row 5) show rapid growth continuing into the 1974–78 period. Our best estimate of the net growth in employment resulting from the creation of plants, less the disappearance of existing ones, indicates a continuous acceleration; the residual nature of this estimate, however, detracts somewhat from the confidence that can be placed in it, especially for the last subperiod.[15] Even if the net creation figure for 1974–78 (table 4-11) is upward biased, there is little doubt that the creation of plants made a greater contribution to employment growth over 1968–78 than before and that this development was due to the SMI boom.

There is direct evidence of considerable turnover (creation and disappearance) among small factories (and perhaps among medium-size ones as well), although these data are not complete enough to provide accurate estimates. With respect to disappearances, the available statistics seldom distinguish between change of locale, change of ownership, and true disappearance. In any case, within a fairly short span of years a significant proportion of plants can no longer be identified. The analysis of the 1956–71 period by Berry and Pinell-Siles suggests a disappearance rate of at least 3–4 percent a year for plants of 10–99 workers and a likely rate of 10 percent or more for the smallest plants of roughly 5–14 workers.[16]

During the fast growth of 1970–75, new establishments appeared in Bogotá and Cali at quite a high rate; data from DANE's industrial directory imply annual rates of 8.8 percent and 7.4 percent, respectively, which are considerably higher than those in most U.S. cities.[17] Although these figures may be upward biased, because some apparent births may be relocations of one sort or another, net creation must be downward biased by DANE's incomplete coverage of small plants in the 1970s. Disappearance (death) rates were 4.9 percent annually in both Bogotá and Cali; these are close to the rates Lee gives for large U.S. cities (Cleveland, Minneapolis–Saint Paul, Boston, New York, Phoenix, and Los Angeles) and are consistent with Berry and Pinell-Siles's figures for 1967–71. Employment birth and death rates were lower, since the establishments involved were below average in size. Lee defines employment birth rate for a given year as the ratio of employment in plants created that year to total employment at the beginning of the year; the employment death rate is defined in a similar way.[18]

Correlates of Establishment Growth

Employment growth rates vary widely from plant to plant, at least over periods of a few years, and actual falls are frequent. In studying the period of slow growth between 1962 and 1966, Todd found that employment in 4,500 plants rose by less than 1 percent a year, but that among the firms identified in both years about the same number reported increases and decreases in employment. There was a positive association between size and rate of employment growth; plants with less than 25 workers in 1962 did not grow on average over the four years; but plants with 25 workers or more averaged 4.5 percent growth over the four years.[19] Berry and Pinell-Siles report that employment in plants identified in both 1970 and 1975 grew at an annual rate of 3.8 percent.[20] Over this period, total factory employment was probably growing at more than 6 percent a year (table 2-2). Plants of all sizes tended to grow faster in 1970–75 than in 1962–66, and a smaller share suffered sharp declines. In contrast to 1962–66, the average percentage growth in employment during the latter period was faster in smaller plants: it was upward of 25 percent (that is, about 4.8 percent a year) for those that had been in the 10–49 range in 1970 and 17.5 percent (3.3 percent a year) for those that had employed 100 workers or more in 1970. Data from another study covering 1971–78 suggest a slightly greater gap between small and large plants—about 5 percent a year for plants of up to 100 workers and about 3 percent for those with more than 100.[21]

One would expect growth to be more variable in smaller firms, with some growing rapidly and a higher proportion suffering sharper declines than large firms. The data do suggest something of this pattern, although only plants of 100 or more workers seem to be relatively free from sharp fluctuations. In both the 1970–75 and 1962–66 periods the rate of change of employment varied greatly within plant-size categories of up to 100 workers, and very large employment increases (say, 70–80 percent) and very large decreases (say, 40 percent) were fairly frequent. Among plants of 100 workers or more, however, the proportion with falling employment appears to have been small. Since the overall employment increase was small, the share of plants with large employment increases must also have been small and the variance less than for smaller plants.

Between 1962 and 1966, a period of slow total growth in manufacturing, not only was employment growth relatively faster in large existing plants than in small ones, but the growth of average labor productivity in manufacturing as a whole was very rapid—almost 3.3 percent in the factory subsector. During the period of rapid growth between 1970 and 1978, however, employment in smaller plants grew faster than in larger ones, overall factory employment grew faster, and labor productivity grew less rapidly (probably by 1–2 percent a year).[22] There are several possible reasons for these differences. Changes in the industrial composition of growth might be thought to play a part, except that the 1962–66 and 1970–75 patterns are rather similar (although metal products were more important in the latter period). A second possibility is that smaller plants may be able to respond more quickly to new opportunities than larger ones and thus could have fared better under the buoyant conditions of the early 1970s. In addition, small and medium industry may face special problems when foreign exchange is in short supply, as in 1962–66, since the rationing of foreign exchange is likely to favor the larger firms; when there is no shortage, however, access may become more equal and SMI may be better able to grow and prosper.

But perhaps the most likely explanation for the differential growth rates has to do with the nature of Colombia's capital market and the different roles it plays in the development of SMI and LI. The capital market is characterized by such imperfections as interest rate controls, subsidized credit programs, and regulations governing the investment behavior of financial intermediaries. Credit, especially longer-term credit, is scarce because its price is low, but it is more readily available to large firms than to SMI. As a result, SMI relies on self-financing more than LI does.[23] Part of the observed difference in this respect could be a matter of preference, but part of it is undoubtedly due to differential access to credit. When investment funds come largely from past earnings, there is likely to be a substantial acceleration in the growth patterns of firms.[24] SMI's dynamism during the 1970s fits this model in the sense that SMI profits were high (from the late 1960s at least). LI growth rates would be less likely to be sensitive to past profit levels, since it has fairly good access to credit at all times—hence the relatively slower acceleration in LI's growth rate during the 1970s in comparison with the 1960s.

The Growth of Small and Medium Metalworking Firms

Data from our metalworking sample provide more detailed information about the growth patterns of firms than can be obtained from the DANE data discussed above.[25] Reported employment growth was very rapid, averaging about 15.5 percent a year between 1973 and 1977 for firms for which data covering both years are available (table 4-12).[26] Employment also grew rapidly before 1973.[27] When they were founded or taken over by their present management, these firms had an average labor force of 14 workers; at the time of the survey, the average labor force was 34.7 workers. These growth rates are extremely high; either this is an atypical set of firms or the increase in employment is overstated.[28] Even if the figures contain some unexplained upward bias, there is no doubt that on the average these firms grew very fast. Our less reliable data on sales imply a somewhat lower average annual growth rate of 8–11 percent over 1973–

Table 4-12. *Average Annual Growth Rate of Employment*
in a Sample of Metalworking Firms, 1973–77,
by Employment Size in 1973
(percent)

Size in 1973 (number of workers)	1973–77	1973–75	1975–77	Number of observations
1–5	38.3	48.6	28.7	9
6–10	24.5	23.9	25.1	9
11–20	24.0	27.1	21.9	12
21–30	13.3	10.8	15.9	10
31+	10.0	8.2	11.9	11
All	15.4	14.4	16.5	51

Note: The table gives weighted averages across the firms in each category; that is, the growth rate of the total employment of the firms in a given category.

77. The implication of these growth rates of employment and sales taken together—that labor productivity was declining over the four-year period at perhaps 6–7 percent a year—is implausible, so the figures for sales growth should be treated with great caution. In any event, whether the employment data or (as we suspect) the sales data are biased, they both suggest that this set of firms grew very rapidly during the reference period.[29]

As with static indicators such as technical efficiency and BC ratios, our survey data on employment growth rates suggest that they vary widely across firms. Two clearly negative correlates of growth (whether measured by sales, employment, or capital) are a firm's age and size.[30] Between 1973 and 1977 employment grew at about 30 percent a year in firms that were 10 years old or less, at an average of 13 percent in those aged 11–25 years, and at 2.6 percent in the few (only five) aged 26 or older (table 4-13). The negative relation is less systematic for sales, but

Table 4-13. *Average Annual Growth Rate of Employment*
in a Sample of Metalworking Firms, 1973–77, by Age of Firm in 1978
(percent)

Firm's age in 1978 (years)	1973–75	1975–77	1973–77	Number of observations
1–5	32.3	23.8	24.0	11
6–10	39.2	28.0	33.5	11
11–15	9.5	27.9	18.3	9
16–25	12.1	9.4	10.8	15
26+	0.3	4.8	2.6	5
All	14.4	16.5	15.4	51

Note: The table gives weighted averages across the firms in each category.

there is a considerable gap between firms up to 15 years old (for which weighted average annual growth rates fall in the 20–30 percent range) and firms older than 15 (whose average growth was less than 4 percent a year). The 1973–77 employment growth rates of these firms seem reasonably typical. Growth patterns for this and earlier periods suggest annual employment growth rates of around 30 percent in firms up to about 10 years of age, but they are much lower for firms of 20 years or so.

The negative association between growth rate and age of firm may be linked to the tendency for employment to grow faster in the smaller firms in our sample.[31] Thus, when firms are classified by their 1973 employment levels, size and the 1973–77 employment growth rate are negatively related (table 4-12).[32] Since our sample is limited to firms that have remained within the SMI size range, the observed relations between age, size, and growth rates are biased; that is, they differ from the relations that would emerge were one to follow over time a group of firms that had fallen within the SMI size range at some given point in the past. Our sample excludes firms that have gone out of business or that started out in the SMI size range but subsequently exceeded it; these exclusions tend to understate the typical growth performance of older firms and of those in the upper part of the SMI size range.

Despite these biases, the qualitative picture these data present remains valid, at least for this industry.[33] It is a picture of initial rapid growth by young, small firms that have been able to move ahead perhaps because the problems inherent in small size create an incentive to grow or perhaps because the opportunity to grow is most likely to arise for very small firms that have little overall effect on the market. Growth gradually slows as the firm ages and expands, in some cases approaching what one might interpret to be an equilibrium size range.[34] The negative relation between growth and age of firm may be due to associations between age of firm and size, between age and profitability, and between the respective ages of the firm and the entrepreneur. When employment growth over 1973–77 is regressed on age of enterprise, employment in 1973, and the private benefit-cost ratio (in 1977), age of enterprise and number of workers in 1973 are significant with a negative sign at nearly a 95 percent confidence level, whereas the PBC ratio has a positive sign but is not statistically significant.[35] A similar relation emerges in the case of sales.

These results suggest that the pattern of decelerating growth for the typical firm is associated with increasing size, an aging entrepreneur, and a relatively low BC ratio; when age of firm is not accompanied by those conditions, it is not a barrier to growth. Although the private BC ratio or some other indicator of profitability could be an important proximate cause of growth and a good predictor of it, our evidence is not conclusive since our PBC figures refer to 1977, and the growth being analyzed occurred before 1977.[36]

Table 4-14. *Initial Difficulties of Metalworking Firms, by Initial Level of Employment*
(percent)

Initial number of workers	Finding clients	Paying debts	Obtaining raw materials	Finding responsible workers	Technical difficulties	Lack of working capital	Number of observations
1-3	25.0	25.0	37.5	43.8	62.5	68.8	16
4-7	18.8	25.0	56.3	62.5	62.5	56.3	16
8-10	30.0	60.0	40.0	30.0	70.0	30.0	10
11-20	33.3	46.7	40.0	46.7	73.3	26.7	15
21+	28.6	35.7	57.1	50.0	71.4	21.4	14
All	26.8	36.6	46.5	47.9	67.6	42.3	71

Entrepreneur's age is negatively related to growth rates, its coefficient being consistently negative and significant in the presence of other variables; this suggests that older entrepreneurs are less inclined or less able to make their firms grow.[37] A clearer negative effect on sales growth than on employment growth suggests either that older entrepreneurs also have greater difficulty in raising efficiency or that they are less inclined to increase labor productivity by raising the K/L ratio.

New small and medium firms typically face a variety of hurdles that are sometimes reflected in below-average BC ratios. An important issue for policy purposes is whether the efficiency disadvantages of small, young firms are likely to be transitory, either because the firms grow out of them or because they resolve them in other ways. Chapter 3 noted that at the time of the survey many of the small metalworking firms in our sample were characterized by relatively low efficiency and high fixed capital per worker (but relatively low working capital).[38] These firms also tended to charge lower prices than their competitors (although this is a result of deliberate policy and is a problem only in the sense that these firms would have preferred the same market share with higher prices) and faced a number of other difficulties. Some idea of whether these problems can be expected to persist can be gained by considering the process of firm growth and change over time.

Most firms had initial technical difficulties, and nearly half of them had problems in obtaining raw materials, hiring responsible workers, and obtaining enough working capital (table 4-14). Finding clients was a less common problem and did not seem to be associated with the original level of employment or sales. The need to pay debts was cited as an initial difficulty by only one-quarter of the firms starting with 7 workers or less but by nearly half of those starting with 8 or more workers. Problems in obtaining raw materials were not particularly related to initial levels of employment or sales, nor were technical difficulties in finding responsible workers. The only initial difficulty that was especially characteristic of small firms was the lack of working capital.

Some of these initial problems appear to have slowed the growth of firms, but usually for only a few years. The growth of employment did seem slower in firms that had difficulties in finding clients in their early years, but over the longer haul no negative effect is apparent (that is, if one judges by the longer-run growth of older firms that experienced this problem at the start). Many firms with initial difficulties probably went into liquidation, however, and were therefore not caught by our survey. A similar picture holds for firms unable to repay their debts or obtain working capital. The existence of technical difficulties is actually correlated with above-average employment growth in the early years (that is, for firms one to five years old at the time of the survey).

Table 4-15. *Initial Difficulties of Metalworking Firms, by Age of Firm in 1978*
(percent)

Age of firm in 1978 (years)	Finding clients	Paying debts	Obtaining raw materials	Finding responsible workers	Technical difficulties	Lack of working capital	Number of observations
1–5	17.6	52.9	35.3	35.3	41.1	64.7	17
6–10	13.3	20.0	53.3	40.0	60.0	46.7	15
11–15	20.0	10.0	20.0	80.0	70.0	30.0	10
16–25	35.0	30.0	45.0	55.0	85.0	40.0	20
26+	50.0	70.0	70.0	40.0	80.0	40.0	10
All	26.4	36.1	44.4	48.6	66.7	45.8	72

Table 4-16. *Reasons for Design Changes Made by Metalworking Firms in the Four Years Preceding the Survey, by Size of Firm*
(percent)

Size of firm (number of workers)	Main reason for change					Small change	No change	Number of firms
	Improve quality	Meet client's demand	Save labor	Adapt foreign design	Substitute for imported parts			
1–10	43.8	12.5	12.5	0	0	12.5	18.8	16
11–20	55.0	10.0	5.0	0	0	15.0	15.0	20
21–40	56.3	0	6.3	0	0	18.8	18.8	16
41–60	15.4	0	23.1	7.7	0	46.2	7.7	13
61+	7.7	7.7	7.7	7.7	7.7	23.1	38.5	13
All	38.5	6.4	10.3	2.6	1.3	21.8	19.2	78

Our survey suggests that the problems facing new metalworking firms have changed somewhat over time. Finding new clients has been a relatively infrequent problem for firms that began operating after 1963: 17 percent of these firms reported it, compared with 40 percent of older firms (table 4-15). This pattern probably reflects both maturation of the market for mechanical products—which makes it easier to assess markets, locate clients, and so on—and the generally buoyant economic conditions and fast growth of demand in the sector since the mid-1970s. Difficulties in paying debts also declined among new firms until the mid-1970s, but were strikingly high for those firms starting in the five years before the survey was made. Lack of working capital was also cited more frequently. This recent development may be related to the higher-than-average initial investment of firms one to five years old, or perhaps to the changing background of their entrepreneurs. Many of the oldest and the newest firms, both of which had atypically frequent problems with debts, were started by skilled workers. Technical difficulties are less frequent in the case of the newer firms, probably because of accumulated knowledge in the industry as a whole. The high proportion of relatively new firms started by skilled workers may have played a part here, but skilled workers were also prominent as entrepreneurs in the oldest firms, where such difficulties were the norm.

As firms grow older, some of their initial problems seem to resolve themselves. For example, although about 15 percent of all sample firms were currently spending time looking for clients, searches of this kind were more common among younger firms (about one-quarter of those up to ten years old were pursuing such searches compared with 7 percent of older firms); among the newer firms, searches for clients were especially common among middle-size units with 11–40 employees.

Most firms adjust to market conditions over time by making design changes and adding new products. About 80 percent of the sample firms reported design changes (table 4-16), including a majority of each size group; the largest plants (61 workers and up) were the least inclined to do so (61 percent did). The reasons for design changes varied somewhat by size of firm. Whereas 52 percent of firms with less than 40 workers made changes to improve quality, only 11.5 percent of the larger ones did so. Small plants (in this case, those with less than 20 workers) were also more likely to make changes to meet clients' demands and were less likely to make them to save labor. Higher proportions of larger plants made what were characterized as "small changes"; since small plants are usually newer than large ones, they are likely to have had less time to make design changes or to add new products. Meanwhile, more than three-quarters of all firms had added new products; employment grew faster in those that did so than in others, apparently regardless of their initial size.

At the time of the survey, about three-quarters of the capital of smaller firms was self-financed (see table 3-25); this share was probably also high in earlier years. Still, the growth of capital stock appears to have been fastest for small firms; they apparently succeeded in building up capital out of profits or by drawing in new partners. Such a buildup must have loosened the working capital constraint, although it would not have completely removed the constraint since output was growing rapidly.

Measuring Firm Efficiency in a Dynamic Context

Our estimates of static benefit-cost ratios by firm size showed that there was a considerable gap between firms with more than 40 workers and smaller ones (see table 3-2). But the growth rates discussed in this chapter suggest that, if inefficiency is due to the small size or young age of a firm, it may not last for long since a small, young firm may grow or be liquidated. It is useful to illustrate how the policy relevance of the efficiency differentials that exist between firms in different size categories could be affected by the patterns of firm growth.

The simplest such calculation compares a firm that is in the most efficient size category and whose efficiency remains constant in the future with one that is in the smallest category and that grows at the average rate for each size category through which it passes until it reaches the most efficient category.[39] The peak level of social efficiency in our sample of metalworking firms is reached by firms in the category of 41–60 workers, so let us assume that, on the average, no further efficiency gains occur above an employment level of 50 workers. A firm starting out with 3 workers and growing at the size-specific rate shown in table 4-12, column 1 would have an SBC of 1.22 (corresponding to the size category of 1–10 workers) for 4.72 years, an SBC of 1.41 for 3.21 years, an SBC of 1.43 for about 6.65 years, and an SBC of 1.72 for about 3 years (SBC values are taken from table 3-2).[40] The average SBC over these 17.6 years would be 1.42, or about 19 percent below the peak level of 1.73. Given the simplifying assumption that total inputs grow at the same rate as employment, the average SBC weighted by total inputs during each year would be about 1.51, or 14 percent below peak level. If another 12.4 years were added to the comparison, during which period the previously small firm continued to produce the level of output that it reached when its SBC hit the peak level, the difference would be only 5.3 percent over this 30-year period.

Thus, if undiscounted comparisons are made between the present and the future, the average longer-run efficiency in the utilization of resources differs very little in a firm that starts small and one that is large, given the growth rates of the firms sampled in the metalworking industry. The difference is increased if one assumes a positive social discount rate and deflates future outputs and inputs to the present. At a 10 percent discount rate, the unit that had started as a small firm would have an efficiency ratio 18.5 percent below that of the unit that had been operating at peak social efficiency throughout the 30 years of the last comparison. With a social discount rate of 5 percent, the differential would be well below 10 percent.[41]

In most industries at most times, of course, small firms would be unlikely to grow as rapidly as the sample of metalworking firms under discussion. The efficiency disadvantage of a firm that started as a small unit would therefore be greater than the above figures suggest. Another complication would be added if SBC and growth tended to be correlated at any given firm size. This would suggest that a fast-growing firm would have a higher-than-average SBC whatever its size and that, other things being equal, its long-run efficiency disadvantage relative to a larger firm would be less than the above calculations indicate. At the same time, firms that grew more slowly would be at a greater disadvantage, and firms that went out of business perhaps even more so.

Neither the findings of chapter 3 nor those of this chapter suggest that small metalworking firms are undesirable because of their below-average SBC ratios. Given that those ratios are above 1, they pass the simple test of producing an output worth more than the estimated social cost of inputs. The desirability of such firms depends on one's assumptions about how the resources they now employ would be used in their absence. Even if they never grew into particularly efficient production units, the case against them would be weak unless it could be shown that the resources they use would otherwise be used by firms that are more efficient than the estimated economywide average that underlies our social opportunity cost assumptions.

Summary

The rapid aggregate expansion of SMI from about the late 1960s (see chapter 2) has been associated with rapid growth of the representative SMI firm (although there are wide differences across firms in this respect) along with the creation of many SMI firms. Although many units seem to have disappeared, net creation of firms accounted for perhaps half of all manufacturing employment growth in Colombia between 1953 and 1978.

The entrepreneur plays the central role in the SMI drama—as organizer, risk-taker, innovator, and often as participant in the production process. SMI entrepreneurs are typically drawn from middle-income backgrounds, and a majority of them have at least some secondary education. Their enterprises are generally quite small at first, with respect to capital, which comes mainly from their own funds (savings and severance pay) and from family loans; official credit institutions play little part in the early capitalization of SMI firms. Entrepreneurs often buy second-hand equipment to keep capital costs down.

In SMI as a whole, a majority of entrepreneurs appear to have had previous experience with self-employment (including earlier business ventures). Former skilled workers make up an important source of entrepreneurial talent in the metalworking sector. Nearly 40 percent of the entrepreneurs in this sector gained their skills by working in other small or medium enterprises before starting their own firms, while another 20 percent gained their skills by working in a large firm.

SMI firms in the metalworking industry had a variety of start-up problems, particularly technical difficulties and problems in obtaining raw materials, responsible workers, and adequate working capital; a lesser problem was the shortage of clients. Nonetheless, these firms registered very fast employment growth rates (an average of 15 percent a year between 1973 and 1977). Rates for SMI as a whole were well below this level but were still high, probably averaging about 5 percent between 1970 and 1978. At least during the rapid expansion of SMI in the 1970s, the employment growth rate tended to be higher in the smaller plants. The growth process thus appears to have been most rapid when firms were young and small and then to have gradually decelerated. During the early 1960s, when the economy as a whole and the manufacturing sector grew more slowly, larger plants had on the average grown more quickly than small ones. Evidence from food processing and (especially) metalworking firms suggests that SMI depends heavily on self-financing. The relatively rapid growth of SMI in the 1970s—both by comparison with the 1960s and by comparison with LI in the 1970s—may have been made possible by the reinvestment of high profits during the latter period.

New SMI establishments are created by a combination of entrepreneurial business capacity and the availability, in many cases, of modest amounts of capital belonging mainly to the entrepreneur or his family. Their growth is a consequence of their ability to respond flexibly to market opportunities, their accumulation of capital within the firm, and, as chapter 5 demonstrates, their significant capacity for improving production technologies.

Notes

1. In the extensive literature on the problems faced by the small-scale sector (including nonmanufacturing units), some models have denied its growth po-

tential and explained its existence by the survival activities of a marginalized labor force. See, for example, Aníbal Quijano, "The Marginal Pole of the Economy and the Marginalized Labor Force," *Economy and Society*, vol. 2, no. 4 (1974). Hubert Schmitz, "Growth Constraints on Small Scale Manufacturing in Developing Countries: A Critical Review," *World Development*, vol. 10, no. 6 (June 1982), p. 445, points out that such an extreme position has no empirical support: "The issue is not *whether* small enterprises have growth and development potential but *under what conditions.*"

2. Corporación Financiera Popular (CFP) and Organización de los Estados Americanos, *Diagnóstico de la Pequeña y Mediana Industria y Bases para una Política de Fomento y Desarrollo en Colombia* (Bogotá, 1972), pp. 38–40. In this study, the CFP obtained data from 195 firms that were among its 1,936 clients. SMI was defined to include companies with less than 100 workers and total assets of less than 15 million pesos in December 31, 1971 (ibid., p. 6). Since they were all clients of CFP, the sampled firms would not be expected to be fully representative of all SMI.

3. There are not many detailed studies of entrepreneurship in Colombia. One recent monograph, including several fascinating stories of individual innovative entrepreneurs, is Fundación para el Fomento de la Investigación Científica y Tecnológica (FICITEC), *Empresarios Colombianos: Un Nuevo Contexto de Desarrollo* (Bogotá, 1976).

4. The majority of the firms in both sectors were founded by their present owners (86 percent of metalworking firms and 61 percent of food processing firms).

5. Both our industry samples have higher proportions of entrepreneurs with primary education than was reported in CFP's 1972 sample. This fact could reflect lower education among owners in these sectors than in SMI as a whole, a less narrowly chosen sample (CFP clients are not fully representative), or a changing pattern over time.

6. Aaron Lipman, *El Empresario Bogotano* (Bogotá: Ediciones Tercer Mundo y Facultad de Sociología, Universidad Nacional de Colombia, 1966), p. 49.

7. Most of these factors are discussed by José F. Escandón, "Análisis de los Factores que han Determinado el Desarrollo de la Pequeña Empresa en Colombia: Una Interpretación Histórica," *Coyuntura Económica*, vol. 11, no. 3 (October 1981).

8. The share of fixed capital in total initial capital may reflect the tightness of an entrepreneur's financial situation. This share was higher for persons with incomplete primary (85 percent), complete primary (60 percent), or incomplete secondary (67.6 percent) schooling than for persons with college education (35 percent). Firms that started small were not systematically high or low in this regard.

9. For all SI firms in all industries, secondhand items accounted for nearly 30 percent of all investment in machinery and equipment (including vehicles) in 1976. The comparable figure for all MI firms was about 19 percent (see tables 2-21 and 2-22).

10. Figures are based on DANE's monthly wage and employment survey. See DANE, *Boletín Mensual de Estadística*, no. 293 (December 1975), p. 22, and no. 348 (July 1980), p. 153. The decline was smaller than average in the metal products

industry (excluding machines) but about average in nonelectrical machinery. These are the three-digit industries to which the firms in our metalworking sample belong.

11. Evidence of the importance of learning by doing in the metalworking industries is provided by Leonard Dudley, "The Effects of Learning on Employment and Labor Productivity in the Colombian Metal Products Sector," in *Essays on Industrialization in Colombia*, ed. Albert Berry (Tempe, Ariz.: Arizona State University, Center for Latin American Studies, 1983). Dudley found the growth rate of labor productivity owing to learning by doing to be 2–3 percent a year over the period 1957–67. In the case of process industries or more technologically sophisticated sectors, knowledge of the operational technology does not easily lead to mastery of the basic design, which is contained in the original blueprints and engineering design specifications.

12. By the late 1960s, when nearly half of the sample firms had been created, SENA had been training skilled workers for more than a decade.

13. Escandón, "Análisis de los Factores que Han Determinado el Desarrollo de la Pequeña Empresa en Colombia."

14. If the plants sampled for DANE's monthly employment index were representative, this share would probably be more than half. Using DANE's figures for total employment growth, with a slight upward adjustment in 1978 (see row 4 of table 4-11), the share is 41 percent; using our best estimates (row 5) it is 54–58 percent. (The share of employment generated by new firms is less, though by how much we do not know, than that created by new plants, since some new plants are parts of old firms.) But DANE's sample is biased toward larger plants; on the basis of the evidence presented below, this may cause it to underestimate somewhat the annual employment growth rate of all existing firms. That rate may have been closer to 3 percent than the 2.5 percent shown here, in which case the contribution of new plants would probably fall below 50 percent.

The studies by Todd for 1962–66 (see note 19) and Berry and Pinell-Siles for 1970–75 (see note 16) imply, respectively, that less than half and more than half of employment growth occurred in existing plants during the periods analyzed.

15. The very slow growth of existing firms in the 1974–78 period also casts some doubt on the validity of our strikingly high estimate of total growth in factory employment over those years, as discussed in chapter 2.

16. See Albert Berry and Armando Pinell-Siles, "Small-Scale Enterprises in Colombia: A Case Study," Studies on Employment and Rural Development no. 5, World Bank, Development Economics Department, Washington, D.C., 1979.

17. Kyu Sik Lee, "Intra-Urban Location of Manufacturing Employment in Colombia," *Journal of Urban Economics*, vol. 9 (1981), p. 224.

18. The average size (at birth) of establishments beginning operations in the period 1970–75 was 33.6 workers, compared with 62.5 workers for continuing establishments and 25.7 workers for those terminating business (or relocating). Kyu Sik Lee, "Distribution of Manufacturing Establishments and Employment in Bogotá and Cali," World Bank, Development Economics Department, Washington, D.C., January 1978, p. 23. From the increasing undercoverage of DANE data during the 1970s it appears that the reported net creation rates (births minus deaths) are downward biased. The average size of establishments at birth and at

death is probably fairly seriously upward biased in the figures presented by Lee owing to undercoverage in the lower size ranges.

19. John Todd, "Efficiency and Plant Size in Colombian Manufacturing," Ph.D. diss., Yale University, 1972, pp. 41–45. Although more of these plants moved to a lower size category than to a higher one, the distribution of firms by size within most categories would suggest that similar numbers moved up and down when intrasize category movements are allowed for.

Note, however, that firms that moved to a different region over the interval studied could not be identified and included. If, as is quite possible, the relation between the likelihood of sale or change of location and the firm's rate of growth varies across sizes, the positive association between size and rate of employment growth might not hold for the whole population of plants.

20. Berry and Pinell-Siles, "Small-Scale Enterprises," p. 62.

21. Lino Jaramillo G., "Crecimiento de la Pequeña, Mediana, y Gran Industria entre los Años 1971 y 1978," Banco de la República, Bogotá, Colombia, 1982; processed.

22. Since most disappearances were recorded for small plants, a decline in the overall rate would probably reflect an improvement in the position of small plants relative to large ones. The disappearance rate estimated for plants during 1967–71 by Berry and Pinell-Siles was lower than that for earlier periods; thus the same might have been true of a comparison between 1970–75 and earlier years (see Berry and Pinell-Siles, "Small-Scale Enterprises," pp. 70–73).

23. As noted, for example, by James R. Tybout, "Credit Rationing and Industrial Growth in Colombia: A Micro-Econometric Analysis," Ph.D. diss., University of Wisconsin-Madison, 1980, chap. 3.

24. This issue is analyzed in depth by Tybout, "Credit Rationing and Industrial Growth," on the basis of a sample of SMI and LI firms.

25. Systematic data on the growth history of firms in our food processing sample were not obtained because we were concerned that the length of the questionnaire would prejudice the overall quality of the data and were working under time and financial constraints. Since all the firms we sampled had only one plant, for the purposes of this discussion firm and plant numbers are the same.

26. This excludes firms created since 1973. For some firms, data for one or the other year had to be estimated. The unweighted average growth rate across firms (that is, the sum of growth rates divided by the number of firms) is usually above the weighted growth rate (growth rate of the sum of the labor force of all firms in a given category). We assume here that the latter is the more interesting figure.

27. Exactly how fast depends on how the growth rate is measured. The unweighted average for 34 firms was 24.0 percent a year; the average of these firms' ages was about 10 years as of 1973. If, however, firms are weighted by their initial size and by the number of years over which growth was recorded before 1973 (or, in a few cases, a later year), the average was only 8.5 percent, since the high growth rates corresponded especially to firms that had started very small and had been created only a few years before 1973.

28. The only other evidence on employment growth rates by size of plant in the metalworking industries over recent years refers to 1970–75. Berry and

Pinell-Siles found that for plants producing metal products other than machinery and equipment (industry no. 381) employment grew by 18 percent, or 3.3 percent a year. For plants producing machinery, transport equipment, or professional equipment (industries no. 382–385) the growth was 31 percent, or 5.5 percent a year. In each case, plants of 10–24 workers in 1970 grew well above the average, at 6.3 percent a year in industry 381 and at 9.1 percent in industries 382–385. See Berry and Pinell-Siles, "Small-Scale Enterprises," table A-21, pp. 162–63.

Overall, existing plants (that is, all sizes together) grew at an annual rate of 3.6 percent over 1973–77 for industry 381 and at a rate of 5.9 percent for industry 382. Since most of the plants in our sample were relatively small in 1973 (an average of 20.8 workers), these growth rates are not impossible but they are above the average for all plants in the two-digit industries from which our sample is drawn and are atypical even for small plants.

29. Although the use of an inaccurate deflator or differences between sales growth and output growth could account for this apparent bias, perhaps the most obvious possible source would be the difficulty respondents experienced in recalling current peso sales for the years before 1977. Some may not have understood the question, and others may have found that the rapid inflation of preceding years confused the issue. Although nearly all the firms (57 of 64) kept books at the time of the interview, some may not have kept them in earlier years, and some did not consult their books when answering the question. If some respondents gave sales figures for earlier years that broadly approximated to 1977 pesos, then our estimated growth rates would be downward biased. It is true that some independent figures suggest declining aggregate labor productivity in the factory sector during the 1970s (at least through 1975), including the metal products sector, but the most extreme aggregate figures indicate a decline much less rapid than that implicit in our survey figures.

30. For the period 1973–77, the simple correlation between age of firm and rate of labor force growth was −0.428. For sales it was −0.287. These correlations were also negative for all subperiods analyzed.

31. This fact may be disguised if one compares growth rates across groups of firms classified by size at the end of the growth period being studied and if the period is longer than a couple of years. Thus, when firms are classified by size in 1977, growth over 1973–77 tended to be higher for the larger firms, though the relationship was not monotonic.

32. A similar though less obvious relationship exists for sales; parallel but perhaps less close relationships appear to have existed for both labor and sales before 1973.

33. If we abstract from firms that go out of existence, the truncation of our sample leads to little or no bias for firms that started both recently and on a small scale. As noted, it does lead to a downward-biased estimate of growth rates for older firms and firms starting fairly high in the SMI size range, the expected degree of bias being greater the older the firm and the larger it started. Thus if a firm started with 50 workers 20 years ago, the fastest its employment could grow without its exiting from SMI (given that our upper limit for the category is 100 workers) would be 3.5 percent a year. If it started with 75 workers 20 years ago, the fastest its employment could grow would be 1.5 percent a year. Only the

slower-growing firms starting under such conditions are still found in SMI. In the case of older firms, an additional biasing factor may be at work. It seems that firms originating farther back in time, especially more than 25 years ago, were larger when founded (the average employment of 22.6 for the ten firms in this last group contrasted with the 14.7 average for the sample).

The magnitude of the truncation bias is not directly measurable with the data at hand. Several pieces of evidence suggest, however, that it is not significant enough to alter our results qualitatively. First, the aggregate employment data for the metal industries as a whole make it clear that the larger and older firms that provide most of total employment do not grow as quickly as the small, young firms in our sample, the subgroup whose growth rate is not significantly biased by truncation. Second, among the subgroups of our sample where the truncation is unlikely to have had much biasing effect, growth is negatively associated with age when size is held constant. Moreover, the negative association with size is consistent with data for the 1970s from other sources, as discussed earlier in this chapter.

Errors of observation or short-term fluctuations affecting the value of a variable in a given year create other difficulties in the analysis of the relation between size and growth. For example, errors of observation in the size variable (in the present case, employment) create a bias toward a negative correlation between size at the beginning of a period and (subsequent) growth, if it is assumed that there are no errors of observation of the size variable at the end of the period (or no end-of-period errors uncorrelated with those at the beginning of the period). Suppose that of four firms two started a period with 20 workers and two with 10, and that all doubled over the period. If the "observed" beginning sizes of the 20-worker firms were 24 and 16, and the "observed" beginning sizes of the 10-worker firms were 14 and 6, and end-of-period observations were all correct, the data would reveal a negative correlation between "observed" initial size and growth rate over the period. Such a spurious relationship might also be manifested in a negative correlation across firms between the growth before and after 1973 or between 1973–75 and 1975–77 growth rates. Fortunately, the simple correlation coefficients show a tendency for the 1973–75 and 1975–77 growth rates of both variables to be positively associated (especially for employment), so that this bias does not appear to be too serious.

34. Apart from the consistency with this proposition of the growth rates observed over 1973–77 for firms of different ages and sizes, it is also true that the typical sample firm underwent a declining growth rate over the period before the survey.

Although some entrepreneurial characteristics are statistically significant in multiple regressions to explain the growth of employment and of sales, size and age of firm generally retain their negative signs and statistical significance; the negative sign of age of enterprise is sometimes reversed in the case of sales growth, however, and size measured by one variable (for example, employment) may not have a negative association with growth of the other variable. This latter finding is not too surprising. Errors of observation would contribute to such a pattern, as would the existence of disequilibrium sales-labor (S/L) ratios that the firm tends to correct in the succeeding period. These phenomena do not appear important enough to negate the conclusion that growth and size are negatively correlated, especially for employment, unless the first-year employment figures are wrong or misleading.

35. The equation is

$$L = 1.62 \text{ PBC} - 0.44A - 0.22N \qquad R^2 = 0.23$$
$$\quad\quad (0.69) \qquad (1.85) \quad (1.86) \qquad\qquad \overline{R}^2 = 0.18$$
$$\qquad\qquad\qquad\qquad\qquad\qquad\qquad\qquad\qquad N = 43$$

where L is the average (geometric) annual growth of employment for 1973–77, PBC is the private benefit-cost ratio in 1977, A is age in 1977, and N is employment in 1973 (t values are in parentheses).

Because of the truncation problem alluded to earlier, the coefficients emerging from this regression could be seriously biased unless firms of relatively large size in 1973 were excluded. We therefore reran the regression excluding firms that had more than 40 workers in 1973 and were older than 15 years. The coefficient of PBC became negative and insignificant but the rest of the picture was unchanged—a result that supports our interpretation of the tendency for growth to decelerate with size.

The new equation is

$$L = -2.40 \text{ PBC} - 0.74A - 0.70N \qquad R^2 = 0.16$$
$$\quad\quad (0.57) \qquad (1.03) \quad (1.62) \qquad\qquad \overline{R}^2 = 0.04$$
$$\qquad\qquad\qquad\qquad\qquad\qquad\qquad\qquad\qquad N = 23$$

The signs of the coefficients for age and 1973 employment remain negative but their levels of significance fall; that of age is now significant (using a one-tail test) only at a 15 percent level of confidence and that of 1973 employment at almost the 5 percent level of confidence.

Even when the two equations are compared, it is impossible to judge precisely how the truncation of the sample has affected our results, since there is no way to deduce from a truncated sample what the characteristics of the universe are without arbitrary assumptions. But we are reasonably confident that the true association of the rate of employment growth with age and with employment level does not differ too seriously from that portrayed in the tables in this chapter and in the first equation above.

36. Growth of sales is likely to raise the PBC ratio, whereas growth of employment may either signal prosperity or imply failure to raise productivity. Consistent with this, the 1977 PBC ratio is a strong predictor of the growth of sales over 1973–77 (the relation is considerably weaker over 1975–77). In the regression explaining labor growth over 1975–77, however, its sign is negative, though this is not very significant. In any case, correlation of growth with PBC measured at a later date may well reflect the effects of profitability on growth.

37. The simple correlation of entrepreneur's age with the rate of growth of sales over 1973–77 is −0.48 and that with the rate of employment growth over 1975–77 is −0.32. Both are statistically significant.

38. The ratio of capital to labor is higher for the smallest firms than for slightly larger ones if size is defined either by number of workers or by sales, but not if it is defined by value of capital stock (see chapter 3).

39. Since our sample does not extend to large industry, it does not provide a basis for comparison with establishments of, say, several hundred workers. The discussion in chapter 3, however, suggests that medium-size plants are as efficient as large ones.

40. In using the simple relation between size and SBCs to predict the evolution of a given firm, this methodology implicitly assumes that all determinants of SBCs vary directly with firm size, so that in whatever size category the firm is found, its SBC is equivalent to the average SBC of the sampled firms in that size category.

41. In this section size has been defined by the level of employment. The calculations could also use the level of sales without changing the basic ideas involved. It is probable that efficiency differences would be somewhat greater when calculated that way, since output is usually more correlated with efficiency than is employment.

5

Technical Change

The prosperity and growth of a small firm—and ultimately its very survival—may often depend on its ability to improve its product line, incorporate technical change, and adopt better administrative and marketing practices. In chapter 2 we estimated that labor productivity in Colombian SMI as a whole rose by 40 percent from the mid-1950s to the late 1970s.[1] Such an increase suggests some degree of technological advance and raises important questions about the process of change, not all of which can be addressed here.[2] In this chapter, we try to illustrate the process of technical change in Colombia's SMI sector by reviewing some of the main features of change in metalworking and food processing. How did the firms that were early starters in these industries acquire their technical knowledge, how was it adapted to local conditions, and how was it later transferred to other firms that in turn incorporated further technical changes and adaptations? Our information on small and medium metalworking and food processing firms suggests that they were able to improve their product and process technology once they had overcome initial financial constraints. The ability of small metalworking firms to adapt product design and quality specifications to the requirements of their clients is of special interest.

The Metal Products Industry

Colombia started to manufacture nonelectrical metal products, such as integrated kitchens, stoves, ovens, agricultural pumps, sprayers, and other related equipment, in the late 1950s when the government restricted imports as a result of balance of payments difficulties. Three types of firms were induced to participate in the expanded, protected market: (1) established firms that had previously acquired relevant experience through repair and reconstruction activities, (2) traders who were confronted with new constraints on imports and consequently sought local alternatives to their foreign suppliers, and (3) new firms specifically created to take advantage of the protected domestic market.

When products had relatively complex designs (as in the case of agricultural implements and pumps) and when trade names were important selling points, production was often initially based on licenses and technical assistance from abroad. Some other products, such as integrated kitchens and ovens, were at first copied from previously imported items or were based on designs from foreign catalogs. Firms with previous experience in repairing or reconstructing imported products tended to be better copiers than other firms. Firms with a background in distributing or repairing were more aware of consumer preferences and better able to adapt foreign designs than were newly created firms.

From the beginning, most firms had to adapt imported designs to local conditions. The adaptations were made for three main purposes: to provide acceptable substitutes for materials and components that were not produced locally and that were difficult to import because of balance of payments problems; to alter the finishing process and final appearance because of difficulties in importing certain kinds of manufacturing equipment; and to adapt products to local practices and preferences. These adaptations involved considerable technical efforts by the first generation of local firms, which were operating with untrained labor and inexperienced managers. Some of the larger firms resorted to foreign technical assistance after failing to solve their technical problems themselves. Some survived because restrictions on imports obliged users to buy local products, even if the latter were lower in quality and higher in price. In time, however, the quality of most local products rose substantially as a result of improved production techniques and better communication between producers and users. The former reflected improvements in labor force skills and the modernization of equipment that firms were able to undertake as their financial situation improved.

A second generation of small metalworking firms emerged during the early 1970s. Many of these new entrants were managed by former production workers and technicians who had left the older, first-generation firms and had started their own businesses with the proceeds of their severance payments and accumulated savings. The new entrepreneurs were familiar with the product designs and production techniques used by the older and larger firms. Some started as subcontractors of the older firms, remaining in the same geographical area; others, particularly those producing agriculture-related items, established their plants close to their potential customers. Some began by doing repair and reconstruction work and only later entered production. Close contact with customers together with experience in repair work made it possible for some of these firms to introduce further design adaptations that have become well accepted by local users over the years. Buyers also value the proximity of repair facilities.

Despite their often relatively primitive production methods, these smaller firms can usually undersell larger, established firms because their proximity to their customers reduces or eliminates distribution and transport costs. Smaller firms also tend to pay out less in labor benefits, are able to escape taxes, and look for lower returns on their investment than the upper-middle-class trader-entrepreneurs characteristic of the first-generation firms. Larger firms have sometimes responded to competition by lowering their prices, but the small firms have been able to retain their local clients by making design improvements. Some of these smaller firms are now well established and employ 50 or more workers. The most successful have improved their products and their production techniques by importing modern equipment. In other cases, however, initial managerial and technical deficiencies have become more evident as production has expanded. Although we lack conclusive statistics, our impression is that the death rate among the smaller, second-generation firms has been higher than among those of the first generation.

The remainder of this section presents some illustrative examples of the process of evolutionary growth of SMI metalworking firms over the past two decades.

Agricultural Implements

The main products of this industry are plows, disks, cultivators, and seeders. The four largest firms started production in the early 1960s. Two of them had been making other metal products for ten or more years. When they entered this new field, however, they decided to obtain licenses and technical assistance from foreign companies. The largest and oldest firm (founded in Medellín in 1925 and employing more than 750 workers by 1977) began production under license from three U.S. firms—Townes (Los Angeles), Service (Dallas), and Ford. It is Colombia's largest producer of disks, which it makes under license from Ingersoll (a U.S. firm). The only other producer of disks in Colombia has 90 workers and operates in Bogotá under license from Taisa (a U.K. firm). The two remaining firms, created in response to import restrictions, also started with foreign licenses and technical assistance. One was founded in Barranquilla by the former president of a General Electric subsidiary; it uses the subsidiary's distribution network to sell agricultural implements. This firm started with a license from Caterpillar, the supplier of the equipment distributed by the General Electric subsidiary. The fourth firm, located in Bogotá and now employing 130 workers, also received technical assistance from an American firm.

These first-generation agricultural implement makers did not locate near their main markets. Medellín, where the largest of them is located, is not situated in an important agricultural zone; the firm's products have to be transported unassembled to distributors in other parts of the country. Similarly, when the Barranquilla firm got started, its main market was the distant Cauca Valley; Atlantic coast agriculture had not yet become mechanized. There was little competition among the four firms; to a large extent, they specialized in different types of products—the Medellín firms, for example, concentrated on light implements and the Barranquilla firm produced mainly heavier implements appropriate for sugarcane fields.

During this early period, a few smaller firms started producing agricultural implements for local markets by using skills acquired in the repair business to copy imported models. Some of these firms never expanded production beyond local markets, often because of technical problems. In our 1978 sample we found two such firms in Barranquilla, two in the Cali-Palmira region, one in Ibagué, one in Tuluá, and one in Bogotá.

The technological efforts of the largest firms working under license have been devoted primarily to improving production processes by acquiring more modern and mechanized equipment, and secondarily to changing the original design. Sometimes such changes have involved developing substitutes for materials that could not be acquired locally; for example, when pressed iron was not available in Colombia, it became necessary to use iron profiles and tubes, which tended to make the implements heavier than imported ones. Also, hard soils coupled with the driving habits of Colombian tractor operators obliged the firms to reinforce some of the parts. During these early years smaller firms that were located close to users tried to modify their product to meet their clients' requirements. Those not bound by licensing agreements—such as the second largest producer, which was located in Bogotá—were able to combine the characteristics of several specialized implements in a single versatile one.

The more significant design modifications were usually introduced by firms that were located near the users and consequently were in close touch with them. For example, a medium-size producer in Tuluá modified the Medellín firm's seeding machine by reducing the distance between the disks and adding a flat plate to prevent the seeds from breaking as they fell. This firm's seeder was also machined rather than welded and thus was stronger. Another producer in Ibagué modified the design of a rice-husk remover imported from Japan by changing the transmission from a pinion to a belt system and strengthening the axis by using rollers with greater capacity. A producer of cultivators in Palmira, finding that imported machines were too rigid for Colombian soil, adapted a basket for each furrow with a spring that bent in uneven fields. He also added a hydraulic attachment to imported seeding machines pulled by tractors, so as to avoid wasting the patch at the end of a plot where the tractor turns. An American producer later incorporated this adaptation into its own design.

The four largest manufacturers dominated the agricultural implements market until a second generation of firms appeared in the early
1970s.[3] The new entrants were based in the main agricultural zones;
seven were in the Cali-Palmira region alone. Many of the former production workers and technicians who founded these establishments started
by providing repair services, having acquired their skills in the first-
generation firms. This experience, together with their physical proximity
to their clientele, encouraged them to adapt the designs they had previously learned. For example, a small producer in Neiva who had worked
for the firm in Ibagué modified a John Deere towage by making the axles
interchangeable; this meant that the entire machine did not have to be removed from a field for repairs if an axle broke. The same producer also
attached a third wheel to the direction system with a fixed ring, so as to
avoid shaking in the rice fields.

The main second-generation producers in the Cali-Palmira region,
where sugarcane is a major crop, concentrated on modifying the
Barranquilla firm's ROME-type rakes (produced under license). The disks
and journal bearings of these rakes tended to break because Colombian
soils—unlike those in the United States—are hard to prepare in summer
for the winter growing period. One local firm solved the problem by rein-
forcing the bridges of the journal bearings and increasing the dimensions
of the axles and disks. Another made the links that attached the rake to
the tractor more flexible and less subject to breakage. A third added a
mechanism that enabled the operator to change the position of the disks
without dismounting from the tractor. One of the Palmira firms now imports agricultural implements from the United States to use as proto-
types; they are then tested on a sugarcane plantation to determine what
modifications would better fit them to local conditions.

These various design improvements together with the lower prices of
local firms sharply reduced the large Barranquilla firm's share of the market for heavy machinery used by sugarcane growers in the Valle region.[4]
The Barranquilla producer and its main distributor in Cali, a subsidiary of
a U.S. firm that also sells electrical appliances, tried to halt production by
the small firms on the grounds that they were illegally copying designs
covered by patents. The local producers were able to demonstrate, however, that the modifications did not infringe on the Barranquilla firm's
patent rights.

Sprayers

Two firms began making agricultural sprayers in Colombia during the
mid-1950s, also as a result of import restrictions. One of the pioneering
manufacturers, a medium-size metalworking firm, was induced to enter

this new market when its owner heard from a friend in the Caja Agraria (the public agricultural credit institution) that there was a scarcity of sprayers in Colombia. Initially, this entrepreneur copied and combined the characteristics of imported models. His firm's output grew from 50 sprayers a month in 1948 to 100 a day by the time of our survey interview (1978). Difficulties in obtaining necessary materials and equipment obliged him to introduce further modifications. For example, the piston-type pump of the sprayer was made in one piece in the imported item. Since this required a special machine that was not available to the Colombian firm, the owner decided instead to make the pump in pieces. The advantage of his approach was that the user could change a broken piece if necessary without replacing the whole pump. This firm has increased its work force from ten to eighty and has gradually modernized its equipment; it now has a turret lathe. But the owner has been careful not to overequip his firm, noting that some other manufacturers in the sector have acquired modern equipment that remains idle for 50 percent of the time.

The other pioneering firm, located in Cali, was founded in 1957 by a farmer who was induced by import restrictions to design a sprayer for his own use, which he based on an imported model. With most of its initial capital supplied by a family loan, this firm is today the largest producer of sprayers in Colombia. By the late 1960s, it had grown to the point where it had become a joint stock company, and the original owner lost control. He left the firm and founded another enterprise in 1968. This firm now has forty workers; it has introduced some design changes (for example, the pump is embedded in the sprayer and thus provides better protection), but weak management has made it less successful than some of its competitors. In 1974, two employees of the original firm— the accountant and one of the skilled workers—also started their own enterprise.

When imports were permitted again, foreign sprayers could no longer compete with locally produced ones; including tariffs, the imported brands cost twice as much as local ones.

Agricultural Pumps

In 1960, an importer of Aurora brand pumps from the United States found it increasingly hard to obtain import permits and decided to start production on his own. He received initial technical assistance from his American supplier and later manufactured under license from a German industrial pump company. With the help of the American licenser (to which it pays 5 percent royalties), the firm has introduced modifications to the design of its pumps. It has also received technical assistance from abroad for foundry work. After a period of difficulty with importing motors and special valves, the firm began production. Its equipment remains rudimentary, however.

The other large producer of pumps in our sample now has ninety workers. In 1969 it started to assemble pumps in Bogotá, using parts imported from the United States and Canada. In 1972 the firm began to manufacture the parts itself, paying royalties to several foreign companies. The success of its efforts enabled it to control 60 percent of the Colombian market. The firm's owner estimates that 80 percent of the small producers of pumps and irrigation equipment in Bogotá are former workers in his firm. As the quality of their pumps is comparable to his own, his firm buys and distributes some of them with its trademark. Competition is fierce, however, and some small firms have started to sell directly to customers at lower prices. In one case, five small firms now manufacture different components that are assembled by a sixth firm and sold at prices 25 percent below those of the larger firm. The latter has expanded its capacity and installed more modern equipment, so as to reduce its costs and compete better with the small producers.

A third, relatively large firm, located in Medellín, started business in 1960 as a distributor and repairer of pumps. Its learning process over the years has included visits by the owner to firms in the United States and Europe, and it has copied models from them and from catalogs that contain technical information. Serious technical problems, however, have kept productivity low (the firm has sixty employees, but sales are only 2 million pesos a year). These problems have recently led the owner to hire a metallurgical engineer.

Most of the technical efforts of pump producers were a response to the need to produce parts that were difficult to import. In some cases even the manufacturing equipment used—presses and simple machine tools—had to be adapted because the firms lacked the resources to buy more modern machinery. These efforts have sometimes generated skills that could be applied in other industries. One entrepreneur with a background in civil aviation has learned to adapt equipment for his small pump shop and is now trying to build a machine to weed and fertilize the soil and thereby speed up banana production.

In another case, two former employees of the large pump producer in Bogotá set up a firm and copied a pump produced under license by the large Barranquilla firm. Mainly through trial and error—together with technical assistance from local metallurgical firms and technical tests undertaken by a university laboratory—this firm became the only Latin American producer of bronze-aluminum turbines outside Mexico. One of the owners took correspondence courses in motors and the firm started reconstructing pumps and compressors; after five years it began producing water pumps and now offers twenty-three models. Another remarkable innovation, designed and produced by a small firm in Bogotá employing only thirteen workers, is a pump that lifts water more than 60 meters, to be used in Colombia's hilly coffee growing areas. According to the owner of this firm, such a pump cannot be obtained abroad.

Other Agricultural Capital Goods

The process of import substitution has also involved innovative adaptations of foreign designs for other agricultural capital items. One medium-size firm, which started producing rice dryers after participating in the installation of a British rice mill, has placed the silos on an incline instead of in the usual horizontal pattern; this makes the handling of rice less labor-intensive and less pollutive, and produces more uniform quality. Another small producer of rice dryers, who had also worked in the Ibagué firm mentioned above, based his adaptive design on an imported Danish machine that he had repaired and on information from American catalogs. His major modification was to change the shape of the base and head of the transporters to avoid grain loss.

Integrated Kitchens

Local production of integrated kitchens (ranges, ovens, sinks, and associated kitchen furniture) started in Colombia in the mid-1960s. Partly as a result of the construction boom of the early 1970s, Bogotá, Cali, and Medellín had some fifty-eight producers by 1978; ten of these were medium or large firms. The first entrants into the market were salesmen who recognized the potential demand for this type of kitchen. A Sears salesman, for example, got the idea from a French catalog that explained the design details; he then left his job to start his own business. At first, his designs were simply copied from the French catalog, but he later introduced modifications according to his customers' specifications.

The most difficult problem faced by first-generation firms in this market was learning to work with new materials—such as stainless steel, which requires special equipment for argon welding. As of the mid-1960s there were no workers trained in argon welding, so manufacturers had to proceed by trial and error. Difficulties in importing equipment induced ingenious substitutions; in the absence of polishing disks, for example, some firms used dental equipment. By the late 1960s, SENA had started training programs in argon welding, polishing, and carpentry. These programs were subsequently cut back, however, because a large number of trainees went directly to Venezuela where they could earn more.

Large producers of integrated kitchens now have engineers and architects in their design teams and work mainly for higher-income clients.

Small firms usually make a less sophisticated product and sell to lower-income groups. Production techniques in the industry are generally more labor-intensive than in other branches of the metalworking sector. Small firms use manual equipment and subcontract to others, since few of them have their own smelting ovens; meanwhile, the shortage of skilled workers is obliging larger firms to mechanize their production processes.

Stoves

The production of gasoline stoves in Colombia was also started by importers with some experience in the metalworking industry. In 1958, the son of an importer set up a business to repair imported stoves, using catalogs and instructions provided by the suppliers. When imports were cut off, this individual (a lawyer and an economist) moved into the production of industrial stoves, improving on the designs with which he was familiar from his repair work. His models were based on the same principle as the imported stoves, but were simpler and sturdier in design. For example, the electric stoves had several elements in each plate, which permitted the user to change a damaged part without changing the whole plate. Improvement in equipment and production methods enabled this firm to cut its work force from fifty to twenty with only a minor reduction in output. One worker from this firm later started his own business; by 1978 he had an even larger firm. Another, more recently established producer (1960), who learned the relevant production process while working for a larger firm, reduced the proportion of imported elements in the stove; previously 60 percent of them were imported, now only the valves come from abroad (Sweden).

Another of the early gasoline stove firms was founded in 1966 by an importer in association with his brother, who ran a foundry shop. Their early models were copies of a Canadian stove (Coleman), which is simple and can be produced by manual techniques. Production grew rapidly from an initial level of 500 stoves a month to 6,000 a month in 1978, making the firm one of the largest in this sector. An important technological improvement was the use of dies to cut sheet metal and thus reduce both production time and wastage of materials. This firm now imports its machinery directly from the United States and has mechanized other areas of production. The acquisition of a semiautomatic welder, for example, reduced the labor required for welding from seven to two workers.

Bakery Ovens

In 1958 the son of an importer of bakery ovens started to manufacture ovens in Bogotá when imports were reduced by high tariff barriers. He

had experience in his own repair firm and used catalogs and repair instructions from foreign suppliers to design his own ovens. His
medium-size firm has now become highly profitable. Workers trained in
this pioneering firm subsequently set up several other companies; one of
them is now a large enterprise, which credits its success to a design modification that eliminates the need to turn the molds while baking the
bread. Production of bakery ovens in Cali was also started by importers
who copied and modified imported equipment. Some modifications reflected the need to substitute local materials and to adapt manufacturing
methods to local working practices. Initially, graphite bearings, which
are made under high pressure, were imported from the United States
when imports were restricted. One firm, which lacked high compression
equipment, developed (with the help of a German technician) a bearing
that does not have to be produced under high pressure but nevertheless
lasts longer than the previously imported item.

As in the case of integrated kitchens, there are significant differences in
the quality and price of bakery ovens made by small and large producers,
so that their products go to different categories of consumers. As in other
metalworking industries, most firms start by operating on a relatively
small scale and gradually acquire new equipment as their financial position improves. Even quite large firms in the sector use relatively
labor-intensive production methods, however.

The Food Processing Industry

Industrial production of cheese, guava paste, and potato chips started in
Colombia in the 1940s but was limited to a few producers. The 1970s
witnessed a surge of small-scale manufacturing activity similar to that
experienced in the metalworking sector. The firms that had existed before this expansion had been established by owners who had acquired
their technical knowledge abroad (cheese, potato chips) or who had
mass-produced a traditional household food product (guava paste). The
firms created in the 1970s were owned by local traders and raw material
producers, who were attracted by the profitability of a sector that en-
joyed tariff protection and, in the case of milk products, controlled raw
material prices. Although these food firms have raised their product
quality and productivity over time, they have generated few of the adaptive innovations characteristic of the metal products sector. This is partly
because the processed food sector produces mainly standardized items
and partly because most entrepreneurs, particularly in the newer firms,
lack technical experience. Most technical improvements have come
from research and training institutions outside the sector or from local
equipment manufacturers. Unlike the situation in the metalworking

sector, technical knowledge is seldom transferred from large firms to smaller ones through the mobility of skilled workers from the former to the latter. One reason for this is that process industries offer fewer opportunities to learn the basic elements of the technology from experience in production.[5]

In food processing, product quality depends on quality control methods at various stages of the process (starting with the raw materials), on the type of production equipment, and on the methods of preserving raw materials and finished products. Performance depends on the scale of production and on the abilities of the entrepreneur. Smaller firms usually lack the skills and equipment necessary for rigorous quality control, resorting instead to simple eye inspection, whereas larger firms have technicians and equipment to measure characteristics such as the acidity and bacteriological content of the products.

The equipment used can also affect both quality and productivity. For example, pasteurization and homogenization improve the quality of fresh cheese, but only large firms can afford the equipment for these processes. Similarly, the overall productivity of a cheese operation is increased by a decreamer, which is used to produce butter as a byproduct, but small firms cannot afford this additional capital. Finally, food preservation methods can have major economic consequences. For example, guava paste producers who know how to preserve the fruit can operate year round without interruption and can maintain the correct proportions of guava and sugar (60 and 40 percent, respectively). Firms that do not preserve the fruit add more sugar when guavas are scarce; the result is an inferior product.

Small food processing firms have less incentive to achieve a high-quality product than their counterparts in the metalworking sector. Users of metal products can usually assess quality fairly easily and can thus encourage firms to make improvements. By contrast, consumers of food products are less aware of the latter's potential health risks, and evaluation is made more difficult by inadequate government controls and by retailers' tendency to sell products of different quality at similar prices.

The equipment used by food processing firms ranges from simple cooking devices, storage containers, and manual tools to integrated and semiautomated plants. Small firms tend to start with simple equipment. As quality is not an important obstacle to growth, they can expand gradually, adding more items of simple (and relatively divisible) equipment until their level of output justifies acquiring more sophisticated plant and machinery. Inadequate access to raw materials can be a serious obstacle to growth, however, especially for small firms that lack the working capital that larger ones can use to secure a relatively stable supply. The remainder of this section gives some examples of technical change in the food processing industry.

Guava Paste

Industrial production of guava paste started in the early 1940s in rural Boyacá and Santander, spreading to Bogotá and Bucaramanga as workers migrated. There are currently four or five large firms in Colombia, each processing about 4,000 kilograms of fruit a day, and a large number of smaller firms that process between 500 and 1,000 kilograms daily. Industry entrepreneurs estimate that there are more than 40 guava paste producers in Bogotá alone.

The first firms were founded by people who knew and adapted traditional household production methods. By contrast, the firms created in the mid-1970s are owned by traders who have been attracted to the profitability of the business. Not being knowledgeable about technical matters, they have had to rely on hired personnel. The "expert" in a typical small firm is an experienced worker called a *puntero*, who tastes the mixture and decides on the proper acidity and cooking time. This traditional method produces batches of variable quality. In larger firms the same task is undertaken by technical personnel, although only two of the largest firms that we visited had refractometers and equipment to measure acidity. The Export Promotion Agency (PROEXPO), which wished to develop an exportable product, launched a major effort to improve quality. To this end, the Institute for Technological Research (IIT) has undertaken research and given technical assistance to a group of firms with the help of a large cooperative (COPINDULCE). One result was a method of preserving guava paste for several months, which has been used by several producers since 1977. The owner of a firm in Pitalito, a chemical engineer, developed his own process independently of the IIT and now specializes in selling preserved guava to other producers.

Equipment for guava paste production ranges from copper cauldrons heated by direct flame to stainless steel pressure cookers heated by a central boiler. An intermediate technique uses a combination of copper cauldrons with pressure and temperature controls, heated by a central boiler. All the equipment is locally produced except for the boilers, which are usually acquired secondhand from abroad. The IIT has worked with several equipment producers to design more efficient cauldrons and has helped some firms to improve the layout of their plants. As firms grow, they acquire better equipment, but very few make technical contributions of their own. One rare exception is a producer in Pitalito who was able to cut fuel consumption by one-third in comparison with firms using similar techniques. Another introduced improvements to his equipment, including a mechanical mixer, which were so well received by other firms that he sold his business and became an equipment producer. The transition from simple to more sophisticated equipment entails a learning process. When a cooperative of fifty producers in Pitalito obtained modern equipment with resources from the Canadian government, its productivity remained much lower than that of other firms in the region—because nobody in the cooperative knew how to use the equipment properly.

Cheese and Yogurt

Industrial production of cheese in Colombia was begun in the mid-1940s by two firms that used foreign capital and technology. These firms now supply about 60 percent of the market. The rest is in the hands of small and medium enterprises that emerged in the 1970s, stimulated at least in part by the existence of price controls on milk but not on milk products. In 1950 there were no more than four producers of yogurt, but by 1978 there were more than thirty small establishments in the Sabana of Bogotá alone. Today the largest firms process between 70,000 and 125,000 bottles of milk a day; medium-size firms process about 10,000, and small firms between 500 and 5,000. (The relation between the input of milk and the output of the final product varies little; entrepreneurs usually describe their output in terms of the amount of milk used.)

Most of these new entrepreneurs were previously owners of pasteurizing firms or distributors of milk and milk products; few had experience in cheese production. New firms typically began by producing fresh cheese, and some of them later incorporated the production of industrial cheese and yogurt. These products are technically easier to produce and require less working capital than the matured cheese produced by the largest firms. (Mature cheese requires up to a year in storage, while fresh cheese can be sold after a few days.) Large firms also produce fresh cheese. Small entrepreneurs learn their skills from other small firms and from courses given by SENA and the universities. Dissemination of knowledge through the mobility of workers is common among small firms, but not between large and small firms. For example, in Zipaquirá, thirteen cheese producers who started after 1974 have apparently learned the technology from each other. All are very small (two to four workers).

When SENA started its dairy program in the Sabana of Bogotá, the objective was to give small farmers technical assistance with the production of milk derivatives. The program's initial focus was on farmers with incomplete primary schooling, but the demand for courses from better-educated farmers obliged SENA to accept people with secondary (or even university) education. Courses are now offered at three levels, the most advanced of which includes the study of microbiology; some students have been able to obtain jobs with the large milk processors.

SENA also has agreements with a number of universities for their staff to help train students who attend its Agricultural Center. With the collaboration of the Dutch government, SENA has developed a set of manuals to teach techniques ranging from pasteurization to the production of different types of cheese.[6] Training time ranges from sixty hours for yogurt or butter production to ninety hours for cheese, and includes both theory and practical lessons in the Agricultural Center's plant. As of 1981, SENA was offering eight courses a year with an enrollment of about 200 students, and nearly 600 people had received training since 1976. They came from different parts of the country and even from abroad (two students were from Honduras in 1979). Some SENA graduates are working as technicians for larger firms, but many others have started their own businesses.

Another SENA program was begun in 1974 with the Colombian Agricultural Institute in Nariño to improve techniques for the extraction and processing of milk. The Dutch government provides technicians and equipment. The emphasis of the program has been on improving the processing of milk rather than milk derivatives. Meanwhile, the National University gives higher-level courses on milk technology. It also provides technical assistance, much of it free, to small cheese producers and to local equipment manufacturers who are adapting imported equipment to a smaller scale of production. SENA also provides free technical assistance to cheese producers.

Domestic production of equipment has grown along with the industry. Several importers of secondhand equipment, most of which comes from Denmark and the United States, have become important sources of technical knowledge for small firms. One such importer has his own cheese and yogurt plant to demonstrate to his customers how to use the equipment. A producer of carton containers similarly uses his yogurt plant for demonstration purposes. At the time of our interviews, however, small producers in rural areas were not aware of the existence of the equipment suppliers in Bogotá and Cali.

Even if large firms with imported technology are not a source of technical knowledge for small firms, they have indirectly helped the latter by introducing the country to a variety of products and by fostering demand for them through advertising. Small firms without money for advertising are less able to introduce new products. For example, a small producer in Bogotá who introduced a European type of yogurt survived for only a year because of lack of consumer acceptance, even though his prices were lower and his packaging better than those of other yogurts. Sometime later the two largest producers introduced a similar yogurt with more success.

The courses given by SENA and some universities have helped to raise the quality of cheese produced in Colombia. Small firms still make lower-quality products, however, because they cannot afford pasteurizing equipment, which is economically justified only for processing more than 5,000 milk bottles a day, and because they usually prepare their own curd, which is cheaper but gives lower-quality cheese than imported curd. Unpasteurized milk not only affects the quality of the product but also presents a health hazard to consumers.

Potato Chips

Industrial production of potato chips dates from the late 1940s, when a U.S. citizen started a small plant with secondhand equipment imported from Houston (mainly peeling and cutting machines). This firm never produced more than 310 kilograms a day (compared with the 6,200 kilograms a day currently produced by the largest firm in Colombia), but it was very important in developing a market for the product and acted as a source of technical information for other firms. After two years, the pioneering company faced competition, first from a former distributor and then from a new firm that now has one-third of the Colombian market. The higher volumes and lower prices of its competitors eventually forced the original producer out of the market. By the late 1960s other firms had appeared, some established by former workers for the largest firm and others by distributors who recognized the potential of the business. The industry currently consists of four or five large enterprises (two with foreign capital) and many small ones, fifty of them in Bogotá alone. The simplest method of production, and the one that is most common among small producers, is a completely manual one; the potatoes are peeled and cut, fried in an open container, and removed all by hand. This method wastes up to 5 percent of the potatoes. An intermediate technology uses simple machines, of the type used by the original small producer, for peeling and cutting and a basket moved by a system of pulleys to transport the fried potatoes. Firms that start small graduate from manual to semimechanized processes as their financial situation improves. Only the largest firms have integrated systems.

Design Capability and Firm Size

In our sample many SMI firms displayed design capability and had improved product quality as discussed in the preceding sections. A majority of metalworking companies in each size category turned out products either designed by themselves or modified from other firms' designs (table 5-1). Even though a firm made no modifications, it may not have lacked design capability but may simply have been manufacturing products that were adequate in quality and needed little or no modification. This is suggested by the fact that design modification is less frequent among larger firms, which tend to manufacture better-quality goods, than smaller ones. It can be difficult to differentiate between modifications and new designs; there are no totally original designs in the sample, but significant product modifications have been made for some time. The continuing efforts of SMI to improve product quality are confirmed by the fact that only 12 of 64 respondents said they had not introduced design changes in the four years preceding the survey. Most design changes by small firms are made to improve quality or to adapt the product to clients' needs. Few make changes that facilitate production, such as standardization of parts for series production or simplification of design to reduce the number of machines. This type of change is more common among larger firms (41–60 workers); one-quarter of this subgroup made modifications to facilitate production during the preceding four years.

Overall, Colombian metalworking firms are still at an early stage in the development of design capability. Small entrepreneurs are doing what their counterparts in more advanced semi-industrial countries such as Argentina did ten or fifteen years ago.[7] In most Colombian SMIs, design

Table 5-1. *Sources of Product Design and Nature of Design Changes in Small and Medium Metalworking Firms, by Size*
(number of firms)

Product design	Number of workers					All
	1–10	11–20	21–40	41–60	61+	
Sources						
Own, modification, and copy	0	2	0	3	1	6
Own and modification	6	6	10	4	0	26
Modification only	3	7	1	2	4	17
Modification and copy	2	0	1	2	1	6
Copy only	1	1	2	0	1	5
License	1	1	1	1	1	5
All	13	17	15	12	8	65
Nature of changes in the past four years						
No change	2	2	3	1	4	12
Quality improvement	6	10	8	2	0	26
Adaptation to client's needs	2	2	0	0	1	5
Facilitation of production	1	1	0	3	0	5
Adaptation of foreign design	0	0	0	1	1	2
Small changes	2	2	3	5	2	14
All	13	17	14	12	8	64

changes are made by entrepreneurs themselves without help from technicians experienced in design; it is relatively rare for these changes to be systematically transferred to blueprints. In the case of agricultural implements and stoves, an entrepreneur's design ability seems to be the result of practical experience rather than theoretical knowledge. Producers of pumps and compressors, however, may have taken either formal or correspondence courses on the subject. Larger firms have design departments that employ technicians and sometimes engineers, but their capacity for design work is far weaker than that of their more experienced counterparts in Argentina.

The small- and medium-size metalworking firms in our sample do not confine themselves to designing their own products; most of them (65 percent) manufacture, and in some cases design, some of their own equipment as well (see table 5-2). This often consists of simple metal-cutting and bending machines, including hydraulic presses, whose design is based on existing equipment. But 30 percent of our sample incorporated design modifications suited to the specific needs or abilities of individual firms. Many very small firms of 1–10 workers design and build their own simple equipment because they lack the money to buy it. Their designs are usually based on equipment already available in the market, but with modifications. Nearly all the sampled firms in the 41–60 worker category also design some of their own equipment, although lack of money is less frequently their motive. The practice is less common (observed in three of eight firms) among the largest units, probably because they use relatively sophisticated basic equipment, which requires auxiliary equipment that is beyond their design capabilities.

Choice of Technique, Technical Change, and Firm Size

It is evident from our two samples that sophistication of equipment is associated with firm size—and, in the case of food processing, with the age of firm as well. Within each sector we have classified a firm's technology as simple if it is uses predominantly manual tools or simple machines in the main stages of its production process; as intermediate if it is uses a combination of manual and automatic machines; and as more sophisticated if most of its equipment is mechanized (see the glossary for definitions of types of technique). These categories are meaningful only within a given sector; they do not permit comparisons between the two sectors. We should also emphasize that the techniques used by all the sample firms are simple and labor-using relative to those of developed countries. Even the most sophisticated Colombian firms use standardized all-purpose equipment, which is easy to operate and maintain.

Table 5-2. *The Capacity of Small and Medium Metalworking Firms to Design Their Own Equipment, by Size*
(number of firms)

Number of workers	No design capability	Copy existing designs	Copy and modify existing designs	Number of firms
1–10	2	4	7	13
11–20	8	7	2	17
21–40	7	6	2	15
41–60	1	5	6	12
61+	5	1	2	8
All	23	23	19	65

In the metalworking sector, nearly 60 percent of the firms with fewer than 20 workers use mainly simple techniques, whereas six of the eight firms with more than 60 workers use relatively sophisticated techniques (see table 5-3). Similarly, in the food sector, the smallest firms use either very simple or intermediate production techniques, while four of the six firms with 30 or more workers use relatively sophisticated techniques. In food processing, sophistication of techniques increases with the age of the firm (see table 5-3).

The association between firm size and sophistication of technology raises the question of whether some types of technical change are closely linked to firm growth and whether firms that stay small are also able to make desired changes in their production processes. This is an important issue if efficient small firms do indeed have certain advantages (linked to their labor intensity) over large enterprises from society's point of view.

Our sample information indicates that changes in production techniques occur mainly with growth, when the new scale of production and the different factor prices faced by the expanding firm justify the change. Certain minor increases in mechanization are profitable even for a small firm, however, and these are undertaken when its financial situation permits. The majority of metalworking firms in all size categories (including the smallest firms with 1–10 workers) had become more mechanized in the three to four years prior to our survey (table 5-4). More than two-thirds of the youngest firms (aged 5 years or less) with more than 10 workers had already increased their level of mechanization, but those that were both young and small had not (see table 5-5). Increases in mechanization usually take place in the firm's main process (table 5-4), while peripheral activities tend to remain labor-intensive even in larger firms. In the food sector, nearly all small firms have recently changed their production processes; the smallest (1–7 workers) did so mainly to

Table 5-3. *Sophistication of Technology in Small and Medium Metalworking and Food Processing Firms, by Size and Age* (number of firms)

Type of firm	Type of technology			Number of firms
	Simple	Intermediate	More sophisticated	
Metalworking firms				
Size (number of workers)				
1–10	9	3	1	13
11–20	7	6	2	15
21–40	3	3	9	15
41–60	2	4	6	12
61+	0	2	6	8
All	21	18	24	63
Age (years)				
1–5	5	4	6	15
6–10	6	4	4	14
11–15	3	1	5	9
16–25	5	5	6	16
26+	2	4	3	9
All	21	18	24	63
Food processing firms				
Size (number of workers)				
1–7	5	5	1	11
8–15	1	6	4	11
16–29	4	3	1	8
30+	0	2	4	6
All	10	16	10	36
Age (years)				
1–5	5	4	3	12
6–15	5	5	5	15
16+	0	7	2	9
All	10	16	10	36

improve quality, and the next category up (8–15 workers) to reduce production costs (table 5-6). As expected, lack of finance is the main obstacle to a small firm's ability to upgrade its production techniques. The very small metalworking firms (1–10 workers) that did not change their processes universally blamed their failure to do so on the lack of finance (table 5-4). A majority of the other firms that had made no change (8 out of 14) indicated that they did not change because they were satisfied with their present production technology.

Given the difference between private profitability and social efficiency, it is important to distinguish changes of technology that raise a firm's SBC from ones that lower it or leave it unaffected. It is often argued that capital-intensive large plants obtain capital at a price that is below its

Table 5-4. *Changes in Production Process in Small
and Medium Metalworking Firms, by Size*
(number of firms)

Aspects of change in production process	Number of workers					Number of firms
	1–10	11–20	21–40	41–60	61+	
Change						
No change	5	5	0	3	1	14
Increase mechanization	7	11	12	8	7	45
Other[a]	1	1	3	1	0	6
All	13	17	15	12	8	65
Reason for change						
Increase production	1	4	4	1	3	13
Increase production or						
add new products	2	3	6	2	2	15
Improve quality	2	1	1	1	0	5
Reduce costs	4	3	3	5	2	17
All	9	11	14	9	7	50
Reason not to change or to limit change[b]						
Satisfied with process	0	4	1	3	0	8
Lack of finance	6	3	0	2	1	12
All	6	7	1	5	1	20
Expansion of facilities						
Yes	4	8	12	5	5	34
No	9	9	3	7	3	31
All	13	17	15	12	8	65
Areas of increase in mechanization						
Main process	4	9	6	5	6	30
Main process and						
finishing	1	2	4	2	0	9
Main process,						
transport, and	0	0	1	1	1	3
finishing	2	0	1	0	0	3
All	7	11	12	8	7	45

Note: Information in the table is for the three to four years preceding the survey.

a. Improvements in the use of existing machinery—for example, programming of the production process or the addition of equipment accessories.

b. The number of responses can exceed the number of firms making no change since firms could cite both reasons, and some firms that made small changes gave their reasons for not making larger changes.

social opportunity cost and that their choice of capital-intensive technologies is socially inefficient even if it is beneficial from the perspective of private profit. Unfortunately, our data do not permit a reliable analysis of this dimension of the technological changes introduced by our samples of firms. If the cost of capital is thought to be high for SMI, especially

Table 5-5. *Increases in the Level of Mechanization in Small and Medium Metalworking Firms, by Age and Size*
(number of firms)

Firm's age (years)	Increase in mechanization	Number of workers					
		1–10	11–20	21–40	41–60	61+	Total
1–5	Yes	0	3	5	0	1	9
	No	4	2	1	1	1	8
6–10	Yes	4	3	1	1	4	13
	No	0	0	1	0	0	1
11–15	Yes	0	0	4	2	1	7
	No	1	1	0	0	0	2
16–25	Yes	3	2	1	3	1	10
	No	0	1	1	3	1	6
26+	Yes	0	3	1	2	0	6
	No	1	2	0	0	0	3
All	Yes	7	11	12	8	7	45
	No	6	6	3	4	1	20

Note: Information in the table is for the three to four years preceding the survey.

SI, it would follow that few of these firms would introduce labor-saving technological improvements to any extent. But if a large proportion of the firm's own capital and borrowed capital (when it is available) can be obtained at a price below what one surmises to be the social opportunity cost of capital, it may be that some of the "improvements" just described have had the effect of lowering SBCs.

Information and Technical Assistance

Metalworking firms of all sizes often tap external sources of technical information. Nearly 90 percent of the entrepreneurs we surveyed either go

Table 5-6. *Reasons for Changes in Production Process in Small and Medium Food Processing Firms, by Size*
(number of firms)

Changes in production process	Number of workers				
	1–7	8–15	16–29	30+	Total
No change	1	1	1	2	5
Improve quality	6	2	2	2	12
Add new product	0	2	2	1	5
Reduce cost	3	6	3	1	13
Satisfied with process	1	0	0	0	1
All	11	11	8	6	36

Note: Information in the table is for the three to four years preceding the survey.

to fairs or read trade catalogs and magazines for this purpose. Producers of agricultural implements frequent agricultural fairs, where they may pick up product design ideas, and technical fairs, where they may get ideas for the best sort of capital equipment to use. Small metalworking firms in Argentina, which are also active in product design, place similar importance on the design information that they get from fairs and foreign producers' catalogs.[8] Fewer of the food firms in our sample (37 percent) use these sources of information.

Technical improvements by small and medium firms reflect mainly the entrepreneur's learning by doing in the firm, knowledge acquired in his previous job, information collected from the sources noted above, or technical assistance. Few of the smallest firms have received technical assistance from any source (see tables 5-7 and 5-9), whereas a majority of those with 10 or more workers have. In the metalworking sector, young and small firms have received assistance more often than older small ones (see table 5-8), even though most firms express a need for more help regardless of age. The main kind of assistance received by firms with fewer than 20 workers has been in administration and management, an appropriate focus given their tendency to weakness in these areas. Larger firms more frequently received assistance in production as well as administration. Food processing firms more often received assistance dealing with the production process or with equipment. This bias reflects the fact that the managers of these firms tend to lack the technical expertise generally found in metalworking SMI firms.

Government agencies have been the main source of technical assistance for the metalworking firms in our sample. SENA, which seems to focus especially on firms with 11–60 workers, has been the source of technical assistance for nearly 60 percent of all firms that have received help of this kind. Other nonprofit sources are Fundación para el Fomento de la Investigación Científica y Tecnológica (2 firms), the Caja Agraria (2 firms), and SENA-ASTIN (3 firms). In the food sector, although fewer firms have received any assistance (only 11 out of 31), much of it has gone to small firms with 8–15 workers (although not to the very smallest group); this pattern reflects the government's efforts to improve the performance of small producers of guava paste for export purposes.

Toward a Model of Technological Change in SMI

The empirical evidence reviewed in previous sections shows that many SMIs have an impressive capacity for technical change, even when external help is not available. In industries such as metalworking, technical change tends to diffuse from one firm to others as a result of labor mobility and the creation of entrepreneurs from among former workers. The

Table 5-7. *Technical Assistance for Small and Medium*
Metalworking Firms, by Size
(number of firms)

Technical assistance and information	Number of workers					Total number of firms
	1–10	11–20	21–40	41–60	61+	
Sources of information						
No sources	2	3	0	2	0	7
One source	3	3	4	1	0	11
Several sources	8	11	11	9	8	47
All	13	17	15	12	8	65
Type of technical assistance received						
Product	0	0	0	2	2	4
Production methods	1	2	2	0	1	6
Administration	2	7	2	1	0	12
Administration and production	1	3	5	6	2	17
No assistance	9	5	6	3	2	25
All	13	17	15	12	7	64
Sources of technical assistance						
Research institute	1	0	0	3	0	4
Family and friends	0	2	0	1	0	3
Government only	1	4	5	3	1	14
Government and others	0	4	1	2	1	8
Suppliers, consultants, or banks	3	1	3	0	2	9
All	5	11	9	9	4	38
Desire for technical assistance						
No	4	4	6	4	2	20
Yes	7	10	7	6	2	32
All	11	14	13	10	4	52
Type of technical assistance needed						
Administration	2	0	0	0	0	2
Production methods	1	4	2	2	2	11
Administration and production	1	2	0	1	0	4
Marketing	0	2	1	1	0	4
Design	0	0	1	1	0	2
Organization	3	1	0	1	0	5
All	7	9	4	6	2	28

Note: Information in the table is for the three to four years preceding the survey.

Table 5-8. *Receipt of Technical Assistance by Small and Medium Metalworking Firms, by Size and Age*
(number of firms)

Firm's age (years)	Technical assistance received	Number of workers					All
		1–10	11–20	21–40	41–60	61+	
1–5	Yes	2	5	3	0	1	11
	No	2	0	3	1	0	6
6–10	Yes	2	2	2	1	2	9
	No	2	1	0	0	2	5
11–15	Yes	0	0	2	1	0	3
	No	1	1	2	1	0	5
16+	Yes	0	5	3	7	2	17
	No	4	3	0	1	0	8
All	Yes	4	12	10	9	5	40
	No	9	5	5	3	2	24

Note: Information in the table is for the three to four years preceding the survey.

assistance that SENA and other agencies provide in such areas as management practices, production techniques, and product design helps individual firms, increases their contribution to the economy, and generates externalities for other firms through the diffusion process. The total benefits of such assistance are very likely to outweigh the costs.

The sort of technology used by SMIs and the extent and nature of technological change in the sector raise important issues for developing countries. Unless it is significantly adapted to the developing-country environment, imported technology can be undesirably capital-intensive. Although large industry is inclined to utilize such technology, one of the advantages often claimed for SMI is its greater labor intensity. The positive feature, however, has led to concern that SMI may fail to improve its technology over time and may therefore be a bad economic bet in the longer run. Both the available data on labor productivity trends in small-scale manufacturing as a whole and the more detailed information from our two industry samples tend to refute such a pessimistic view, and although the cottage shop sector is not our chief concern here, it seems that it, too, may be characterized by more technological innovation and change than has often been assumed.

Nelson's model of the process of technological change in manufacturing in developing countries hypothesized that LI technology is in general more efficient than that of smaller industry and that these relatively efficient LI processes gradually become disseminated to smaller establishments and raise their productivity.[9] (Nelson illustrated his model using Colombian data.) Although this type of diffusion clearly explains some of the productivity increases in SMIs, it is obviously not the main mecha-

Table 5-9. *Use of Outside Sources of Information
and Type of Technical Assistance Received
in Small and Medium Food Processing Firms, by Size*
(number of firms)

Technical assistance and outside information	Number of workers				Total number of firms
	1–7	8–15	16–29	30+	
Use of outside sources of information					
No	8	6	5	1	20
Yes	2	4	2	4	12
Total	10	10	7	5	32
Technical assistance received					
Type of product	2	4	0	1	7
Equipment	2	5	0	1	8
Production methods	2	4	0	2	8
Administration and finance	2	2	2	1	7
No assistance	8	3	6	3	20
Total	10	8	8	5	31

Note: Information in the table is for the three to four years preceding the survey.

nism at work in improving either products or processes. Consider first how changes in process technology occur within SMI. From our samples it appears that small firms in the metalworking and food industries tend to start with very simple production techniques; as they grow, they adopt more sophisticated processes, which become increasingly similar to those used by larger firms—though not identical to them unless a smaller firm actually joins the "large firm" category.[10] But in general superior technology does not seem to be diffused from larger to smaller firms as the latter find out about technologies that are better than the ones they previously used. Rather, a smaller firm seems to adapt its technology to changes in its financial situation and in the factor prices it faces; in other words, technological changes reflect objective changes in a firm's economic circumstances.

In the metalworking sector, entrepreneurs who said that they had acquired some or all of their skills by working in large firms (22 percent) or by being apprentices in training institutions such as SENA (18 percent— see table 4-9) would be expected to be familiar with the relatively sophisticated techniques used in larger firms.[11] The 38 percent who acquired some or all of their skills working in small or medium firms and the 46 percent who were partly or wholly self-taught might or might not, but our general impression is that such information was rather widely known.[12] Nevertheless, SMI entrepreneurs start with simple techniques and change them only when their firm's growth justifies it. In the food sector, entrepreneurs in small firms have typically not had prior experience in other firms, large or small, in the industry; much of their technical knowledge derives from the traditional production process, from training institutes (SENA, IIT, and others), or from other small firms through worker mobility. But in food processing plants the evolution of technology in response to changes in firm size and factor prices appears similar to that in the metalworking industry.

The positive relationship that we find between the capital-labor ratio and firm size (at least above a certain level) is consistent with a belief that firms choose factor proportions according to the patterns of factor prices or market access that they face, although it is also consistent with Nelson's hypothesis, since our data do not permit us to reject the possible coexistence of different production functions across firm size. But direct observation in the metalworking and food processing industries suggests that the former interpretation is often closer to the mark.[13] A related inconsistency between our evidence and Nelson's diffusion model lies in our finding that intermediate technologies are more efficient than relatively capital-intensive ones. Baily reports the same conclusion in her analysis of the brick industry in Colombia.[14]

The data indicate that the basic product designs used by small firms are copied from imports or LI products. The owners of small firms have often been able to design their own products as a result of skills acquired by working in larger firms—but a small firm's design innovations usually precede those made by larger ones. Important adaptations can make it possible for small firms to penetrate market sectors previously controlled by large ones. The dynamic role of small firms in design innovation may reflect their close contact with final users, together with the flexibility that results from their relatively low levels of capital investment and their owners' direct involvement in day-to-day management.

Thus, in general, although owners of small firms often learn their skills by working for larger firms, the technical improvements they introduce have more to do with their business circumstances (factor prices, clients' demands, financial position) than with a recognizable general pattern of technological diffusion from larger to smaller firms. Direct contacts between firms are important in the process of technology diffusion. This process generally occurs within firms of a similar type, however, with the big division being between capital-intensive and labor-intensive units.[15] Thus, although previous experience in another firm can be an important source of technological information for the SMI entrepreneur, it does not automatically lead him to adopt a previous employer's technology. Other sources of information for small firms include skilled individuals with experience in another firm who are brought in on contract, local equipment producers and distributors, importers of secondhand equipment, training and technical advice provided by SENA, and catalogs and other information obtained at fairs. Distributors tend to be biased in favor of capital-intensive techniques, which are more profitable for them. Baily reports that one machinery distributor, which produced a labor-intensive cementing machine for shoe soles because it was unable to sell a more capital-intensive one, nevertheless complained of the "irrational behavior" of its clients in preferring the labor-intensive machinery.[16]

Design work on capital goods can be a fruitful source of technological capacity. Capital goods that are manufactured domestically reflect the simpler technologies used by SMI more often than the sophisticated ones used by LI. Both our research and Baily's study found that domestically produced machinery was practically nonexistent in the most modern capital-intensive categories of firms, except for occasional simple motors and conveyor belts, but became more important in the less capital-intensive categories. Colombian machinery is generally a simplified version of the corresponding imported item. For example, some cheese producers buy a simplified locally made version of Danish equipment that has been imported secondhand. Sometimes this equipment is made by the users themselves; metalworking firms, for example, produce their own presses and cutting equipment. In industries where users lack the necessary skills, equipment is produced by other firms according to their own or users' specifications.

It is impossible to determine precisely how much of SMI's output gains from technological change are due to the diffusion of technology from more efficient large firms (the Nelson hypothesis) or to improvements arising in other ways, including innovation within SMI itself.[17] The evidence presented in this chapter does suggest, however, that these gains are often unrelated to diffusion from large to small firms—in fact, a not insignificant number may constitute a reverse flow from small to large companies if we judge from the history of agricultural implements. We noted in chapter 3 that overly sophisticated techniques usually pay off less well than intermediate technologies in small and medium-size metalworking and food processing firms; thus it is unlikely that a straightforward transfer of technology from large modern firms to SMI would be the main way to increase their efficiency. At the very least, transfers of that sort would require adaptation to SMI's scale of operations.

Our surveys of metalworking and food processing, together with other evidence, such as Baily's studies of the brick and men's leather shoe industries, illustrate the importance of distinguishing between choice of technology (how factor prices determine the technology used) and improvements in the production function (technological change). There is no evidence to support the view that the techniques used by large firms are generally better than those used by SMI firms, in the sense of being superior for all relevant factor prices. It appears that if a given SMI firm moves to a more sophisticated technology (which may indeed come from larger firms), it does so because changes in access to or prices of factors dictate the choice of a different technique. At a given point in a firm's evolution, the optimal technology from a private point of view will not generally be the most sophisticated one. Moreover, since the firm's factor prices will not generally correspond to the social opportunity costs of factors, this climbing of the ladder of technological sophistication may or may not raise the firm's social efficiency—or may raise it until a certain level of technology is reached and then lower it.

We therefore believe that technological change, understood as the improvement of an existing process or product, is a more likely source of increases in SMI's social efficiency than is a switch to a different already known process or product because the former raises the firm's efficiency at the factor prices the firm faces. It is with respect to this sort of change that SMI seems to be surprisingly independent of LI. This is not to deny that much of the improvement in SMI factor productivity over time may be the result of improvements in capital equipment, plant layout, or other factors that were first applied in the country in LI (usually through transfers from abroad) and that were diffused through purchase of secondhand equipment or through other channels. But significant improvements are generated within SMI itself—and, even more important, only some of the techniques that maximize private profit for LI will also raise private profit in SMI or social efficiency in either category.

Notes

1. As noted in chapter 2, these figures do not reflect the performance of individual plants over time, since many new plants are created and some others change size category.

2. The overall rate of technological change in SMIs cannot be estimated since aggregate data on the capital stock over time by plant size category are not available. But the 40 percent figure indicates an important process of capital deepening (raising K/L) or technological improvement in small and medium plants. Those firms that did not graudate to the "large" category were on the average much more productive at the end of the period than at the beginning, or were replaced by more productive ones.

3. Our sample included 25 firms producing agricultural implements; these firms employed 732 workers in 1977. DANE's *Industria Manufacturera, 1978,* p. 86, lists 53 plants with 2,153 workers in industrial group 3822 (agricultural implements); these employment figures refer to November 1978. The 1970

volume, *III Censo Industrial, 1970,* p. 20 lists 38 plants with 1,344 workers. Comparison of the figures for the two years implies a 1970–78 average annual employment growth rate of 6 percent. *Industria Manufacturera, 1967,* p. 28, which predates the reduced coverage of smaller plants around 1970, reports 81 plants with 1,543 workers. On the basis of the more complete information that was used in 1967, there would almost certainly have been more than 100 plants by 1978; many of these establishments, however, would probably have been engaged mainly in repair activities. We believe that our sample included a high proportion of all SMI output and employment in the industry. Our 732 workers (not including the 750 in the industry's largest firm, which did not permit us to conduct detailed interviews) constitute about half of those reported by DANE (if the largest firm's workers are excluded).

4. The firm informed us that the share of its own sales going to the region fell from 50 to 10 percent. It had previously had a near-monopoly in this region.

5. SENA plays an important role in the training of technicians for cheese production, and IIT has undertaken research in guava paste production (see below).

6. Two of the former course organizers studied in Holland. The one in charge at the time of the survey studied in Switzerland.

7. Mariluz Cortes, "Argentina: Technical Development and Technology Exports to Other LDCs," World Bank, Development Economics Department, Washington, D.C., March 1978; processed.

8. Ibid.

9. Richard R. Nelson, "A Diffusion Model of International Productivity Differences," *American Economic Review,* vol. 58, no. 5, part 1 (December 1968), pp. 1219–48.

10. In both the sectors surveyed, some of the larger firms acquired their technical knowledge abroad from their licensers or through technical assistance.

11. Baily reports that the great majority of decisionmakers in labor-intensive shoe firms had previously worked for another shoe producer, but she does not say whether the experience typically occurred in large firms. Mary Ann Baily, "Technology Choice in the Brick and Men's Leather Shoe Industries in Colombia," Yale University, Economic Growth Center, New Haven, Conn., August 1977; processed, p. 228.

12. These percentages add to more than 100 because some respondents cited more than one source.

13. It also coincides substantially with Baily's findings for the brick industry in Colombia; she concludes that factor price differences, not a simple process of technological diffusion, explain a more or less permanently wide range of factor proportions in that industry. (Mary Ann Baily, "Brick Manufacturing in Colombia: A Case Study of Alternative Technologies," *World Development,* vol. 19, no. 2 [February 1981].) To support this proposition, she argues that older rather than newer firms have more modern equipment and that intermediate technologies are in fact the most efficient. The capital market imperfections cited (though not quantified) by Baily are undoubtedly an element in the coexistence of such varying factor proportions. Her emphasis on labor market imperfections is perhaps harder to accept as a general proposition (numerous other studies indicate that

firm size has relatively little explanatory power in accounting for wage differences). But major imperfections in only one factor market are sufficient for her argument.

14. Baily, "Brick Manufacturing in Colombia."

15. This is particularly evident in the case of cheese producers and among the brick producers studied by Baily. As noted in chapter 2, although plants of 100 workers or more are the major sellers of used capital goods, plants of 50–99 workers are large buyers but sell very little. This might suggest that such a division exists in manufacturing as a whole and that most smaller firms are so much more labor-intensive than MI firms that it does not pay to buy used machines from them. In the abstract one might expect that each size category would buy used machinery mainly from larger plants and sell used machinery mainly to smaller plants. All but the largest, and perhaps the smallest, would both buy and sell in considerable quantities.

16. Baily also notes that such sources as foreign technical assistance contracts, foreign private consultants, foreign trade fairs, and machine catalogs are more important for capital-intensive firms, since a producer must have greater educational sophistication or greater fixed cost to use these sources. Baily, "Technology Choice," pp. 132–36.

17. The answer would depend on what prices are used to weight inputs and outputs. As noted earlier. factor prices differ across size classes of firms.

6

An Interpretation of the Success of SMI

As the preceding chapters have shown, SMI was a dynamic, growing, profitable, and innovative sector during most of the 1970s.[1] The much more limited data on earlier periods give the impression that growth and profitability were less in evidence then. This chapter is concerned with the main characteristics of SMI firms, some possible explanations for their special dynamism during the 1970s, and the general implications of our findings for public policy.

The historical analysis of chapter 2 showed that the secular downward trend in SMI's share of manufacturing employment and output was reversed during most of the 1970s (at least until 1978). In these years, SMI grew faster than large industry did as new small enterprises began appearing at an increasingly fast pace at the same time that established ones were expanding rapidly. This impressive advance appears to have been caused primarily by favorable economic conditions rather than by any direct involvement of government or special steps to encourage it. Although the support given by public institutions such as CPF and SENA was a great help to some firms, the decade witnessed no special change in public policy that might help to explain the increased dynamism of SMI.

Beginning in the late 1960s, however, incomes rose rapidly and consequently the demand for manufactured goods increased, as did the availability of such vital inputs as entrepreneurship, capital goods, credit, and labor. New SMI entrepreneurs included many former blue-collar workers who started their own businesses after accumulating production skills (and entitlement to severance payments) while working in larger firms created during the import-substitution period. Many new white-collar entrepreneurs began their new businesses as sidelines or second sources of income. The acquisition of capital equipment was facilitated by Colombia's favorable balance of payments position. As larger firms were encouraged to replace their old equipment by the reduced price of imported machinery, local supplies of secondhand equipment grew. By the early 1970s, rising demand also favored the establishment of a number of local importers of secondhand equipment. Credit availability improved with the relaxing of foreign exchange constraints and the growth of the extra-bank system, which was fueled by, among other things, the incomes generated from illegal exports. At the same time, the urban labor force was growing rapidly and becoming better skilled as a result of accumulated experience, higher levels of education, and the contribution of training institutions (especially SENA, whose programs had begun in the 1960s).

Characteristics and Performance of SMI

SMI has played an important role in the Colombian economy in recent years, most notably as a source of employment (where it was comparable to LI in the mid-1970s), but also as a contributor to total industrial output. It has also generated healthy profits: in 1976 the ratio of profits (before direct taxes) to the sum of the value of inventories plus the book value of fixed assets was almost 0.35, which is about equal to that of large industry (see table 2-19); the return to correctly measured capital (that is, adjusted for inflation) might be somewhat lower, but not dramatically so. To judge by our samples in the metalworking and food sectors, this impressive average performance represented the mean of a wide range of individual outcomes; some firms were doing poorly, whereas others were registering sparkling successes. Similarly, the average growth rate of SMI has been strong but has varied widely from firm to firm. DANE's data show that between 1970 and 1975 the employment of firms with 5–99 workers (in 1970) grew at an annual average of 4.6 percent; their output probably rose a little faster. To judge by aggregate employment figures for SMI (which suggest an average annual growth of 9 percent or so between 1970 and 1978 (see table 2-2), new firms must have played a major role in the aggregate growth of SMI.[2]

SMI was much more dynamic in some sectors than in others; the metalworking activities covered in our sample represented an outstanding example of rapid growth. These nearly eighty firms began with an average of fourteen employees and a small capital stock. In general capital, employment, and output grew rapidly, although short- or longer-term contractions also occurred. Growth was based largely on the reinvestment of profits and on technological improvements that the SMI firm often helped to create. Aggregate labor productivity in SMI as a whole appears to have risen markedly since World War II. In short, most of our evidence shows SMI to be a growing, changing sector; SMI firms in some as yet unstudied industries may of course turn out to be different.

Both aggregate DANE data and our survey of SMIs at the micro level suggest that smaller firms in the SMI category tend to be less efficient than larger ones.[3] Nevertheless, DANE data on labor productivity suggest that the static efficiency disadvantage of small firms may vary considerably by industry and in some cases is absent or unimportant. In any event, an efficiency disadvantage need not imply a pessimistic conclusion about the potential of these firms, for several reasons. First, data on the efficiency of the smallest firms are influenced by the performance of those (often young ones) that will and often should fail. (Since few new companies start large, such transitory firms do not push down the efficiency indicators for larger units.) Average efficiency is probably considerably higher for small firms with reasonably good managers. Second, in many sectors, including the two that we studied in detail, factors other than size appear to be more important in determining the efficiency of firms. Further, with growth rates of the kind observed in the metalworking sector, a typical firm does not stay small for long, so that a longer-run assessment of its efficiency may be considerably more favorable than one taken when it is young and inefficient. In addition, there is ample evidence that firms can raise their productivity via mechanization and technical improvements without growing (at least in terms of employment).

Sixteen of the roughly 100 firms in our surveys had private benefit-cost ratios below or equal to one. In a few of them the entrepreneurs were considering shutting down. Most (9 of the 16) were covering variable costs, so that one would not expect them to exit from the market unless they received an attractive offer for the business or for their capital. A large majority of these entrepreneurs also reported that their economic situation had improved as a result of having started their businesses. Many of those with blue-collar origins would have had limited alternatives and could therefore be expected to remain in the market as long as current and expected returns to their labor did not fall below the incomes they could obtain as skilled workers or technicians in larger firms.

Differences in the benefit-cost ratios of firms appear to be largely due to differences in technical efficiency, especially in the metalworking sector. Allocative or price efficiency is harder to isolate; it doubtless plays a role, but is probably less important. Differences in the input costs and output prices of firms also help to explain differences in their economic performance. In both the sectors that we studied, small firms benefit from lower labor costs, which stem largely from their lower contributions to social security and some other fringe benefits. Differences in the cost of borrowed capital are probably relatively unimportant for our small- and medium-size firms, since retained earnings constitute their main source of capital. Access to borrowed funds to complement other resources probably contributes to better economic performance, although this is hard to confirm by statistical analysis.[4] Such access allows firms to have more working capital and to increase their flexibility. Small firms tend to charge lower prices than their competitors, in some cases because their products are lower in quality, in others because they are trying to enter markets dominated by larger firms. At the same time, they tend to pay more for raw materials because they buy them in small quantities and, in the case of food processing, because they are less able to sustain a steady inflow during the year.

A firm's technical efficiency and BC ratios are affected by the characteristics and quality of the entrepreneur and the sophistication of the production technology used. In both metalworking and food processing, persons with more than a primary education seem to have an advantage; when these sectors are considered separately, however, persons with secondary schooling do very well in food processing but do less well in the metalworking sector than persons with primary schooling only. The two sectors also differ in the skill combinations that tend to pay off; in metalworking, persons with only production skills do less well than others, but in the food sector this is not the case. Apparently production skills are relatively abundant in the metalworking sector (where many entrepreneurs are former mechanics), whereas administrative skills are scarce. In food processing, however, few entrepreneurs have had prior experience in production activities and the opposite is the case. In both sectors and in most of the size categories we distinguished, the use of moderately sophisticated technology is associated with higher technical efficiency and BC ratios than the use of the simplest or the most sophisticated technologies—despite the fact that the most sophisticated technology used by firms in both samples is simple by international standards. Technologies that are sophisticated by Colombian standards are, however, quite efficient in the largest mechanical firms (those with more than 60 workers), while simple technologies produce the best results in firms with 10 or fewer workers.

The availability of inexpensive secondhand equipment contributes significantly to the creation of small firms by greatly reducing their initial investment. Secondhand equipment is extensively used by larger firms as well. In the metalworking sector, the use of a high proportion of secondhand equipment is not associated with reductions in BC ratios or technical efficiency, as some critics of the use of such equipment in developing countries fear, possibly because Colombian skilled workers are able to repair and produce spare parts. Our regression analysis indicates that the use of secondhand equipment in the food sector may have a slight, but statistically insignificant, negative effect on the PBC ratio.

Small firms in Colombia have a striking capacity to grow and improve technically over time. Many of those in the metalworking sector design their own products and adapt existing designs to the needs of their clients. These design skills originate in the repair and reconstruction services initially provided by most firms. Close contact with their clients permits them to respond to users' needs more effectively than larger firms can. In fact, their ability to change designs helps very small firms compete with larger ones. Small firms are also willing to improve their production processes when their financial situation permits.

Causes of the SMI Boom in the 1970s

Until the late 1960s, SMI's share of manufacturing output and employment was roughly constant in the manufacturing sector as a whole, including CS, but was falling in relation to LI's share. SMI's labor productivity was much lower than LI's and was rising more slowly. During the 1970s, overall manufacturing employment grew rapidly, continuing a trend begun earlier; SMI sector employment accelerated markedly, with growth appearing to be most rapid in the SI size range.[5] Aggregate SMI labor productivity fluctuated, showing no net gain between the late 1960s and 1977–78, so output grew at about the same rate as employment.

The 1970s saw marked changes in the pattern of Colombia's economic development, some of which may have been related to the surge in SMI activity. Until about 1967, the economy and the manufacturing sector were growing at acceptable but not impressive rates. Then began a period of sustained high growth, during which both national income and manufacturing output rose at about 7 percent a year. Before 1972, steady growth was accompanied by modest inflation. During the rest of the decade, however, the inflation rate was in the 20–30 percent range, a level not reached on a consistent basis during the previous half century. As inflation accelerated, real wages in most (perhaps all) occupational categories fell, and the share of wages in national income declined noticeably.[6] Urban employment grew very rapidly, in part because of a rise in female participation rates, and the rate of urban unemployment fell from its high levels of the late 1960s.[7] Manufacturing employment grew even faster than total urban employment; within the manufacturing aggregate, SI appears to have been the most dynamic source of new jobs.

The subsections that follow examine the main demand and supply factors that seem to account for the pace and pattern of growth in the manufacturing sector during the 1970s. We also consider whether some of the salient features of the Colombian economy during the decade—the very rapid growth of urban employment, constant or declining real wages, and constant or declining (at least for several years) labor productivity in manufacturing—are causally linked, and whether together they could have contributed to the SMI boom.

The Demand Side

During the decade that began in the late 1960s per capita income in Colombia rose rapidly, at about 5 percent a year. The demand for manufactured goods must have been rising rapidly, given their high income elasticity. Total supply appears to have expanded a little less rapidly, with the result that the relative prices of manufactured goods, especially those produced domestically, increased (see appendix table 25).[8] The contribution of the large-scale sector to domestic supply was damped somewhat by the fact that, at least during the first part of the period, the sector had shifted its efforts into the export market because of the rising real exchange rate and other incentives. This presumably helped to open the domestic market to smaller-scale producers in the early 1970s. By the middle of the decade, the growth of the LI sector was slowing; the ratio of investment in new fixed assets to value added, which had been relatively high in the early 1970s compared with the 1960s, fell somewhat between 1974 and 1978. This ratio had formerly been a little higher in LI than in SMI, but by 1976–78 it was considerably lower (see table 2-20). Profits in LI remained attractive, but prospects for the future may have appeared less positive.[9]

By the mid-1970s the exchange rate was devaluing too slowly to maintain the attractiveness of the foreign markets that had opened up in the previous decade. Businesses may have become more risk averse, perhaps because they lacked confidence in the prospects for the continued protection of domestic industry or were concerned about rising taxes and about the future stability of an economy whose income growth was based partly on unusually high coffee prices and on possibly transitory drug revenues.[10] Some observers noted a tendency among large corporations to put mergers and purchases of existing plants ahead of investment in new capital goods.[11] They did so perhaps because good bargains could be obtained at the time or because they expected a slowdown in the growth of demand. Large industry with some degree of monopoly or oligopoly power normally has no interest in expanding to the point of pushing prices down; SMI may have entered many industries under the ample monopoly price umbrella of LI.

Whatever the factors affecting LI's investment decisions, it seems reasonable to suppose that its failure to expand capacity more aggressively opened up market opportunities for SMI. Although we do not have reliable year-by-year figures on the rate of output growth in SI during the

1970s (because of the serious undercoverage in DANE's figures), our employment estimates (table 2-2) and the figures for investment (table 2-20) suggest that acceleration continued through 1978. With the recession of the early 1980s this growth has no doubt been slowed or reversed.

The Supply Side

The rapid expansion of SI can also be traced to a number of supply-side factors. Prominent among these was the supply of willing and capable entrepreneurs and the availability of capital and machinery.

ENTREPRENEURSHIP AND LABOR. One traditional source of entrepreneurship in CS, and probably in SI as well, has been the children or protégés of existing entrepreneurs, who learn the business mainly through on-the-job experience. This source has probably continued to contribute to the success of small-scale activities. Nevertheless, as our samples show, it could hardly have been responsible for the rapid expansion of SI activities in the 1970s, especially in relatively new activities such as metalworking. Apparently many former employees or partners moved out on their own after having built up skills and experience in their previous jobs. The supply of such people can be viewed as a function of accumulated experience in manufacturing and other sectors over the previous couple of decades. Meanwhile, the expansion of the formal education system has contributed to the supply of persons with relatively high levels of education, which generally seem to pay off in high returns to entrepreneurship.[12] Both these factors might be expected to generate a gradual increase in the available supply of entrepreneurial talents and in the growth of SMI; in fact, however, SMI seems to have experienced a sudden growth spurt around the beginning of the 1970s. The explanation for this appears to lie in the rapid expansion of demand and in other supply-side phenomena.

One such phenomenon is the fall in real wages during the 1970s. Both white- and blue-collar wages in manufacturing and other sectors fell in the early 1970s and did not regain their earlier levels until the end of the decade; at the same time, average per capita income was rising rapidly. This meant not only that real wage costs were lower than before and thus provided an inducement to the entrepreneur, but also that real wages of potential entrepreneurs (for example, the employees of larger plants) were falling and thus increasing the inducement for such persons to go into business for themselves. Starting a business would normally mean giving up wage or salary employment, although some white-collar workers and professionals continued to be employed while managing or otherwise participating in a small firm.

The tax reforms of the late 1960s and the 1970s may have caused some people to exchange wage or salaried employment for entrepreneurial profits. The reforms made it more difficult for salaried personnel to avoid income taxes and increased, if only temporarily, the general tax burden. Since income from capital invested in a small business is much harder to tax than wage income from a larger firm, a person's disposable income could be raised considerably simply by shifting its source. Whether it was because real incomes were declining or were falling short of aspirations and expectations, a growing trend of the 1970s was to increase family incomes by adding new sources of revenue. In such a setting, many people would be on the lookout for possible opportunities in small business.

Falling or stagnant real wages in the early 1970s were at least partly the result of a price-wage lag, but because inflation had never before reached such high levels, the institutional mechanisms for minimizing the lag had not yet been developed. Falling wage levels may also have reflected the unusually rapid growth in the urban labor force, fueled by rising female participation rates. In 1964 women constituted only 22–23 percent of the urban manufacturing labor force; in June 1978 the figure was 35 percent. The expansion of manufacturing employment was most notable among the younger workers. Between 1964 and 1978 the proportion of manufacturing employment accounted for by urban employees aged 15–29 rose from about 20 percent to about 28 percent (table 6-1).[13] The apparently elastic supply of labor may have worked more to the advantage of SI than MI or LI, since SI is less affected than the others by labor legislation and is also typically more labor-intensive.[14]

If the main exogenous factor in the 1970s was a rapid increase in labor supply that tended (with the assistance of rapid inflation) to push real

Table 6-1. *Manufacturing Employment as a Share of Total Employment, by Age: Urban and Rural, 1964, and Urban, 1978*
(percent)

	July 1964 (urban and rural)			June 1978 (urban)	
Age	Distribution by age	As share of total employment	Age	Distribution by age	As share of total employment
Under 15	1.67	4.80	Under 15	0.95	9.90
15–19	12.81	11.09	15–19	11.07	23.72
20–24	18.08	14.85	20–29	38.74	29.72
25–44	49.91	14.89	30–39	23.08	24.14
45–64	15.70	10.45	40–49	15.88	24.14
65+	1.84	7.30	50–59	7.12	18.70
All ages	100.00	12.78	60+	3.13	14.63
			All ages	100.00	24.71

Source: The 1964 population census and DANE's June 1978 household survey.

wages down, neither the sharp expansion of manufacturing employment nor the fall in labor productivity would in principle be surprising.[15] Yet the speed with which these effects followed the decline in real wages does seem surprising, especially in the case of LI. Falling real wages are, of course, likely to be especially helpful to SI with its high labor intensity; nevertheless, the view that labor market factors impinge most strongly on the SI sector does not fit well with the tentative evidence for a reduction in the wage differential between SI and larger plants in the early 1970s, unless the prices of other SI inputs were also falling at this time.

AVAILABILITY OF CAPITAL AND MACHINERY. Both capital and foreign exchange became more readily available in Colombia after the late 1960s. The market for secondhand machinery also broadened, and an extra-bank credit market evolved, fueled by inflation (which tended to lower real interest rates on most traditional financial assets) and large revenue inflows from the drug (and perhaps also coffee) bonanzas.

To judge by our food and metalworking sector samples, entrepreneurs' savings are not only the prime source of start-up capital for small firms, but also their main source of finance for later growth. The fact that aggregate family savings appear to have grown rapidly with the economic boom beginning in the late 1960s is therefore directly relevant to this study.[16] The accelerating inflation of the early 1970s led to a marked decrease in the return to financial assets; by 1974 the only financial investments to earn a positive real return were probably extra-bank market loans and UPACs (Unidad de Poder Adquisitivo Constante).[17] Given a large flow of savings and generally unsatisfactory returns on financial assets, investment in new business ventures and in real estate was likely to become increasingly attractive.

An important savings instrument for skilled workers was their accumulated severance pay (cesantía). By the late 1960s, many workers had accumulated enough such savings to meet the modest initial capital requirements of many of the firms in our food and metalworking samples.[18] This form of forced savings enabled many former workers to start up businesses of their own; thus in retrospect it seems an important institutional influence on SMI development.

Both aggregate statistics and our industry samples show that, once a small firm became established, a profit rate equal to the industry average provided a substantial source of savings for subsequent expansion. Since the performance levels of firms varied widely, there were likely many exceptions to this pattern, especially in sectors that were less profitable than the two we studied, and other time periods were no doubt less advantageous than the 1970s in this respect. As discussed in chapter 4, the rate of mortality among small firms has generally been high.

Given the dominant role of self-financing in the creation and growth of SMI firms, the importance of the capital market to them is unclear. Inadequate access to credit has often been viewed as a major barrier to new entrants, and many firms in our metalworking sample cited the lack of working capital as an important initial problem. The impressive growth record of many of these same firms suggests, however, that this view might be overdrawn in reference to the recent situation in Colombia— although the unusual circumstances of the 1970s probably enabled firms to reinvest profits at a higher rate than would normally be possible. Moreover, in the metalworking and food industries the proportion of investment that is self-financed declines with the age and size of the firm (see table 3-25), so that credit appears to play a more important part in the expansion rather than in the creation of firms and in the founding of middle-size rather than very small ones.

Thus there seems no reason to doubt that credit can make a significant difference, and that SMI would have done less well had credit been less available. Official credit to SMI—provided mainly by the Corporación Financiera Popular, the commercial banks, and the development finance companies (financieras)—appears to have increased rapidly in the late 1960s and early 1970s, just after the CFP and Caja Agraria programs were initiated (table 6-2); before that it probably rose slowly.[19] Extra-bank credit to SMI probably also rose rapidly in the early 1970s, albeit from a low base; SMI makes proportionately more use of this source of credit than does LI.[20] The flexibility of extra-bank credit may have been an important plus for SMI. A firm that is temporarily short of working capital may find a real annual interest rate of 12 percent an acceptable price to pay for the important boon of ready access to credit.

At a best guess, the ratio of formal sector loans outstanding to SMI to the value added by SMI was less than 10 percent in 1968; by 1978 the figure had probably risen closer to 15 percent. If the extra-bank credit were taken into account, the increase would be somewhat greater. The coincidence of timing between the fast growth of SMI and the rapid increase in availability of both official and extra-bank credit is intriguing. The available data do not permit us to probe the causal relations, but a closer look would seem appropriate once additional information becomes available.

Until the late 1960s, Colombia's financial system was under considerable government control and appeared to be biased in favor of large borrowers. In 1967, when the government adopted a crawling peg exchange rate, the dominant institutions were the Central Bank (Banco de la República), the commercial banks, the Agricultural Credit Bank (Caja Agraria), the Central Mortgage Bank (Banco Central Hipotecario), and the Development Finance Corporations (Corporaciones Financieras).

Table 6-2. *Loans Outstanding to Small and Medium Industry, by Institutions, 1968–78*
(current pesos except as noted)

Year	Commercial banks	Corporación Financiera Popular	Development finance companies	Caja Agraria	Instituto de Fomento Industrial (IFI)	Total	Total (1978 pesos)	Increase in total loans outstanding	Increase in total loans outstanding (1978 pesos)
1968	188	8.4	200	n.a.	n.a.	423[a]	2,199	—	—
1969	210	47.3	256	29.3	n.a.	579[a]	2,783	156	750
1970	218	94.7	368	35.3	n.a.	764[a]	3,345	185	810
1971	240	190	450	46.5	n.a.	989[a]	3,922	225	892
1972	265	290	585	142	n.a.	1,368[a]	4,784	379	1,325
1973	561	370	657	200	120	1,908	5,467	540	1,547
1974	791	457	747	250	142	2,387	5,359	479	1,075
1975	988	571	1,018	300	158	3,035	5,640	648	1,204
1976	1,108	850	1,366	350	179	3,853	5,791	818	1,229
1977	1,406	995	2,009	463	206	5,079	5,949	1,226	1,436
1978	2,122	1,499	2,520	510	224	6,875	6,875	1,796	1,796

n.a. Not available.

a. Assumes that IFI's share of the total was the same (6.3 percent) as in 1973.

Source: Figures kindly supplied by Thomas Bentley of the World Bank. The figures for the commercial banks, the development finance corporations, and IFI are all approximations based on rough guesses as to the percentage of their loans to manufacturing that went to SMI.

Previous attempts to direct credit, finance government expenditure, and control foreign exchange had produced restrictions and distortions in the system, including interest rate ceilings on deposits and loans, forced investment requirements, and directed credit. Interest rate controls led to credit rationing and probably also to lower savings rates. The SMI sector—especially the SI subgroup—did badly under this system. As of 1970, only about 8–9 percent of commercial bank credit went to borrowers with assets below the median initial investment of metalworking firms in our sample.[21] SMI access to formal sector credit was limited and a number of observers considered this a serious obstacle to the sector's growth.[22]

During the late 1960s and early 1970s the financial system grew more diverse and flexible.[23] Interest rate ceilings were raised, the UPAC was set up with a fixed real interest rate to channel savings into construction, and the extra-bank market evolved, with much higher interest rates than those previously paid in the official system.[24] In 1974 the government began a systematic effort to ease restrictions and to reduce the role of the Central Bank in development banking while promoting its function as a monetary authority. Some of the liberalizing effects of these changes were offset by the rising inflation of the early 1970s; others were adversely affected by steps taken during the 1977 stabilization program. Since 1980, the extra-bank market has been rather more tightly regulated and its competitiveness has diminished. Taken as a whole, the country's financial system remains inadequate in many respects, as evidenced by a 1982 crisis that induced the Superintendency of Banks to nationalize one commercial bank and intervene in another. Nevertheless, it is fair to say that the system did become more supportive of SMI from the late 1960s through most of the 1970s. Whether recent changes, including a return to directed credit, will reverse that trend remains to be seen.

Capital Equipment

Most items of machinery and equipment used in Colombia's manufacturing industry are still imported in LI and probably in SMI as well. The rapid expansion of SMI in the 1970s may therefore owe something to the buoyant state of the balance of payments and the greater availability of imports. This improvement over the chronic balance of payments problems of the 1960s was partly due to exogenous factors—high coffee prices and drug exports—but also to the more skillful management of the foreign exchange policy, beginning with the adoption of a floating exchange rate in 1967. As foreign exchange became more readily available, large firms imported capital equipment to replace old machinery (and to increase output); the used machinery and equipment were then put up for sale at prices SMI firms could afford.

In general, an exchange rate reasonably close to equilibrium probably benefits SMI, both by generating increased flows of total imports (because total exports are greater) and by helping to avoid rationing of foreign exchange.[25] More specifically, any broadening of the market in secondhand equipment benefits SMI greatly, as discussed in chapter 4. In addition, a more liberal foreign exchange regime encourages specialized intermediaries to import secondhand machinery and to repair and rehabilitate it.

After the Boom

Since our data were collected, the growth of the Colombian economy as a whole and that of the manufacturing sector in particular has slowed dramatically. Manufacturing output fell in 1981 and 1982, remained unchanged in 1983, and only in 1984 began to regain some of the lost ground. Until 1982, the open unemployment rate remained roughly constant, while real wages in construction and manufacturing (for which data are available) continued on an upward trend. In 1983 and 1984, however, the unemployment rate moved up sharply, and by 1984 all real wage series had turned down. Systematic figures are not yet available to indicate how this recession has affected SMI, but the general impression among observers is that both SMI and LI have been seriously hit. For 1978–80, however, available evidence suggests continued fast employment creation in SMI. According to a sample survey of 700 establishments, the annual absorption of blue- and white-collar workers into SMI was greater than 10 percent. Output growth estimates for SMI as a whole were lower but still higher than those of LI. Experience from a number of other countries suggests that smaller firms are better able to hold their own or grow during a recession than are larger ones, but this may be more true of very small (cottage-shop) establishments than of SMIs. Certainly these more difficult times will test the mettle of many of the firms that rode the wave of the 1970s and will help policymakers and outside observers understand how the state of the economy as a whole affects and is affected by SMI. If SMI is now shrinking, will it be poised to expand again when sustained growth reappears? Not knowing the answers to such questions limits our ability to draw conclusions from the 1970s; the special circumstances of those years must be borne in mind.

Public Policy and SMI Development

On balance, public policy appears to have been neither a major support for SMI nor a strong deterrent. On the one hand, it has contributed to (or at least failed to remedy) restrictions on the sector's access to credit from financial institutions. And it seems likely that trade policy has favored LI, both because protection is usually required by and directed disproportionately toward the more capital-intensive sectors (in which LI tends to be strongly represented) and because (even when trade strategy does not reflect this bias) the greater political clout of LI is likely to produce the same outcome. On the other hand, official regulations dealing with minimum wages, unionization, fringe benefits, social security, and taxes have no doubt helped SMI indirectly because they impinge more lightly on it than they do on LI. For example, unions are not permitted in firms with less than 25 workers, and the minimum wage and associated social legislation is not rigorously enforced in the SMI sector. Having the flexibility to contract the work force or to expand it with the confidence that it can later be contracted may be very important indeed, as we saw in chapter 4. SMI firms undergo large fluctuations even when their growth in the aggregate is quite rapid. If, for example, they could not contract when necessary, their dynamism might be seriously reduced.

The tax system favors an SMI entrepreneur over a person who earns the same income in the form of a salary, since the former can more easily evade taxes. The tax reform of 1974–75, which raised income tax rates, may have increased this advantage. Taxes are also probably collected more efficiently from larger units of production (especially if they are incorporated) than from smaller ones. To the extent that SMI is considered to be making a valuable contribution to the Colombian economy, these various distortions in its favor may be condoned, especially if they help to offset a different set of distortions working in the opposite direction. Another (presumably inadvertent) contribution of public policy to the formation of SMI units has come from the severance pay system of forced savings that helps low-income individuals accumulate the capital needed to set up an enterprise of their own. SMI's contribution to economic mobility is based in part on this phenomenon.

Policies dealing with credit, technical assistance, and imported equipment (especially secondhand equipment) are already tailored somewhat to the needs of SMI and could be more so. As noted earlier, credit has hitherto been more important for the expansion of SMI firms than for their creation. As far as we can judge, the CFP has made a useful contribution to SMI; it should continue its activities, broadening them as appropriate. Some of the credit it supplies leads to expansion of both output and employment, while some promotes labor-saving technical change so that employment may fall or stagnate as output expands. The rapid growth of the extra-bank market in the 1970s has probably alleviated some of SMI's need for working capital, but it seems unlikely that this market could be a substitute for CFP's support in the acquisition of fixed capital.

More generally, the contributions of CFP and the extra-bank market—which should certainly be given their due—might well have been substantially less important had the rest of the financial system been freer of imperfections, many of which were caused by government regulation. If the SMI boom of the 1970s was in large part a result of the greater availability of investment funds out of high profits, one wonders whether the boom could have occurred earlier and whether the sector could have made a greater contribution to the economy as a whole if the official credit system had been less biased against it. Designing a financial system that responds flexibly and efficiently to the needs of SMI is a complex task, and it might seem presumptuous to suggest that promoting a healthy SMI sector is a sufficient reason for making the effort. But an efficient SMI sector does provide real economywide benefits, which are even more important in countries not as far along the development path as Colombia.

Without historical data it is hard to judge the effect of technical assistance on the performance of firms, but our results suggest that managerial and production assistance are important for many smaller firms. The lack of administrative skills is a serious problem in metalworking and other SMI sectors. Although several institutions (CFP, SENA, and FICITEC) provide technical help in this area, the large number of firms in our industry samples that have not received such assistance and would like to get it suggests that much remains to be done. We are unable to judge, however, whether the type of assistance that these entities can provide will necessarily pay off for SMI as a whole, since there is little evidence on how well such assistance meets SMI's needs.

SENA and other training institutions have done a great deal for the Colombian economy by helping to develop the basic skills needed for industrial development. Most SMI firms give preference to SENA graduates when they look for workers with specialized abilities, such as welding, lathe operation, and other skills requiring substantial training. Despite SENA's efforts, however, many of the most urgently needed skills remain in short supply, and firms have to compensate by training their own workers. In the case of semiskilled workers, many firms prefer on-the-job training in order to avoid what they consider to be the bad habits that workers may acquire in training institutions. For example, some entrepreneurs say that these institutions introduce the labor code before they teach the trainees to operate a machine; others consider the training too "general" to be of much practical use. In our metalworking sample, the most favorable attitudes toward worker training institutions were found among employers in the smallest establishments of 1–10 workers (about half of whom responded this way, as opposed to only 20 percent in the larger establishments). The attitude in small firms may be related to the emphasis they place on not having to undertake on-the-job training.

One of the positive things that governments can do for SMI is to promote markets for secondhand equipment. Discrimination against imports of secondhand machinery, a policy some countries pursue deliberately and others more randomly, makes it more difficult for skilled workers to start their own businesses with a small investment. Since the equipment has a low foreign exchange cost, there is no serious argument for curtailing such imports when the balance of payments situation is difficult; the import of expensive new equipment is a more logical place for belt-tightening.

Summary

Colombia's small- and medium-size manufacturing sector expanded impressively in the decade before 1978, the year in which our surveys of metalworking and food processing firms were undertaken. The SMI sector was more dynamic than large industry and seems to have contributed significantly to the rapid expansion of output and urban employment during the decade, the extent of its contribution depending on the spillover effects of SMI's growth on other sectors. This was the period when the Colombian economy, to the surprise of many observers, was able to raise employment levels fast enough to avoid the crisis of open and disguised joblessness that had been predicted by the ILO in 1969.[26]

Our interpretation of the role of SMI in Colombia's economy, especially of the reasons for its surge of growth during the 1970s, is inevitably incomplete. But we believe that some of our firmer conclusions are important and that some emerging hypotheses point in interesting directions.

SMI can play a significant, dynamic role in middle-level developing countries such as Colombia. Almost all these countries are well into an import-substituting phase of development or have already begun to encourage manufactured exports. This role seems to be fostered by the accumulated experience of earlier industrialization (in Colombia's case, import-substituting industrialization). That experience promotes entrepreneurial, technical, and manual skills; contributes to a market for secondhand machinery and equipment; and helps to define markets. Indeed, our observations in the metalworking and food processing industries show the earliest group of producers (now relatively large in most cases) playing the same role of "market definition" for SMI that, according to Hirschman, imports perform for the first domestic manufacturers of a product.[27] In some industries, the earliest (and now large) producers have probably contributed significantly to SMI growth through subcontracting, although this phenomenon was not an important feature of the specific industries covered by our survey.

Small size is evidently not too serious a barrier either to efficiency or to growth, at least under the conditions that have prevailed in Colombia. While Colombia's industrial policy has been more evenhanded than that of many developing countries, it has nevertheless favored large industry in most respects. Why, then, did SMI flourish during the period under discussion?

One important factor—perhaps the critical one—was the generally successful growth of Colombia's economy, which created a rapidly rising demand for many products and healthy profit rates for both SMI and large industry. Although our analysis implies that medium-size metalworking and food processing firms had a higher average benefit-cost ratio than small firms, the average was well above unity even for the latter group. Aggregate data for manufacturing also confirm that the profit rate as of 1976 was high both in SMI and in LI. Furthermore, our analysis suggests that technical economies of scale were not important enough to constitute a major obstacle to SMI. The higher average benefit-cost ratios of the larger firms in our samples are statistically explained by such correlates of size as the entrepreneur's skills, access to finance, and type of technology used, rather than by size itself. The histories of the firms we surveyed reveal that most of them began operations with impressively low levels of capital invested—often because they were able to obtain secondhand machinery at low prices. If equipment indivisibilities were important, they had bearing only at very low levels of capital stock.

Thus SMI in Colombia has not been unduly hampered by diseconomies of small-scale operation. In fact, it has shown a good deal of dynamism and versatility, in that many firms have improved the designs of their products, have responded flexibly to buyers' needs, have made their own machinery, and the like. As a result, individual firms have grown quite fast. Thus the sector does *not* correspond to the picture sometimes drawn of a stagnant manufacturing backwater.

Nevertheless, SMI has had its share of problems and drawbacks. Job security and wages are somewhat lower than in large industry. SMI's lack of political clout, together with vigorous competition in some industries, may make it vulnerable to macroeconomic difficulties such as the current recession of the early 1980s. Given its relative isolation from formal sector financial markets, SMI's growth may well depend on a healthy profit rate; this hypothesis is consistent with the surge of growth in the 1970s.

The available evidence leaves little doubt, however, that countries such as Colombia can reap considerable output and employment benefits from SMI. To the extent that rapid growth of demand is a prerequisite of SMI dynamism, one can perhaps draw no conclusions about appropriate policy except that, if an initial growth impulse can be developed, SMI potential can help to magnify it and ensure the satisfactory expansion of employment. The greater the importance attached to the growth of demand, of course, the harder it would be effectively to manipulate policy instruments to achieve high rates of SMI expansion in its absence. Still, our impression is that a well-conceived and successfully implemented public policy—one that provides access to credit and imports, vocational training (such as that of SENA), technical assistance (more often on the financial and business sides than on the production side), and support of the market for secondhand equipment—should enhance the sector's performance enough to be worthwhile. Countries in an early stage of development might ponder the example that Colombia provides of a hardy SMI sector that can successfully fend for itself provided that the government does not discriminate too severely against it. Furthermore, countries in which the expansion of education has created aspirations that cannot be met by public or private wage employment would find it beneficial if large numbers of capable entrepreneurs moved into SMI, as they have in Colombia. Governments should ensure that their systems of incentives encourage such socially desirable behavior.

An interesting hypothesis for future research would be the notion that public policies that encourage entrepreneurship, improve access to capital, provide more information on technology, and so on are of limited importance to the success of SMI when demand is healthy but that they become *more* important when demand is sluggish. The most pessimistic hypothesis, in some sense, is that policy can never have much effect. At present, neither of these views can be dismissed.

Notes

1. Given the lack of precise evidence on failure rates, some caution should be exercised in describing the success of SMI even during the 1970s. But we do know that many firms grew fast and that SMI output and employment grew fast in the aggregate.

2. These figures are somewhat suspect, as discussed in chapter 2, but the fact that growth was fast seems beyond much doubt.

3. See Todd's estimates in table 3-7 of this book. Also, table 2-19 suggests that in 1976 plants with less than 20 workers were of below-average efficiency, given that both their profit rates and their labor costs were below average. These data are at most suggestive, however, in view of their aggregate nature and numerous other statistical weaknesses.

4. In our multiple regressions for the food sector, access to any external source of credit, especially private banks, was associated with better economic performance. In the metalworking sector, the only obvious relation was a negative one

with loans from moneylenders or suppliers. But no definite conclusions are warranted since it is difficult to judge the direction of causation.

5. Some lingering doubt surrounds this result, however, since DANE's annual manufacturing survey has not indicated rapid growth in the SI labor force. See the discussion in chapter 2.

6. For more details see Albert Berry and Ronald Soligo, "The Distribution of Income in Colombia: An Overview," in *Economic Policy and Income Distribution in Colombia*, ed. Albert Berry and Ronald Soligo (Boulder, Colo.: Westview Press, 1980).

7. The highest levels of open urban unemployment recorded in Colombia occurred in 1967. The subsequent pattern consisted of significant fluctuations, but the trend was mainly downward until 1978; in June of that year, the urban unemployment rate was below 8 percent.

8. As inflation control became a major objective of government policy in the López administration (1974–78), Finance Minister Botero argued that import liberalization was needed to reduce inflation. This proved politically impossible, and the domestic market remained largely a protected preserve of domestic industry.

9. During 1970–77 profits in factory manufacturing as a whole (which mainly reflect those of LI because of its heavy weight in the total) represented about 31–37 percent of capital, defined as the sum of the book value of fixed assets plus the value of inventories, and perhaps 25–30 percent of a more accurate measure of capital. Comparable figures are not available for earlier periods, although data on the share of labor in manufacturing and more detailed data on the corporations suggest that the relevant rates were also high then. See Albert Berry, "A Descriptive History of Industrialization in Colombia," in *Essays on Industrialization in Colombia*, ed. Albert Berry (Tempe, Ariz.: Arizona State University, Center for Latin American Studies, 1983), pp. 66–70.

10. The imposition of a value added tax was probably the main element in the rise in the "tax share" of gross value added in manufacturing, from less than 2 percent in 1971 to an average of 16.4 percent in 1977–79.

11. See, for example, Rudolf Hommes R., *La Organización Industrial y la Pequeña Industria* (Bogotá: Servicio Nacional de Aprendizaje [SENA], n.d.), p. 57.

12. With the possible exception of secondary schooling in the metalworking industry, according to our survey data.

13. The 1964 figure is a "best guess" since we have no separate urban figures for that year.

14. We do not know to what extent changes in the age structure of manufacturing employment (including CS) also characterized firms in the factory sector for which the wage movements noted above have been calculated. By sex, the female share of recorded factory employment was 27.5 percent in 1970 and 30.4 percent in 1978, a smaller increase than in manufacturing employment as a whole. We do not know the incidence by plant size of the compositional changes cited, so it is hard to judge how they may have influenced the growth of SMI compared with that of LI. An analysis of earnings by age, sex, and level of education would help to clarify the events of the 1970s.

15. The decline in real wages and in labor productivity could be partly due to a decrease in the average skill level of the manufacturing labor force in association with the lower average age of employees during the 1970s, the departure of some skilled workers to Venezuela and elsewhere, and the increasing share of women in the labor force.

16. National accounts estimates of family savings are notoriously prone to error when, as in Colombia, they are calculated as a residual. Nevertheless the dramatic reported increase in these savings—from an average of 0.72 percent of national income in 1969–71 to an average of 5.84 percent in 1975–77—almost certainly reflects real trends. Actual family savings have generally been greater than national accounts estimates for them. For alternative estimates, see James Hanson, "Estimación del Ahorro Familiar en Colombia," rev., Department of Economics, Brown University, 1973; processed, table 1.

17. The UPAC is a construction-related asset whose real return was originally fixed but was later adjusted so that it, too, had a negative real return for a time. For further comments on the decrease in the return to financial assets, see Albert Berry, "The Effects of Inflation on Income Distribution in Colombia: Some Hypotheses and a Framework for Analysis," in *Economic Policy*, ed. Berry and Soligo.

18. Since the value of the accumulated cesantía was indexed for inflation, the decline in real wages in the early 1970s did not lower its value, although subsequently it accumulated at a slower rate.

19. According to our estimates, real credit outstanding to SMI during 1968–73 rose at a rate of nearly 20 percent a year. Before 1968, real credit to manufacturing grew less rapidly, and the increasing role of the development finance companies would suggest, if anything, a declining share for SMI. That share rose significantly in 1968–73 and then increased a little more in 1973–78, if the assumptions used in table 6-2 are reasonably accurate.

20. The extra-bank market includes loans to firms by individuals or by specialized financial intermediaries, which, although entirely legal, do not operate under the restrictions and controls imposed by banking legislation. The interest rate these institutions pay to savers and charge to borrowers therefore tends to be an equilibrium one.

Gómez and Villaveces present the results of a 1975 Fedesarrollo survey of sources of finance in LI and of a 1976 survey for SMI; these show the share of own funds in totals invested to be 30.1 and 52.5, respectively; domestic bank credit, 15.0 and 20.0 percent; Corporación Financiera Popular, 0.0 and 12.4 percent; development finance companies, 21.7 and 4.4 percent; foreign credit, 20.4 and 0.0 percent; and extra-bank credit, 1.9 and 5.2 percent. (Hernando Gómez and Ricardo Villaveces, *La Pequeña y Mediana Industria en el Desarrollo Colombiano* [Bogotá: La Carreta, 1979], p. 147.) The data for SMI are unlikely to be very accurate since the sample was not representative, but the other figures are generally plausible, so the extra-bank figure is probably reasonably valid.

21. Based on a comparison of the median initial investment figure of 550,000 1978 pesos and data presented by Berry and Urrutia on the distribution of commercial bank loans by assets of borrower in 1970. Albert Berry and Miguel

Urrutia, *Income Distribution in Colombia* (New Haven, Conn.: Yale University Press, 1976), p. 210.

22. See, for example, Genaro Payán López and John Eddison, "El Impacto del Crédito sobre el Empleo en la Pequeña y Mediana Industria," *Revista del Banco de la República*, vol. 43, no. 517 (November 1970), pp. 1619–28.

23. For a discussion, see Francisco Ortega, "Notas sobre la Reciente Evolución Económica e Institucional del Sector Financiero," *Ensayos sobre Política Económica*, no. 1 (March 1982), pp. 21–43.

24. See Joaquín de Pombo, "Algunos Aspectos del Mercado Libre de Dinero en Colombia," *Revista del Banco de la República*, vol. 45, no. 539 (September 1972), pp. 1574–98.

25. A relation between import liberalization and rapid SMI growth has been noted in the Philippines. International Labour Organisation, *Sharing in Development: A Programme of Employment, Equity and Growth for the Philippines* (Geneva, 1974), p. 140.

26. International Labour Organisation, *Towards Full Employment: A Programme for Colombia* (Geneva, 1970).

27. Albert O. Hirschman, *The Strategy of Economic Development* (New Haven, Conn.: Yale University Press, 1958), p. 123.

Methodological Appendix

This appendix briefly describes the data collection procedures and analytical concepts and techniques used in our examination of the metalworking and food processing industries.

The Data Base: Coverage and Collection Procedures

The data base for our industry-specific analyses of SMI performance includes small and medium metalworking enterprises (sampled in 1978) and food processing enterprises (sampled in 1979) in or near areas of Bogotá, Medellín, Cali, Palmira, Buga, Cartago, Tuluá, Pereira, Manizales, Armenia, Barranquilla, Ibagué, Neiva, Sabaneta, Pitalito, Chiquinquirá, Moniquirá, Paipa, Zipaquirá, Madrid, and Duitama. The sample of firms is not a truly random one. Rather, it is designed to provide reasonable coverage of most of the variations in the SMI category with respect to work force, size, age of plant, and location. We thus included a relatively large proportion of the medium-size firms—in some instances, nearly all the units in this subcategory. In the subcategory of small firms the sample departs from randomness in a different way. Since the universe of firms in this subgroup is not known (DANE's reporting is incomplete, especially for the smaller SI firms), our use of plants listed by DANE and the Corporación Financiera Popular makes our initial sample frame less than fully random. We complemented the DANE and CFP lists, however, by asking the firms we interviewed who their competitors were or who else they knew to be producing similar items and then added these firms to the list of potential interviewees. Subject to these various constraints, we tried to make the samples as random as possible.

Questionnaires were administered to 79 small and medium enterprises in the metalworking sector in 1978 and to 42 firms in the food processing sector in early 1979. The 25 producers of agricultural implements included in the metalworking subsample account for about 80 percent of Colombia's output of these goods. The firms included in the other metalworking product groups also account for a substantial share of total output of their respective products. The 42 firms in the food processing sector represent a much smaller segment of this market; their exact share of output is difficult to judge since DANE's coverage of these products is weak.

Interviews were carried out by a team of Colombians with the relevant technical expertise under the supervision of World Bank staff. Questionnaires sought information not only about outputs and inputs, but also about entrepreneurship, methods of production, technological characteristics, and growth prospects and constraints faced by the firms in the sample; cross-checks to test the quality of responses to some questions were built into the design. Interviews lasted up to three hours. It was usually possible to develop an atmosphere of mutual confidence between interviewers and respondents, with the result that relatively few responses were likely to include deliberate misstatements.

Assessing Industry and Firm Performance: The Conceptual Framework

Under the simplest set of neoclassical assumptions, all firms in an industry have perfect information, operate in a perfectly competitive and riskless environment, and maximize profits; all firms are consequently efficient from both a private and a social point of view, and the ratio of output to inputs does not vary among firms. Empirical evidence suggests, however, that efficiency does vary greatly among firms operating in the same physical environment. Microeconomic studies usually distinguish between allocative inefficiency (which results from a firm's failure to choose an optimal set of inputs given the factor prices it faces) and technical inefficiency (which is due to the firm's failure to maximize output from a given set of inputs). Although the conventional theory of the firm focuses on allocative or price inefficiency, some economists have argued that losses from technical inefficiency may far exceed those from price inefficiency.[1]

When prices diverge from the social opportunity cost of factors because of market imperfections, it is necessary to distinguish between private allocative inefficiency (which arises when a firm fails to choose the combination of inputs that would minimize private cost at a given level of output) and social allocative inefficiency (which occurs when the firm's inputs fail to minimize the social opportunity cost of production). This distinction is important since, under factor market distortions, efficiency in keeping private costs low will typically not imply social efficiency. The factor prices that firms face may be distorted by employment laws, government investment incentives, and taxes. These imperfections may affect firms in different ways according to their location, size, or the social connections of their managers. It is widely believed that such distortions induce firms to choose capital-intensive techniques even if this is an inappropriate choice from the social point of view.

Both private and social allocative inefficiency may result from incomplete knowledge of the range of existing techniques and of the quality of productive inputs. The costs of technology search may differ from one firm to another, depending on such factors as size and connections with foreign firms. Differences in the abilities, motivations, and preferences of entrepreneurs may also lead them to choose different production techniques and scales of operation. In their selection of techniques, entrepreneurs may have to choose between higher expected profits and lower risks, or between the level of profits and the satisfactions of using speedy, modern capital-intensive techniques. In addition, interfirm differences in the time frame for initial investment, which imply differences in available techniques and in factor prices at the moment of investment, can account for different factor combinations. In this case, what may at first glance appear to be an inefficient choice of factors may not be so. If one uses historical or replacement costs of capital to measure the "quantity" of capital, however, what might have seemed to be rational choices at the time they were made may turn out to be inefficient in the light of present factor prices. The commercial value of capital is often a more appropriate measure, but it may depend greatly on the state of the market.

Since differences in efficiency may have many sources, there appears to be no single "right" way to measure allocative efficiency; rather, various definitions exist, each of which tells us different things about the performance of firms. The choice between alternative concepts of efficiency is frequently a practical one. In principle, raising output by applying better entrepreneurial or managerial inputs is more appropriately viewed as the result of a higher level of resource inputs than as a consequence of a more efficient deployment of available inputs. In fact, however, inputs of such qualities as human motivation and ability are hard to measure, so that analysis may instead focus on a more easily measured output-input ratio that does not incorporate variables of this kind and is thus more akin to a measure of engineering efficiency than of allocative efficiency in its widest sense.

Interfirm differences in technical efficiency have received relatively little attention in the microeconomic literature, despite the mounting evidence that they contribute heavily to variations in the economic performance of firms. Technical inefficiency can be explained by poor management training, inadequate education, or lack of information.[2] Leibenstein developed the concept of X-efficiency, which encompasses not only technical efficiency, but also other sources of inefficiency not explained under the maximization postulate. He introduced motivation as a separate input that cannot be purchased in the market.[3]

Several recent studies of firms in developing countries have applied the concepts of X-inefficiency and technical inefficiency and report major differences in the technical efficiency of different firms belonging to the same industrial sector.[4] Meller finds no correlation between size of establishment and technical efficiency, whereas Page and Tyler suggest that small firms are less efficient than larger ones. Some studies tend to conclude that certain managerial attributes—such as education, experience, and owner operation—have a positive influence on the firm's technical efficiency, but a general consensus has not yet emerged.

Methodology and Measurement

In this study we assess the economic performance of a firm by benefit-cost (BC) ratios, which measure the ratio of value of output to the cost of inputs, and technical efficiency indices (TEI), which measure the ability of a firm to maximize output from a given set of inputs. Three benefit-cost ratios are used: the entrepreneurial (EBC), the private (PBC), and the social (SBC). When outputs and inputs are measured at social prices (or social opportunity cost), a BC ratio greater than one implies that the firm's existence has a positive effect on the total output of the economy.[5] A ratio of less than one implies the opposite. When measured at market prices, the BC ratio reflects either the firm's overall profitability (if the ratio used includes all inputs in the denominator) or the profitability of the entrepreneur's inputs (if only these inputs are included in the denominator). The coexistence of firms with different BC ratios implies that factor or product markets are imperfect, that firms have differing levels of X-efficiency or risk aversion, or (when reference is to observed rather than true BCs) that measurement errors are distorting the picture. These imperfections can be identified by analyzing information on the market conditions faced by firms. By comparing BC ratios at social and market prices, we can ascertain the extent to which factor price differences account for the existence of some socially inefficient firms.

While the BC ratio captures a firm's allocative and technical efficiency, the TEI is in principle independent of the firm's choice of factor proportions and of relative factor prices.[6] Instead, the TEI measures the efficiency with which a firm uses a given combination of resources; its value is conventionally assumed to be unity for those members of any given set of firms that are on the technical efficiency frontier, in other words, the ones that have the highest ratios of output to input with a

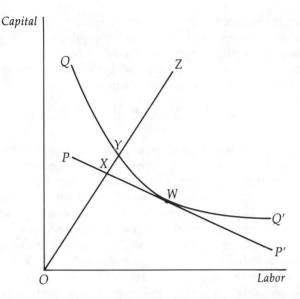

given capital-labor ratio. In the accompanying figure if the line QQ' represents the technical efficiency frontier (which may be estimated in a variety of ways) and each point corresponds to the input combination required to produce one unit of output, then the amount by which a firm's TEI is lower than one indicates the firm's distance from the technical efficiency frontier. For example, the TEI for firm Z in the figure is given by the ratio OY/OZ. Although the TEI is not a measure of overall economic efficiency, it is an interesting variable in its own right and one that is likely to be an important correlate of economic efficiency. Some entrepreneurial or technical characteristics affect the firm's BC ratios through their effect on its TEI; other factors, such as the absolute level of input and output prices, affect the firm's BC ratios directly.

We assume that the entrepreneur's basic objective is to maximize the return to his own capital and labor inputs in the enterprise. When each of these inputs is important, as in the case of owners of small firms who were previously production workers, the most interesting ratio is likely to be the EBC, defined as

$$\text{EBC} = \frac{VA - [r_b K(b) + W_h L(h)]}{r_o K(o) + W_o L(o)}$$

where VA is value added; $r_b K(b)$ is the cost of borrowed capital and includes $r_1 K_1$, which is the cost of borrowed fixed capital, and $r_2 K_2$, which is the cost of borrowed working capital; $W_h L(h)$ is the cost of hired labor;

and $r_oK(o)$ is the opportunity cost of the entrepreneur's self-financed capital.[7] It also includes fixed and working capital costs; $W_oL(o)$ is the opportunity cost of the entrepreneur's own labor input.[8]

By varying this formulation slightly we can measure the implicit return to self-financed capital. The formula would be

$$r_o = \frac{VA - [r_bK(b) + W_hL(h)] - W_oL(o)}{K(o)} .$$

Because many owners of small firms were previously technicians and skilled workers in large firms, the opportunity cost of their labor is likely to be close to the wage they would earn in a large firm.

Similarly, we can calculate the implicit return to the entrepreneur's labor given an assumed opportunity cost for self-financed capital. Since it is hard to separate the opportunity cost of an entrepreneur's labor from that of his capital, especially in small firms, estimates of the return to both factors together (as with estimates of the EBC) are likely to be more accurate than those for either separately.

Another variable of interest to the entrepreneur and to other investors is the ratio of total benefits accruing to factor owners (including people other than the entrepreneur) to the total private cost of resources employed by the firm, including those not owned by the entrepreneur. This ratio can be expressed by

$$PBC = \frac{VA}{rK + WL}$$

where r is a weighted average of the interest rates corresponding to the firm's various sources of credit (including the entrepreneur's own funds), and W is a weighted average of the wages of different skill categories (including the opportunity cost of the entrepreneur), so that WL is simply the wage bill including the entrepreneur's opportunity cost.

In addition, we can calculate a "social" benefit-cost ratio (SBC) using a single estimate of the social opportunity cost of capital (r_s) applied to all sources of finance and using the sectoral average wage for each skill category as the cost to each firm of using that labor:[9]

$$SBC = \frac{VA}{r_sK - W_sL} .$$

Because this formula does not apply shadow prices to outputs or raw material inputs (unlike many estimates of "social" indicators, our calculations rely on domestic prices rather than border prices for tradables), we can only use it to compare the SBCs of firms in the same sector that have similar input and output mixes.

The differences between PBC and SBC ratios offer some clues to the possible effects on a firm's profitability of removing market distortions, particularly those in the capital market; they also give an idea of the extent to which market distortions explain the existence of socially inefficient firms.

Our analysis makes more use of PBCs than EBCs, largely for practical reasons. The most elusive data in the formulas for these ratios are the opportunity costs of the entrepreneur's own labor and capital. Furthermore, EBC is more sensitive than PBC to errors in the measurement of these variables.[10] Consequently, the former may turn out to be a less accurate indicator than the latter, even in the case of returns to the entrepreneur's own inputs. When factor markets are imperfect, the entrepreneur may be almost as interested in maximizing PBC as EBC, since his access to borrowed capital is certain to depend on the confidence of his creditors—a factor that in turn depends on the overall productivity of the resources used by the firm, not just on the productivity of the entrepreneur's resources. Empirically, EBC ratios tend to vary more than PBCs.[11] The two indicators are highly correlated, however, so that the results of an analysis using EBC as the dependent variable are unlikely to differ much from one using PBC; where there is any doubt, we have used both measures. In any event, when one of these indicators exceeds, equals, or is less than one, the same is necessarily true of the other.[12]

Technical Efficiency and Price Efficiency

The concepts of price efficiency and technical efficiency can be most readily understood when an industry is characterized by a linear homogeneous production function in two factors—capital and labor—whose efficiency frontier (QQ' in the figure) is known, and when all its firms face the same relative price of the two factors.[13] Technically efficient firms such as Y achieve unit output using one of the input combinations represented by QQ'. A firm using combination Z is inefficient since firm Y, which uses the two factors in the same ratio as does Z, produces the same output using only a fraction (OY/OZ) as much of each factor. Thus the technical efficiency of firm Z can be defined as OY/OZ. Now let $P'P$ be an isocost curve. Firm W is seen to be price efficient (or allocatively efficient, the terms being used interchangeably), whereas firm Y is technically efficient but not price efficient. Firm W's costs of production are only a fraction (OX/OY) of firm Y's costs. The price efficiency of firm Y can thus be defined as OX/OY. Firm Z's price efficiency is the same. Relative to the efficient firm W, Z has an overall efficiency of OX/OZ, a technical efficiency of OY/OZ, and a price efficiency of OX/OY. Overall efficiency is thus the product of price efficiency and technical efficiency.[14]

Private price efficiency, which is sensitive to errors in reported factor prices, cannot be measured accurately without more detailed price data than were available in this study. Because relative factor prices differ from firm to firm, separate price information is needed for each firm. Technical efficiency, however, requires only information on quantities of a firm's inputs and outputs and knowledge of the efficiency frontier. Consequently it is relatively simple to estimate the firm-specific index that can then be used to explore the determinants of technical efficiency.

Nonparametric approaches to the estimation of the efficiency frontier were popular for a time after Farrell's pathbreaking work.[15] Since then, however, techniques have been developed to estimate a parametric frontier by imposing a functional form. The one we use, which was proposed by Aigner and Chu, relies on a homogeneous Cobb-Douglas production frontier that requires all observations to be on or beneath the frontier.[16] The model can be written as

$$\ln Q = \ln f(K,L) + u$$
$$= a_0 + a_1\ln K + a_2\ln L + u$$

where the error term u is constrained to be nonpositive, and this one-sided error term forces $Q \leq f(K,L)$. The parameters a_0, a_1, a_2 may be estimated by using linear programming, that is, by minimizing the linear sum of the values of the residuals, subject to the constraint that each residual be nonpositive.[17] When estimated by ordinary least squares, the equation above represents an average production function, and the error term, u, is stochastic. In Aigner and Chu's approximation of the production frontier, however, the disturbance term is presumed to reflect technical efficiency differences, and all measurement errors are assumed to be negligible. If all u_i's are constrained to be nonpositive, the estimated production surface depicts a best-practice frontier or envelope. The technical efficiency of each observation can be computed directly from the vector of residuals, since u represents technical inefficiency. That is, the ratio of the observed output of a firm to its efficiency frontier output provides the technical efficiency index.

One advantage of the parametric approach is its adaptability to nonconstant returns to scale (a_1, a_2 need not be restricted to add to one). The programming approach, like Farrell's, is sensitive to extreme observations, though not to the same degree. At the same time, the specification of a production function imposes a structure on the frontier that may be unwarranted. The parameter estimates obtained have none of the standard statistical properties such as confidence intervals and t ratios. Since no statistical assumptions are made about the unexplained residual u in the equation above, no inferential results can be obtained. The residual is referred to as technical inefficiency. But u may also be due to the omission of variables (for example, management) in the production function or to errors in the measurement of variables. The former is commonly known as the "management bias" problem and the latter as the "errors in variables" problem.[18]

Despite these limitations, we rely on technical efficiency indices calculated using the linear programming estimate of a nonstochastic production function. But we also calculate firm TEIs using Farrell's methodology. The two approaches produce similar TE indices, with correlation coefficients for four product categories above 0.95 and for two other product categories of 0.83 and 0.73. (For the items in these categories, see the glossary.) As noted above, the linear programming method can be applied under conditions of nonconstant returns to scale. But when we estimated "average" Cobb-Douglas production functions, the hypothesis of constant returns to scale could not be statistically rejected. Hence, constant returns to scale were explicitly assumed in this linear programming approach. (As noted above, separate Farrell-type efficiency frontiers for different size groups crossed each other.)

Measurement of Inputs and Outputs

Our BC and TEI calculations require that a firm's outputs and inputs be measured and valued. Data for the metalworking sector refer to mid-1977, those for the food sector to January 1979. In the metalworking sector, value added and the cost of paid labor refer to all of 1977 and are thus the sum of current-price monthly figures that reflect the inflation in the Colombian economy during 1977. The average prices, however, are approximately those of mid-1977. For the food sector, our statistical information refers to the first months of 1979, and value added and physical output correspond to one month's production. We convert value added, wage bill, fixed capital, and inventories to the prices of January 1979, then multiply by twelve to obtain an annual figure; some adjustments are made for the seasonality of production.

A firm's wage bill, calculated as the average daily wage costs times the total number of days in operation, includes social security payments to workers and an estimate of the imputed wage of the manager or entrepreneur. Each entrepreneur's labor is costed at the average earnings of persons in Bogotá with the same level of education and labor market experience except that, in the metalworking sector, a floor (which amounts to the average wage of a skilled worker in the sector) was imposed on this labor cost.[19] Fixed capital inputs are more difficult to estimate, particularly in the case of small firms that do not record the book value of their plant and equipment on a consistent basis. In choosing between the replacement or commercial value of fixed capital, each of which is appropriate for a different set of research questions, we generally opt for commercial value as a more accurate reflection of the future capital costs of firms at the time.[20] In the food sector we include transport equipment in our estimate of fixed capital because the delivered price of the products includes an imputed return to this capital. Since we have only the commercial value of transport equipment, we do not have the option of using the replacement value of fixed capital in this sector. Historical cost, a third possible measure, was also unavailable; it would have been useful in the analysis of overall entrepreneurial efficiency, since efficiency in the purchase of capital goods is as relevant from a private (and sometimes a social) point of view as any other type of efficiency. By exaggerating capital costs, we may well have underestimated the PBC of some firms that have acquired secondhand equipment at bargain prices. Very small firms often buy inexpensive secondhand equipment that is in poor condition and repair it themselves.

Working capital is another critical input. Shortages of this item may explain poor industry performance, particularly in small firms that lack access to the needed financing.[21] In a study of capacity utilization in Colombia, Thoumi finds that most managers perceive working capital shortages to be an important cause of underutilization of fixed capital.[22] Our estimates of working capital are based on inventories of finished products and raw materials and on credit arrangements with suppliers of inputs and buyers of output.[23] In each sector, about 60 percent of a typical firm's working capital is accounted for by inventories. The ratio of working capital to fixed capital averages 0.41 in the metalworking samples and 0.36 in the food processing samples. Both fixed and working capital, initially valued as of the dates of interviews, were deflated to mid-1977 and to January 1979 for the metal and food industries, respectively. The difference in the timing of our two surveys constitutes a possible source of noncomparability between the BC ratios for the two sectors.

In the case of fixed capital, the formulas for BC ratios and TEIs include both depreciation allowances and interest payments. To estimate depreciation in the metal products industry, we assume that the life of new equipment is fifteen years and that of secondhand equipment ten years. In estimating private BC ratios for the firm's various sources of credit (self-financing, public banks, private banks, moneylenders, and suppliers), we apply average real interest rates, calculated as the effective rates paid at the time of the interview minus the average rate of inflation during the preceding four years. These real rates are self-financing,

1 percent; public banks, 4 percent; private banks, 8 percent; and money-lenders and suppliers, 12 percent. Between 1975 and 1978 the average annual increase in consumer prices was about 24 percent. Because this figure was also close to the longer-run average, we considered it a reasonable prediction of future rates. For commercial (that is, private) banks, whose nominal interest rates were between 20 and 30 percent, we estimated the average effective rate at 34 percent. The Corporación Financiera Popular (the public bank of relevance for SMI) had a nominal rate of 24 percent for loans to SMI, an effective rate of 28 percent for loans to finance fixed capital investment, and 24–28 percent for working capital loans.[24] The difference between the nominal and effective rates depends on arrangements with respect to compensating balances and on commissions and fees charged. The rate for moneylenders (the extra-bank market) has been estimated by Bentley (personal communication) as 30–36 percent for large industry and 36–60 percent for SMI. Rates for suppliers vary a great deal. We have assumed an average of 36 percent for the two sources together. The opportunity cost of the entrepreneur's own funds is the hardest figure to estimate and obviously may vary widely. For small savers whose alternatives are limited to investing in financial assets such as savings deposits or even UPAC accounts in savings and loan institutions, all average real rates of return between 1975 and 1977 were negative—usually from −6 percent to −1 percent. These individuals would often have other, better ways to use money, such as real estate investment. But it seems likely that none would provide a real return approaching the levels of the average return to private sector capital. The figure of 1 percent that we have chosen is a compromise between the rates of 5–10 percent that small investors might average on nonfinancial nonmanufacturing capital and the negative rates they would get on financial assets.

In our benchmark SBCs we assume the social opportunity cost of capital to be 12 percent, which is a rough estimate of the average return to capital in Colombia in the late 1970s.[25]

Technical efficiency indices for the metal product firms use data on value added and two inputs: labor, defined as man-days of unskilled labor equivalent per year, and capital services, defined as the cost of replacement capital at "social" prices (that is, applying the 12 percent opportunity cost of capital used in estimating SBCs).[26] Separate technical efficiency frontiers are calculated by both the linear programming and the Farrell methods for each of the three categories of metalworking firms; each category includes firms that produce similar products and that use broadly similar production techniques. In the food sector, physical output instead of value added is used as the measure of output; this choice was dictated by our belief that physical output was a better indicator of value added than our estimate of value added, which incorporates potentially serious errors in input prices. Since the ratio of material input to output (both variables were measured by weight) was stable across firms in each subsector, it seems likely that true value added is a stable percentage of value of output. When TEI using value added as normally calculated was employed in regressions, the fits were very bad. Independent technical efficiency frontiers are calculated for two of the three product groups in the sample, cheese and guava paste; in the case of potato chips, problems in the measurement of output precluded such a calculation. Although the product group frontiers avoid aggregation among dissimilar products, they are based on a relatively small number of firms, so that part of what is gained by making the frontier product-specific may be lost as a result of the instability of the frontier.

How accurate are our measurements of inputs and outputs, and hence our estimates of BC ratios and TEI, likely to be? Although some variables and relationships may be questionable, the main conclusions appear to be reasonably robust. Collecting accurate input and output data from very small firms in the informal sector is notoriously difficult for a number of reasons, including the lack of accounts in many cases. Most of our sample firms are drawn from a higher size range, however, and nearly all those in the metalworking sector (57 of the 65 on which our BC analysis is based) did keep books, as did 20 of the 30 in food processing. Furthermore, the interviewers made every effort to elicit accurate information and to assure respondents that the data provided would not fall into the hands of tax authorities. In fact, the sample data (for example, wage rates and labor productivity) and many of their implications (such as the fast growth of SMI firms, the high average level of profits but their marked fluctuation from one firm to another, and the positive association of PBC with size) were consistent with other information (such as the aggregate data presented in chapter 2). As a result, we are confident that the quality of the information collected permits reasonably accurate measurement of BC and TEI ratios and analysis of their determinants. Where uncertainties are present, sensitivity analysis has been used to test the extent to which our results may be affected by plausible errors of observation (see chapter 3).

Notes

1. See, for example, Harvey Leibenstein, "Allocative Efficiency versus 'X-Efficiency,'" *American Economic Review*, vol. 56 (1966), pp. 392–415.

2. The effect of poor management training is discussed by Howard Pack, "The Substitution of Labour for Capital in Kenyan Manufacturing," *Economic Journal*,

vol. 86 (1976), pp. 45–58. For further comments on inadequate education, see John M. Page, "Technical Efficiency and Economic Performance: Some Evidence from Ghana," *Oxford Economic Papers*, vol. 23, no. 2 (July 1980), pp. 319–39. For a discussion of lack of information, see Kenneth H. Shapiro and Jurgen Muller, "Sources of Technical Efficiency: The Roles of Modernization and Information," *Economic Development and Cultural Change*, vol. 25 (1977), pp. 293–310.

3. Because decisionmaking is not completely in the hands of the entrepreneur and contracts may be incomplete (the entrepreneur hires labor time, not worker effort), Leibenstein insists that a firm has "inert areas" that permit individuals to behave in nonmaximizing ways. External pressures in the form of competition and pressures on profits may induce owners to reduce inert areas. See Leibenstein, "Allocative Efficiency," and "X-Efficiency versus Allocative Efficiency," in *Beyond Economic Man*, ed. Harvey Leibenstein (Cambridge, Mass.: Harvard University Press, 1976).

4. Among the most important studies in this area are Joel Bergsman, "Commercial Policy, Allocative and X-Efficiency," *Quarterly Journal of Economics*, vol. 88, no. 3 (1974), pp. 409–33; Donald J. Lecraw, "Choice of Technology in Low-Wage Countries: A Non-neoclassical Approach," *Quarterly Journal of Economics*, vol. 93, no. 4 (1979), pp. 631–54; Patricio Meller, "Efficiency Frontiers for Industrial Establishments of Different Size," *Exploration in Economic Research*, vol. 3, no. 3 (1976), pp. 397–407; Samuel A. Morley and Gordon W. Smith, "The Choice of Technology: Multinational Firms in Brazil," *Economic Development and Cultural Change*, vol. 25, no. 2 (January 1977), pp. 239–64; W. G. Tyler, "Technical Efficiency in Production in a Developing Country: An Empirical Examination of the Brazilian Plastics and Steel Industries," *Oxford Economic Papers*, vol. 31 N.S. (1979), pp. 477–95; and Lawrence J. White, "Appropriate Technology, X-Efficiency, and a Competitive Environment: Some Evidence from Pakistan," *Quarterly Journal of Economics*, vol. 90, no. 4 (1976), pp. 575–89. Bergsman, Morley and Smith, and Tyler concentrate on Brazil, Lecraw on Thailand, Meller on Chile, and White on Pakistan.

5. The social opportunity cost of factors reflects, among other things, the unemployment situation. With widespread unemployment, for example, the social opportunity cost of labor could be zero. A BC ratio greater than one might also imply that the firm's existence has a positive effect on the present value of future output or future consumption, depending on how one defines the social welfare function and on whether one attempts to take into account effects of this period's economic activity on future outcomes. The present study does not take into account future period outcomes in the definition of SBC.

6. This is not quite true in our analysis since we have to aggregate different types of labor and capital into the two aggregates used—labor and capital—by the use of relative prices. Were one able to describe the efficiency frontier in terms of homogeneous factors, this would not be necessary.

7. In the case of fixed capital, r is calculated by the formula

$$r_1 = \frac{i}{\dfrac{1}{1 - (1+i)^n}}$$

where n is the expected life of the equipment and i is the rate of interest.

8. With respect to the entrepreneur's labor input, our estimate for each individual is based on the earnings in the Bogotá labor market of people with the same education and experience; see the discussion later in this appendix.

9. In principle, the social opportunity cost of capital may differ across sources, but we did not have enough information to draw such fine distinctions. The entrepreneur's labor input is estimated as noted above.

10. Consider, for example, a firm that uses little of these two factors. If their value was overestimated by a factor of two, PBC would nevertheless be nearly accurate, but EBC would be misestimated by a factor of nearly two, since these two values make up the denominator of the ratio.

11. This would tend to be true unless the share of own resources in total resources was a substantially increasing function of PBC, in contrast to the relationship observed in our sample.

12. If $r_b K(b) + W_h L(h)$ is defined as R and $r_o K(o) + W_o L(o)$ as T, then EBC $= (VA - R)/T$ and PBC $= VA/R + T)$. If EBC exceeds one, for example, then $VA - R > T$. When R is added to each side of the inequality, it is evidently also true that $VA > R + T$, that is, that PBC exceeds one.

13. For discussions of the concept of technical efficiency and ways in which it can be calculated, see M. J. Farrell, "The Measurement of Productive Efficiency," *Journal of the Royal Statistical Society,* ser. A, vol. 120 (1957), pp. 253–81; and C. P. Timmer, "On Measuring Technical Efficiency," *Food Research Institute Studies in Agricultural Economics, Trade, and Development,* vol. 9 (1970), pp. 99–171. Farrell was concerned with comparing technical efficiency across industries. Timmer expanded the methodology and developed firm-specific relative technical efficiency indices for comparisons of different firms within an industry at a given period in time. For an application to increasing returns to scale, see M. J. Farrell and M. Fieldhouse, "Estimating Efficient Production Functions under Increasing Returns to Scale," *Journal of the Royal Statistical Society,* ser. A, vol. 75 (1962), pp. 252–67. For extension to the n-factor case see Farrell, "Measurement of Productive Efficiency."

14. In other words, the welfare loss of an inefficient firm is the loss of output due to the failure to maximize output given a set of inputs times the cost overruns per unit of output due to the failure to minimize costs in choosing inputs.

15. In Farrell's technique the unit output efficiency frontier is made up of the linear segments connecting pairs of (K,L) observations defined by the fact that no other observation lies inside the line connecting a pair of observations. Nonconstant returns to scale can be dealt with by segmenting the sample by size and calculating different frontiers for each size group. See Farrell and Fieldhouse, "Estimating Efficient Production Functions." In testing whether different size groups of our samples have different efficiency frontiers, we found, however, that the resulting efficiency frontiers cross each other; thus economies of scale may not be very important within the size range of our samples. Another limitation of Farrell's technique is that since only a relatively small percentage of observations are used to estimate the efficiency frontier, results may be quite sensitive to extreme observations that are due to measurement errors. Moreover,

the efficiency index for firms that are extremely capital- or labor-intensive tends to be sensitive to the observations for the few firms that fit that description and also lie close to the efficiency frontier.

16. D. J. Aigner and S. F. Chu, "On Estimating the Industry Production Function," *American Economic Review*, vol. 57 (1968), pp. 826–39.

17. The programming problem can be stated as follows.

Minimize
$$\sum_{i=1}^{n} \hat{u}_i$$

subject to $\hat{a}_0 + \hat{a}_1 \ln k_i + \hat{a}_2 \ln L_i \geq \ln Q_i$

and $\hat{a}_0, \hat{a}_1, \hat{a}_2 \geq o$, where $\hat{a}_0, \hat{a}_1,$ and $\hat{a}_2$ are the estimated values of the three parameters involved. For elaboration, see Timmer, "On Measuring Technical Efficiency," and "Using a Probabilistic Frontier Production Function to Measure Technical Efficiency," *Journal of Political Economy*, vol. 79 (1971), pp. 776–94.

18. For elaboration, see F. R. Forsund, C. A. K. Lovell, and Peter Schmidt, "A Survey of Frontier Production Functions and of Their Relationship to Efficiency Measurements," *Journal of Econometrics*, vol. 13 (1980), pp. 5–25.

19. The earnings data are based on Rakesh Mohan, *The Determinants of Labor Earnings in Developing Metropolises: Estimates from Bogotá and Cali, Colombia*, World Bank Staff Working Paper 498 (Washington, D.C., October 1981), pp. 28–34.

20. Commercial value of the equipment reflects what the entrepreneur would receive if he sold his equipment on the market. Its replacement value reflects what he would have to pay at the moment of the interview to set up a plant with similar equipment, which may or may not be new, depending on his inclinations. The difference between the two values in the metalworking sector averaged about 2 to 1; it tends to be larger for firms with a higher proportion of older equipment.

21. Kenneth shows that working-capital and fixed-capital ratios in the United States are markedly higher for small manufacturing firms than for larger ones. See D. A. Kenneth, "The Working Capital Needs of Small Enterprises," World Bank, Industry Development and Finance Department, Washington, D.C., 1979; processed.

22. Francisco Thoumi, "La Utilización del Capital Fijo en la Industria Manufacturera Colombiana," *Revista de Planeación y Desarrollo*, vol. 10, no. 3 (1978), pp. 36-37.

23. See the methodology outlined by Roger R. Betancourt and Christopher Clague, "Working Capital and Shift Work in Imperfect Capital Markets," University of Maryland, Department of Economics, College Park, 1976; processed. See also, by the same authors, *Capital Utilization: A Theoretical and Empirical Analysis* (Cambridge, Eng.: Cambridge University Press, 1981).

24. Data on nominal interest rates between 1963 and 1977 are presented, for example, in Fernando Gaviria C., "El Mercado Extrabancario y las Tasas de Interés en Colombia," *Revista del Banco de la República* (June 1978), p. 786. There

is no organized evidence on effective rates; our estimates of the differentials between the nominal and effective rates are based on evidence kindly supplied by Thomas Bentley of the World Bank.

25. Information on the average return to capital in Colombia suggests something in the range of 10–15 percent. In one of the more detailed studies, Harberger estimated a rate of 8–10 percent for the mid-1960s. Arnold C. Harberger, "La Tasa de Rendimiento de Capital en Colombia," *Revista de Planeación y Desarrollo*, vol. 1, no. 3 (October 1969), pp. 13–42. By the mid- to late 1970s the rate was somewhat higher, since the labor share of GNP had fallen and the marginal output-capital ratio had risen. From 1975 to 1979 the ratio of increase in output to gross investment was about one-third, and the capital share (one minus the paid plus imputed labor shares) was only a little under 50 percent. The average return to capital net of depreciation was probably at least 12 percent at this time. The marginal return would be lower, of course, how much lower depending on how one defined it. For the manufacturing sector, the profit rate gross of taxes appears to have been in excess of 20 percent. See Berry, "A Descriptive History," p. 66. The figures of appendix table 22 show that during the 1970s the ratio of net income of capital to the sum of inventories and the book value of fixed capital ranged from 21 to 37 percent. If we allow for some understatement of capital in these figures, the true ratio is probably in the range of 15–25 percent in most years. This figure, like that for the private sector as a whole, would tend to overstate returns to capital in the economy since public investment does not enter the denominator.

In an economy with a relatively perfect capital market, the returns to various types of financial assets would constitute useful information for estimating the private returns to capital. But in Colombia these returns are probably far below the true returns to capital, and thus we do not pretend to base an estimate of the social opportunity cost of capital on them. Labor market imperfections should also be allowed for in estimating the social opportunity cost of capital, but we were unable to do so in the absence of evidence on their extent.

26. See table 3-1 for statistics on man-days per year and unskilled equivalent man-days per year. Man-days per year is the product of the number of workers employed in a firm and the number of days it operates in a year. To obtain unskilled equivalent man-days per year, we weighted each skill category by the ratio of its wage rate to the unskilled wage rate. In the food sector we include transport equipment in our estimate of fixed capital because the delivered price of the products includes an imputed return to this capital.

Statistical Appendix

Table 1. Trends in the Industrial Sector during the Twentieth Century

| Item | 1870 | 1900 | 1925–27 | 1929–31 | 1939–41 | 1949–51 | 1959–61 | 1969–71 | 1978 | Annual average growth rates | |
										1900 to 1969–71	1900–78
All manufacturing											
Employment (thousands)	275–325	300–400	406–439	422–460	451	473	607	853	1,300[a]	1.1–1.5	1.5–1.9
Output (market prices, millions of 1958 pesos)	n.a.	104–167	473	520	1,010	2,113	4,131	7,425	12,315[b]	5.5–6.3	5.7–6.3
Labor productivity (1958 pesos)	n.a.	346–418	1,076–1,116	1,130–1,233	2,239	4,467	6,800	8,705	9,473	4.3–4.7	4.1–4.3
Physical capital stock (millions of 1958 pesos)	n.a.	n.a.	3,465	4,487	5,076	8,336	13,023	18,816	n.a.	4.0[c]	n.a.
Output/capital	n.a.	n.a.	0.13	0.12	0.20	0.25	0.32	0.39	n.a.	—	—
Share of total employment (percent)	20.0[b]	18.5[b]	15.9–17.2	15.4–16.8	13.5	12.1	13.1	14.9	16.2	—	—
Output/GNP (percent)											
Current prices	n.a.	n.a.	n.a.	n.a.	13.3	16.9	18.2	18.8	20.7	—	—
Constant 1958 prices	n.a.	n.a.	8.9	8.2	10.6	14.5	17.8	19.0	19.2	—	—
Factory manufacturing											
Employment (thousands)	n.a.	n.a.	≤70	n.a.	95–115	178.8	267.1	395.4	723.0	≥4.5[c]	≥4.6[c]
Output (market prices, millions of 1958 pesos)	n.a.	n.a.	n.a.	n.a.	660	1,575	3,304	6,287	10,796	7.8[d]	7.6[d]
Labor productivity (1958 pesos)	n.a.	n.a.	n.a.	n.a.	5,740–6,950	8,808	12,369	15,900	14,932	2.9–3.6[d]	2.0–2.6[d]

Physical capital stock (millions of 1958 pesos)	n.a.	n.a.	n.a.	n.a.	7,033	11,509	16,950	n.a.	n.a.	n.a.
Output/capital	n.a.	n.a.	n.a.	n.a.	0.22	0.29	0.37	n.a.	0.55[c]	0.86[c]
Share of total employment (percent)	n.a.	$\leq$2.74	n.a.	2.84–3.44	4.57	5.75	6.90	9.01	3.95[d]	3.94[d]
Output/GNP (percent)										
Current prices	n.a.	n.a.	n.a.	8.7	12.6	14.6	16.2	17.8	—	—
Constant 1958 prices	n.a.	n.a.	n.a.	6.9	10.8	14.2	16.3	17.0	—	—
Cottage shop manufacturing										
Employment (thousands)	n.a.	350–90	n.a.	336–56	294.2	340.4	457.6	577.0	—	—
Output (market prices, millions of 1958 pesos)	n.a.	n.a.	n.a.	350	538	827	1,099	1,519	—	—
Share of manufacturing output (percent)	n.a.	n.a.	n.a.	34.7	25.5	20.0	15.4	12.3	—	—
Share of total employment (percent)	n.a.	n.a.	n.a.	10.1–10.7	7.5	7.3	8.0	7.2	—	—

n.a. Not available.

— Not applicable.

Note: The official national accounts estimates of output used here for the period after 1950 appear to provide a seriously downward biased estimate of cottage shop output; its share in manufacturing output in this table is substantially below the probably more accurate figures of appendix tables 5, 6, and 7 for 1953, 1964, and 1975, respectively.

a. Chosen arbitrarily to be near the middle of the range defined by the figures in table 2-2.

b. Provisional.

c. For the period beginning in 1925–27.

d. For the period beginning in 1939–41.

Sources: For details, see Albert Berry, "A Descriptive History of Industrialization in Colombia," in *Essays on Industrialization in Colombia*, ed. Albert Berry (Tempe, Ariz.: Arizona State University, Center for Latin American Studies, 1983), table 2-1.

Table 2. Distribution of Establishments, Employment, Wages, Production, and Value Added, by Manufacturing Sector, for Very Small Firms, Second Industrial Census, 1953 (monetary values in thousands of 1953 pesos)

Manufacturing sector	Number of establishments	Employment (number)			Wages and fringe benefits	Value of production	Value added
		Total	Paid	Nonpaid			
Food	2,470	5,890	1,790	4,100	1,069	21,995	7,129
Beverages	260	520	210	310	222	1,742	919
Tobacco	800	1,910	770	1,140	463	3,993	1,971
Subtotal	3,530	8,320	2,770	5,550	1,754	27,730	10,019
Textiles	1,770	4,070	510	3,560	313	9,530	3,601
Clothing and footwear	18,260	28,380	6,520	21,860	6,551	116,399	47,482
Leather	840	1,420	380	1,040	368	5,591	2,338
Subtotal	20,870	33,870	7,410	26,460	7,232	131,520	53,421
Wood	2,040	3,520	1,050	2,470	856	10,351	5,793
Furniture	2,980	5,050	1,620	3,430	2,182	16,432	9,575
Subtotal	5,020	8,570	2,670	5,900	3,038	26,783	15,368
Paper	10	10	0	10	—	48	31
Printing	240	660	430	230	590	2,789	1,994
Subtotal	250	670	430	240	590	2,837	2,025

Rubber	60	100	10	90	7	128	112
Chemicals	470	1,040	350	690	247	3,887	1,569
Subtotal	530	1,140	360	780	254	4,015	1,681
Nonmetallic minerals	1,460	3,930	1,750	2,180	1,489	6,462	4,306
Base metals	50	110	50	60	107	511	371
Metal products	1,330	2,330	850	1,480	1,055	7,608	4,663
Nonelectrical machinery	80	160	50	110	59	430	280
Electrical machinery	650	1,030	300	730	309	4,222	2,490
Transport equipment	920	2,300	1,090	1,210	1,086	7,507	4,401
Subtotal	2,980	5,820	2,290	3,530	2,509	19,767	11,834
Other	1,420	2,130	370	1,760	571	8,986	5,576
Total	36,110	64,560	18,100	46,460	17,544	228,611	104,601

— Not applicable.

Note: Very small firms defined as those having less than 5 workers and less than 24,000 pesos of output in 1953.

Source: DANE, *Boletín Mensual de Estadística*, no. 72 (March 1957), pp. 15–17.

Table 3. Distribution of Establishments, Employment, Wages, Raw Materials, and Production, by Manufacturing Sector, for Very Small Firms, 1970
(monetary values in 1970 pesos)

Manufacturing sector	Number of establishments	Employment			Remuneration		Raw materials	Value of production
		Total	Paid	Nonpaid	Wages	Fringe benefits		
Food, beverages, tobacco	3,901	10,951	5,279	5,672	30,512	1,188	374,356	557,319
Textiles, clothing and footwear, leather	10,415	20,095	6,483	13,612	47,214	1,384	294,811	563,431
Wood, furniture	4,876	10,309	4,006	6,303	35,722	876	141,147	313,112
Paper, printing	733	1,969	1,048	921	9,321	403	23,494	59,453
Rubber, chemicals, oil and coal, plastics	326	877	478	399	3,761	162	27,985	50,440
Nonmetallic minerals	848	2,318	1,335	983	11,673	303	28,905	70,405
Base metals	126	375	208	167	1,805	110	6,016	13,000
Metal products, nonelectrical machinery, electrical machinery, transport equipment	2,423	5,888	2,868	3,020	26,432	779	120,759	241,705
Other	481	1,191	505	686	3,586	110	18,352	36,266
Total	24,129	53,973	22,210	31,583	170,055	5,316	1,035,826	1,905,132

Note: From sample of 3,925 establishments having less than 5 workers.
Source: Unpublished DANE data.

Table 4. Employment in Household Industries, 1973

Manufacturing sector	Number of households with industry[a]	Total employment	Number of workers in household					
			1	2	3	4	5	6+
Food, beverages, tobacco	35,697	104,271	11,300	18,250	16,787	16,374	11,773	29,787
Textiles, clothing, leather	43,105	93,928	21,953	22,925	12,777	10,168	5,980	20,125
Wood, furniture	11,068	26,752	5,424	4,937	3,913	2,973	1,626	7,879
Paper, printing	1,459	4,066	411	946	1,038	239	314	1,118
Chemicals, oil and coal products, rubber and plastics	1,895	6,452	501	1,106	478	699	1,248	2,420
Nonmetallic minerals	3,920	12,549	1,280	2,311	1,137	1,823	1,011	4,987
Base metals	243	403	130	132	141	0	0	0
Metal products, machinery	2,914	10,640	1,105	1,227	1,505	1,082	761	4,960
Other	3,133	7,974	1,245	1,832	1,217	784	737	2,159
Information lacking	21,763	52,009	9,145	13,351	7,224	6,004	3,209	13,076
Total	125,197	319,044	52,494	67,017	46,217	40,146	26,659	86,511

Note: A household industry is one that produces in the household manufactured goods for sale. This category does not include shops, stores, beauty parlors, and the like.

a. The total number of households in 1973 was 3,471,834.

Source: DANE, *XIV Censo Nacional de Población y III de Vivienda, 1973, Muestra de Avance y Resúmenes Departamentales,* table 13, pp. 52–53. The original data have been expanded according to the underenumeration reflected in the 1973 census. The population totals for *cabecera* (municipal seat) and *resto* (the rest of the municipality) are taken from DANE, *Boletín Mensual de Estadística,* no. 314 (September 1977), p. 30. The number of household industries and employment have been expanded separately in cabecera and resto by the same proportions by which the latest revisions exceed the original population estimates in cabecera and resto.

Table 5. *Composition of Output, by Size, 1953*

Size of establishment (number of workers)	Workers	Average labor productivity (pesos per year)	Output (value added, millions of pesos)	Percentage of total output	Labor share of value added (percent)
Independent workers	146,450[a]	2,020[b]	295.8	15.34	—
2–4					
Our estimate	135,618	1,453[c]	197.1	10.22	—
Reporting to DANE	64,560	1,620	104.6	5.54	60.50
5–9	23,550	3,470	81.7	4.23	44.01
10–14	13,698	4,400	60.3	3.12	42.57
15–24	15,870	5,010	79.5	4.12	41.14
25–49	21,623	6,860	148.3	7.69	34.52
50+	106,189	10,040	1,066.1	55.27	26.93
CS	282,068	1,747	492.9	25.55	—
SI	74,741	4,948	369.8	19.17	39.35
MI and LI	106,189	10,040	1,066.1	55.27	26.93
Factory	180,932	7,937	1,436.0	74.45	30.13
All	463,000[a]	4,166	1,889.3	100.00	—

— Not applicable.

Note: Data in this table are not fully consistent with those of table 2-2 since DANE figures for establishments of 5 workers and up have not been adjusted.

a. Interpolated between the 1951 and 1964 population census figures and then reduced by 4.74 percent to be consistent with the unadjusted estimates for the factory sector. Since most of the undercoverage would pertain to SI, we have probably understated its share of employment and output at this time.

b. Earnings assumed to be 1.5 times that of paid workers in CS, which might have been 875 pesos (it was 980 pesos for persons in the very small establishments that did report), thus 1,313 pesos. We assume these earnings are 65 percent of value added (the ratio for reporting very small plants was 60 percent although family workers may have been numerous).

c. Nonreporting persons are assumed to be 80 percent as productive as those included, whose average was reported in the DANE survey as 1,610. Since those reported include many independent workers (average number of workers per establishment was 1.8), the average productivity figure involves both independent workers and workers in plants of 2–4 workers. This would suggest that average productivity in the latter would be less than shown here, but we made no further adjustment to allow for this. Understatement would probably exceed any upward bias from this source.

Table 6. *Distribution of Manufacturing Value Added, by Size, 1964*

Sector	Number of workers (thousands)	Average labor productivity (pesos per year)[a]	Output[a] (millions of pesos)	Percentage of total output
All	637.5	18,390	11,723	100.00
CS	327.5	8,000[b]	2,620	22.35
SI	125.7	15,910	2,000	17.06
MI	33.1	28,030	928	7.91
LI	151.2	40,840	6,175	52.67
Factory	310.0	29,360	9,103	77.65

a. Where DANE data are used (that is, for SI, MI, and LI), the figures are scaled down by the ratio of 0.852 to correspond to the ratio of the Banco de la República's estimate of value added in factory manufacturing to DANE's estimate.

b. Urrutia and Villalba have 7,625 in their table 4b. See Miguel Urrutia and C. E. Villalba, "El Sector Artesanal en el Desarrollo Colombiano," *Revista de Planeación y Desarrollo,* vol. 1, no. 3 (October 1969), p. 76. This is based on independent workers, which could bias it up, but fails to include any value added apart from earnings or any understatement of earnings. On balance, it is probably downward-biased by 5–10 percent for these reasons. We raised it by 6 percent. We assume that no adjustment is necessary of the sort the Banco de la República makes to DANE data in estimating the national accounts.

Table 7. *Distribution of Manufacturing Value Added, by Size, 1975*

Plant size	Number of workers	Average labor productivity (pesos per year)[a]	Output (billions of pesos)	Percentage of total output
Independent workers	285,000[b]	31,040[c]	8.847	8.51
2–4	265,000	25,880[d]	6.859	6.60
5–9	35,400	60,000	2.124	2.04
10–14	37,000	70,000	2.590	2.49
15–19	33,000	75,648	2.496	2.40
20–24	25,000	75,772	1.894	1.82
25–49	55,000	87,929	4.836	4.65
50–74	37,384	107,990	4.036	3.88
75–99	25,600	137,607	3.523	3.29
100–199	71,715	172,885	12.398	11.93
200+	229,901	236,403	54.349	52.28
All	1,100,000	97,620	103.950	100.00
CS	550,000[e]	28,556	15.706	15.11
SI	185,400	75,189	13.940	13.41
MI	62,984	120,010	7.559	7.27
LI	301,616	221,298	66.747	64.21
Factory	798,384	110,528	88.244	84.89

(Table continues on the following page.)

Table 7 *(continued)*

a. Figures for plants of 10 workers and up are those from DANE's reported plants. The DANE figure for firms of 5–9 workers is lowered as the DANE plants are unrepresentative. We presume smaller plants reporting to DANE underreport value added substantially; however, those who report are likely to be atypically productive compared with all plants in the same size category. Which bias would be the greater is not clear.

b. The number of urban independent workers in late 1974 was 198,000 according to DANE's household survey (EH9); it appears that there were a few more in 1975, say 205,000–210,000. The rural independent workers fell from 100,000 in 1972 to 64,000 in 1978, which suggests there were about 80,000 in 1975, for a total of about 285,000.

c. Assumes Bourguignon's figure, raised by 15 percent to allow for underreporting, but recognizes that his figures for seven cities would exceed the national urban figures by a few percentage points. See François Bourguignon, "Pobreza y Dualismo en el Sector Urbano de las Economías en Desarrollo: El Caso de Colombia," *Desarrollo y Sociedad*, no. 1 (1979), p. 52: Assumes a labor share of 90 percent (we use 50 percent for very small plants). Possibly a little more of the income of these people comes from sources other than their job. About 28 percent of independent workers are, according to our estimates, in rural areas and have much lower incomes; we assume an average income half as high as in urban areas. (In 1970 the figure for all persons earning an income in manufacturing was 50 percent as high in rural as in urban areas. See DANE, *Boletín Mensual de Estadística*, no. 237 [April 1971], p. 71.) The average income for urban independent workers was thus about 32,500 pesos.

d. Bourguignon permits an estimate of 34,800 blue-collar paid workers in traditional manufacturing (seven cities), 16,700 white-collar workers, 10,730 owners and managers, and 73,500 independent workers (Bourguignon, "Pobreza y Dualismo," p. 52). This seems to be a very high ratio of white- to blue-collar workers, higher than for modern sector manufacturing, according to Bourguignon's sample (where this ratio seems too low). Here we assume the ratio to be 4:1 for this category. The average income figure is raised by 15 percent to allow for underreporting, lowered by 5 percent to allow for the lower incomes of the perhaps 10 percent of these workers found in rural areas, and becomes 16,393 pesos. We assume that all the family helpers not in the factory sector are included in the category of workers in establishments of 2–4 workers. (This exaggerates the differential average labor productivity between the two, but we have no way of knowing how many family helpers assist independent workers.) As a result the composition of this group is roughly: paid, 72.10 percent; owner and manager, 17.33 percent; and family helper, 10.57 percent.

Most employees, even in CS, are urban, so we assume an average income of 80 percent of that reported by Bourguignon, that is, 48,096 pesos. Average earnings in the sector then become 20,154 pesos. This may be an underestimate, since some owners are probably classified in other occupational categories, although the inclusion of plants of 5 workers in the Bourguignon data tends to make it an overestimate. Here we assume 22,000 pesos. We then assume that the ratio of included earnings to value added is 85 percent.

e. It is difficult to calculate a precise figure for this group since their composition is not fully known.

Table 8. *Labor Productivity in Manufacturing, 1951–78*

Year	Output at market prices (millions of 1958 pesos)	Employment (thousands)	Output per worker (1958 pesos)	Average annual increase in labor productivity — Period	Average annual increase in labor productivity — Percent
1951	2,246.8	480	4,681	1951–78	2.31–2.84
1964	5,188.2	638	8,138	1951–64	4.35
1970	7,404.1	853	8,680	1964–70	1.08
1973	9,557.1	985	9,703	1970–78	0–1.78
1975	10,157.4				
1978	12,291.4	1,232–1,417	8,674–9,977		

Sources: Output figures are from Banco de la República, *Cuentas Nacionales*. Employment figures are from table 2-2 except that for 1951, which is interpolated from figures
from the same source.

Table 9. *The Importance of Cottage Shop in Manufacturing
Output, Depending on Assumptions Used, 1970 and 1977*

Source of factory output estimate[a]	1970 — Billions of pesos	1970 — Percent	1977 — Billions of pesos	1977 — Percent
DANE (market prices)				
Factory	26,315		167,389	
Cottage shop	5,658	17.7	31,664	15.91
Total	31,973		199,053	
Banco de la República				
Market prices				
Factory	21,632		138,658	
Cottage shop	5,658	20.7	31,664	18.59
Total	27,290		170,322	
Factor costs				
Factory[b]	17,709		124,723	
Cottage shop[b]	5,251	22.87	30,000	19.39
Total	22,960		154,723	

a. Cottage-shop output figures are, in each case, those of the Banco de la República,
Cuentas Nacionales.

b. Assuming the tax burden on cottage shops is half as high as on the factory subsector
(taxes are high on beverages, tobacco, and the like). The overall burden is 13.4 percent.

Table 10. Labor Productivity and Earnings of the Cottage-Shop and Factory Subsectors, by Industry, 1953

Industry	Percentage of CS in employment (registered)	Value added per worker			Average size of establishment (number of workers)		Ratio of value added to value of production		Average earnings (pesos)		
		Factories (F)	Cottage shops (CS)	CS/F[a]	Factory	CS	Factory	CS	Factory	CS	CS/F
Food	12.43	6,581	1,210	0.184	14.72	2.38	0.173	0.324	1,955	597	0.306
Beverages	4.50	30,854	1,767	0.057	44.34	2.00	0.725	n.a.	4,426	1,057	0.239
Tobacco	22.41	8,458	1,032	0.122	17.59	2.39	0.590	n.a.	2,064	601	0.291
Textiles	9.95	7,239	885	0.122	65.57	2.30	0.487	n.a.	2,567	614	0.239
Clothing and footwear	49.79	3,481	1,673	0.482	10.39	1.55	0.397	n.a.	1,578	1,005	0.637
Wood and coal products (except furniture)	45.30	3,963	1,646	0.415	9.01	1.73	0.406	n.a.	1,741	815	0.468
Wood furniture	55.17	3,471	1,896	0.545	9.20	1.69	0.589	n.a.	1,958	1,347	0.688
Paper and products	0.50	7,830	3,100	0.396	38.78	1.0	0.511	n.a.	2,660	—	—
Printing	7.77	5,450	3,021	0.554	22.70	2.75	0.600	n.a.	2,915	1,372	0.471
Leather and products	26.11	6,523	1,646	0.252	13.81	1.69	0.367	n.a.	2,901	968	0.334

Rubber and products	3.39	12,482	1,120	0.090	39.56	1.67	0.555	n.a.	2,981	700	0.235
Chemicals	9.44	8,925	1,509	0.169	20.62	2.21	0.532	n.a.	2,695	706	0.262
Petroleum and coal derivatives	0	15,538	—	—	122.15	—	0.278	n.a.	5,851	—	—
Nonmetallic mineral products	18.04	5,534	1,096	0.198	18.21	2.69	0.633	n.a.	2,061	851	0.413
Base metal industries	7.20	5,877	3,373	0.574	21.48	2.20	0.395	n.a.	2,900	2,140	0.738
Metal products, except machinery	25.85	4,432	2,001	0.452	17.36	1.75	0.506	0.651	2,198	1,241	0.565
Nonelectric machinery	9.24	4,383	1,750	0.399	12.19	2.0	0.456	n.a.	2,164	1,180	0.545
Electric machinery	36.31	5,856	2,417	0.413	15.44	1.58	0.526	n.a.	2,430	1,030	0.424
Transport equipment	29.04	4,947	1,913	0.387	13.51	2.50	0.620	n.a.	2,545	996	0.391
Miscellaneous	41.93	5,393	2,618	0.486	13.66	1.50	0.593	n.a.	2,280	1,543	0.677
All	24.48	7,527	1,620	0.215	17.71	1.79	0.390	0.458	2,375	969	0.408

n.a. Not available.

— Not applicable.

Note: Because the CS data are based on a 10 percent sample, in small cells there is some variance between the figure shown and the true value.

a. The unweighted average of this ratio for the four industries with more than 40 percent of employment in CS was 0.482; for the five industries with 20–39 percent of employment in CS it was 0.325; and for the ten industries with less than 20 percent employment in CS it was 0.274.

Source: DANE, *Boletín Mensual de Estadística*, no. 72 (1957), pp. 16–18.

Table 11. *Manufacturing Employment, by Two-Digit Industry and by Factory and Cottage-Shop Subsectors, 1938 and 1964*

Industry	1938	1964
Food	29,387	73,889
Factory	≥6,153	41,561
Cottage shop	≤23,234	32,328
Beverages	6,358	19,216
Factory	≥1,975	16,420
Cottage shop	≤4,383	2,796
Tobacco	10,167	8,574
Factory	≥5,059	3,803
Cottage shop	≤5,108	4,771
Textiles	114,684[a]	62,362
Factory	≥11,551	44,099
Cottage shop	≤103,133	18,263
Clothing and footwear	160,788	153,265
Factory	≥2,790	31,510
Cottage shop	≤157,998	121,755
Wood and products	44,356	78,245
Factory	n.a.	10,989
Cottage shop	≥44,356	67,256
Paper and products	—[b]	5,613
Factory	—	5,485
Cottage shop	—	128
Printing	7,132	16,935
Factory	n.a.	11,812
Cottage shop	≤7,132	5,123
Leather and products	7,024	9,488
Factory	n.a.	4,482
Cottage shop	≤7,024	5,006
Rubber and products	—[b]	7,900
Factory	—	6,900
Cottage shop	—	1,000
Chemicals	4,722	25,752
Factory	≥2,761	19,819
Cottage shop	≤1,961	5,933
Petroleum and coal products	—[b]	4,880
Factory	—	2,026
Cottage shop	—	2,854
Nonmetallic mineral products	16,517	36,907
Factory	≥2,807	25,493
Cottage shop	≤13,710	11,414
Metal and metal products	25,226	136,951
Factory	≥1,417	51,549
Cottage shop	≤23,809	85,402
Total	435,863	655,961[b]
Factory	80,000–100,000	283,571
Cottage shop	335,863–355,863	372,390

n.a. Not available.

— Not applicable.

a. Includes 90,559 persons listed in the 1938 census (p. 154) under "Industries of Animal and Vegetable Fibers," of which 81,409 were men.

b. These industries either did not exist in 1938 or were not separated out in the data.

c. Includes 15,984 people listed in the 1964 census under "other."

Sources: For 1938, total employment in each industry, the population census, República de Colombia, Contraloría General de la República, Dirección Nacional de Estadística, *Censo General de Población*, vol. 16 *(Ultimo), Resumen general del país* (Bogotá: Imprenta Nacional, 1942), pp. 154–55; and for a minimum estimate of factory employment, República de Colombia, Contraloría General de la República, Dirección Nacional de Estadística, *Anuario General de Estadística, 1938* (Bogotá: Imprenta Nacional, 1939), p. 48. For 1964, total employment, the population census, República de Colombia, Departamento Administrativo Nacional de Estadística, *XIII Censo Nacional de Población, Resumen General* (Bogotá: Imprenta Nacional, 1967), pp. 134–36; and for factory employment, DANE, *Anuario General de Estadística, 1964*, vol. 4 (Bogotá: DANE, n.d.), pp. 572–75.

Table 12. *Labor Productivity, by Industry and by Plant Size, 1975*
(absolute figures in thousands of pesos)

Industry	Plant size (number of workers)									All plants	Plant-size categories			Labor productivity indices (average = 1.00)[b]		
	5–9	10–14	15–19	20–24	25–49	50–74	75–99	100–99	200+		SI	MI	LI	SI	MI	LI
Food	144.0	93.3	137.4	103.4	115.5	176.7	245.2	201.0	228.6	190.3	115.0	208.5	221.0	0.60	1.10	1.16
Beverages	79.0	105.8	98.7	53.9	249.3	219.9	503.2	395.8	560.9	489.5	104.2	332.5	513.9	0.38	0.68	1.05
Tobacco	18.3	42.5	23.1	72.2	0	12.9[a]	0	466.1	549.1	472.8	50.9	12.9[a]	533.1	0.11	0.03[a]	1.13
Textiles	47.0	50.2	66.9	67.8	66.1	77.6	73.2	81.2	155.0	134.0	64.0	75.8	146.9	0.48	0.57	1.10
Footwear and clothing	42.3	49.3	41.1	42.6	43.8	43.9	53.0	65.0	78.5	61.1	44.1	48.4	73.7	0.72	0.79	1.20
Wood	51.6	47.9	41.4	41.1	65.6	36.8	70.4	324.4	163.3	110.8	53.6	49.3	214.0	0.48	0.44	1.93
Wood furniture	36.3	37.8	49.8	50.0	45.0	47.1	49.6	86.8	96.1	59.5	43.8	48.2	91.1	0.74	0.81	1.53
Paper	36.7	93.3	78.5	84.3	82.7	77.7	197.0	229.7	358.5	232.2	83.0	125.6	315.5	0.36	0.54	1.36
Printing	47.7	54.1	56.2	65.3	65.8	77.4	142.2	122.9	167.5	123.9	61.1	94.9	155.9	0.49	0.77	1.26
Leather	75.9	46.4	46.9	43.6	50.6	51.4	43.5	63.7	127.3	85.3	49.2	47.0	101.5	0.58	0.55	1.19
Rubber	36.2	122.5	102.0	72.2	111.8	73.2	118.8	128.5	256.5	203.4	103.1	92.7	246.8	0.51	0.46	1.21

Chemicals	258.7	105.7	118.7	146.0	214.3	214.2	190.7	300.8	335.4	300.3	182.9	247.4	329.8	0.61	0.82	1.10
Industrial	764.4	174.2	132.8	315.9	375.5	545.8	304.0	554.2	364.8	400.6	330.5	503.1	309.4	0.85	1.26	1.00
Other	131.4	98.8	112.9	80.8	136.7	145.0	158.3	239.9	317.1	251.1	121.2	151.9	291.8	0.48	0.60	1.16
Oil and products																
Nonmetallic minerals	43.6	38.2	45.3	63.1	58.1	67.9	71.1	107.9	207.5	145.5	54.4	69.2	191.9	0.37	0.48	1.32
Clay	31.2	35.0	24.3	48.4	30.7	44.3	44.5	31.8	97.2	82.3	32.2	44.4	94.0	0.39	0.54	1.14
Glass	28.2	32.7	69.9	79.1	49.1	32.6	59.7	80.1	170.7	130.8	55.9	42.7	149.9	0.43	0.33	1.15
Other	37.8	38.7	43.8	61.8	63.7	78.6	77.4	137.2	274.1	167.9	56.9	78.1	219.5	0.34	0.46	1.31
Base metals																
Metal products	46.1	69.0	51.4	52.5	80.9	87.0	102.4	128.0	198.8	125.1	70.2	92.5	174.9	0.56	0.74	1.40
Nonelectrical machinery	44.8	64.0	59.8	67.1	98.1	98.9	208.9	135.0	159.0	126.9	80.5	141.6	150.7	0.63	1.12	1.19
Electrical machinery	86.0	82.8	74.9	53.6	92.4	160.9	129.6	168.7	168.9	148.4	84.8	146.3	168.9	0.57	0.99	1.14
Transport equipment	75.5	54.7	76.3	82.3	65.5	107.3	85.8	117.1	336.4	243.7	68.7	99.9	304.2	0.28	0.41	1.25
Plastic	87.0	59.8	64.9	51.1	83.3	90.1	86.3	111.4	138.5	107.9	74.7	89.0	125.9	0.69	0.82	1.17
All	81.5	69.7	75.6	75.8	87.9	108.0	137.6	172.9	236.4	179.1	81.7	120.2	221.4	0.46	0.67	1.24

a. Based on a very small number of plants, which are clearly atypical or for which data were incorrectly reported.

b. Averages refer to the specific industry, not to all manufacturing.

Source: Unpublished DANE data from the 1976 survey of manufacturing.

Table 13. *Average Annual Wage Earnings,*
by Plant Size and Job Category, 1975
(pesos)

Plant size (number of workers) and job category	DANE annual survey of manufacturing		DANE seven-city household survey (September-October)	
	With fringe benefits	*Without fringe benefits*	*Traditional sector*	*Modern sector*
1–4	26,410	20,893		
5–9	24,416	19,852		
10–14	26,261	20,839		
15–19	26,674	21,041		
20–24	29,038	22,489		
25–49	32,184	24,503		
SI (5–49)	29,902	23,082		
50–74	38,304	27,774		
75–99	41,556	30,138		
MI (50–99)	39,645	28,750		
100–199	50,421	34,437		
200+	74,222	46,265		
LI (100+)	68,612	43,476		
All[a]	57,107	37,485		
Blue-collar	43,954	28,879 ⎱	16,296	23,424
White-collar clerical	79,684	52,376 ⎰		
Technicians	167,646	102,324 ⎱	21,096	57,156
Directors	204,536	141,473 ⎰		
All nonblue-collar	99,467	65,126	n.a.	n.a.
Independent workers	—	—	27,612	—
Owners and managers	—	—	60,120	240,996

n.a. Not available.
— Not applicable.
a. In December 1975 the average annual earnings of all manufacturing workers was 32,862 pesos according to the Ministerio de Trabajo y Seguridad Social, Instituto Colombiano de Seguros Sociales, *Series Estadísticas, Años 1949–1975* (Bogotá: ICSS, n.d.), p. 49.
Sources: DANE annual survey of manufacturing data are from DANE, *Industria Manufacturera,* 1975 (Bogotá, 1978), pp. 29–35. DANE household survey data are calculated from the figures presented in François Bourguignon, "Pobreza y Dualismo en el Sector Urbano de las Economías en Desarrollo: El Caso de Colombia," *Desarrollo y Sociedad,* no. 1 (1979), pp. 52, 54.

Table 14. *Earnings (Excluding Fringe Benefits) in the Modern and Traditional Sectors of Manufacturing, 1975*
(pesos)

	Paid blue-collar workers		Paid white-collar workers	
Sector	Bourguignon	DANE	Bourguignon	DANE
Modern	23,424	28,879	57,156	65,126
Traditional	16,296	18,000	21,096	23,400
Modern/traditional	1.44	1.60	2.71	2.78

Note: Bourguignon's figures are compared with DANE figures on earnings excluding fringe benefits on the presumption (supported by the numbers) that the former are not likely to include many, if any, of those fringe benefits.

Sources: François Bourguignon, "Pobreza y Dualismo," p. 54, and DANE figures presented in table 2-12.

Table 15. *Average Annual Remuneration (Including Fringe Benefits) and Share of Fringe Benefits in Total Remuneration, by Plant Size, 1976*

Plant size (number of workers)	Total		Managers and directors		Technicians				Clerical workers		Blue-collar workers		Apprentices	
	Pesos	FB/T	Pesos	FB/T	National (pesos)	FB/T	Foreign (pesos)	FB/T	Pesos	FB/T	Pesos	FB/T	Pesos	FB/T
Less than 5	29,702	23.41	46,807	21.07	—	—	—	—	31,749	21.28	31,668	23.85	—	—
5–9	31,919	22.09	64,608	23.21	56,904	24.33	59,528	22.33	31,060	21.56	29,217	22.04	24,039	19.93
10–14	33,018	22.89	72,921	21.58	68,906	25.35	57,028	20.46	37,650	22.96	29,744	22.95	13,833	18.28
15–19	34,329	24.15	85,436	22.51	65,917	24.72	187,067[a]	24.14	42,456	24.59	29,902	24.25	16,713	21.24
20–24	35,862	24.52	96,290	24.24	76,865	24.72	107,423[a]	20.44	42,325	25.55	30,367	24.29	14,115	21.16
25–49	41,321	26.90	129,873	25.96	103,334	27.45	107,404	25.28	58,500	27.81	33,060	26.73	18,982	23.13
50–74	47,221	29.18	168,880	28.30	126,237	31.49	241,242	30.47	70,284	30.00	36,879	28.86	28,616	27.31
75–99	55,708	29.82	227,583	30.44	122,239	28.46	211,949	24.59	79,868	30.04	42,129	29.82	24,594	25.31
100–199	65,495	33.26	279,934	32.76	181,958	37.79	209,300	28.07	92,433	32.13	48,066	33.60	23,667	31.55
200+	92,502	38.76	410,441	37.19	258,947	44.07	423,704	35.08	125,772	38.16	72,294	38.69	35,908	35.34
All	72,238	35.78	254,774	33.66	207,026	41.18	292,664	32.75	102,205	35.72	55,737	35.58	29,086	32.85
SI	38,151		107,726		87,962		127,903		51,522		37,200		18,009	
MI	50,695		192,729		124,224		225,417		74,595		38,992		19,370	
LI	86,314		365,568		243,681		373,421		116,786		66,735		32,992	
SMI	43,295		138,113		104,694		163,724		61,379		34,668		18,583	

— Not applicable.

FB/T = the percentage of total remuneration received in the form of fringe benefits.

a. Very small sample.

Source: Unpublished data from DANE's 1976 survey of manufacturing.

264

Table 16. *Average Annual Blue-Collar Wage (Including Fringe Benefits), by Plant Size in the Clothing Industry, 1976*

Plant size (number of workers)	Average annual blue-collar wage (pesos)	Percentage of blue-collar workers	Plant size (output in millions of pesos)	Average annual blue-collar wage (pesos)	Percentage of blue-collar workers
Less than 5			≥0.2	9,704	0.07
5–9	24,437	0.53	0.2+ to <0.4	12,476	0.39
10–14	23,580	2.59	0.4+ to <0.6	15,797	0.60
15–19	24,375	2.68	0.6+ to <0.9	17,855	0.97
20–24	23,801	2.69	0.9+ to <1.5	22,043	3.21
25–49	24,151	14.33	1.5+ to <2.0	22,840	1.89
50–74	23,769	11.78	2+ to <4	23,852	9.41
75–99	27,694	5.96	4+ to <10	23,522	18.12
100–199	29,507	15.08	10 to <50	30,432	30.93
200+	41,160	44.34	≥50	42,642	34.40
All	32,680[a]	100.00	All	31,933[a]	100.00

a. The two averages for all workers differ because data for some firms were available under one size classification but not under the other.
Source: Unpublished DANE data from the 1976 survey of manufacturing.

Table 17. *Average Daily Earnings (Including Fringe Benefits),*
by Skill Category of Workers in Metalworking and Food Processing Firms

Firm size (number of workers)	Supervisors and technicians		Skilled workers		Semiskilled workers		Unskilled workers		All	
Metalworking firms (December 1977 pesos)										
1–10	—	(0)	234	(13)	167	(8)	98	(11)	156	(13)
11–20	297	(3)	242	(20)	165	(17)	122	(17)	161	(17)
21–40	471	(6)	309	(16)	180	(8)	121	(9)	189	(15)
41–60	363	(2)	277	(13)	189	(10)	135	(11)	190	(12)
61+	473	(2)	300	(10)	178	(8)	131	(7)	185	(8)
All	415	(13)	270	(72)	174	(51)	121	(55)	175	(65)
Food processing firms (January 1979 pesos)										
1–7	—	(0)	154	(5)	122	(7)	104	(11)	137	(11)
8–15	229	(2)	194	(10)	160	(5)	136	(10)	165	(11)
16–29	399	(4)	211	(6)	163	(6)	131	(7)	139	(8)
30+	755	(3)	229	(6)	178	(6)	156	(6)	179	(6)
All	480	(9)	198	(27)	155	(24)	128	(34)	153	(36)

— Not applicable.

Note: The daily wages include social security, SENA contributions, and other fringe benefits. Figures in parentheses denote number of firms.

Table 18. *Composition of the Labor Force, by Plant Size, 1976*
(percent)

Plant size (number of workers)	Unpaid[a]	White-collar (paid)				Blue-collar (paid)	Apprentices
		Total	Executive	Technical	Clerical		
1–9	16.50	15.37	2.88	1.41	11.08	68.11	n.a.
10–14	10.26	18.19	3.37	1.47	13.35	71.55	n.a.
15–19	7.23	18.84	3.48	1.43	13.93	73.92	n.a.
20–24	5.41	19.03	3.30	1.72	14.01	75.56	n.a.
25–49	3.17	20.57	3.07	1.64	15.86	76.26	n.a.
50–74	1.91	19.79	2.68	1.63	15.48	78.30	n.a.
75–99	0.78	23.15	2.63	2.41	18.11	76.07	n.a.
100–199	0.59	25.69	2.37	2.08	21.24	73.72	n.a.
200+	0.09	25.93	1.35	2.46	22.12	73.96	n.a.
All	1.46	23.98	2.05	2.17	19.76	74.56	n.a.
SI	5.62	30.16	13.54	1.24	14.00	69.73	11.10
MI	1.44	16.78	11.70	0.92	10.44	47.96	8.09
LI	0.21	49.43	70.19	4.18	78.42	225.48	51.61
SMI	3.95	46.94	25.14	1.96	24.43	117.69	19.19

n.a. Not available.

a. Owners, associates, and unpaid family helpers.

Source: Unpublished DANE data from the 1976 survey of manufacturing.

Table 19. *Kilowatt-Hours of Electricity Consumed Annually per Worker, by Plant Size, Selected Industries, 1976*

Plant size (number of workers)	Food	Textiles	Clothing	Printing	Metal products[a]
Less than 10	7,950	2,460	1,921	2,428	2,192
10–14	6,511	1,770	1,068	1,766	2,368
15–19	7,116	2,058	1,056	2,074	1,880
20–24	9,569	1,703	827	1,377	2,314
25–49	6,401	2,390	770	1,429	2,471
50–74	6,224	2,645	802	1,955	2,764
75–99	7,971	3,194	903	2,110	2,918
100–199	5,666	3,448	973	1,781	4,319
200+	12,309	11,684	1,394	2,239	5,761
All	9,057	9,344	1,116	1,978	3,851
SI	7,131	2,208	878	1,647	2,351
MI	6,936	2,914	836	2,026	2,823
LI	10,667	10,698	1,282	2,126	5,245
SMI	7,054	2,554	860	1,739	2,521

a. Excluding machinery; International Standard Industrial Classification (ISIC) category 381.

Source: Unpublished DANE data from the 1976 survey of manufacturing.

Table 20. *The Ratio of Book Value of Fixed Capital to Value Added and of Energy Consumption to Value Added, by Plant Size, Selected Industries, 1976*

Plant size (number of workers)	Printing (342)		Food products (311–312)		Metal products (381)[a]	
	BV/VA	CE/VA	BV/VA	CE/VA	BV/VA	CE/VA
1–4	0.988	0.046	0.607	0.050	1.229	0.030
5–9	0.963	0.047	1.138	0.097	0.724	0.033
10–14	0.851	0.027	0.737	0.079	0.663	0.038
15–19	1.376	0.030	0.528	0.052	0.588	0.029
20–24	0.574	0.018	0.808	0.083	0.465	0.032
25–49	0.661	0.018	0.465	0.035	0.531	0.027
SI (5–49)			0.568	0.050	0.550	0.029
50–74	1.490	0.017	0.439	0.031	0.587	0.023
75–99	0.525	0.011	0.231	0.016	0.336	0.023
MI (50–99)			0.308	0.022	0.487	0.023
100–199	0.954	0.016	0.548	0.031	0.458	0.024
200+	0.338	0.010	0.830	0.045	0.519	0.034
All	0.524	0.013	0.626	0.039	0.505	0.029

Note: BV, book value of fixed capital; VA, value added; and CE, consumption of energy in kilowatt-hours. Figures for the ratio CE/VA refer to kilowatt-hours per peso of value added. Figures in parentheses are ISIC categories.

a. Excluding machinery.

Source: Unpublished DANE data from the 1976 survey of manufacturing.

Table 21. *Purchases of Used Machinery and Equipment as a Percentage of Gross Investment in Machinery and Equipment, by Industry, Selected Years*

ISIC category	Industry	1973	1975	1976	Weighted average (1973, 1975, 1976)
311–312	Food	23.8	8.2	11.0	12.1
313	Beverages	30.0	4.4	2.6	6.0
314	Tobacco	5.1	47.5	2.7	13.5
321	Textiles	3.2	15.2	10.5	8.4
322	Clothing	34.6	18.6	16.5	24.8
323	Leather	14.0	5.1	13.1	9.6
324	Footwear	28.5	24.6	30.6	28.2
331	Wood products (except furniture)	43.3	36.7	28.0	41.0
332	Wood furniture	31.7	37.1	10.8	26.0
341	Paper	4.2	5.2	2.0	3.6
342	Printing	11.6	20.7	9.9	14.0
351	Industrial chemicals	70.1	8.7	6.2	48.9
352	Other chemicals	30.1	18.7	8.6	19.6
353–354	Petroleum refining and coal	14.9	1.0	0.1	3.1
355	Rubber	4.3	6.7	9.4	6.2
356	Plastics	14.7	5.6	11.8	11.3
361	Ceramics	0.6	6.3	5.2	4.0
362	Glass	5.4	8.7	5.1	6.2
369	Other nonmetallic minerals	15.3	17.2	37.0	24.4
371	Base metals	1.2	5.1	2.7	3.2
372	Nonferrous metals				
381	Metal products	17.7	20.0	19.8	19.2
382	Nonelectric machinery	20.8	15.5	33.1	23.0
383	Electrical machinery	21.8	3.4	7.5	10.2
384	Transport equipment	12.2	9.8	16.6	12.5
Total		24.3	10.6	10.7	15.2

Source: DANE, *Industria Manufacturera*, 1973, 1975, and 1976.

Table 22. *Indicators of the Returns to Capital in Manufacturing,*
1970–78

Item	1970	1971	1973	1975	1976	1977	1978
Percentage of value added[a] going to:							
1. Labor, including imputed earnings of self-employed	36.29	34.06	34.08	31.88	31.07	30.31	33.34
2. Publicity, insurance, professional services, other	11.41	11.69	13.17	11.57	12.19	12.97	17.73
3. Rent, interest, and royalties	6.74	7.08	8.77	10.04	9.39	9.86	9.11
4. Depreciation	4.73	4.68	5.78	6.18	5.30	4.89	5.42
5. Indirect taxes	1.49	1.65	2.41	5.96	10.48	15.40	18.20
All capital used by plant[b]	52.30	54.25	52.75	56.55	56.74	56.72	48.93
Capital owned by plant[c]	45.56	47.17	46.97	46.51	47.35	46.86	39.82
Capital owned by plant, less depreciation[d]	40.83	42.49	41.19	40.33	42.05	41.97	34.40
Capital owned by plant, less depreciation and indirect taxes	39.34	40.84	38.78	34.37	31.57	26.57	16.20
GI/BV	41.87	41.38	47.72	42.68	55.19	56.04	52.39
NI/BV	37.53	37.38	37.26	37.01	49.02	50.19	45.26
NIT/BV	36.16	35.83	35.08	31.54	36.80	31.78	21.31

Note: GI, gross income of capital operated by plant; BV, book value of fixed assets plus inventories; NI, net income of capital operated by plant; NIT, net income of capital operated by plant, after indirect tax.

a. Includes some small items which should not be included, with the result that the value added figures are biased upward by a few percentage points.

b. 100 minus rows 1 and 2. This share of value added includes payments to capital not owned by the establishment.

c. 100 minus rows 1, 2, and 3. This share of value added includes only payments to capital owned by the establishment.

d. 100 minus rows 1, 2, 3, and 4.

Table 23. *Factory Employment Indices for a Fixed Set of Plants: Blue-Collar, White-Collar, and Total, Compared with Employment Index Based on DANE's Annual Manufacturing Survey (All Plants), 1953 to 1970–71*

Year	Blue-collar Spliced series (1)	Blue-collar New series (2)	White-collar Spliced series (3)	White-collar New series (4)	Total Spliced series (5)	Total New series (6)	Implicit index of paid employment based on DANE Unadjusted (7)	Implicit index of paid employment based on DANE Adjusted (8)
1953	100.0		100.0		100.0		100.0	100.0
1955[a]	107.0		120.7		109.6		100.6	106.6
1956	109.9		132.3		113.2		111.0	116.9
1957	115.6		148.8		120.2		120.6	127.2
1958	114.7		154.1		120.1		124.5	130.6
1959	118.7		160.9		124.5		131.2	137.1
1960	122.2		168.6		128.8		134.7	140.2
1961	123.9		173.0		130.9		140.2	146.3
1962	126.0	100.0	175.4	100.0	133.0	100.0	146.0	152.3
1963	126.4	100.3	182.6	104.1	134.5	101.1	148.6	154.7
1964	126.5	100.4	187.2	106.7	135.3	101.7	150.3	156.5
1965	125.9	99.9	189.6	108.1	135.1	101.6	155.9	162.3
1966	127.6	101.3	192.8	109.9	137.1	103.1	158.9	165.2
1967	126.2	100.2	195.2	111.3	136.5	102.6	156.1	162.1
1968	126.4	100.3	198.9	113.4	136.9	102.9	160.7	165.6
1969	131.8	104.6	205.7	117.3	142.7	107.3		180.3
1970	137.1	108.8	216.3	123.3	148.4	111.6		191.5
1970–71	139.7	110.9	220.5	125.7	150.9	113.5		

Note: Columns 1, 3, and 5 are based on a splicing (in April–May of 1962) of the early series, with base 1953, and the new series beginning in May 1962. Column 7 gives the index implicit in the annual industrial survey statistics published in DANE, *Anuario General de Estadística*, and more recently in *Industria Manufacturera*. Column 8 gives an adjusted version of that index after its changing levels of coverage over time have been taken into account.

a. No data are available for 1954.

271

Table 24. Factory Employment Indices for a Fixed Set of Plants Compared with Total Reported Manufacturing Employment, 1970–78
(indices, 1970–71 = 100)

Year	Total reported manufacturing employment[a]			DANE employment indices[b]			Change in employment index ÷ change in total reported employment	
	Total	White-collar	Blue-collar	Total	White-collar	Blue-collar	Years	Ratio
1970–71	100	100	100	100	100	100		
1971	101.4	103.5	100.9	102.4	101.9	102.5	1972/1970	0.64
1972	110.0	117.7	107.0	106.4	108.5	105.8	1973/1972	0.42
1973	121.3	132.2	118.4	111.1	115.4	109.7	1974/1973	0.73
1974	128.6	n.a.	n.a.	116.4	122.0	114.6	1975/1974	0.75
1975	131.0	151.3	125.7	118.2	127.4	115.0	1976/1975	0.65
1976	134.7	156.0	129.0	120.6	131.4	117.3	1977/1976	0.60
1977	139.7	165.2	132.5	122.0	131.6	119.5	1978/1977	0.36
1978	143.5	175.9	134.7	124.5	134.4	121.3	1978/1970–71	0.56

n.a. Not available.

a. DANE, Annual Survey of Manufacturing.

b. Based on a sample of about 800 plants, with many large ones always chosen and smaller ones selected on a random basis. For a description of the methodology see DANE, Boletín Mensual de Estadística, no. 333 (April 1979), p. 69, and no. 293 (December 1975), p. 9. Indices are based on the period July 1970 to June 1971. Figures for subsequent years also refer to these months.

Table 25. *The Relative Price of Manufacturing Value Added, 1964–79, and the Wholesale Price Index of Manufactured Goods, 1970–79*

| Year | Price of manufacturing value added ÷ price of GDP[a] | Wholesale price index of manufactured goods[b] | | |
		Produced and consumed in Colombia	Imported	Exported
1964	1.094			
1965	1.059			
1966	1.026			
1967	1.042			
1968	1.005			
1969	1.004			
1970	1.000	100.0	100.0	100.0
1971	1.018	112.6	109.8	102.6
1972	1.018	134.1	128.4	126.1
1973	1.038	170.6	164.1	171.7
1974	1.102	226.3	232.7	254.1
1975	1.126	288.7	294.8	297.7
1976	1.122	366.8	345.3	489.2
1977	1.066	489.9	387.5	761.7
1978	1.084	575.7	461.2	675.5
1979	1.128	729.4	553.8	726.2

a. Measured at market prices; from the national accounts.
b. From *Revista del Banco de la República,* various issues.

Bibliography

Aigner, D. J., and S. F. Chu. "On Estimating the Industry Production Function." *American Economic Review*, vol. 57 (1968), pp. 826–39.

Anderson, Dennis. "Small Industries in Developing Countries: A Discussion of Issues." *World Development*, vol. 40, no. 11 (November 1982), pp. 913–48.

Anderson, Dennis, and Farida Khambata. *Small Enterprises and Development Policy in the Philippines: A Case Study.* World Bank Staff Working Paper 468. Washington, D.C., 1981.

Anderson, Dennis, and Mark W. Leiserson. "Rural Non-Farm Employment in Developing Countries." *Economic Development and Cultural Change*, vol. 28, no. 2 (January 1980), pp. 227–48.

Baily, Mary Ann. "Technology Choice in the Brick and Men's Leather Shoe Industries in Colombia." Yale University, Economic Growth Center, New Haven, Conn., August 1977. Processed.

_____. "Brick Manufacturing in Colombia: A Case Study of Alternative Technologies." *World Development*, vol. 19, no. 2 (February 1981), pp. 201–14.

Bain, Joe S. *Barriers to New Competition: Their Character and Consequences in Manufacturing Industries.* Cambridge, Mass.: Harvard University Press, 1956.

Banerji, Ranadev. "Small-Scale Production Units in Manufacturing: An International Cross-Section Overview." *Weltwirtshchaftliches Archiv*, vol. 114 (1978), pp. 62–84.

_____. "Average Size of Plants in Manufacturing and Capital Intensity: A Cross-Country Analysis by Industry." *Journal of Development Economics*, vol. 5, no. 2 (June 1978), pp. 155–66.

Baumol, W. J. *Business Behavior, Value and Growth.* Rev. ed. New York: Harcourt, Brace and World, 1967.

Becker, Gary S. *Human Capital.* New York: Columbia University Press, 1964.

Betancourt, Roger R., and Christopher Clague. "Working Capital and Shift Work in Imperfect Capital Markets." University of Maryland, Department of Economics, College Park, Md., 1976. Processed.

_____. *Capital Utilization: A Theoretical and Empirical Analysis.* New York: Cambridge University Press, 1981.

Bergsman, Joel. "Commercial Policy, Allocative and X-Efficiency." *Quarterly Journal of Economics*, vol. 88, no. 3 (1974), pp. 409–33.

Berry, Albert. "The Relevance and Prospects of Small-Scale Industry in Colombia." Economic Growth Center Discussion Paper 142. Yale University, New Haven, Conn., 1972.

————. "Predicting Income Distribution in Latin America during the 1980s." In *Latin American Prospects for the 1980s: Equity, Democratization, and Development*, ed. David H. Pollock and A. R. M. Ritter. New York: Praeger, 1983.

————. "The Limited Role of Rural Small-Scale Manufacturing for Late Comers: Some Hypotheses on the Colombian Experience." Development Studies Program Working Paper B4. University of Toronto, Toronto, Ont., 1984.

————, ed. *Essays on Industrialization in Colombia.* Tempe, Ariz.: Arizona State University, Center for Latin American Studies, 1983.

Berry, Albert, and Armando Pinell-Siles. "Small-Scale Enterprises in Colombia: A Case Study." World Bank Studies on Employment and Rural Development 56, Washington, D.C., July 1979. Processed.

Berry, Albert, and Ronald Soligo, eds. *Economic Policy and Income Distribution in Colombia.* Boulder, Colo.: Westview Press, 1980.

Berry, Albert, and Miguel Urrutia. *Income Distribution in Colombia.* New Haven, Conn.: Yale University Press, 1976.

Bhalla, A. S. "Galenson-Leibenstein Criterion of Growth Reconsidered: Some Implicit Assumptions." *Economia Internazionale*, vol. 17 (1964), pp. 241–49.

————. *Technology and Employment in Industry: A Case Study Approach.* Geneva: International Labour Office, 1975.

Bourguignon, François. "Pobreza y Dualismo en el Sector Urbano de las Economías en Desarrollo: El Caso de Colombia." *Desarrollo y Sociedad*, no. 1 (1979), pp. 37–72.

Bryce, Murray D. *Industrial Development: A Guide for Accelerating Economic Growth.* New York: McGraw-Hill, 1960.

Child, F. C., and Hiromitsu Kaneda. "Links to the Green Revolution: A Study of Small-Scale, Agriculturally Related Industry in the Pakistan Punjab." *Economic Development and Cultural Change*, vol. 23, no. 2 (January 1975), pp. 249–75.

Chuta, Enyinna, and Carl Liedholm. "The Economics of Rural and Urban Small-Scale Industries in Sierra Leone." African Rural Economy Paper 14. Michigan State University, Department of Agricultural Economics, East Lansing, Mich., 1976.

————. "Rural Non-Farm Employment: A Review of the State of the Art." Rural Development Paper 4. Michigan State University, East Lansing, Mich., 1979.

Corporación Financiera Popular and Organización de los Estados Americanos. "Diagnóstico de la Pequeña y Mediana Industria y Bases para una Política de Fomento y Desarrollo en Colombia." Bogotá, 1972. Processed.

Cortes, Mariluz. "Argentina: Technical Development and Technology Exports to Other LDCS." World Bank, Development Economics Department, Washington, D.C., March 1978. Processed.

Cortes, Mariluz, and Ashfaq Ishaq. "The Market of Secondhand Equipment in Colombia." World Bank, Development Economics Department, Washington, D.C., 1979. Processed.

Dhar, P. N., and Harold Lydall. *The Role of Small Enterprises in Indian Development.* Bombay: Asia Publishing House, 1961.

Díaz-Alejandro, Carlos. *Foreign Trade Regimes and Economic Development: Colombia.* New York: Columbia University Press, 1978.

Escandón, José F. "Análisis de los Factores que han Determinado el Desarrollo de la Pequeña Empresa en Colombia: Una Interpretación Histórica." *Coyuntura Económica,* vol. 11, no. 3 (October 1981), pp. 113–39.

Farrell, M. J. "The Measurement of Productive Efficiency." *Journal of the Royal Statistical Society,* ser. A, vol. 120 (1957), pp. 253–81.

Farrell, M. J., and M. Fieldhouse, "Estimating Efficient Production Functions under Increasing Returns to Scale." *Journal of the Royal Statistical Society,* ser. A, vol. 75 (1962), pp. 252–67.

Fei, John C. H., and Gustav Ranis. *The Labor Surplus Economy: Theory and Policy.* Homewood, Ill.: Irwin, 1964.

Forsund, F. R., C. A. K. Lovell, and Peter Schmidt. "A Survey of Frontier Production Functions and of Their Relationship to Efficiency Measurement." *Journal of Econometrics,* vol. 13 (1980), pp. 5–25.

Fundación para el Fomento de la Investigación Científica y Tecnológica (FICITEC). *Empresarios Colombianos: un Nuevo Contexto de Desarrollo.* Bogotá, 1976.

Galenson, Walter, and Harvey Leibenstein. "Investment Criteria, Productivity, and Economic Development." *Quarterly Journal of Economics,* vol. 69, no. 3 (August 1955), pp. 343–70.

Gaviria G., Fernando. "El Mercado Extrabancario y las Tasas de Interés en Colombia." *Revista del Banco de la República,* June 1978, pp. 776–806.

Gerry, Chris. "Petty Production and Capitalist Production in Dakar: The Crisis of the Self-Employed." *World Development,* vol. 6, no. 9-10 (1978), pp. 1147–60.

Gilbrat, Robert. *Les Inégalités Economiques.* Paris: Recueil Sirey, 1931.

Gold, Bela. "Changing Perspectives on Size, Scale and Returns: An Interpretative Survey." *Journal of Economic Literature,* vol. 14, no. 1 (March 1981), pp. 5–33.

Gómez, Hernando, and Ricardo Villaveces. *La Pequeña y Mediana Industria en el Desarrollo Colombiano.* Bogotá: La Carreta, 1979.

Harberger, Arnold C. "La Tasa de Rendimiento del Capital en Colombia." *Revista de Planeación y Desarrollo,* vol. 1, no. 3 (October 1969), pp. 13–42.

Hanson, James. "Estimación del Ahorro Familiar en Colombia." Brown University, Department of Economics, 1973. Processed.

Hirschman, Albert O. *The Strategy of Economic Development.* New Haven, Conn.: Yale University Press, 1958.

Ho, Samuel P. S. *Small-Scale Enterprises in Korea and Taiwan.* World Bank Staff Working Paper 384. Washington, D.C., April 1980.

Hommes, Rudolf. *La Organización Industrial y la Pequeña Industria.* Bogotá: Servicio Nacional de Aprendizaje (SENA), n.d.

Hoselitz, Bert F. "Small Industry in Underdeveloped Countries." *Journal of Economic History*, vol. 19 (1959), pp. 600–18.

———, ed. *The Progress of Underdeveloped Areas*. Chicago, Ill.: University of Chicago Press, 1952.

India, Government of. Ministry of Commerce and Industry. *Small Industry in a North Indian Town*. New Delhi, 1956.

International Labour Organisation. *Towards Full Employment: A Program for Colombia*. Geneva, 1970.

———. *Employment, Incomes and Equality: A Strategy for Increasing Productive Employment in Kenya*. Geneva, 1972.

———. *Sharing in Developing: A Program of Employment, Equity and Growth for the Philippines*. Geneva, 1974.

Jaramillo, Lino. "Crecimiento de la Pequeña, Mediana y Gran Industria entre los Años 1971 y 1978." Instituto Colombiano de Comercio Exterior (INCOMEX), 1982. Processed.

Jewkes, John. "The Size of the Factory." *Economic Journal*, vol. 62 (June 1952), pp. 237–52.

Kaneda, Hiromitsu. "Development of Small and Medium Enterprises and Policy Response in Japan: An Analytical Survey." University of California, Department of Economics, Davis, Calif., 1980.

Kenneth, D. A. "The Working Capital Needs of Small Enterprises," World Bank, Industry Development and Finance Department, Washington, D.C., 1979. Processed.

Kilby, Peter. *Industrialization in an Open Economy: Nigeria, 1945-1966*. London: Cambridge University Press, 1969.

———, ed. *Entrepreneurship and Economic Development*. New York: Free Press, 1971.

King, Kenneth. "Kenya's Machine Makers: A Study of Small-Scale Industry in Kenya's Emergent Artisan Society." *World Development*, vol. 2, no. 4 (1974), pp. 9–28.

Kugler, Bernardo, Alvaro Reyes, and Martha I. de Gutiérrez. *Educación y Mercado de Trabajo Urbano en Colombia: Una Comparación entre Sectores Modernos y No Modernos*. Bogotá: Corporación Centro Regional de Población, July 1979.

Langdon, Steven. "Multinational Corporations, Taste Transfers, and Underdevelopment: A Case Study from Kenya." *Review of African Political Economy*, no. 2 (1975), pp. 12–35.

Lecraw, Donald. "Choice of Technology in Low-Wage Countries: A Non-neoclassical Approach." *Quarterly Journal of Economics*, vol. 93, no. 4 (1979), pp. 631–54.

Lee, Kyu Sik. "Distribution of Manufacturing Establishments and Employment in Bogotá and Cali." World Bank, Urban and Regional Division, Development Economics Department, Washington, D.C., January 1978. Processed.

———. "Intra-Urban Location of Manufacturing Employment in Colombia." *Journal of Urban Economics*, vol. 9 (1981), pp. 222–41.

Leff, N. H. "Entrepreneurship and Development: The Problem Revisited." *Journal of Economic Literature*, vol. 17, no. 1 (March 1979), pp. 46–64.

Leibenstein, Harvey. "Allocative Efficiency versus 'X-Efficiency.'" *American Economic Review*, vol. 56 (1966), pp. 392–415.

_____. *Beyond Economic Man*. Cambridge, Mass.: Harvard University Press, 1976.

_____. *Economic Theory and Organizational Analysis*. New York: Harper, 1960.

Lipman, Aaron. *El Empresario Bogotano*. Bogotá: Universidad Nacional de Colombia, Ediciones Tercer Mundo y Facultad de Sociología, 1966.

Lipton, Michael. "Family, Fungibility, and Formality: Rural Advantages of Informal Non-Farm Enterprises versus the Urban-Formal State." Paper presented at the meetings of the International Economic Association, Mexico City, 1980.

Little, Ian, Tibor Scitovsky, and Maurice Scott. *Industry and Trade in Some Developing Countries*. London: Oxford University Press, 1970.

Lockwood, W. W. *The Economic Development of Japan, 1868–1933*. Princeton, N.J.: Princeton University Press, 1955.

Marris, Robin. *The Economic Theory of Managerial Capitalism*. Glencoe, Ill.: Free Press, 1964.

Mazumdar, Dipak. "A Descriptive Analysis of the Role of Small-Scale Enterprises in the Indian Economy." World Bank, Development Research Department. Washington, D.C., 1980. Processed.

McGreevey, William P. *An Economic History of Colombia: 1845–1930*. Cambridge, Eng.: Cambridge University Press, 1971.

Mead, Donald C. "Of Contracts and Subcontracts: Small Firms in Vertically Disintegrated Production/Distribution Systems in LDCs." *World Development*, vol. 12, no. 11-12 (November-December 1984), pp. 1095–1106.

Meller, Patricio. "Efficiency Frontiers for Industrial Establishments of Different Sizes." *Exploration in Economic Research*, vol. 3, no. 3 (1976), pp. 379–407.

Meller, Patricio, and Manuel Marfán. "Small and Large Industry: Employment Generation, Linkages and Key Sectors." *Economic Development and Cultural Change*, vol. 19, no. 2 (January 1981), pp. 263–74.

Mellor, J. W. *The New Economics of Growth: A Strategy for India and the Developing World*. Ithaca, N.Y.: Cornell University Press, 1976.

Mendels, Franklin. "Proto-Industrialization: The First Phase of the Industrialization Process." *Journal of Economic History*, vol. 32 (1972), pp. 241–61.

Mohan, Rakesh. *The Determinants of Labor Earnings in Developing Metropolises: Estimates from Bogotá and Cali, Colombia*. World Bank Staff Working Paper 498. Washington, D.C., October 1981.

Morley, Samuel A., and Gordon W. Smith. "The Choice of Technology: Multinational Firms in Brazil." *Economic Development and Cultural Change*, vol. 25, no. 2 (January 1977), pp. 239–64.

Myrdal, Gunnar. *Asian Drama: An Inquiry into the Poverty of Nations*. London: Allen Lane, Penguin Press, 1968.

Nelson, R. R. "A Diffusion Model of International Productivity Differences." *American Economic Review*, vol. 58, no. 5, part 1 (December 1968), pp. 1219–48.

Nelson, R. R., and Edmund S. Phelps. "Investment in Humans: Technological Diffusion and Economic Growth." *American Economic Review*, vol. 56 (May 1966), pp. 69–75.

Nelson, R. R., T. P. Schultz, and R. L. Slighton. *Structural Change in a Development Economy: Colombia's Problems and Prospects*. Princeton, N.J.: Princeton University Press, 1971.

Nelson, R. R., and Sidney Winters. *An Evolution Theory of Economic Capabilities and Behavior*. Cambridge, Mass.: Harvard University Press, 1982.

Nieto, Luis E. *Economía y Cultura en la Historia de Colombia*. Bogotá: Ediciones Tercer Mundo, 1962.

―――――. *El Café en la Sociedad Colombiana*. Bogotá: Ediciones la Soga al Cuello, 1971.

Ortega, Francisco. "Notas sobre la Reciente Evolución Económica e Institucional del Sector Financiero." *Ensayos sobre Política Económica*, no. 1 (March 1982), pp. 21–43.

Otsuki, T., I. Ohara, H. Iwayama, T. Miki, M. Hondai, and A. Hasida. *Industrial Development in South East Asian Countries: Small and Medium Industries— Republic of Indonesia*. Tokyo: International Development Center of Japan, 1977–78.

Pack, Howard. "The Substitution of Labour for Capital in Kenyan Manufacturing." *Economic Journal*, vol. 86 (1976), pp. 45–58.

Page, John M. "Firm Size, the Choice of Technique and Technical Efficiency: Evidence from India's Soap Manufacturing Industry." World Bank, Development Economics Department, Washington, D.C., 1979. Processed.

―――――. "Technical Efficiency and Economic Performance: Some Evidence from Ghana." *Oxford Economic Papers*, vol. 23, no. 2 (July 1980), pp. 319–39.

―――――. *Small Enterprises in African Development: A Survey*. World Bank Staff Working Paper 363. Washington, D.C., 1979.

Parker, W. N. "Industry." In *The New Cambridge Modern History*, ed. Peter Burke. Vol. 13. Cambridge, Eng.: Cambridge University Press, 1979.

Payán López, Genaro, and John Eddison, "El Impacto del Crédito sobre el Empleo en la Pequeña y Mediana Industria." *Revista del Banco de la República*, vol. 43, no. 517 (November 1970), pp. 1619–28.

Penrose, Edith. *The Theory of the Growth of the Firm*. Oxford: Blackwell, 1972.

de Pombo, Joaquín. "Algunos Aspectos del Mercado Libre de Dinero en Colombia." *Revista del Banco de la República*, vol. 45, no. 539 (September 1972), pp. 1574–98.

Portes, Alejandro. "The Informal Sector and the World Economy: Notes on the Structure of Subsidized Labour." *IDS Bulletin*, vol. 9, no. 4 (1978), pp. 35–40.

Pryor, Frederick. "The Size of Production Establishments in Manufacturing." *Economic Journal*, vol. 82 (1972), pp. 547–66.

Quijano, Aníbal. "The Marginal Pole of the Economy and the Marginalized Labor Force." *Economy and Society*, vol. 2, no. 4 (1974), pp. 393–428.

Ranis, Gustav. "Investment Criteria, Productivity and Economic Development: An Empirical Comment." *Quarterly Journal of Economics*, vol. 76 (May 1962), pp. 298–302.

Sandesara, J. C. "Scale and Technology in Indian Industry." *Bulletin of the Oxford University Institute of Economics and Statistics*, vol. 28 (August 1966), pp. 181–98.

Schmitz, Hubert. "Growth Constraints on Small-Scale Manufacturing in Developing Countries: A Critical Review." *World Development*, vol. 10, no. 6 (June 1982), pp. 429–50.

———. *Manufacturing in the Backyard: Case Studies on Accumulation and Employment in Small-Scale Brazilian Industry*. London: Frances Pinter, 1982.

Schumacher, E. F. *Small Is Beautiful*. London: Sphere Books, 1974.

Shapiro, Kenneth H., and Jurgen Muller. "Sources of Technical Efficiency: The Roles of Modernization and Information." *Economic Development and Cultural Change*, vol. 25 (1977), pp. 293–310.

Silva, Jaime. "Direct Foreign Investment in the Manufacturing Sector of Colombia." Ph.D. dissertation. Northwestern University, 1976.

Simon, H. A. *Models of Man*. New York: Wiley, 1957.

Singh, Ajit, and Geoffrey Whittington. "The Size and Growth of Firms." *Review of Economic Studies*, vol. 17, no. 129 (January 1975), pp. 15–26.

Staley, Eugene, and Richard Morse. *Modern Small Industry for Developing Countries*. New York: McGraw-Hill, 1965.

Steele, B. F. *Small-Scale Employment and Production in Developing Countries: Evidence from Ghana*. New York: Praeger, 1977.

Stewart, Frances. *Technology and Underdevelopment*. 2d ed. London: Macmillan, 1978.

Sutcliffe, R. B. *Industry and Underdevelopment*. Reading, Mass.: Addison-Wesley, 1971.

Thoumi, Francisco. "La Utilización del Capital Fijo en la Industria Manufacturera Colombiana." *Revista de Planeación y Desarrollo*, vol. 10, no. 3 (1978), pp. 11–95.

———. "Estrategias de Industrialización, Empleo y Distribución del Ingreso en Colombia." *Coyuntura Económica*, vol. 9, no. 1 (April 1979), pp. 119–42.

Timmer, C. P. "On Measuring Technical Efficiency." *Food Research Institute Studies in Agricultural Economics, Trade, and Development*, vol. 9 (1970), pp. 99–171.

———. "Using a Probabilistic Frontier Production Function to Measure Technical Efficiency." *Journal of Political Economy*, vol. 79 (1971), pp. 776–94.

Todd, John E. "Efficiency and Plant Size in Colombian Manufacturing." Ph.D. dissertation. Yale University, 1972.

Tybout, R. "Credit Rationing and Industrial Growth in Colombia: A Micro Econometric Analysis." Ph.D. dissertation. University of Wisconsin, 1983.

Tyler, W. G. "Technical Efficiency in Production in a Developing Country: An Empirical Examination of the Brazilian Plastics and Steel Industries." *Oxford Economic Papers*, vol. 31 N.S. (1979), pp. 477–95.

Tyler, W. G., and L. F. Lee. "On Estimating Stochastic Frontier Production Functions and Average Efficiency: An Empirical Analysis with Colombian Micro Data." *Review of Economics and Statistics*, vol. 61 (1979), pp. 436–38.

United Nations. *Measures for the Economic Development of Underdeveloped Countries*. New York, 1951.

Urquhart, M. C., and K. A. H. Buckley, eds. *Historical Statistics of Canada*. Toronto: Cambridge University Press, 1965.

Urrutia, Miguel. *Winners and Losers in Colombia's Economic Growth in the 1970s*. New York: Oxford University Press, 1985.

Urrutia, Miguel, and C. E. Villalba. "El Sector Artesanal en el Desarrollo Colombiano." *Revista de Planeación y Desarrollo*, vol. 1, no. 3 (October 1969), pp. 43–78.

White, Lawrence J. "Appropriate Technology, X-Efficiency, and a Competitive Environment: Some Evidence from Pakistan." *Quarterly Journal of Economics*, vol. 90, no. 4 (1976), pp. 575–89.

————. "The Evidence on Appropriate Factor Proportions for Manufacturing in Less Developed Countries: A Survey." *Economic Development and Cultural Change*, vol. 27, no. 1 (October 1978), pp. 27–60.

Wogart, J. Peter. *Industrialization in Colombia: Policies, Patterns and Perspectives*. Tübingen: J.C.B. Mohr (Paul Siebeck), 1978.

Watanabe, Susumu. "Reflections on Current Policies for Promoting Small Enterprises and Subcontracting." *International Labour Review*, vol. 110, no. 5 (November 1974), pp. 405–22.

————, ed. *Technology, Marketing and Industrialization: Linkages between Large and Small Enterprises*. New Delhi: Macmillan, 1983.

Welch, Finis, "Education in Production." *Journal of Political Economy*, vol. 78, no. 1 (January-February 1970), pp. 35–59.

Index

The most recent World Bank publications are described in the catalog *New Publications*, which is issued in the spring and fall of each year. The complete backlist of publications is shown in the annual *Index of Publications*, which is of value principally to libraries and institutional purchasers. The latest edition of each is available free of charge from Publications Sales Unit, The World Bank, 1818 H Street, N.W., Washington, D.C. 20433, U.S.A., or from Publications, The World Bank, 66, avenue d'Iéna, 75116 Paris, France.